Where to watch birds in

Yorkshire

(including the former North Humberside)

Where to watch birds in

Yorkshire

(including the former North Humberside)

Second edition

John R. Mather
Illustrated by D.I.M. Wallace & Mark Whorley

Christopher Helm

A & C Black • London

Second edition 1998
First edition 1994

© 1998 John R. Mather
Illustrations by D.I.M. Wallace and Mark Whorley
Maps by John R. Mather

Christopher Helm (Publishers) Ltd, a subsidiary of A & C Black (Publishers)
Ltd, 35 Bedford Row, London WC1R 4JH

ISBN 0-7136-4634-9

A CIP catalogue record for this book is available from the British Library

Typeset and designed by D & N Publishing
Membury Business Park, Lambourn Woodlands, Hungerford, Berkshire

Printed in Great Britian by Redwood Books, Trowbridge, Wiltshire

CONTENTS

Contents

Contents

FOREWORD

The need and demand for this series of books on *Where to Watch Birds* has become a viable and commercial project because of the amazing upsurge in birdwatching as a popular and, nowadays, a well organised hobby and pastime. This is well illustrated by a bird which I was lucky enough to see in 1953; in November of that year, a Yellow-billed Cuckoo, from America, turned up in a garden at Cloughton, a small village some six miles north of Scarborough. Fortunately, the owner was interested in natural history, realised the bird was something unusual and let my father, at that time recorder for birds in the Scarborough Field Naturalists' Society, know of its appearance. The bird stayed for about a week and during that time was seen by no more than ten birdwatchers. If it had arrived today and news of its presence was announced on 'Birdline', something in the order of 500 birdwatchers would come from far and wide to see it.

To offer this large and growing number of birdwatchers a comprehensive survey of the best places to see birds in Yorkshire, a county so large that it is divided into four administrative regions and into five Watsonian Vice-counties, divisions which are still used for recording purposes by The Yorkshire Naturalists' Union, requires an author of outstanding knowledge and merit. John R. Mather is just such an ornithologist. He has lived for all but four years of his life in Knaresborough, at the very centre of the county, giving him the easiest access of anyone to all parts of this huge area. He has been involved in the recording of birds in the county for the last 41 years. It was in the YNU Ornithological Report for 1952 that his name first appeared as a contributor; in 1964 he was appointed recorder for Vice-county 64, a position he held until 1979; in 1970 he became Editor of the annual Yorkshire Bird Report, a task he fulfilled for ten years to 1979 when he became Chairman of the YNU Bird Records Committee, a position he held until his retirement from office in October 1993. In 1986, he published his book *The Birds of Yorkshire*, a definitive work which will stand for very many years before it is brought up to date. He served on the *British Birds* Rarities Committee from 1976 to 1984, and on the British Ornithologists' Union Records Committee for eight years up to 1993 including three years as Chairman.

There can be no-one better able to introduce present day birdwatchers to some of the best habitats in Yorkshire, to enhance their days in the field in pursuit of their chosen hobby.

Athol J. Wallis

ACKNOWLEDGEMENTS

Having been born and lived in Yorkshire for over 65 years, it became very clear when I embarked on this guide that there were many areas about which I knew very little apart from their name and ornithological reputation. I therefore visited all the 92 sites included in the first edition, travelling 10,000 miles (16,000 km), learning much about this vast county in the process. Whilst researching for this second edition, I visited many of the original sites and also 12 new ones which are now included.

The whole exercise would have been most difficult without the willing assistance of several people, some of whom accompanied me on site visits, have supplied written details of their particular areas, or who have checked my draft manuscripts for sites with which they are familiar. Special thanks must go to Miss Ann Mettam of Harrogate who acted as my chauffeuse for much of the long distances travelled and who also checked the entire manuscript. I am also very grateful to John E. Dale of Huddersfield, John Martin of West Ardsley, Brian Shorrock of Settle and Athol J. Wallis of Scarborough who have given freely of their time in helping me both in the field and with written information. No less important were the contributions made by the following who supplied details of the places they know well or who helped in other ways; I am most grateful to them all: Ron Appleby of Scarborough, June Atkinson of Harrogate, Sally Barrow of Bridlington, Pat Clayton of Wass, W.F. Curtis of Atwick, the late Derek Cutts of South Cave, L.G. Dewdney of Ilkley, Clive Featherstone of Thorne, G.T. Foggit of Harrogate, Ian Forsyth of Cottingham, Peter Griffin of Oulton, Nick Morgan of Ainderby Steeple, Paul Morris of Leeds, John Newbould of Rotherham, Frank Oates of York, Christine Parkin of Staveley, Hugh Parkin of Doncaster, David Procter of Ossett and Peter Treloar of Knaresborough. Thanks must also go to the Yorkshire Wildlife Trust for helpful advice on their reserves through Miss Helen Jackson of Harrogate. The drawings are the work of D.I.M. Wallace and Mark Whorley and I am very grateful to them for these.

I must also thank Robert Kirk of Christopher Helm (Publishers) Ltd for his encouragement and help during the preparation of this second edition.

INTRODUCTION

The area covered by this guide is the traditional county of Yorkshire with the exception of four small regions in the west which in 1974 became part of Cumbria, Lancashire and Greater Manchester, namely the extensions of Mickle Fell, Sedbergh, the Forest of Bowland and the Saddleworth district, and also that part south of the River Tees which is now included in the new county of Cleveland. This last named area is dealt with by another guide in the *Where to Watch* series. North Humberside, an area which enjoyed the dubious status of being part of a separate county for a mercifully short period, has reverted to being part of the traditional Yorkshire...how sensible!

Yorkshire lays claim to being the largest county in the British Isles and can boast a variety of habitats surpassing any other region. Within these vast areas, from the wild and barren moorlands of the Pennine Chain running along the entire western boundary with over 200 reservoirs, eastwards through the dales and the wooded gills and cloughs of the foothills onto the central plain and the vales, to the variable coastline with its contrasting characters of the high-terraced basaltic cliffs at Ravenscar, the impressive chalk heights of the Buckton and Bempton cliffs which fall away to the Flamborough Headland, and southwards along the 36 miles (57.6 km) of low and crumbling boulder-clay ramparts of Holderness, terminating at the sand dunes of Spurn Point, are contained a proliferation of excellent bird haunts, many of which are featured at the 105 sites in this book, 12 of which have been added since the first edition.

The sites have been chosen for ease of access as well as for their birdwatching opportunities. There are many other sites which are on private land or are difficult to reach and these have been omitted. Local naturalists often have permission to visit such areas as the result of long and sometimes difficult associations and negotiations and the privacy of such sites must be respected. There are many areas, including parks, stands of woodland, lakes and ponds which have public access or can be viewed from public roads or footpaths and these can be investigated by those who are able to recognise the ornithological potential of the various habitats. It would have been impossible to include even a small proportion of such places. The countryside is continually changing and some of the sites included in this guide may well alter over the years, perhaps for the worse, but we are fortunate in having many areas which are protected by reserve status. The RSPB administers four very important reserves; at Fairburn Ings, Blacktoft Sands, Hornsea Mere and the seabird colonies at Bempton Cliffs. The Yorkshire Wildlife Trust either owns or has administrative responsibility for no fewer than 60 reserves and the National Trust and The Woodland Trust take care of 50 sites, at least 36 of which are valuable bird habitats. There are several Country Parks with excellent areas set aside for birds, which are administered by the various local authorities who are to be commended on this initiative.

Since I wrote *The Birds of Yorkshire* in 1986, the status of some species has changed. These changes were happening at that time but in the absence of organised surveys were not immediately obvious in some cases. Turtle Dove, Song Thrush and Tree Sparrow are three species which have undergone a marked reduction in numbers during the last decade. Yellow Wagtails are generally scarcer than formerly, noticeably in the York district and also in most areas of the southwest. Corn Buntings have become thinly scattered over much of central Yorkshire, being now relatively numerous only in the southeastern part of the county. Hooded Crows, once a regular feature along the coast in winter, are now very scarce. On the credit side, the Pied Flycatcher population in some of the Pennine and Hambleton foothills has increased during recent years, aided in part by the provision of nesting boxes. Some birds of prey are showing signs of an encouraging increase and, if left alone by those ill-informed people who seek to eliminate them from the countryside, would establish a firm foothold in several parts of the county. The Forestry Commission is to be applauded for its enlightened attitude in this respect. The Magpie, a much maligned bird, especially by those people living in suburbia, where it has found a safe and well-provisioned niche, is being dubiously successful throughout.

A county list of 426 species reflects the excellent variety of habitats within the Yorkshire boundaries. The vast accumulation of records, submitted by a wealth of very competent birdwatchers, whose observations have appeared in the reports of local societies and also in the County Bird Report over the years, has provided much of the raw material for the 'Species' sections in this guide.

For many years, long before being asked to write this book, I went through the process of making a mental note of various landmarks which would enable others to locate a particular site and have drawn on this experience. Having had subsequent recourse to Ray Moore's very helpful *Where to Watch Birds in Kenya*, it was often frustrating to be uncertain whether or not one had driven too far or had missed some obscure turning, and with this in mind, I have attempted to be as detailed as possible in the sections dealing with 'Access' and have personally checked the distances and every instruction under that heading. When writing the sections on 'Timing' and 'Calendar', I have been mindful of those readers, particularly keen beginners, families and visitors from overseas who may have little or no knowledge of the birds which a particular habitat may hold, or perhaps more importantly, the time of year in which they are most likely to be seen, and have therefore, in addition to the season, given the actual months of usual occurrence and included all the common resident species.

An American friend, on hearing that I was preparing this book, said recently: 'Don't make the mistake of assuming that everyone will know that Blackbirds and Blue Tits can be seen almost everywhere – include them in the lists'. From my experiences abroad, that was sound advice and I have therefore treated each site on its own merits and listed all the birds which one can reasonably expect to see there. It is unlikely that the watcher will actually see all the birds shown for each location and the 'Species' lists are inevitably optimistic, but given suitable weather at the right time of year, it should be possible to see a good percentage of those indicated. Although chosen primarily for their birds, some of the sites included herein are also botanically and entomologically very rich and many are scenically impressive.

In spite of the oft short-sighted criticism being levelled at the changes to the English names of birds proposed by the British Ornithologists' Union for use in a World Checklist, an exercise with which I was associated, the changes will inevitably come and be accepted; it is human nature to object to change. I have therefore used the new English names published by the editors of *British Birds* magazine in 1993, for use in the British context, which is, in my opinion, a reasoned and acceptable compromise by a well established and respected journal. Besides, are not Horned Lark and Red-billed Chough splendid names?

John R. Mather
Eagle Lodge
Knaresborough
August 1997

> *Alas, that Spring should vanish with the Rose,*
> *That youth's sweet-scented manuscript should close,*
> *The Nightingale that in the Branches sang,*
> *Ah, whence, and whither flown again, who knows.*

Omar Khayyam (died 1123)

The 105 major sites in this guide have been divided into 11 different regions, based mainly on their geographical grouping, thus indicating neighbouring places which can be visited on the same day. The coast is somewhat different, in that I have included all the 17 localities from Whitby at the northern end southwards to Spurn Point, in the one grouping.

The five sections within each site chapter: 'Habitat', 'Species', 'Timing', 'Access' and 'Calendar' are given the same treatment in every case except where the habitat is not particularly important in which case I have combined 'Habitat' and 'Species' into one section, which for certain sites is more meaningful in any case.

Habitat

This section gives a broad outline of the location, its geological character and altitude where relevant, the vegetation, and any other important features within the site and its environs. At many sites there is more than one distinct type of habitat, each with its own differing bird populations, and these habitats are described; for example at Broomhead Moor and Reservoir, there are areas of open heather moorland, the reservoir, and extensive conifer plantations. As time passes, some areas will undergo vegetative change, particularly at gravel pits and reservoirs, and also forestry plantations as they mature. In this last situation particularly, some birds may be lost as a result: Black Grouse, Short-eared Owl and European Nightjar being three species which have been so affected in the past.

Species

The most important birds likely to be seen are detailed in this section, usually in species order but giving the temporal distribution where this is important. It aims to give a general picture of the birds of the particular locality and those mentioned may be seen at the appropriate season. It is, of course, impossible to guarantee their presence and factors such as adverse weather, the wrong time of day or previous disturbance will influence those which are present at any one time (see 'Calendar' paragraph below). The northern breeding specialities such as Red Grouse, European Golden Plover and Ring Ouzel can be found on the high ground in the west and northeast, particularly the North York Moors, the Northwestern Dales, Upper Nidderdale and the Southern Pennines. The main seabird colonies are concentrated between the towns of Scarborough and Bridlington.

Timing

This is not too important in some cases except for the season of the year, but where there are advantages in visiting early in the day for example, or to coincide with a particular happening such as pre-roosting assemblies or likely movements of seabirds and passerines in certain weather conditions, then this is mentioned. The wind direction is important during the spring and autumn migration seasons and one should have regard for this when planning a visit to the coast. In April and May, look out for winds from the southern quarter when the summer migrants should arrive in force and southern rarities may overshoot into Britain. In the autumn, if the wind is in the east, immigrant chats, warblers and fly-catchers will arrive along the east coast, mainly during August and September, with the rarer eastern pipits, warblers and thrushes arriving during October and early November.

Access

I have attempted to be as detailed as possible in this important section. The directions to each site usually start at easily located points such as motorway exits, towns or villages and include the accurate distances which are given in both miles and kilometres. I have mentioned obvious landmarks, such as public houses, radio towers or geological features with the aim of reassuring visitors that they are on the right track. When used in conjunction with the OS Landranger maps, these directions will enable readers to plan their journey times and, hopefully, locate each site with ease.

Most of the National Parks, Country Parks and Forestry Commission areas have visitor centres or information boards showing the recommended walks. Information leaflets are usually available at these centres and visitors should avail themselves of the facilities. Coach parties intending to visit reserves administered by the Royal Society for the Protection of Birds or The Yorkshire Wildlife Trust, should inform the warden or the secretary in advance (see List of Organisations for addresses). Access to some privately owned sites is along permissive footpaths and these should be respected. The managed grouse moors are diligently 'keep-ered' and in no circumstances should visitors leave the roads or recognized tracks to walk across the heather moors. This is particularly important during the late spring and summer months when the Red Grouse are nesting, and again during the grouse shooting season from mid-August to December.

Calendar

This section consists of a straightforward list of all the species which one can reasonably expect to encounter at each site during an adequately prolonged visit at the appropriate season. Quite obviously there will be days when one's luck is out, and others on which unexpected birds will be seen, but most of those listed occur in normal circumstances. There are some exceptions however; the rarer divers and grebes and also some seabirds may be seen only sporadically depending on the weather, but those listed have occurred with some regularity during recent years. Passing shearwaters and skuas may be absent on some days during their migration periods if the weather is not suitable, but, if the correct conditions prevail, as outlined in the relevant 'Species' and 'Timing' sections, then some will certainly be present.

Small passerines, particularly the rarer warblers, occur more frequently in some years than others but there is a fair chance of encountering them at the recommended sites if, as for most migrant species, the winds are from the correct direction during the spring and autumn migration periods. Other weather factors will influence the occurrence of several species, particularly during the winter months, when prolonged periods of frost or snow may bring large flocks of Northern Lapwings, Wood Pigeons, thrushes or finches into new areas, often for only a short time as they exploit a temporary food supply.

Key to the maps

	Large towns and urban areas	▬▬	Main roads
		──	Minor roads
	Deciduous woodland	++++++	Railways
	Coniferous woodland	─ ─ ─	Track (may be motorable)
	Sea	······	Footpath
	Lakes, reservoirs and ponds	≈≈≈	River or canal
		─⌄─	Stream or dyke
●●	Small towns and villages	Ⓟ	Parking area

THE AREA COVERED BY THIS GUIDE

Map of Yorkshire showing the five Watsonian Vice-county divisions: areas of roughly the same size, devised originally by H.C. Watson in 1873 to facilitate botanical recording and still used by The Yorkshire Naturalists' Union. The five small shaded areas have now become part of (anti-clockwise) Cleveland, Cumbria, Lancashire (2) and Greater Manchester.

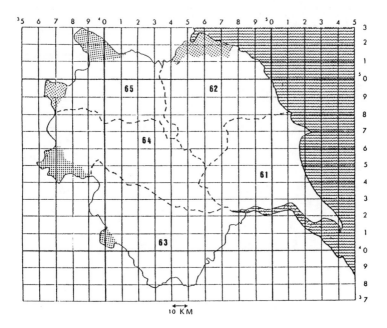

10 KM

THE COAST

1 Whitby Harbour and Sands
2 Ravenscar, Beast Cliff, Stoupe Brow and Robin Hood's Bay
3 Long Nab, Burniston
4 The Scarborough Area
5 Burton Riggs Reserve
6 Filey Brigg and Bay
7 Filey Dams Reserve
8 Bempton Cliffs RSPB Reserve
9 Flamborough Head
10 Bridlington Harbour and South Beach
11 Fraisthorpe Beach and Fields
12 Barmston Beach
13 Hornsea and Mappleton
14 Hornsea Mere
15 Tophill Low Nature Reserve
16 Brandesburton Ponds
17 Spurn Point Bird Observatory and Easington Lagoons

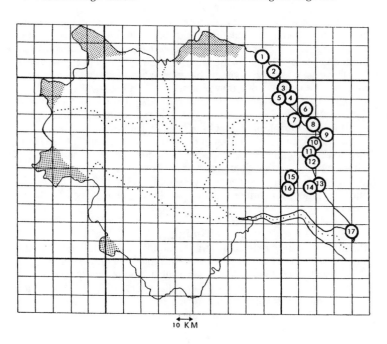

10 KM

1 WHITBY HARBOUR AND SANDS

OS Landranger map 94
Whitby

Habitat and Species

Whitby Harbour is situated at the mouth of the River Esk and is enclosed by piers which shelter small areas of mud at low tide. The main harbour is a busy fishing port and thus attracts many gulls, particularly during the winter months when the resident population of Herring Gulls is joined by large numbers of this species from further north, including the slightly larger and darker birds from across the North Sea. Also present are Black-headed Gulls, Common Gulls and many Great Black-backed Gulls in addition to occasional Iceland, Glaucous or Mediterranean Gulls. Some Kittiwakes are always present. The outer piers provide shelter for seabirds, especially during periods of severe weather when solitary Shags, Common Eiders, Common Scoters, Common Guillemots or Razorbills may enter the harbour in addition to an occasional Red-throated or Great Northern Diver, Great Crested Grebe or any one of the three rarer grebes. Great Cormorants can usually be seen as they fish in the harbour. Watching from the end of the west pier during the winter may produce any of these species in addition to Fulmars, Northern Gannets and passing flocks of Eurasian Wigeons and Common Teals. It is also possible to see Long-tailed Duck, Greater Scaup, Red-breasted Merganser and perhaps Little Auk at this time.

The wide expanse of Whitby Sands, stretching for 1 mile (1.6 km) from the west pier, attracts several species of waders during the autumn and winter months. During September, October and November, especially during rough weather, skuas may be seen from the pier, mainly Arctic, but Long-tailed, Pomarine and Great are possibilities. Rock Pipits frequent the harbour and the piers during the winter months.

Timing

The main attraction here is the large assembly of gulls during the winter months, when a visit at any time between September and March will provide the watcher with excellent views of all the commoner species as well as the chance of seeing an Iceland or Glaucous, especially during prolonged periods of severe weather; divers, grebes, sea ducks and auks are also most likely to be seen at this time.

Access

Whitby is situated some 17 miles (27.2 km) north of Scarborough and is reached by taking the A171 northbound which enters the town centre to cross a bridge over the River Esk. Turn right immediately over the bridge and drive alongside the harbour where there is ample parking space during the winter months. The main harbour area can be easily viewed from the roadside. Walk along the 0.25 mile (0.4-km) long west pier to look for passing skuas during the autumn and for divers, grebes, sea ducks and auks during the winter.

Approaching from the north, proceed along the A174 which runs alongside the wide expanse of Sansend Beach 2 miles (3.2 km) before entering Whitby, where it joins the A171 to reach the bridge over the river in the town centre.

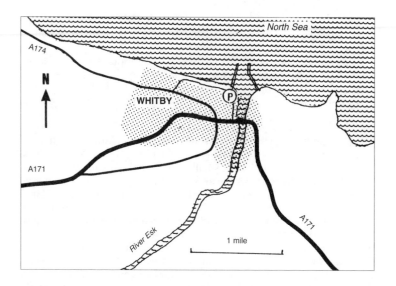

Calendar

This includes the harbour, the beach and the offshore waters.

Autumn and winter (September to March): Any one of the divers, Great Crested Grebe, any one of the three rarer grebes, Fulmar, Northern Gannet, Great Cormorant, Shag, Eurasian Wigeon, Common Teal, Mallard, Greater Scaup, Common Eider, Long-tailed Duck, Common Scoter, Common Goldeneye, Red-breasted Merganser, Oystercatcher, Great Ringed Plover, Grey Plover, Northern Lapwing, Red Knot, Sanderling, Purple Sandpiper, Dunlin, Bar-tailed Godwit, Eurasian Curlew, Common Redshank, Turnstone, Pomarine Skua, Arctic Skua, Long-tailed Skua, Great Skua, Mediterranean Gull, Black-headed Gull, Common Gull, Herring Gull, Iceland Gull, Glaucous Gull, Great Black-backed Gull, Kittiwake, Common Guillemot, Razorbill, Little Auk, Rock Pipit.

2 RAVENSCAR, BEAST CLIFF, STOUPE BROW AND ROBIN HOOD'S BAY

OS Landranger
Maps 94 and 101
Whitby and
Scarborough

Habitat

The cliffs at Ravenscar, which reach a height of around 585 feet (178 m), are steep and terraced with grassy slopes, some exposed crags and an ample scattering of bushes and gorse. The Beast Cliff is clothed in deciduous woodland.

The minor road along Stoupe Brow is bordered by heather moor to the west and by bush-covered grassy slopes with lots of gorse, tumbling steeply down to sheep pasture along the lower cliff top.

Lying immediately north of Ravenscar is Robin Hood's Bay, a wide arc backed by cliffs of boulder clay and a rocky shoreline, stretching for 2 miles (3.2 km) to the village of the same name. Stoupe Beck enters the Bay along a steep-sided wooded valley, 1.5 miles (2.4 km) north of Ravenscar.

Species

This spectacular area is certainly worth a visit, particularly during the late spring and summer for breeding Fulmars, Herring Gulls and passerines, and also during the autumn for small migrants and passing seabirds. Visits during the winter months can also be productive, when divers and sea ducks find food and shelter in Robin Hood's Bay. During February, March and early April, good numbers of Red-throated Divers often assemble in the Bay whilst on their journey north to the breeding grounds in northern Scotland and beyond. At any time between August and early November, there is a fair chance of seeing passing skuas in the Bay, especially during rough weather with winds from the northern quarter. Several species of waders can be found during the autumn and winter months amongst the rocks around the Bay including Oystercatchers, Red Knots, Purple Sandpipers, Dunlins, Eurasian Curlews and Turnstones. Passing Sandwich, Arctic and Common Terns frequent the Bay whilst on migration. Fulmars breed along the cliffs and also in the disused Stoupe Brow Quarry, about 0.5 miles (0.8 km) from the sea, and are regularly present during the winter months also.

Herring Gulls are particularly numerous and breed along the entire stretch of cliffs. There is a small breeding colony of Great Cormorants at Blea Wyke Point, halfway between the village of Ravenscar and the old coastguard lookout to the south. Eurasian Jackdaws are common in the

Fulmars

22

area and breed along the cliffs as do feral pigeons, many of which resemble pure Rock Doves.

The bush-covered slopes at Ravenscar and along Stoupe Brow, and also the wooded slopes of Stoupe Beck, are good for migrant passerines in the spring and autumn, particularly the latter period when both passage and 'fall' migrants should be looked for. Common Swifts, Sand Martins, Barn Swallows and House Martins can often be seen streaming south along the cliff tops at this time. The month of October usually brings 'falls' of immigrant thrushes and Common Starlings, usually when the winds are easterly with rain or mist, at which time there is always the chance of finding an eastern rarity. An occasional migrant Eurasian Sparrowhawk or Merlin may be seen as they hunt for small birds along the cliffs. A lone Peregrine Falcon is sometimes present during the winter.

Most of the common resident passerines occur in the woods or on the bush-covered slopes in addition to Common Redstarts, Common Whitethroats, Blackcaps, Chiffchaffs and Willow Warblers during the summer. A pair or two of Common Kestrels are resident. Both Green and Great Spotted Woodpeckers frequent the woods on Beast Cliff or anywhere along the adjoining slopes. Typical breeding birds in the bushy areas and gorse patches along the cliffs are Meadow Pipits, Chaffinches, Goldfinches, Linnets and Yellowhammers. Rock Pipits breed along the lower part of the cliffs and may be seen on the upper slopes in the summer and also during the winter months. In some years, a few Dotterels may be seen in the ploughed fields along Stoupe Brow, especially near the radio mast (see 'Access' below).

Timing

This complex has something to offer the birdwatcher throughout the year. The best time to visit for the highest number of species is perhaps during the period late August to October when both the resident birds and the migrants will be present. The wooded slopes, at Stoupe Beck particularly, should be checked for 'fall' migrants during this time. Winter and early spring can be good for divers, sea ducks and waders in Robin Hood's Bay. The area is popular with tourists and may be very crowded during the summer months.

Access

Ravenscar lies 7 miles (11.2 km) north of Scarborough and is reached by taking the A171 Scarborough to Whitby road, or the A165 coast road, from Scarborough which joins the A171 at Burniston about 2 miles (3.2 km) to the north. Continue through Burniston to Cloughton where the main road bears left, and take the minor road straight ahead signed Staintondale and Ravenscar. This undulating road continues for 4.5 miles (7.2 km) to a junction and bears right to the village of Ravenscar (straight on at this junction leads to Stoupe Brow – see below). After entering Ravenscar, the road bears right at the Raven Hall Hotel and becomes Station Road. There is a National Trust Information Centre on the left just before the entrance to Raven Hall Hotel. Just past the hotel grounds is a track to the left down which one can drive to park and walk the short distance to the cliff top. Alternatively, one can drive along Station Road (cul de sac) to another track and parking area opposite a large isolated building (Tea Rooms). The 'Cleveland Way', a coastal footpath, runs along the whole length of the cliffs and overlooks the impressive vegetated slopes and terraced basaltic crags. Walk south for about 1 mile (1.6 km), passing the disused

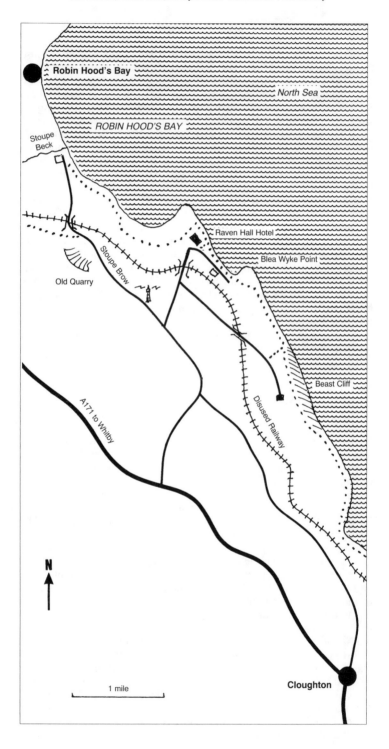

coastguard lookout, to the wooded Beast Cliff. As an alternative to returning along the cliff top from here, look for a Public Footpath sign at a stile near a gate, from where the path crosses a field to join a minor road running northwards back to Ravenscar. Follow this road and just before crossing a small bridge, pass through a gap in the fence on the left which leads to the disused railway track, continuing under the bridge and back to Ravenscar near the Tea Rooms. This is a recommended circular walk in both late spring and autumn.

Another good walk starts from near the entrance to Raven Hall Hotel, just to the left of which is a path leading across the golf course, before passing through a small area of woodland to join the disused railway track, from where one can return to the main road or walk northwards for 1.5 miles (2.4 km) to Stoupe Beck.

To reach Stoupe Brow and Robin Hood's Bay beach by car, leave Ravenscar and return to the junction referred to above after 0.75 miles (1.2 km) signed Stoupe Brow. Turn right here and, during the month of May, look over the ploughed fields on the right between the junction and the radio mast for Dotterels. Continue along the narrow and often steep winding road for 1.5 miles (2.4 km) to reach the old Stoupe Brow Quarry on the left. Park on the roadside here and take a wide track which leads up to the left below the quarry and onto the high ground. This track is worth investigating for migrants during the spring and autumn as well as being good for the breeding scrubland birds during the summer. On returning to the car, continue for 0.5 miles (0.8 km) to the end of the narrow road at Stoupe Brow Farm, immediately past which is a small car park. Steps lead from here for 300 yards (270 m) down the side of the wooded valley to Stoupe Beck and Robin Hood's Bay beach.

Calendar

This includes the cliffs, the woodland and the Bay.

All year: Fulmar, Great Cormorant, Common Kestrel, Herring Gull, Rock Dove, Wood Pigeon, Green Woodpecker, Great Spotted Woodpecker, Rock Pipit, Pied Wagtail, Wren, Hedge Accentor, Robin, Blackbird, Mistle Thrush, Long-tailed Tit, Blue Tit, Great Tit, Magpie, Eurasian Jackdaw, Carrion Crow, Common Starling, House Sparrow, Tree Sparrow, Chaffinch, Greenfinch, Yellowhammer.

Summer (April to August): Sky Lark, Common Redstart, Song Thrush, Common Whitethroat, Blackcap, Chiffchaff, Willow Warbler, Goldfinch, Linnet.

Spring and autumn passage (April to early June and late July to October): Eurasian Sparrowhawk, Merlin, Dotterel (Spring), Arctic Skua, any of the other three skuas, Sandwich Tern, Common Tern, Arctic Tern, Common Cuckoo, Common Swift, Sand Martin, Barn Swallow, House Martin, Meadow Pipit (also in summer), Whinchat, Northern Wheatear, Ring Ouzel, Goldcrest, Spotted Flycatcher, Pied Flycatcher.

Winter (October to March): (mainly Robin Hood's Bay) Red-throated Diver, Black-throated Diver, Greater Northern Diver, Eurasian Wigeon, Common Teal, Mallard, Common Eider, Common Scoter, Common Goldeneye, Red-breasted Merganser, Peregrine Falcon, Oystercatcher, Turnstone, Black-headed Gull, Common Gull, Great Black-backed Gull, Kittiwake, Fieldfare, Redwing.

3 LONG NAB, BURNISTON

Habitat

Long Nab is a small promontory lying 4 miles (6.4 km) to the north of Scarborough. The adjacent land is mainly arable and the cliffs reach a height of around 80 feet (25 m). The cliffs just to the north of the Nab are rocky and steep and have a small breeding colony of Common Guillemots and Kittiwakes. A gully near the small car park offers shelter for migrants, the slopes being clad with bracken, hawthorn, willow scrub and some *Phragmites* reeds. The arable fields are bordered by hedgerows and are also worth checking for migrants.

Species

Seawatching from the area of the Nab will produce all the seabirds and waterfowl which pass elsewhere at other coastal watchpoints. Birds moving south tend to pass fairly close inshore before swinging out to pass the Scarborough Marine Drive headland. What has been written in detail in the section on Flamborough Head regarding weather and species involved in sea movements applies to Long Nab but on a smaller scale. The arable fields attract Sky Larks and Yellowhammers during the autumn and winter months and Twites, Lapland Longspurs and Snow Buntings in small numbers during the late autumn. During times of spring and autumn migration, the gully running south from the car parking area is worth checking for passerines, as are the adjacent hedgerows and also the stubbles in autumn.

Timing

Sea-watching during the winter months can be good for divers, grebes, Fulmars, Northern Gannets, waterfowl and waders. Late summer and autumn will provide the watcher with movements of shearwaters, gulls, terns and skuas in the right weather conditions. The arrival of immigrant thrushes and other passerines during October and November can be well seen here as elsewhere.

Access

To reach Long Nab, travel north from Scarborough on either the A165 or the A171 Burniston and Whitby roads. Burniston lies 4 miles (6.4 km) north of Scarborough. Look for the Three Jolly Sailors public house in the village of Burniston at the junction of the A165 and A171. Approaching along the A165, turn right onto the A171 and turn right again immediately at the side of the pub into Rocks Lane. Continue along on good undulating tarmac, passing under a bridge for 1 mile (1.6 km) and take the right bend at Cliff Top House to reach a small car parking area (free) after 200 yards (180 m). Walk north from here along the cliff-top footpath to reach Long Nab, identified by a white observation hut. Watch the sea from the cliff top or from the grassy slopes below. Walk a little further north from the Nab to view the small seabird colony. The gully to the south is reached from the car park; a narrow tarmac path leads down through the bushes and *Phragmites* reeds and finally to the boulder beach. Check this

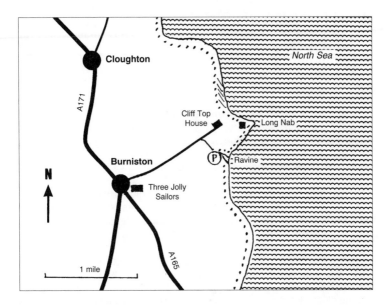

area for migrants in both spring and autumn. The arable fields and stubbles adjacent to the car parking area and the surrounding hedgerows should also be checked, especially during late autumn. Watch from the paths and do not walk over the land.

Calendar

Winter (October to March): Red-throated Diver, Black-throated Diver, Great Northern Diver, Red-necked Grebe, Slavonian Grebe, Fulmar, Northern Gannet, Great Cormorant, Shag, Grey Heron, Eurasian Wigeon, Common Teal, Mallard, Common Eider, Common Scoter, Common Goldeneye, Red-breasted Merganser, Common Kestrel, Oystercatcher, Purple Sandpiper, Dunlin, Eurasian Curlew, Common Redshank, Turnstone, Common Gull, Herring Gull, Great Black-backed Gull, Common Guillemot, Razorbill, Little Auk, Rock Dove, Stock Dove, Sky Lark, Rock Pipit, Tree Sparrow, Linnet, Twite, Snow Bunting, Yellowhammer, Reed Bunting, Corn Bunting.

Spring and autumn passage (April to early June and August to October): Red-throated Diver, Black-throated Diver, Sooty Shearwater, Manx Shearwater, occasional Cory's, Great and Mediterranean Shearwaters, European Storm Petrel, Leach's Storm Petrel, Northern Gannet, Great Cormorant, Shag, Common Shelduck, Eurasian Wigeon, Common Teal, Common Scoter, Merlin, Eurasian Sparrowhawk, waders, Pomarine Skua, Arctic Skua, Long-tailed Skua, Great Skua, Sandwich Tern, Common Tern, Arctic Tern, Common Swift, Sand Martin, Barn Swallow, House Martin, Meadow Pipit, Tree Pipit, Robin, Common Redstart, Whinchat, Northern Wheatear, Blackbird, Fieldfare, Song Thrush, Redwing, warblers, Goldcrest, Spotted Flycatcher, Pied Flycatcher, Linnet.

Summer (March to August): Great Cormorant, Northern Lapwing, Kittiwake, Common Guillemot, Razorbill, Puffin, Common Kestrel, Rock Dove, Sky Lark, Wren, Barn Swallow, Tree Sparrow, Yellowhammer, Corn Bunting.

4   THE SCARBOROUGH AREA

OS Landranger Map 101
Scarborough

Habitat and Species

One of the most popular holiday resorts of the east coast of England, the Scarborough area has also much to offer the birdwatcher throughout the year and the following eight sites provide a varied selection of habitats, each having a wide range of seasonal attractions.

The Harbour Sheltered by enclosing piers which protect it from rough seas, the harbour often attracts divers, grebes, Shags, sea ducks and Common Guillemots which seek shelter during the winter months. Large numbers of gulls are attracted by the fishing cobles which land their catches along the west pier, and this is the best place to see Iceland and Glaucous Gulls which appear almost annually amongst the assemblies of Herring Gulls, Great Black-backed Gulls and Kittiwakes. A few Great Cormorants are usually present, either sitting on buoys anchored in the harbour or fishing close to the tied-up fishing boats. Turnstones feed on fish scraps along the piers during hard weather and Rock Pipits are regular visitors at such times. Up to 200 Purple Sandpipers regularly roost along ledges on the seaward side of the east (outer) pier at high tide during the winter months, at which time flocks of Sanderlings feed on the deserted South Bay beach on high tides after dark when they can be watched in the illumination of the street lights. A few pairs of Kittiwakes nest on ledges of the buildings opposite the west pier.

Scarborough Harbour

The Marine Drive This coast road, which links the south and north bays, runs along the base of the Castle Hill cliff where upwards of 2,000 pairs of Kittiwakes breed annually. This colony is rather special in that the busy road runs between it and the sea, affording a unique opportunity to sit and watch the activities of the birds from below. Some pairs of Fulmars and Herring Gulls also nest on the cliffs. Eurasian Jackdaws are common

28

during the breeding season and a pair of Common Kestrels is usually present. After the young Kittiwakes have left their nests during August, feral Rock Doves take over the cliff and are present throughout the winter. The road abuts the sea and is therefore an excellent place from which to watch passing seabirds. Movements of shearwaters, terns, skuas and auks, which are evident at all the watchpoints along the coastline during the spring and autumn migration periods, can be seen well from here, and there is the added advantage of being able to watch from one's car in wet weather. If the sea becomes too rough, usually with strong winds from the northeastern quarter, the Marine Drive is closed to traffic. Closure is indicated by flashing red lights at each end, beyond which it is an offence to proceed.

Kittiwakes

The Castle Hill This imposing promontory, which dominates the town, is a favourite place for watching migrant passerines. The south-facing slopes of the hill are clothed in trees and bushes with brambles and are thus very attractive to tired migrants. Several rare birds have been seen on the hill including Pied Wheatear, Booted Warbler, Icterine Warbler, Barred Warbler, Pallas's Leaf Warbler, Yellow-browed Warbler and Firecrest. The autumn arrivals of thrushes can be spectacular, especially in misty or rainy conditions. Watching from the Marine Drive often allows observers to witness flocks of Blackbirds, Fieldfares, Song Thrushes, Redwings and Common Starlings struggling in low over the sea to make their first landfall on the slopes of the Castle Hill. An occasional Long-eared or Short-eared Owl may be seen at this time.

Scalby Mills Situated at the northern end of the North Bay, this site is interesting in that the Scalby Beck runs out across the boulder beach and attracts hundreds of gulls and terns which assemble to bathe in the fresh water at low tide. Some birds are present during most of the year and include all the commoner gulls in addition to Mediterranean and Little Gulls which are regular here. In 1976, 11 different species of gulls were seen on one winter's day. During the periods of spring and autumn passage, sea terns assemble here and include Sandwich, Common and Arctic with an occasional Roseate. Waders are normally present and include Purple Sandpiper, Eurasian Curlew, Common Redshank, Turnstone and sometimes a Grey Phalarope during the autumn and winter. The lower part of the narrow Scalby Beck, as it passes through a deep gully, regularly has Common Sandpiper, Common Kingfisher, Rock Pipit, Grey Wagtail and Dipper at the appropriate season.

Jackson's Bay This small bay lies round the headland immediately north of Scalby Mills. Waders feed on the sheltered beach and sea ducks feed close inshore along the bay in winter. Since the recent construction of a long sewage outfall offshore at this point, replacing the old pipe which discharged much closer to the shore, the significance of the bay as a feeding area for birds has declined considerably. Large areas of gorse and blackthorn on the slopes of Scalby Beck, on the left as one climbs the steps to overlook Jackson's Bay, should be checked for Goldfinches, Linnets and Yellowhammers and also for migrants during the autumn.

Peasholm Park This park with its large lake and well-wooded gardens lies on the north side of the town and being close to the sea sometimes attracts an occasional sea duck during bad weather. It can be very good for migrant passerines during the main spring and autumn passage periods and is worth checking for falls of thrushes, especially during October and November when eastern vagrants are also likely to occur.

Scarborough Mere The Mere is situated in the southwestern area of the town, just off the main A64 York road. It is very busy during the summer months with boating and water skiing, but is well worth a visit. Despite this disturbance, one or two pairs of Reed Warblers breed in the small patches of *Phragmites* at what is their most northerly station in England. Common Pochards and Tufted Ducks are present each winter and Moorhens and Common Coots are numerous at this time when a solitary Water Rail may also be seen. Great Crested Grebes nest annually and Common Kingfisher is often present. The mature trees and shrubs around the perimeter often hold both early and late migrants, and the fruiting trees and shrubs attract Bohemian Waxwings during invasion years.

Cornelian Bay This small bay, situated south of Scarborough, is worth a visit during the winter months. The beach attracts large numbers of waders and there have been counts of up to 700 Oystercatchers (January 1981), and up to 300 Purple Sandpipers and 200 Turnstones in recent years. The bay is frequented by sea ducks during the winter months.

Timing

Winter is the best time to visit the harbour when severe weather often brings seabirds into the shelter of the piers and when the Iceland and Glaucous Gulls are likely to be present. Spring and autumn are obviously the best periods for migrants on the Castle Hill. The breeding Kittiwakes are present on the Marine Drive cliffs from April to August and the Fulmars until September. Scalby Mills and Jackson's Bay are worth investigating at any time of the year, but terns, including an occasional Roseate, are best seen during the late spring and autumn, and especially during the evenings if the tide is out. There is little disturbance to the boulder beach from holiday makers at Scalby Mills and the birds can be watched at fairly close range from the sea wall as they bathe in the Scalby Beck outflow.

During July and August, when the main seabird movements take place, parking along the Marine Drive may be difficult (pay machines) and early morning or in the evening are the best times to go there. As with all the locations along the east coast, the light can be a problem early in the day and it is best to park at the northeastern corner of the Drive and watch the sea in that direction. The light in the evenings is from behind and perfect for seawatching.

Access

The harbour area is easy to find at the northern end of the main South Bay sea-front. Parking in the winter is no problem and it is possible to walk along the three piers. Look for the Iceland and Glaucous Gulls on the roofs of the buildings along the west pier where they often sit with Herring and Great Black-backed Gulls, or as they sit on the sea in the harbour. Access to the outer east pier is near the fun fair at the entrance to the Marine Drive. During the winter months this pier is linked to the central Vincent Pier by a narrow temporary footbridge next to the lighthouse. This is the best area from which to watch the harbour complex.

The Marine Drive is a continuation of the sea-front road and runs round the base of the Castle Hill to the North Bay. Access to the slopes of the Castle Hill is easiest from the northern end of the Marine Drive near a small café and gift shop, where one can park and walk up the paths to the castle walls and to the right under an archway (visible from the road) to the wooded south slopes.

Peasholm Park is obvious at the end of the North Bay road next to a roundabout on the A165 Burniston road. There is a large car park (pay machines) adjacent to the nearby swimming baths, which is reached by taking the second exit off the roundabout into Northstead Manor Drive. Turn into the car park on the right after 200 yards (180 m). One can then walk back across the road into the park and walk around the tarmac pathways which circle the lake and gardens.

To reach Scalby Mills from the Marine Drive, continue along the North Bay sea-front road and turn right at the roundabout onto the A165 to Burniston and Whitby. After 1 mile (1.6 km) turn right into Scalby Mills Road at The Ivanhoe Inn, signed 'Sea Life Centre', and continue for 0.5 miles (0.8 km) to the sea-front parking area (pay machines) from where one can look over the low sea wall to the boulder beach and the Scalby Beck outflow.

Jackson's Bay can be reached from here by crossing a footbridge over the beck and climbing the steps to the top of the promontory. View the beach and bay from the cliff top.

Scarborough Mere lies under the eastern slopes of Oliver's Mount, a large hill at the southwestern edge of the town. The best way to reach the Mere is to take the main A64 York road out of Scarborough and after 1 mile (1.6 km) look for a large timber merchants opposite Scarborough Football Ground, after which turn left at a roundabout into Queen Margaret's Road, signed A165 Filey and Bridlington. Cross over a road bridge and reach the Mere entrance on the right after 300 yards (275 m). An

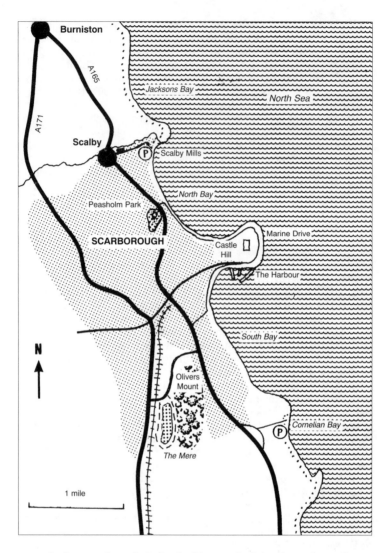

unmade, but good, road circles the Mere and rejoins the main road near the bridge.

Cornelian Bay is reached by travelling south on the A165 coast road and before leaving the last suburbs look for Cornelian Drive, a loop-road on the left. Turn into the Drive at either entrance and follow it round until a rough track branches off towards the sea between fields and passes a large farm building on the right. Park just beyond this building under some pine trees near the cliff top. A path runs down the steep cliff on the left, or one can look down into the bay from the top of the cliff. The Cleveland Way runs along the cliff top and upper slopes of Cornelian Bay southwards to Knipe Point before reaching Cayton Bay. The slopes are covered by a dense area of bushes and trees which attract large numbers of passerines during times of migration. Both Green and Great Spotted Woodpeckers breed in the woods along this stretch of cliff.

Calendar

This includes all eight sites.

Winter (October to March): Red-throated Diver, Black-throated Diver, Great Northern Diver (rare), Great Crested Grebe, Red-necked Grebe, Slavonian Grebe, Fulmar, Northern Gannet, Great Cormorant, Shag, Grey Heron, Eurasian Wigeon, Common Teal, Common Pochard, Tufted Duck, Common Scoter, Common Goldeneye, Red-breasted Merganser, Common Kestrel, Oystercatcher, Grey Plover, Northern Lapwing, Red Knot, Sanderling, Dunlin, Bar-tailed Godwit, Eurasian Curlew, Common Redshank, Turnstone, Grey Phalarope, Mediterranean Gull, Little Gull, Black-headed Gull, Common Gull, Herring Gull, Iceland Gull, Glaucous Gull, Great Black-backed Gull, Kittiwake, Common Guillemot, Razorbill, Little Auk, Rock Dove, Common Kingfisher, Rock Pipit, Grey Wagtail, Pied Wagtail, Bohemian Waxwing (sporadic) and Dipper in addition to the common resident passerines.

Spring and autumn passage (March to early June and late July to October): (Several species of winter seabirds, particularly ducks, also occur on passage in both spring and autumn.) Divers, Fulmar, Cory's Shearwater, Great Shearwater, Sooty Shearwater, Manx Shearwater, Mediterranean Shearwater, Northern Gannet, waders, all four skuas, Sandwich Tern, Roseate Tern (rare), Common Tern, Arctic Tern, auks, Common Swift, Sky Lark, Sand Martin, Barn Swallow, House Martin, Meadow Pipit, Yellow Wagtail, Pied Wagtail, Robin, Black Redstart, Common Redstart, Whinchat, Northern Wheatear, Ring Ouzel, Blackbird, Fieldfare, Song Thrush, Redwing, Icterine Warbler, Barred Warbler, Lesser Whitethroat, Common Whitethroat, Garden Warbler, Blackcap, Pallas's Leaf Warbler, Yellow-browed Warbler, Chiffchaff, Willow Warbler, Goldcrest, Firecrest, Spotted Flycatcher, Red-breasted Flycatcher, titmice, finches.

5 BURTON RIGGS RESERVE

OS Landranger Map 101
Scarborough

Habitat

Burton Riggs is a restored gravel pit complex formerly known as Seamer Gravel Pits and is administered jointly by the Yorkshire Wildlife Trust and the North Yorkshire County Council. There are two large sheets of water surrounded by sandy gravel banks and an abundance of tree and shrub cover. The water is deep and in consequence the shoreline has no significant areas of mud suitable for feeding waders except at the southern end where wader pools have been created. The site is well used by dog walkers and one should tread carefully: there are plans, however, to designate a dog-free zone at the southern end of the Reserve.

Species

Because of its close proximity to the coast, this site has the potential to attract birds normally associated with the sea, particularly if storm driven or at times of spring and autumn migration. Over the years, there have been several such records including Red-necked, Slavonian and Black-necked Grebes, Little Egret, Purple Heron, Common Eider, Long-tailed Duck, Red-breasted Merganser, Arctic Skua, Kittiwake, Sandwich Tern and White-winged Black Tern, all of which have been recorded on single occasions.

A few waders drop in to rest and feed for brief periods during the spring and autumn migration seasons and most of the regular passage species have been recorded. There is an old record of Lesser Yellowlegs. Common and Arctic Terns occur in both spring and autumn, and Black Terns may feed over the water on occasions, particularly during easterly winds in May. Waterfowl are well represented with a resident population of Canada Geese and feral Barnacle Geese as well as many Mallards, some of which show signs of domestication. These species combined, however, form an attraction for other, less usual ducks and geese. Whooper and Tundra Swans may call in occasionally during the late autumn and winter months when Eurasian Wigeons, Gadwalls, Common Teals, Northern Pintails, Common Pochards, Tufted Ducks, Common Goldeneyes and Goosanders may occur in good numbers varying annually. Garganey is a possibility during the spring, at which time a few Northern Shovelers may also pass through.

Gulls are attracted to the fresh water, often in large numbers, to rest and bathe including mainly Great Black-backed, Herring, Common and Black-headed with a few Lesser Black-backed and an occasional Glaucous or Iceland Gull.

Birds of Prey are sometimes seen on the Reserve with Hen Harrier, Merlin and Hobby being on the list in addition to the resident Eurasian Sparrowhawk and Common Kestrel. Both Little and Tawny Owls frequent the general area but are seen on the Reserve only occasionally. A solitary Short-eared Owl may be seen during the autumn and winter months when Barn Owl is also a possibility.

At times of passage during both spring and autumn, large numbers of hirundines and Common Swifts may assemble low over the water to feed, especially if the weather is cold or with rain coinciding with their main arrival periods in spring.

No fewer than 177 species have been recorded at the Reserve, 33 of which are known to have bred. Three of these, Greylag Goose, Common Kingfisher and Long-tailed Tit, have done so on only one occasion and Whinchat and Yellow Wagtail do so only very rarely. Little Grebes breed and a pair of Great Crested Grebes nested in 1994 with two pairs in 1995. The Mallards breed commonly and produce some young of dubious ancestry as evidenced by the varying amounts of piebald plumage. Moorhens and Common Coots nest annually. Little Ringed Plovers attempt to nest in some years but disturbance by dogs is a limiting factor.

Most of the commoner resident passerines nest on the Reserve in addition to the summer visitors which include Sand Martin, Sedge Warbler, Common Whitethroat, Garden Warbler, Blackcap and Willow Warbler. Lesser Whitethroat stays to nest only occasionally. Common Cuckoo is regularly heard and seen in the spring and doubtless breeds. During times of post-juvenile dispersal and passage migration, which starts as early as late June and continues into August and early September, several warblers pass through and augment the resident populations. Rarer ones over the years have been Great Reed Warbler, Savi's Warbler and Icterine Warbler as well as the locally unusual Grasshopper Warbler, Reed Warbler (a potential breeder), Wood Warbler and Chiffchaff. There are single records of European Bee-eater and Red-backed Shrike during the autumn migration season with Great Grey Shrike being recorded in some years during the late autumn and winter months. During the autumn, particularly in late September and early October, Meadow Pipits pass through in some numbers with an occasional Tree Pipit. The rare Richard's and Water Pipits have each been seen on one occasion. Finches gather to feed on the weed seeds during July, August and September including Greenfinches, Goldfinches and Linnets with Yellowhammers and Reed Buntings also in evidence.

Timing
A visit at any time of year can be of interest but the periods of spring and autumn migration from late April to early June, particularly with easterly winds, and from July to October, are perhaps the best for the greatest number of species. Visits during the late autumn and winter months may produce the unusual but, depending on the weather, this period can be relatively quiet for birds apart from the waterfowl and gulls. It is best to be there as early as possible in the morning before the birds are disturbed by anglers and walkers, the passerines not being thus affected however.

Access
To reach this site from Scarborough, leave the town on the A64 York/Malton road and after passing Morrison's supermarket on the left, come to a roundabout and take the third exit, marked with a no through road sign. This short stretch of road leads into a car park alongside the railway lines and a signal box from where a path continues under the road bridge onto the Reserve.

If approaching from York and Malton on the A64, come to the Staxton roundabout, 7 miles (11 km) from Scarborough and take the first exit. After 2 miles (3.2 km), cross over the railway bridge, come immediately to the roundabout as above, and take the first left into the Reserve car park, identified by a Yorkshire Wildlife Trust sign. Paths circle both lakes, the one around the north lake being wide and suitable for wheelchairs.

Calendar
All year: Little Grebe, Great Crested Grebe, Mute Swan, Canada Goose, Greylag Goose, Mallard, Tufted Duck, Eurasian Sparrowhawk, Common Kestrel, Red-legged Partridge, Moorhen, Common Coot, Stock Dove, Wood Pigeon, Sky Lark, Pied Wagtail, Wren, Hedge Accentor, Robin, Blackbird, Song Thrush, Mistle Thrush, Long-tailed Tit, Marsh Tit, Willow Tit, Coal Tit, Blue Tit, Great Tit, Eurasian Treecreeper, Magpie, Eurasian Jackdaw, Rook, Carrion Crow, Common Starling, House Sparrow, Tree Sparrow, Chaffinch, Greenfinch, Goldfinch, Linnet, Bullfinch, Yellowhammer, Reed Bunting.

Spring and autumn passage (April to early June and July to October): Common Shelduck, Common Teal, Garganey (occasional), Northern Shoveler, waders, gulls, Common Swift, Barn Swallow, House Martin, Sand Martin, Tree Pipit, Meadow Pipit, Northern Wheatear, Reed Warbler, Chiffchaff, Goldcrest, Spotted Flycatcher.

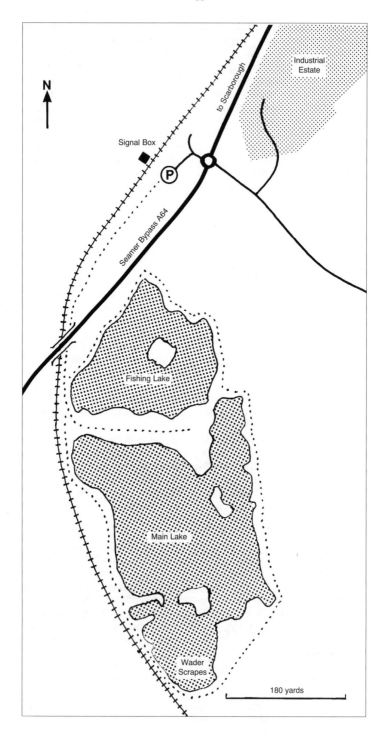

Summer (breeding): Little Ringed Plover, Common Cuckoo, Sand Martin, Sedge Warbler, Lesser Whitethroat (occasional), Common Whitethroat, Garden Warbler, Blackcap, Willow Warbler (also on passage, in addition to the resident passerines).

Winter (October to March): Rarer grebes, Great Cormorant, Tundra and Whooper Swans (occasional), Eurasian Wigeon, Northern Pintail (occasional), Common Pochard, Common Goldeneye, Goosander, gulls, Northern Lapwing, Grey Wagtail, Redwing, Fieldfare, Brambling, Siskin, Corn Bunting.

6 FILEY BRIGG AND BAY

OS Landranger Map 101
Scarborough

Habitat

The finger of Filey Brigg pointing south eastwards towards the Flamborough Headland lies at the tip of the high and eroded boulder-clay cliffs of the Carr Naze approximately 1 mile (1.6 km) northeast of Filey town. Lying in a direct line between the Scarborough Marine Drive and Flamborough Head, it is very well placed as a seawatching point and is regularly watched by both local and visiting birdwatchers.

A large open car parking area and caravan park on the cliff top at the base of the peninsula has beds of shrubs and small trees around the perimeter which attract migrant passerines. Cliff-top fields adjacent to this area are mainly arable. The eroded cliffs of the Carr Naze have little cover and the south side, facing Filey Bay, is mainly bare boulder-clay. The actual Brigg is a long thin point of shelving rocks, almost covered at high tide. A wide valley cut into the cliffs running down to the beach in Filey Bay, known as Arndale, has plenty of tree and scrub cover and is a good place for newly arrived migrants. Filey Bay is a large sheltered bay much favoured by seabirds, especially during severe weather. Running north from the coble landing is Church Ravine, a deep valley well clad with high deciduous trees.

Species

Filey is an excellent place from which to watch passing seabirds and what has been written on this subject in the Flamborough chapters applies equally well here. Most of the seabirds moving south which eventually pass Flamborough Head can be seen well from the Brigg and the same species are usually represented at each site. The actual Brigg is a good place to see assemblies of waders, gulls and terns which rest and feed on the rocks or feed along the surf. Rarities have included White-billed Diver, Surf Scoter and Ross's Gull in recent years and the rarer grebes appear annually.

The beach and rocks adjacent to the cliffs at the northern end of the bay are used by waders including good numbers of Purple Sandpipers and an occasional Grey Phalarope. The general areas of the Brigg, Carr Naze, Arndale and the car parking area are excellent places to witness falls of immigrant passerines during the autumn. All the usual birds are involved, with several sub-rarities being seen each year. The large trees in Church Ravine should be checked at such times and are often the best place to see the eastern leaf warblers.

Timing

The best times to visit are during the spring (April/May) and autumn (September/October) for migrant and vagrant passerines, and also during late autumn (October/November) for thrushes and the rarer pipits and buntings. Movements of waders and seabirds are evident each spring and autumn and one should have regard for the wind direction and strength before deciding when to visit. The largest seabird movements normally occur on winds of some strength from the northern quarter. Periods of easterly winds, especially with rain, or overcast conditions are best for falls of migrant passerines in October and November.

Access

To reach Filey, travel south from Scarborough on the A165 and bear left at a roundabout onto the A1039 (north junction). Continue for 0.5 mile (0.8 km) to a second roundabout and after 200 yards (180 m) turn left into Church Cliff Drive for a Caravan site and North Cliff Country Park (pay machine). Park at the far right-hand corner of the area and walk along the promontory to the right. To reach the actual Brigg from here necessitates clambering down a boulder-clay ridge which can be very slippery in wet weather. Alternatively, one can walk part-way along the promontory to some railings where a set of steps leads down to the beach and Brigg on the bay side.

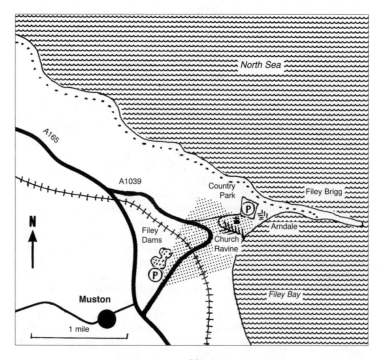

To view the stubbles and hedgerows, and also the breeding Great Cormorants, walk north along the cliffs from the car park. The ravine known as Arndale, runs south to the beach from the Country Park Stores, through a gate signed 'Filey Sailing Club'. To reach Church Ravine from the car park, leave your car near the park entrance and walk towards the bay round a fenced field to the ravine path and then right to the Church area and finally back to the Country Park entrance. On leaving the Park by car, turn left and proceed downhill and under a footbridge on the Ravine Road towards the coble landing. Park along the Ravine Road and walk left along the beach to the Brigg. This is a good approach during the winter when the northern part of the Bay can be searched for divers, grebes, sea ducks and auks. Approaching Filey from the south, turn right at a roundabout on the A1039 (south junction) and continue into the town, turning left for the Country Park shortly after crossing the railway lines.

Calendar

Winter (October to March): Red-throated Diver, Black-throated Diver, Great Northern Diver, White-billed Diver (rare), Red-necked Grebe, Slavonian Grebe, Black-necked Grebe, Fulmar, Northern Gannet, Great Cormorant, Shag, Brent Goose, Eurasian Wigeon, Common Teal, Greater Scaup, Common Eider, Long-tailed Duck, waders including good numbers of Purple Sandpipers, Common Scoter, Velvet Scoter, Common Goldeneye, Red-breasted Merganser, Iceland Gull, Glaucous Gull, Great Black-backed Gull, Herring Gull, Common Gull, Kittiwake, Common Guillemot, Razorbill, Puffin, Black Guillemot (occasional), Little Auk, Rock Dove, Rock Pipit, Sky Lark, Lapland Longspur, Snow Bunting, Yellowhammer, Corn Bunting.

Spring and autumn passage (March to May and July to October) (mainly autumn)*:* Divers, grebes, Sooty Shearwater, Manx Shearwater, occasional Cory's, Great, Mediterranean and Little Shearwaters, occasional European and Leach's Storm Petrels, Common Shelduck, Eurasian Wigeon, Common Teal, Northern Pintail, sea ducks, passage waders, Pomarine Skua, Arctic Skua, Long-tailed Skua, Great Skua, Little Gull, Sabine's Gull, Sandwich Tern, Common Tern, Arctic Tern, Little Tern, the three breeding auks, Common Cuckoo, Common Swift, Wryneck, Sand Martin, Barn Swallow, House Martin, Richard's Pipit, Tawny Pipit, Tree Pipit, Meadow Pipit, Yellow Wagtail, Pied Wagtail, Bluethroat, Black Redstart, Common Redstart, Whinchat, Common Stonechat, Northern Wheatear, Ring Ouzel, Blackbird, Fieldfare, Song Thrush, Redwing, Sedge Warbler, Reed Warbler, Icterine Warbler, Barred Warbler, Lesser Whitethroat, Common Whitethroat, Garden Warbler, Blackcap, Pallas's Leaf Warbler, Yellow-browed Warbler, Chiffchaff, Willow Warbler, Goldcrest, Firecrest, Spotted Flycatcher, Red-breasted Flycatcher, Pied Flycatcher, Red-backed Shrike, Common Starling, Chaffinch, Brambling, Greenfinch, Goldfinch, Siskin, Linnet, Common Redpoll, Common Rosefinch, Bullfinch, Reed Bunting.
   Note: only the regular species and the most likely sub-rarities are mentioned here but rare vagrants are always a possibility and one or two occur annually.

Spring and Summer (March to August): Breeding – mainly along the cliffs to the north of the Brigg and the area of Carr Naze. Fulmar, Great Cormorant, Red-legged Partridge, Herring Gull, Kittiwake, Common Guillemot, Razorbill, Puffin, Rock Dove, Sky Lark, Meadow Pipit, Rock Pipit, Wren, Reed Bunting.

7 FILEY DAMS RESERVE

Habitat

Filey Dams is an area of approximately 15 acres (6 ha) lying to the west and adjacent to the town of Filey. The land is very wet and waterlogged for much of the year with the water table just 3 feet (1 m) below the surface. A large excavated scrape consisting of two connecting main pools provides areas of open water throughout the year. The surrounding land is mainly pasture with scattered trees and old hedgerows, mainly hawthorn and alder with some stands of larger timber. There are areas of *Juncus* rush around the edges, some muddy shoreline frequented by waders at the appropriate season, and two very good hides overlooking the main pools. The land is owned by the Scarborough Borough Council and administered as a reserve by The Yorkshire Wildlife Trust.

Species

This small oasis of what is very localised wetland habitat along this part of the coastline, is an excellent place for birdwatching, especially during the periods of spring and autumn migration. Little Grebes are present during most of the year (usually absent in December and January) and the species breeds on the Reserve. An occasional Great Cormorant may drop in to feed and Grey Herons are regularly present. A flock of Canada Geese is often joined by a few Greylag Geese.

During the spring migration period (March to early June) Common Shelducks may pass through along with other waterfowl including Common Teal, Northern Shoveler and an occasional Garganey. Mallards are resident and small numbers of Tufted Ducks, a few Common Pochards and an occasional Northern Pintail can be seen during the winter months. Eurasian Sparrowhawk and Common Kestrel are resident and regularly seen, and a passing Merlin is a possibility on migration. The site is good for Water Rail and this species is often seen during the winter months. Moorhens and Common Coots are resident.

Waders are well represented and most of the regular passage species may be encountered at the appropriate season. The more unusual ones are always a possibility and rare species seen in recent years have been Black-winged Stilt (May 1991), Pectoral Sandpiper (September 1991) and Red-necked Phalarope (November 1991). Black-headed, Common and Herring Gulls are usually present and small numbers of Lesser Black-backed Gulls pass through, mainly during the spring and early summer.

Stock Doves, Wood Pigeons and Collared Doves are resident and a few Turtle Doves occur on migration. Common Swifts feed over the pools, especially during spells of cool and damp weather, as do Sand Martins, Barn Swallows and House Martins, particularly if these conditions prevail during periods of peak passage. Great Spotted Woodpecker is sometimes seen. Passage of Meadow Pipits, Yellow Wagtails and Pied Wagtails can be witnessed here, mainly during late April and May and also during the autumn; the Blue-headed and Grey-headed races of the Yellow Wagtail have been seen in recent years and White Wagtails occur almost annually during the spring. Flocks of Fieldfares and Redwings are often seen passing over during October and November, usually when easterly winds prevail, at which time immigrant Blackbirds and Song Thrushes may also be numerous in the area.

Timing

Although Filey Dams has something to interest the birdwatcher through-out the year, the best times to visit, especially for the more unusual migrant species, are during late April to early June for the spring migrants, and from September to November for passage migrants, vagrants and winter immigrants. Both the hides face north or north east and the light is from behind and consequently good for viewing at any time of day. Early morning is perhaps the best time to visit as many passage species quickly move on in fine weather. Periods of adverse weather, especially with rain during the autumn, may bring down passage waders and passerines.

Access

Being so close to the town of Filey, this small reserve is worth combining with a visit to Filey Brigg. Approaching from the south on the A165, turn right at a roundabout onto the A1039 signed for Filey. Proceed for 0.5 miles (0.8 km) and turn left into Wharfedale, a long loop-road through a housing estate which eventually returns to the A1039 nearer the town centre. Pass a phone box and turn left, after which the road bears right to reach the Reserve car park after approximately 500 yards (460 m).

Approaching from Filey town, follow the road for Bridlington and after crossing the railway lines, turn right after 150 yards (135 m) to take the first entrance into Wharfedale. Follow the road, which eventually bears left, to reach the Reserve car park after about 650 yards (595 m). The first hide, overlooking the Main Pool, is adjacent to the car park and the East Pool hide is signed to the right along 80 yards (75 m) of well-made hard-core path and a further 100 yards (90 m) of boardwalk. Please stay on the pathways and be as quiet as possible whilst walking to the East Pool hide. See map for site 6.

Calendar

Winter (October to March): Includes several resident species which are present throughout the year. Little Grebe, Great Cormorant, Grey Heron, occasional Tundra and Whooper Swans, Greylag Goose, Canada Goose, Eurasian Wigeon, Gadwall (scarce), Common Teal, Mallard, Northern Pintail (scarce), Tufted Duck, Common Pochard (scarce), Eurasian Sparrowhawk, Common Kestrel, Water Rail, Moorhen, Common Coot, European Golden Plover, Northern Lapwing, Common Snipe, Common Redshank, Black-headed Gull, Common Gull, Herring Gull, Great Black-backed Gull, Stock Dove, Wood Pigeon, Collared Dove, Sky Lark, Wren, Hedge Accentor, Robin, Blackbird, Fieldfare, Song Thrush, Redwing, Mistle Thrush, Long-tailed Tit, Blue Tit, Great Tit, Magpie, Eurasian Jackdaw, Rook, Carrion Crow, Common Starling, Chaffinch, Greenfinch, Common Redpoll, Yellowhammer, Reed Bunting, Corn Bunting.

Spring and autumn passage (April to early June and August to early November): Common Shelduck, Garganey, Northern Shoveler, passage waders, Turtle Dove, Common Swift, Sand Martin, Barn Swallow, House Martin, Meadow Pipit, Yellow Wagtail, Pied Wagtail, Whinchat, warblers, Spotted Flycatcher, Pied Flycatcher, Goldfinch, Linnet.

Habitat

The spectacular chalk cliffs along the north side of the Flamborough headland reach an average height of around 400 feet (120 m). The stretch of cliffs at Bempton, now administered as a reserve by the RSPB, is host to the largest concentration of breeding seabirds on the English mainland. The area adjoining the cliff tops is entirely agricultural comprising both arable and grazing land with hedgerows, the best place for migrants being Hoddy Cows Lane which runs from Buckton to the cliff-top fields. The cliffs are too high for effective seawatching but passing skuas and terns are sometimes evident during the autumn.

Bempton Cliffs

Species

Long famous for its great colonies of breeding seabirds, Bempton provides the visitor with one of the most exciting bird spectacles in England. Until recently, the only place on the British mainland where Northern Gannets nested, the colonies of that species now number over 1,000 pairs. Between 25,000 and 29,000 Common Guillemots have been counted on the cliffs in recent years, Razorbills have numbered over 7,000 birds and Puffins around 6,000. The most numerous seabird is the Kittiwake and there are now up to 75,000 breeding pairs on the reserve stretch of the cliffs and very many more along the whole range. 700 pairs of Fulmars nested in 1989 as well as 950 pairs of Herring Gulls. Several pairs of Shags breed along the base of the cliffs. Large numbers of Rock Doves, many of which are ostensibly pure in both shape and plumage, frequent the cliffs, usually after the seabirds have left for the open sea during late July and August, when up to 500 pairs settle in to breed. Eurasian Jackdaws find nesting crevices amongst the seabird cliffs and several pairs of Tree Sparrows also nest there.

During the spring and autumn passage periods, the cliff-top fields and hedgerows attract migrant passerines and are always worth investigation, sub-rarities and vagrants being a possibility.

Timing

The best time to visit Bempton is from late April to July when the breeding activity is at its height. Visits during the autumn (September to November), after most of the seabirds have left the colonies, can produce migrants along the cliff tops and particularly along Hoddy Cows Lane.

Access

The Reserve can be reached from either the north or south. Travelling south from Filey on the A165, take the B1229 road opposite The Dotterel Inn, and continue for 5 miles (8 km) to the village of Bempton. Approaching from the south, travel to Flamborough and take the B1229 road to reach Bempton after 3 miles (4.8 km). Look for The White Horse Inn, easily identified by its glazed blue tile roof and turn into Cliff Lane alongside the pub. After just over 1 mile (1.8 km) enter the Reserve car park and proceed to the reception area. From here one can walk to the cliffs and along the cliff-top paths in both directions to view the colonies. The cliff edges are mainly long grass and can be very slippery and dangerous, especially during wet weather. There are several obvious viewing points on the small prominences.

Continuing north along the cliff-top path for about 0.5 miles (0.8 km) brings you to Hoddy Cows, an area of scrub and marshy ground some little way back from the cliff top which is worth investigating in the spring and autumn for migrants. A minor road next to a pond at the northern end of Buckton village leads along Hoddy Cows Lane to this area (see map for site 9). See the Bridlington chapter (site 10) for details of cruises to view the breeding seabird colonies from below the cliffs.

Calendar

This includes the cliff-top fields and hedgerows.

Spring and summer (March to August): Fulmar, Northern Gannet, Great Cormorant, Shag, Common Kestrel, Northern Lapwing, Herring Gull, Kittiwake, Common Guillemot, Razorbill, Puffin, Rock Dove, Stock Dove, Common Swift, Sky Lark, Meadow Pipit, Wren, Eurasian Jackdaw, Tree Sparrow, Linnet, Yellowhammer, Corn Bunting.

Spring and autumn passage (April and May, and August to October): Skuas, terns, Turtle Dove, hirundines, Yellow Wagtail, Common Redstart, Black Redstart, Northern Wheatear, immigrant thrushes, warblers, Spotted Flycatcher, Pied Flycatcher, immigrant finches.

9 FLAMBOROUGH HEAD

OS Landranger Map 101
Scarborough

Habitat

The imposing headland of Flamborough juts out into the North Sea for some 6 miles (9.6 km) from its base near Bridlington and, in consequence, acts as a major landfall area for many incoming autumn migrants and as a last jumping-off place on their return journey in the spring at which time incoming migrants also arrive on the headland.

From the village of Flamborough, halfway along the peninsula, the headland is mainly arable farmland with hedgerows and some small plantations of mature deciduous trees as at Old Fall Plantation. A golf course and a large pond close to the point provide good habitat frequented by several migrants including occasional ducks and waders. The coastline is composed entirely of deeply eroded chalk, cut by the sea into caves, pinnacles and arches and reaching a height of around 250 feet (76 m). The bushes on the grassy slopes below the lighthouse, above Selwick Bay, are good for migrants.

On the south side of the peninsula lies the deep wooded valley of South Landing where migrants find food and shelter on arrival. This is perhaps the best place for seeing unusual passerines and for witnessing the hordes of thrushes which pile into the trees and bushes during October and November on easterly winds. Running from north to south and cutting right through the peninsula is Danes Dyke, an ancient fortification which is now cloaked in mature deciduous trees, attractive to migrants in both spring and autumn and a favourite place to see the eastern leaf warblers, especially at the southern end where the wide ravine drops down to the beach from the car park.

Species

Having attracted the attentions of birdwatchers for many years, the headland has more recently become the object of prolonged and intensive study by the Flamborough Ornithological Group who have concentrated particularly on the movements of seabirds off this unique location. Every autumn sees the arrival of thousands of thrushes, warblers, flycatchers and finches and there is always the chance of finding a rarity.

During the winter months, seawatching from the point can produce divers, grebes, sea ducks (including good numbers of Common Eiders on some days) and gulls including occasional Iceland or Glaucous Gulls. Shag has its county stronghold here and over 100 birds are regularly present. Common Guillemots and Razorbills are usually evident in the winter and movements offshore can often involve several thousand birds (as on 7th January 1980 when 10,300 Common Guillemots flew north); 37,000 Puffins were counted on 17th March 1990. Little Auks appear during northerly gales in late October and November and at times their numbers can be exceptional; 6,337 flew south during a northeaster on 29th October 1983. Brent Geese can often be seen in small numbers as they move up and down the coast. Rock Pipits frequent the cliffs and feral pigeons, many of which are ostensibly pure Rock Doves, are always present in good numbers.

44

Spring passage, from late March, sees the arrival of the first Sandwich Terns followed by Commons and Arctics which continue to pass throughout April and May. A movement of divers takes place during February, March and early April when good numbers of Red-throated and fewer Black-throated and Great Northerns move north. The arrival of passerines during the spring period can be impressive and the short grassland at the point is host to Northern Wheatears, pipits and wagtails. The wooded ravine at South Landing should be checked at this time for warblers, flycatchers and possible rarities.

During the breeding season, mainly during June and July, offshore movements of Common Guillemots and Puffins can be spectacular with counts of several thousands passing, often during the evenings. Smaller numbers of Razorbills are usually involved. During the summer, all three species of breeding auks afford excellent views as they sit on the ledges, often at very close range or as they sit on the sea at the base of the cliffs. Many Kittiwakes and Herring Gulls breed on the cliffs and Shags nest in caves and crevices close to the sea. Large numbers of Great Cormorants are usually present during the autumn but do not breed here. July sees the start of the return passage of terns and movements of shearwaters and skuas which peaks in August and September and continues until November. Manx Shearwaters are usually in evidence depending on the wind conditions, a factor which affects the movements of all the seabirds. Sooty Shearwaters are to be seen every autumn and large numbers are sometimes involved, for example, 1,000 on 26th August 1978. A few Cory's, Great, Mediterranean and Little Shearwaters also occur and some southern hemisphere petrels have been seen. Small numbers of skuas pass north during the spring period but autumn is the best time to see this group. Passage is often spectacular but may be of brief duration and the intending visitor should have regard for the weather conditions. Winds of

Gannets

45

some strength from the northern quarter are necessary to bring the largest movements down the coast and belts of rain are often preceded or followed by large numbers. Up to 1,000 Arctic Skuas have been counted during a day's watch and Long-tailed Skuas reached a total of 350 on one autumn day in 1988.

Fulmars breed along the cliffs and Northern Gannets are usually offshore passing to and from their breeding cliffs at nearby Bempton or further north. Both species can also be seen during the autumn and winter.

The arrival of immigrant chats, starts, thrushes, warblers, Goldcrests, flycatchers and finches can be witnessed to advantage at Flamborough during late September, October and November, usually on cold grey days with mist or rain. On winds from the east, it is possible to see thrushes coming in low over the sea and making a landfall on the rocks and upper slopes of the cliffs and in the bushes, or coming in high and tumbling out of the sky into the gullies and trees at South Landing and Dane's Dyke. Many birdwatchers assemble at this time and the chance of a rarity being found is enhanced in consequence.

Timing

A visit at any time during the winter months can be rewarding for seabirds especially if the weather is rough and the sea is running. The spring and autumn passage periods are obviously the best times for seawatching and for seeing migrant passerines. Evening seawatches often produce good numbers of shearwaters, skuas and terns during the autumn. Have regard for the weather when deciding to visit. The seabird movements peak during periods of strong winds from the northern quarter and the immigrant thrushes and other passerines usually arrive on easterly winds and misty or overcast conditions during October and November.

Access

To reach the Flamborough Headland, leave Bridlington on the B1255 road signed Flamborough 4. After 3 miles (4.8 km) the road passes through Danes Dyke (signed on the right) and continues through the centre of Flamborough. After a left-hand bend, turn right onto the B1259 signed for South Landing and the lighthouse. To reach South Landing, take the first right into South Sea Road and proceed for 0.5 miles (0.8 km) to the car parking area (pay machine). From here walk down the valley on a tarmac road which leads to the boulder beach, just before which a signed footpath crosses the ravine and eventually returns to the car park.

To reach the lighthouse and point, return to the B1259 and turn right, following the tarmac road which continues for 2 miles (3.2 km) straight to the lighthouse car parking area (pay machine – tickets from South Landing car park are valid, and vice versa). Park, and walk along a tarmac track past the lighthouse to the fog station at the point, below which several ledges are convenient places from which to watch the sea. An open grassy area to the south of the fog station, near a wooden seat, is also a good watchpoint. During strong westerly or northwesterly winds in the autumn and winter, it is possible to sit out of the wind on the slopes below the cliff top. A footpath along the cliff top on the south side of the peninsula passes Old Fall Plantation and then right along New Fall hedgerow (a little under 1 mile (1.5 km) from the fog station) coming out on the main road 350 yards (320 m) west of the old lighthouse tower.

North Landing Ravine can be reached by returning to Flamborough village, turning right at the 'T' junction onto the B1255, and continuing to

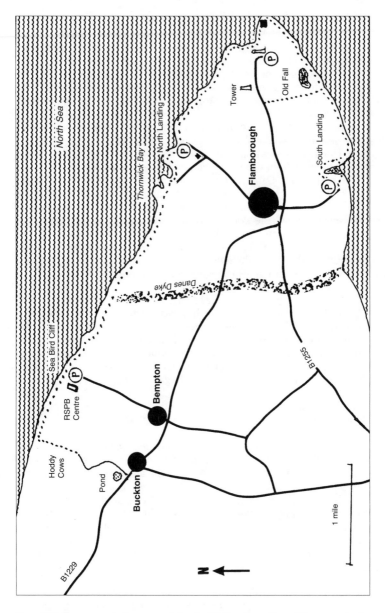

the cliff-top car park (pay machines). Walk along the cliff-top paths in both directions.

Between Easter and the end of August, there are regular boat trips from North Landing in three Yorkshire cobles (clinker-built fishing boats based on Viking long-ship design). These cobles leave on a regular basis (weather permitting) to the seabird colonies around the north side of the headland. With this size of boat, one has the advantage of being able to enter 'Smugglers Cave', one of the largest caves on the Yorkshire coast, renowned in history for the smuggling of contraband from similar small

boats whilst hidden from the view of customs and excise officers. There
is a small hole at the back of this large cave through which it is said contraband was hauled from the boats onto waiting donkeys with cloth-shod
feet to ensure silence. The average boat trips last for 30 minutes but special arrangements can be made for parties wishing to view the birds for
longer periods. For more information and booking details contact the
skipper: Richard Emmerson, Westcarr, Woodcock Road, Flamborough
(Tel: 01262 850575).

Approaching North Landing from Flamborough, look for an unmade
track on the left at The Viking Hotel which leads to Thornwick Bay and
cafe. This track passes a small reedbed on the left before reaching the car
park at the cafe from where one can look down into the Bay.

The entrance to Danes Dyke is signed at a dip in the road, 0.75 miles
(1.2 km) west of Flamborough village. A tarmac road leads through the
wooded dyke to a car parking area (with shop and toilets) from where
one can walk down the wooded ravine to the beach. The road continues
in a loop to rejoin the main B1255 road 700 yards (640 m) further east.

Just before the main car parking area at the lighthouse on the Headland
is the Cliff End Café, on the right, opposite the coastguard station. This is
well worth a visit as it is also a regular rendezvous for birdwatchers.

Calendar

Winter (October to March): Red-throated Diver, Black-throated Diver,
Great Northern Diver, White-billed Diver (rare), Great Crested Grebe,
Red-necked Grebe, Slavonian Grebe, Fulmar, Northern Gannet, Great
Cormorant, Shag, Brent Goose, Eurasian Wigeon, Common Teal, Greater
Scaup, Common Eider, Long-tailed Duck, Common Scoter, Velvet Scoter,
Common Goldeneye, Red-breasted Merganser, Iceland Gull, Glaucous
Gull, Great Black-backed Gull, Herring Gull, Common Gull, Kittiwake,
Common Guillemot, Razorbill, Little Auk, Rock Dove, Rock Pipit,
Eurasian Jackdaw.

*Spring and autumn passage (March to May and July to October (mainly
autumn)):* Divers, grebes, Cory's Shearwater, Great Shearwater, Sooty Shearwater, Manx Shearwater, Mediterranean Shearwater, Little Shearwater,
European Storm Petrel, Leach's Storm Petrel, Great Cormorant, Shag, Com-
mon Shelduck, Eurasian Wigeon, Common Teal, Northern Pintail, Com-
mon Eider, Common Scoter, Red-breasted Merganser, passage waders,
Pomarine Skua, Arctic Skua, Long-tailed Skua, Great Skua, Little Gull,
Sabine's Gull, Common Gull, Herring Gull, Great Black-backed Gull, Kitti-
wake, Sandwich Tern, Common Tern, Arctic Tern, Little Tern, Common
Guillemot, Razorbill, Black Guillemot, Puffin, Common Cuckoo, Common
Swift, Wryneck, Sky Lark, Sand Martin, Barn Swallow, House Martin,
Richard's Pipit, Tawny Pipit, Tree Pipit, Meadow Pipit, Red-breasted Pipit,
Yellow Wagtail, Pied Wagtail, Robin, Bluethroat, Black Redstart, Common
Redstart, Whinchat, Common Stonechat, Northern Wheatear, Ring Ouzel,
Blackbird, Fieldfare, Song Thrush, Redwing, Sedge Warbler, Marsh Warb-
ler, Reed Warbler, Icterine Warbler, Barred Warbler, Lesser Whitethroat,
Common Whitethroat, Garden Warbler, Blackcap, Pallas's Leaf Warbler,
Yellow-browed Warbler, Chiffchaff, Willow Warbler, Goldcrest, Firecrest,
Spotted Flycatcher, Red-breasted Flycatcher, Pied Flycatcher, Red-backed
Shrike, Common Starling, Tree Sparrow, Chaffinch, Brambling, Greenfinch,
Goldfinch, Siskin, Linnet, Common Redpoll, Common Crossbill, Common
Rosefinch, Bullfinch, Yellowhammer, Reed Bunting.

Note: Only the regular species and the most likely sub-rarities are mentioned here but rare vagrants are always a possibility and one or two occur almost annually.

Spring and summer (March to August): Northern Gannet, Great Cormorant, Shag, Herring Gull, Kittiwake, Common Guillemot, Razorbill, Puffin, Rock Dove, Common Swift, Sky Lark, House Martin (nests on the sea cliffs at Thornwick Bay), Meadow Pipit, Rock Pipit, Wren, Eurasian Jackdaw, Tree Sparrow, Yellowhammer, Corn Bunting.

10 BRIDLINGTON HARBOUR AND SOUTH BEACH

OS Landranger
Map 101
Scarborough

Habitat and Species

Bridlington is a favourite seaside resort and during the summer months is very crowded. The busy harbour is enclosed by piers and in the winter months offers shelter for divers, grebes, Great Cormorants, Shags, sea ducks and auks during periods of severe weather. A large area of mud, exposed at low tide, is favoured by waders, particularly Dunlins and Common Redshanks. The fishing cobles unload their catches on the south pier and the gulls assemble in this area. Iceland and Glaucous Gulls sometimes join the large gatherings of Herring and Great Blackbacked Gulls during the winter and a few Kittiwakes are usually present throughout this period. The rocks at the base of the south pier on the seaward side often have Purple Sandpipers and Turnstones, the latter also frequenting the harbour walls. The piers are a good place to see Rock Pipits in winter.

The South Beach, immediately south of the harbour, is a good place for watching gulls and waders; at low tide it is a favourite loafing area for gulls and the waders feeding here include Oystercatchers, Great Ringed Plovers, Grey Plovers, Sanderlings, Dunlins, Common Redshanks and Turnstones. Sanderlings and Turnstones often number over 100 birds, the latter usually being most numerous when there is ample seaweed washed up along the shore. Carrion Crows scrounge along the beach daily.

Timing

Winter is the best time to visit this area, especially during hard weather when seabirds are most likely to seek shelter in the harbour. The South Beach is very popular with dog walkers and the birds are often disturbed in consequence; the gulls and waders are best seen here on falling and low tides. Boats leave the harbour to visit the seabird colonies at nearby Flamborough and Bempton cliffs on a regular basis between mid-May and mid-September (see below).

Access

This area is easy to find and is well signposted. On entering the town on the A166 from the west or on the A165 from either the north or the south, follow signs for South Beach. There is adequate car parking space adjacent to the harbour (pay machines) and plenty of side street parking during the winter months also. The South Beach lies adjacent to the harbour and stretches south alongside the sea-wall and beyond.

The harbour is the starting point for cruises to the seabird colonies at the nearby Flamborough and Bempton cliffs and from mid-May to mid-September the *MV Yorkshire Belle* sails regularly from the North Pier. She can carry 200 passengers and has full facilities on board including a saloon bar, a snack bar and toilets. The cruises last for about 2½ hours and pass close under the impressive cliffs where thousands of seabirds, including Fulmars, Northern Gannets, Shags, Kittiwakes, Common Guillemots, Razorbills and Puffins can be seen sitting on the sea or flying to and from their breeding ledges. Cruises can be arranged for private parties, details of which are available from the skipper; P Richardson, 28 Roundhay Road, Bridlington (Tel 01262-673582).

During recent years, the RSPB has commissioned a series of cruises on Saturdays and/or Sundays, lasting for up to 3 or 4 hours depending on the weather, from May to July visiting the breeding colonies and from August to October for pelagic trips. During the latter, birds are attracted close to the boat by the use of 'chum', a mashed-up mixture of smelly fish, thus offering excellent photographic opportunities. On good days, usually with winds from the northern quarter, varying numbers of both Manx and Sooty Shearwaters and also Arctic Skuas can be seen, often passing close to the boat. The other skuas, Pomarine, Long-tailed and Great, may also occur in addition to Sandwich, Common and Arctic Terns and also many gulls. The RSPB cruises are very popular and one should book in advance if possible. Details can be obtained from the visitor centre at the Bempton Cliffs Reserve or from the RSPB North of England Regional Office, Milburn House, Dean Street, Newcastle-upon-Tyne NE1 1LE.

Calendar

This includes The Harbour, South Beach and the inshore waters.

Winter (October to March): Occasional divers and grebes, Great Cormorant, Shag, Common Eider, Common Scoter, Oystercatcher, Great Ringed Plover, Grey Plover, Sanderling, Dunlin, Common Redshank, Turnstone, Grey Phalarope (occasional), Black-headed Gull, Common Gull, Herring Gull, Iceland Gull, Glaucous Gull, Great Black-backed Gull, Kittiwake, Common Guillemot, Razorbill, Little Auk (sporadic during storms), Rock Dove (many feral types), Rock Pipit, Pied Wagtail, Common Starling, House Sparrow.

For details of the birds on the seabird cliffs at the Bempton Reserve during the summer months see site 8.

11 FRAISTHORPE
BEACH AND FIELDS

OS Landranger Map 101
Scarborough

Habitat and Species

Lying some 4 miles (6.4 km) south of Bridlington, this area is a continuation of the wide sandy beach which runs southwards from the town along the whole length of Bridlington Bay to Spurn Point. The beach is backed by low and eroding boulder-clay cliffs with grazing and arable land up to their edges. The Auburn Beck runs across the beach here, attracting many gulls which bathe in the fresh water. The beach is also favoured by waders, particularly Sanderlings which occur in good numbers. Other waders regularly present are Oystercatchers, Great Ringed Plovers, Grey Plovers, a few Red Knots, Dunlins, Common Redshanks and Turnstones.

The sea can be very productive as divers and gatherings of Great Crested Grebes fish offshore during the winter months. Small flocks of Common Scoters and the occasional Common Eider are often present. Seawatching during July, August and September will produce shearwaters, terns and skuas especially during strong winds from the north or northeast but in smaller numbers than further south as at Hornsea (see that chapter).

Winter flocks of European Golden Plovers and Northern Lapwings frequent the fields just south of Fraisthorpe village. These fields are certainly worth investigating during the spring and autumn migration periods as well as during the winter months. Northern Wheatears regularly feed on the ploughed land in spring when the hedgerows may hold other migrant passerines. Red-legged and Grey Partridges are usually to be seen in the area and flocks of Eurasian Jackdaws, Rooks, Stock Doves and Wood Pigeons are commonplace in the fields south of the village during the winter months. The hedgerows in this part often have flocks of Tree Sparrows, Linnets, occasional Twites, small flocks of Yellowhammers and a few Corn Buntings.

The cliff-top fields immediately south of the car parking area can be very productive during the autumn and winter when gatherings of Sky Larks, occasional Horned Larks, Twites, Lapland Longspurs and a few Snow Buntings may be seen. The upper beach often has Rock Pipit and Pied Wagtail.

Timing

The Fraisthorpe area is best visited during the spring and autumn for migrant waders and passerines, and also during late autumn and winter for waders, gulls and flocks of plovers, pigeons and corvids in the fields as well as the larks, finches and buntings. Early morning is often best for viewing the beach areas as they are disturbed by dog walkers and bait diggers for much of the day. The waders are only temporarily displaced however and soon settle back to feed on the wide expanses of the beach. They are best seen on an incoming tide at which time small parties fly along the shoreline as they shift location. The divers, grebes and sea ducks drift much closer inshore when the tide is rising.

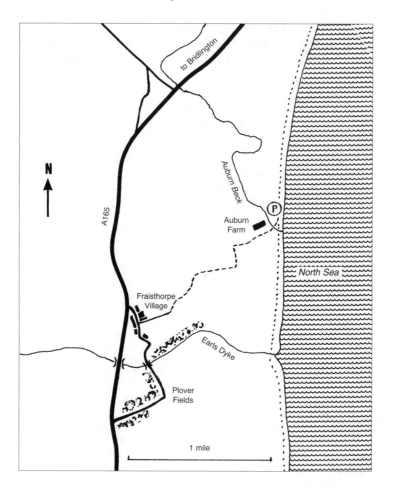

Access

To reach Fraisthorpe, leave Bridlington on the A165 Hull road and after 4 miles (6.4 km) look for the sign to Fraisthorpe Beach shortly after which is a left turning opposite a second sign. Turn left here into the small village and take the first left, again signed Fraisthorpe Beach, and proceed along the narrow winding tarmac road which runs between open arable land to Auburn Farm. The road passes the farm and leads to a private car parking area on the short grass at the top of the beach. Parking is free during the winter months but a charge is made by the farmer during the summer. Walk south from here, crossing over Auburn Beck and along the cliff top to view the beach and the fields.

On leaving the site, and before reaching the main road, come to the 'T' junction in Fraisthorpe village and turn left. This road takes you through the good agricultural area south of the village and finally back to the A165 after just under 1 mile (1.5 km). Shortly after leaving the houses, come to a small bridge and during the autumn, stop to check the hedgerow which runs eastwards along a ditch, for migrants. Further along this route, just beyond where the road bears sharp right, stop to view the large field on the left for European Golden Plovers, Northern Lapwings, corvids and pigeons in winter. The hedgerows along the last section from here to the main road regularly attract Tree Sparrows, Yellowhammers and Corn Buntings.

Calendar
This includes the sea, the beach and the fields.

Winter (October to March): Red-throated Diver, Black-throated Diver (occasional), Great Northern Diver (occasional), Great Crested Grebe, Red-necked Grebe and Slavonian Grebe (rare), Northern Gannet, Great Cormorant, Shag, Common Eider, Common Scoter, Common Kestrel, Red-legged Partridge, Grey Partridge, Moorhen, Oystercatcher, Great Ringer Plover, European Golden Plover, Grey Plover, Northern Lapwing, Red Knot, Sanderling, Dunlin, Common Redshank, Turnstone, gulls, Common Guillemot, Razorbill, Stock Dove, Wood Pigeon, Collared Dove, Sky Lark, Horned Lark, Meadow Pipit, Rock Pipit, Pied Wagtail, Magpie, Eurasian Jackdaw, Rook, Carrion Crow, Common Starling, House Sparrow, Tree Sparrow, Chaffinch, Linnet, Twite, Lapland Longspur, Snow Bunting, Yellowhammer, Reed Bunting, Corn Bunting.

Spring and autumn passage (April to early June and August to October): Manx Shearwater (the rare shearwaters are a possibility), all four skuas, Sandwich Tern, Common Tern, Arctic Tern, Common Swift, Sand Martin (some pairs breed in the boulder-clay cliffs), Barn Swallow, House Martin, Northern Wheatear.

12 BARMSTON BEACH

OS Landranger Map 101
Scarborough

Habitat and Species
Lying 6 miles (9.6 km) south of Bridlington, Barmston Beach is an extension of the Fraisthorpe area and a convenient place to visit. A large area of marshy ground adjacent to the low dunes at the top of the beach is occasionally inundated by the sea during high tides accompanied by easterly gales. A series of reed-filled drainage dykes attracts migrant *Acrocephalus* warblers and Reed Buntings. The marshy ground is worth checking for surface-feeding ducks and waders which drop in during migration. Jack Snipe and Common Snipe are regular here in autumn. The arable fields to the west and north are good for Northern Wheatears in spring and during the autumn when Sky Larks, occasional Horned Larks, Linnets, Twites, Lapland Longspurs, Yellowhammers and Corn Buntings also occur on the stubbles. The pebbly upper beach and low dunes are favourite places for Snow Buntings. The grass fields and

stubbles are sometimes visited by small numbers of White-fronted, Barnacle and Brent Geese during the winter months. Seawatching may produce all the species mentioned in the section on Fraisthorpe.

Timing
Spring, autumn and winter are the best times to visit (see under Fraisthorpe).

Access
To reach Barmston, continue south from Fraisthorpe on the A165 for 2 miles (3.2 km) when the village is signed to the left at a sweeping right-hand bend in the main road. Continue for 1 mile (1.6 km) to the cliff top and park on the right in an open area in front of a cafe. From here, walk north along the cliff top past a caravan site, beyond which is a large arable field. The marshy area lies adjacent to this field and runs along the top of the beach. Walk around the inland perimeter of the marshy ground which borders stubbles. The amount of water varies greatly depending on the rainfall or inundation from the sea. More stubbles continue north from here to an old concrete pill box on a ridge.

One should also walk south along the cliffs, at least as far as Barmston Main Drain, some 0.5 miles (0.8 km) from the car park.

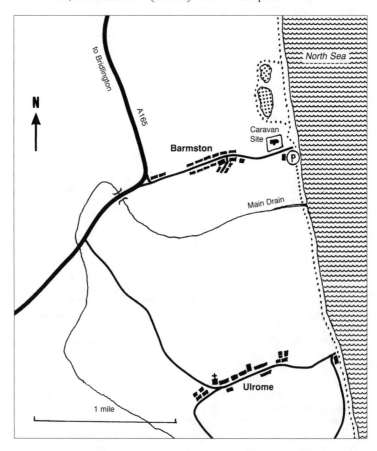

Calendar

Spring (April and May): Migrant waders and passerines.

Autumn and winter (September to March): Horned Lark, Twite, Lapland Longspur, Snow Bunting, in addition to the waders and seabirds (see under Fraisthorpe Beach for details).

13 HORNSEA AND MAPPLETON

OS Landranger Map 107
Kingston-upon-Hull

Habitat

The low boulder-clay cliffs along this part of the coastline reach a height of between 30 and 40 feet (9 to 12 m) and provide a good vantage point from which to watch the sea. Hornsea and Mappleton are ideal for this as they provide vehicular access to the cliff tops. Lying 14 and 17 miles (22.5 and 27.3 km) respectively, south of the Flamborough Headland, both sites provide the watcher with the chance to witness movements of seabirds, particularly during the autumn. Seabirds moving south off Flamborough continue out at sea for some way after passing the projecting headland but approach the shore as they move south and come within sight of land in the region of Hornsea. Birds moving north tend to hug the coastline up to this area, before starting to move out to pass the Flamborough Headland.

Species

Seawatching can be very productive and when the wind is of some strength from the northern quarter during April/May and particularly from July to November, large movements of shearwaters and skuas are regularly seen. Fulmars, Northern Gannets, waterfowl, waders, gulls and terns also pass at the appropriate season. During the winter months, movements of divers, waterfowl and auks are commonplace and are often most evident early in the day. In addition to the regular autumn movements of Manx and Sooty Shearwaters, there are records of Cory's, Great, Mediterranean and Little Shearwaters. Movements of Arctic, Pomarine and Long-tailed Skuas often reach three figures with good numbers of Great Skuas also. This is perhaps the best area to see European Storm and Leach's Storm Petrels during strong northerly gales in autumn (September/October) when birds may fly along the beach over the surf. Movements of Little Auks can reach treble figures during October and November in these same conditions.

Timing

Spring and autumn passage periods (April/May and July to November) are obviously the best times to watch the sea. Peak movements occur with the right weather conditions, discussed in detail in the Flamborough chapter. Movements can start at any time of day if the wind swings or strengthens. Early mornings or evenings are generally the best times to watch although

Pomarine Skuas

movement may continue throughout the day in the right conditions. The light tends to be a problem early in the day unless there is cloud cover.

Access
To reach Hornsea, travel south from Bridlington on the A165 and fork left onto the B1242 just after Barmston. On entering the town, after a sharp left-hand bend, turn left again, signed 'Town Centre and Seafront', and then left again at the main road signed 'Floral Hall'. After 530 yards (485 m), turn right into Morrow Avenue and park at the end on the left. Seawatch from the cliff top or from the brick shelter. This can be very crowded at times of peak seabird movement and a team of local birdwatchers regularly maintains all-day vigils here. Please do not enter if the shelter is crowded as this will impede viewing.

To reach the watchpoint at the southern end of the town, drive to the main seafront area and proceed south along a short tarmac road running parallel with, and adjacent to, the beach and park on a rise in front of the Oasis public house. It is possible to watch from the car here during inclement weather.

Lying some 3 miles (4.8 km) south of Hornsea, Mappleton is more secluded and is a very good place from which to watch the sea. Continue south from Hornsea on the A165 and enter the village of Mappleton. Look for the Maple Garage on the left, immediately after which, turn left and come to a car parking area, with toilets, after 200 yards (180 m). Watch from the cliff top in front of the car parking area or from the slopes below (see map for site 14).

Calendar
Spring and autumn (March to May and July to October): (Mainly autumn.) Red-throated Diver, Fulmar, Cory's Shearwater, Sooty Shearwater, Manx

Shearwater, European Storm Petrel, Leach's Storm Petrel, Northern Gannet, Great Cormorant, Shag, Common Shelduck, Eurasian Wigeon, Common Teal, Northern Pintail, Greater Scaup, Common Eider, Common Scoter, Velvet Scoter, Red-breasted Merganser, Oystercatcher, Great Ringed Plover, European Golden Plover, Grey Plover, Northern Lapwing, Red Knot, Sanderling, Dunlin, Bar-tailed Godwit, Whimbrel, Eurasian Curlew, Turnstone, Pomarine Skua, Arctic Skua, Long-tailed Skua, Great Skua, Little Gull, Sabine's Gull, Kittiwake, Sandwich Tern, Common Tern, Arctic Tern, Little Tern, Common Guillemot, Razorbill, Puffin.

Winter (October to March): Red-throated Diver (marked northward passage during February and early March), Black-throated Diver, Great Northern Diver, Fulmar, Northern Gannet, Great Cormorant, Shag, Brent Goose, Eurasian Wigeon, Common Teal, Greater Scaup, Common Eider, Long-tailed Duck, Common Goldeneye, most of the passage waders listed above, Great Black-backed Gull, Kittiwake, Common Guillemot, Razorbill, Little Auk.

14 HORNSEA MERE

OS Landranger Map 107
Kingston-upon-Hull

Habitat

Hornsea Mere is the largest natural lake in Yorkshire and is 1.5 miles (2.4 km) long and approximately 0.5 miles (0.8 km) wide running east to west only 1 mile (1.6 km) from the sea. The lake shore is varied in character: the eastern end is mainly open, bordering onto grass fields with muddy edges and the western end has large beds of *Phragmites* and *Typha*. The northern shore is bordered by mature deciduous woodland and that of the south by reeds and scrub. The surrounding area to the north and west is mainly arable and grazing land and the town of Hornsea abuts the eastern end. The Mere is administered as a reserve by the RSPB with a resident warden.

Species

Being so close to the sea, the Mere is a prime site for divers, grebes, sea ducks, waders, gulls and terns which seek food and shelter on this large sheet of fresh water at the appropriate season. The Mere is especially good for waterfowl, both diving and surface-feeding ducks occurring in large numbers. Flocks of Common Pochards and Tufted Ducks often reach up to 1,000 birds during the late autumn and the Mere is Yorkshire's principal water for Common Goldeneyes with peak counts of up to 400 and sometimes more during the winter. Small numbers of Goosanders, which were formerly much more numerous are often present and a few Ruddy Ducks now frequent the Mere.

The adjacent grazing land bordering the south side attracts many Eurasian Wigeons and up to 900 have been recorded during the early months of the year. Gadwalls regularly number up to 200 birds. There is a large resident flock of Greylag Geese and Canada Geese, which is often

57

joined by small numbers of Barnacle Geese (feral) and occasional Pink-footed Geese. Mute Swans assemble in large numbers to moult during late summer and regularly number 150 birds. The resident pinioned Whooper Swan at Kirkholme Point has a predilection for vehicles and can be a pest, albeit an interesting one.

Strategically placed for watching visual migration, several species of birds of prey have been recorded including harriers, Ospreys, Honey-buzzards and Hobbies. The extensive reedbeds hold one of the two largest breeding colonies of Reed Warblers in the region. Several rare warblers have occurred including Cetti's, Savi's and Great Reed. Bearded Tits sometimes appear during the autumn and winter. During the autumn (September/October) when fall migrants are coming in over the sea, the area attracts many Common Starlings, Blackbirds, Redwings, Fieldfares and some Ring Ouzels as well as warblers, wheatears, chats, starts and finches. A large mixed corvid roost at the western end regularly holds up to 200 Carrion Crows and more on occasions. A roost of Wood Pigeons regularly has between 5,000–10,000 birds during the winter.

In early autumn, mainly during August, gatherings of Little Gulls can be impressive and this is the best place in the area for watching the species. A large and traditional roost of Great Cormorants in trees on a small island on the north side often holds up to 100 birds and is present throughout the year. Movement of terns, including Common, Arctic and Black, occurs in most years depending on wind direction, in both spring and autumn. A large gull roost includes several hundred birds, mainly Black-headed and Common, but including Herring and Great Black-backed with an occasional Iceland or Glaucous. Many waders pass through during spring and autumn and feed along the open shorelines at the eastern end.

Timing

Anytime between August and May is worthwhile for seeing passage in progress or to see the winter waterfowl, but there is much to interest the birdwatcher throughout the year. Boating tends to disturb the waterbirds at the eastern end around Kirkholme Point but the water is large and there are always some undisturbed areas even here. A line of buoys across the Mere separates the boats from the western end and the secluded bays in this section are better for surface-feeding ducks. A wide channel on the northern side of the boating point is relatively quiet and good for ducks at all times.

Access

The town of Hornsea can be easily reached on the B1242 main coast road or on the B1244 from the west. The best viewing areas at the Mere are the open fields on the southeast corner and the boating point at the eastern end. To reach the open field area, known as 'The first field', leave Hornsea on the B1242 travelling south and turn right onto the Hull road opposite a garage before leaving the town. After 700 yards (640 m) on reaching the open fields, park in Mere View Avenue opposite the field gate. Walk along the edge of the field keeping to the public footpath which continues along the length of the Mere to the western end at Wassand. The boating area on Kirkholme Point is reached by turning into a track between two white brick posts, signed 'The Mere and Car Park' off the main B1242 as it passes through the town centre. Car parking space is available on the point and there is a café and toilet facilities. The RSPB centre is on the left at the entrance to the boating complex and visitors may call in for information.

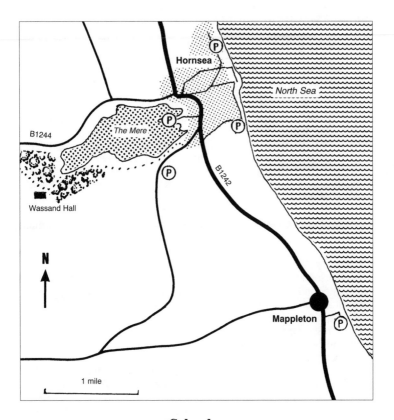

Calendar

Winter (October to March): Divers, grebes, Grey Heron, swans, Greylag Geese, Eurasian Wigeon, Gadwall, Common Teal, Northern Pintail, Northern Shoveler, Common Pochard, Tufted Duck, Common Goldeneye, Long-tailed Duck, Goosander, Ruddy Duck, Water Rail, European Golden Plover, Northern Lapwing, Dunlin, Common Snipe, Common Gull, Black-headed Gull, Herring Gull, Great Black-backed Gull, Iceland Gull, Glaucous Gull, Stock Dove, Wood Pigeon, Collared Dove, Great Spotted Woodpecker, Sky Lark, Rock Pipit, Fieldfare, Redwing, Bearded Tit (sporadic), Eurasian Jay, Tree Sparrow, Corn Bunting, Siskin, Common Redpoll.

Spring and autumn passage (April to early June and August to October): Honey-buzzard, Marsh Harrier, Osprey, Merlin, usual waders, Little Gull, Common Tern, Arctic Tern, Black Tern, Turtle Dove, Common Swift, Tree Pipit, Meadow Pipit, Rock Pipit (Scandinavian race in spring), Yellow Wagtail, Pied Wagtail, Black Redstart, Common Redstart, Whinchat, Northern Wheatear, warblers, Goldcrest, Pied Flycatcher.

Spring and Summer (April to August): Great Crested Grebe, Little Grebe, Great Cormorant, Mute Swan, Greylag Goose, Canada Goose, Gadwall, Common Teal, Mallard, Northern Shoveler, Common Pochard, Tufted Duck, Ruddy Duck, Eurasian Sparrowhawk, Common Kestrel, Red-legged Partridge, Grey Partridge, Moorhen, Common Coot, Common Swift, Common Kingfisher, hirundines, Yellow Wagtail, Sedge Warbler, Reed Warbler.

15 TOPHILL LOW NATURE RESERVE

Habitat

Tophill Low Pumping Station is situated alongside the River Hull and is surrounded by flat agricultural land which was once part of a large area of carrland along the course of the river. The site has been managed, with wildlife in mind, for several years and there are now excellent habitats for birds including shallow lagoons, marshy areas, scrub and small patches of woodland in addition to the large sheets of deep open water in the two reservoirs. Yorkshire Water and The Tophill Low Wildlife Group have worked closely together in recent years to create this very important wildlife area which is now designated as a reserve.

Species

The diverse habitats, situated just 9 miles (14.4 km) from the east coast and in the shallow valley of the River Hull, attract many birds and provide an annual total of around 170 species. Numbers of waterfowl and waders can be spectacular at the appropriate season. The open, deep water of the two reservoirs regularly attracts the rarer grebes in addition to both Little and Great Crested. Great Cormorants are a feature of the reservoirs and can number up to 50 birds, mainly during the autumn. Grey Herons are present throughout the year in varying numbers and allied rarities have been Purple Heron and Eurasian Spoonbill. Small numbers of both Tundra and Whooper Swans call in regularly between October and March when occasional grey geese join the resident flock of Greylag Geese which sometimes numbers up to 500 birds. A few pairs of Common Shelducks nest annually following a spring passage during February, March and April, when numbers often reach 30 to 40 birds.

The site is excellent for ducks and the following species occur annually (some recent maxima are shown): Eurasian Wigeon (500 to 1,000 October to March), Gadwall (up to 50, sometimes more, September to February), Common Teal (main passage in September when up to 700), Mallard (1,000 to 2,000 September to February), Northern Pintail (50 to 100 mainly September and October), Garganey (only very small numbers during May and August/September), Northern Shoveler (up to 100/200 mainly September and October), Common Pochard (100 to 350 mainly during October to January), Tufted Duck (500 to 800 mainly during September, October and November), Common Goldeneye (up to 50, occasionally more, mainly during November to March) and Ruddy Duck (up to 50 mainly during November to March). The sea ducks occasionally appear with Greater Scaup, Long-tailed Duck and Common Scoter occurring in small numbers almost annually. A few Smews and Goosanders are also seen during the winter months.

Eurasian Sparrowhawks and Common Kestrels are breeding residents. Other birds of prey seen during recent years have been Black Kite, Red Kite, Marsh Harrier, Hen Harrier, Montagu's Harrier, Common Buzzard, Rough-legged Buzzard, Osprey, Red-footed Falcon, Merlin, Hobby and Peregrine Falcon. Both Red-legged and Grey Partridges can be seen in the agricultural land and Water Rails are regular around the lagoons where the species has bred successfully. Spotted Crakes are seen occasionally with three individuals recorded in 1991 and a bird seen in September 1993. All the usual passage waders, including Oystercatcher, Little Stint, Curlew Sandpiper, Dunlin, Ruff, Black-tailed and Bar-tailed Godwits, Whimbrel, Spotted Redshank, Common Greenshank, Green, Wood and Common Sandpipers, may pass through during the spring, and especially autumn, migration periods, Ruffs being a particular feature in some years. A pair or two of Little Ringed Plovers breed annually. Winter flocks of European Golden Plovers and Northern Lapwings often reach 1,000 of each and sometimes more. The rarer waders in recent years have been Avocet, Temminck's Stint, White-rumped Sandpiper and Pectoral Sandpiper. All three species of phalaropes have occurred.

A large gull roost on the main reservoir attracts many birds during the winter months as follows: Black-headed Gull (10,000 to 15,000), Common Gull (10,000 to 15,000), Herring Gull (100 to 500) and Great Black-backed Gull (200 to 600, but a phenomenal 3,300 on 5th October 1992). Good numbers of Lesser Black-backed Gulls pass through, mainly during the autumn when they attend the roost. Common and Arctic Terns feed over the water in both spring and autumn with a few Sandwich Terns occasionally. The passage of Black Terns is often evident during May and early June if the winds are from the southeast, and also during August and September.

Five species of owls are recorded annually: Barn Owl is scarce and seen only occasionally, Little Owl is most frequently seen along the approach road, two pairs of Tawny Owls breed each year, and a few Long-eared Owls attend a roost during the winter months when a lone Short-eared Owl may also be seen quartering the ground. Feeding assemblies of Common Swifts can number 1,000 birds and more at any time between May and July. Common Kingfisher is regularly seen along the dykes or around the pools. Hirundines feed over the reservoirs during periods of cool and damp conditions in spring and autumn, especially if these conditions coincide with peak migration, when their combined numbers may be impressive.

Meadow Pipits, Yellow Wagtails and Pied Wagtails pass through on migration and, in spring, often include examples of the various races of Yellow Wagtail and also White Wagtails. A few Northern Wheatears are seen during both seasons. From October, flocks of Redwings and Fieldfares frequent the area, and Blackbird numbers increase as immigrants arrive.

The site is very good for breeding warblers with nine species occurring annually. Grasshopper Warbler, Sedge Warbler, Reed Warbler, Lesser Whitethroat, Common Whitethroat, Garden Warbler, Blackcap, Chiffchaff (sporadic) and Willow Warbler can all be seen between mid-April and June when they are in song and showing to advantage. Rarer warblers in recent years have been Savi's Warbler, Icterine Warbler, Yellow-browed Warbler and occasional Wood Warblers, a rare species away from the high ground in the hills to the west. Bearded Tits are seen from time to time, usually during October and November. Flocks of finches are a common sight during the autumn when Greenfinches, Goldfinches and Linnets assemble to feed on the weed seeds amongst the rough ground. Small flocks of Yellowhammers and Corn Buntings are regularly present in the agricultural areas during the autumn and winter months.

Timing

Tophill Low has something to offer the birdwatcher throughout the year but the periods of spring and autumn migration are the best times for the largest number and diversity of species. Wader passage can be very good during the period July to September, especially if the water levels are low and mud is exposed. The winter months can be good for waterfowl, flocks of plovers and also immigrant thrushes. Visits at any time of day can be equally rewarding as there is normally little disturbance to the lagoons which are overlooked by hides.

Access

This site lies to the east of the A164 Beverley to Great Driffield road, 6 miles (9.6 km) north of Beverley and 5 miles (8 km) south of Great Driffield. The narrow and winding approach road runs eastwards from a large loop layby at the southern end of the village of Watton, and passes through flat agricultural land. After 2 miles (3.2 km), where the road turns sharp left to Hutton Cranswick, keep straight on to reach the pumping station entrance after a further 2 miles (3.2 km).

The Reserve is open from 9 am to 6 pm from April to September and from 10 am to 3 pm from October to March. It is closed on Mondays and Tuesdays except for Bank Holidays. There is an admission charge payable at the gate. Anyone requiring further information should contact The Warden, Tophill Low Nature Reserve, Watton Carrs, Hutton Cranswick, Driffield, East Yorkshire YO25 9RH, enclosing a s.a.e.

Calendar

Winter (October to March): Occasional rarer grebes, Tundra Swan, Whooper Swan, occasional grey geese, Canada Goose, Eurasian Wigeon, Gadwall, Common Teal, Northern Pintail, Greater Scaup, Long-tailed Duck, Common Scoter, Common Goldeneye, Smew, Goosander, Ruddy Duck, occasional birds of prey, European Golden Plover, Common Snipe, Jack Snipe, Woodcock, Common Redshank, Common Gull, Herring Gull, Great Black-backed Gull, Long-eared Owl, Short-eared Owl, Rock Pipit (Marsh), Fieldfare, Redwing, Bearded Tit (sporadic), Siskin, Brambling, Common Redpoll.

Summer (April to August): Includes several species which also occur on passage in both spring and autumn. Turtle Dove, Common Cuckoo, Common Swift, Sand Martin, Barn Swallow, House Martin, Yellow Wagtail, Grasshopper Warbler, Sedge Warbler, Reed Warbler, Lesser Whitethroat, Common Whitethroat, Garden Warbler, Blackcap, Chiffchaff (occasional), Willow Warbler, Spotted Flycatcher.

Spring and autumn passage (April to early June and July to October): Black-necked Grebe (occasional), Garganey, Osprey, Spotted Crake (rare), most of the usual passage waders, Little Gull, Lesser Black-backed Gull, Sandwich Tern, Common Tern, Arctic Tern, Black Tern, Tree Pipit, Whinchat, Northern Wheatear.

All year: Great Cormorant, Grey Heron, Mute Swan, Greylag Goose, Mallard, Northern Shoveler, Common Pochard, Tufted Duck, Eurasian Sparrowhawk, Common Kestrel, Red-legged Partridge, Grey Partridge, Common Pheasant, Water Rail, Moorhen, Common Coot, Northern

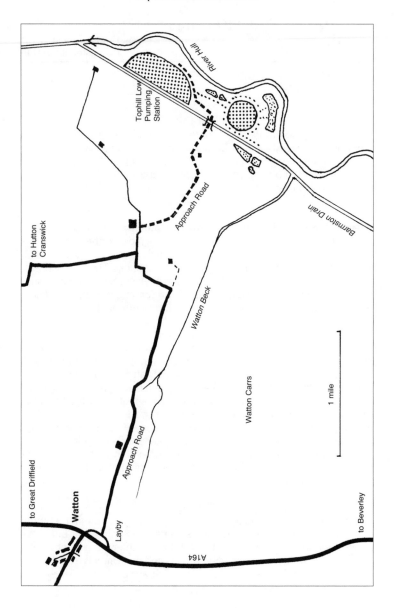

Lapwing, Black-headed Gull, Stock Dove, Wood Pigeon, Collared Dove, Barn Owl (scarce), Little Owl, Tawny Owl, Common Kingfisher, Great Spotted Woodpecker, Sky Lark, Meadow Pipit (also on passage), Grey Wagtail, Pied Wagtail, Wren, Hedge Accentor, Robin, Blackbird, Song Thrush, Mistle Thrush, Goldcrest, Willow Tit, Coal Tit, Blue Tit, Great Tit, Eurasian Treecreeper, Eurasian Jay, Eurasian Jackdaw, Rook, Carrion Crow, Common Starling, Chaffinch, Greenfinch, Goldfinch, Linnet, Bullfinch, Yellowhammer, Reed Bunting, Corn Bunting.

16 BRANDESBURTON PONDS

OS Landranger Map 107
Kingston-upon-Hull

Habitat

This site comprises three large ponds and a rubbish tip adjacent to the A165 dual-carriageway near Brandesburton, and a series of ten other ponds running alongside a minor road to the north of that village, some of which are used by anglers and one for water sports. There are significant areas of *Phragmites*.

Species

The ponds hold all the usual waterfowl, including Great Crested and Little Grebes during the non-breeding season, the most northerly pond near Hempholme being the best for Eurasian Wigeons and grey geese which feed on the adjacent fields, and also for diving ducks. The fishing ponds near Brandesburton have good areas of *Phragmites* reed and also bushes and scrub where both Reed and Sedge Warblers and the other expected resident and migrant passerines can be found during the summer and autumn.

Being situated relatively near to the east coast and also to Tophill Low Reserve, this site has great potential for unusual migrants during the autumn and for the rarer geese and ducks during the winter months. A rubbish tip adjacent to the main road ponds attracts large numbers of gulls during the late autumn and winter which sometimes include Glaucous and Iceland Gulls. There are no significant areas of mud and the site is not particularly good for migrant waders in consequence, although a few are inevitably attracted to the more open water margins. At times of spring and autumn passage, particularly in spring, easterly winds may bring Black Terns into the area, when they linger to feed over the ponds before continuing their journey. Common and Arctic Terns are also often involved.

Timing

The most productive time for a visit is during the late summer, autumn and winter months. During the late summer, passerines will be in evidence around the fishing ponds including warblers and finches; the autumn will produce some passing waders and the winter is excellent for waterfowl. As with most aquatic sites which are prone to disturbance, early morning and also in the evening are the best times to visit.

Access

Take the A1035 northeast from Beverley, continue for 6 miles (9.6 km) to the start of the new A165 dual-carriageway and continue to the second roundabout at the junction with the B1244 Leven/Catwick road. Look for a lay-by on the left just after this roundabout and park here to view the tip and the surrounding fields for gulls in the winter. A telescope is recommended.

Three large ponds lie adjacent to both sides of the main road 0.5 miles (0.8 km) beyond the lay-by. Parking is not permitted along the roadside and one must walk, either from the lay-by, or park in Brandesburton and

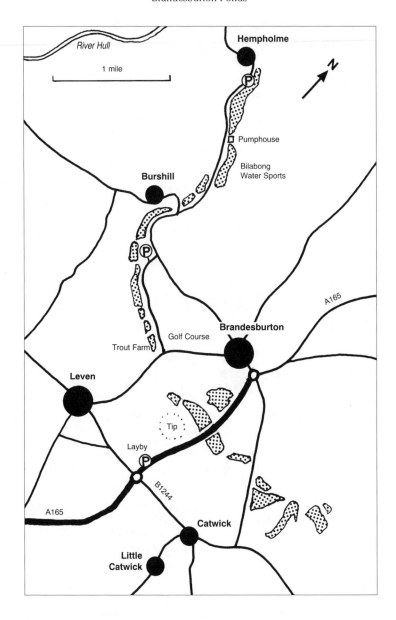

walk back south for 0.5 miles (0.8 km). The northern pond is not visible from the roadside but can be viewed from the bank top.

To reach the series of roadside ponds, some of which are large, to the northwest of Brandesburton, drive into the village and follow signs for Bilabong Water Sports. At the western edge of the village, look for Hainsworth Park Golf Course on the right, immediately after which take a minor road to the right. The first pond on the left is a trout farm and others lie adjacent to the road for the next 3 miles (4.8 km) as far as the small village of Hempholme.

There are several wide verges and gateways along the first stretch where one can park off the road. Towards the end of this first series of ponds, the road takes a right-hand bend where a track goes off to the left ahead, into a large open area where one can park overlooking one of the ponds. This area is sometimes used by motorcyclists for scrambling at weekends and is best avoided at this time. On leaving this car park, turn left and continue on the main road for a short distance and come to a 'T' junction. Turn left here for Burshill and just before the village, take a road to the right signed Hempholme, No Through Road and Bilabong Water Sports. The last and largest pond on the right, after the water sports, is the best for waterfowl and geese during the winter months. There is a convenient elevated lay-by on the right at a left-hand bend just before Hempholme from where one can look over the water and the surrounding fields.

Calendar
This includes the surrounding agricultural land.

Winter (October to March): Occasional rarer grebes, Tundra and Whooper Swans, rarer grey geese (occasional), Eurasian Wigeon, Common Teal, Common Pochard, Common Goldeneye, Goosander, Smew (sporadic), European Golden Plover, Common Snipe, Common Gull, Herring Gull, Great Black-backed Gull, Glaucous and Iceland Gulls (occasional), Short-eared Owl, Fieldfare, Redwing.

Spring and summer (April to August/September): Includes several species which also occur on passage in both spring and autumn. Turtle Dove, Common Cuckoo, Common Swift, Sand Martin, Barn Swallow, House Martin, Yellow Wagtail, Grasshopper Warbler, Sedge Warbler, Reed Warbler, Lesser Whitethroat, Common Whitethroat, Garden Warbler, Blackcap, Willow Warbler.

Spring and autumn passage (April to early June and July to October): Garganey, Osprey, several passage waders, terns, Lesser Black-backed Gull, Meadow Pipit, Northern Wheatear.

All year: Little Grebe, Great Crested Grebe, Great Cormorant, Grey Heron, Mute Swan, Greylag Goose, Canada Goose, Mallard, Tufted Duck, Eurasian Sparrowhawk, Common Kestrel, Red-legged Partridge, Grey Partridge, Common Pheasant, Moorhen, Common Coot, Northern Lapwing, Common Redshank, Black-headed Gull, Stock Dove, Wood Pigeon, Collared Dove, Barn Owl (scarce), Little Owl, Common Kingfisher, Pied Wagtail, Wren, Hedge Accentor, Robin, Blackbird, Song Thrush, Mistle Thrush, Blue Tit, Great Tit, Magpie, Eurasian Jackdaw, Rook, Carrion Crow, Common Starling, House Sparrow, Tree Sparrow, Chaffinch, Greenfinch, Goldfinch, Linnet, Yellowhammer, Reed Bunting, Corn Bunting.

17 SPURN POINT BIRD OBSERVATORY AND EASINGTON LAGOONS

OS Landranger
Map 113
Grimsby

Habitat and Species

The unique geological finger of unstable land which forms Spurn Point has been a regular focal point for students of bird migration since 1945 when the observatory first became operative. It had been investigated by collector naturalists long before then and there are several old records of rare birds being collected along the peninsula. It is now owned by the Yorkshire Wildlife Trust and administered jointly by them and the Spurn Bird Observatory Committee.

The promontory is composed of unstable sand dunes which are regularly ravaged by the North Sea during the winter months. A widespread and invasive covering of sea buckthorn has taken over much of the original marram grass dunes but does little to protect them from the sea during easterly gales and many yards have been eroded away over the years.

Anywhere along the peninsula can be good for birds during the main migration periods but obviously some areas are more suitable than others. Starting from the northern end of the actual reserve area owned by the YWT is a large and mature hawthorn hedge known as 'Big Hedge', which runs from east to west across the base of the peninsula, some 100 yards (90 m) north of the entrance gate. This hedge and the bushes and trees around the observatory headquarters at nearby Warren Cottage offer food and shelter for many migrants during both seasons. Warren Cottage is the site of one of the main observatory ringing traps. Continuing southwards for approximately 0.75 miles (1.2 km) brings you to the 'Narrow Neck', the narrowest part of the peninsula and only about 30 yards (27 m) wide. Most of the migrants moving south down the coast or

Spurn Point – looking north from the lighthouse area

67

along the Humber shore are funnelled here to pass overhead or low along the road and beaches, sometimes in spectacular numbers.

A regular watch is maintained here by those people staying at the observatory. During the spring, between April and early June, many passerines fly south along the promontory, an unusual direction for that season, and the summer migrants may be reorientating back into Western Europe having overshot too far west and north into Britain. Those species that have wintered in the British Isles, such as Northern Lapwings, Eurasian Jackdaws, Rooks, Common Starlings and Chaffinches, numbers of the last named species often reaching four figures in a day at this time of year, are probably coasting down the peninsula and beyond looking for a place to cross the North Sea and back into Europe. Common Swifts, Barn Swallows, House Martins, Goldfinches, and Linnets also feature in these reverse movements. Small numbers of birds of prey including Hen, Montagu's and Marsh Harriers, Eurasian Sparrowhawk, Common Buzzard, Osprey, Common Kestrel, Merlin and Hobby pass at both seasons but mainly during the autumn.

The 'Narrows' are, without doubt, the best place to watch visible autumn migration anywhere on the east coast, and any time from July through to October/November and mainly in the early mornings, it is possible to witness streams of birds passing through. The movements start as early as late June with hirundines, Meadow Pipits and Linnets. During August and September more and more species are involved including a few Grey Wagtails, Greenfinches, Goldfinches, Siskins and Common Redpolls. Early October brings the first big exodus of House Martins, some Reed Buntings and Sky Larks which pass in large numbers. August and September are the main months for the arrival of Common Redstarts, Pied Flycatchers, Whinchats, Northern Wheatears and warblers including Barred and Icterine and occasional Red-backed Shrikes and Wrynecks. During late September and October, Robins and Goldcrests come over the North Sea, sometimes in very large numbers, and the buckthorn bushes are often alive with 'crests'. The visitor may be surprised to see large numbers of House Sparrows and fewer Tree Sparrows moving purposefully south during October and November. There are several ringing recoveries of both species showing that they have moved up to 125 miles (200 km) to the south of Spurn.

During October, on easterly winds, the winter immigrants start to arrive. The largest falls of thrushes, Common Starlings, Chaffinches and Bramblings usually occur when low cloud and rain forces them down on arrival over the coast. In fine clear weather many pass straight over and are not so evident. Falls of Blackbirds can be spectacular and may number several thousand birds. Fieldfares, Redwings, Song Thrushes and Common Starlings also come over in large numbers at this time. October and November is the best period to see Woodcocks along the peninsula as well as many Goldcrests, an occasional Firecrest, Pallas's Leaf Warbler, Yellow-browed Warbler and Great Grey Shrike. Other sub-rarities and vagrants from the east are always a possibility at this time. During the winter months in periods of severe weather, especially if there is snow cover in the area, large numbers of Northern Lapwings, Sky Larks, thrushes, pipits, Common Starlings, finches and buntings may move south, sometimes in spectacular numbers (30,000 Sky Larks on 12th January 1963 and 22,400 on 3rd February, on which date 58 Lapland Longspurs also passed).

Just over 1 mile (1.8 km) to the south of the 'Narrows' is an area known as Chalk Bank, constructed of boulders of chalk, built during the middle of the nineteenth century to prevent flooding and erosion of the peninsula. Today it is a favourite place for pipits and Northern Wheatears which assemble in this area whilst on migration. Near here, on the Humber shore and overlooked by a hide, is a raised sand and shingle beach, used as a high-tide roost by large numbers of Oystercatchers in addition to other waders and terns. Near the end of the peninsula is the lighthouse, beyond which is the 'Point Camp' where a large area of stunted sycamore and elderberry trees surrounding the old army parade ground affords shelter for many fall migrants.

Returning to the north of the peninsula, outside the entrance gate is an area of farmland consisting of grazing and arable with hedgerows and ditches. This is bordered on the west side by a bank and water-filled dyke known as 'The Canal Zone'. A large scrape has recently been excavated and an observation hide built from which waterfowl and waders can be viewed. Running north from the east/west road at the start of the peninsula and to the left of a large caravan park is Beacon Lane, lined with wide hedges, always a good place to look for migrants. Continuing north along the coast from here are Beacon Lane Ponds and Easington Lagoons partly owned and administered by The South Holderness Countryside Society. Being so close to the sea, these areas of fresh water attract many passing birds, particularly waterfowl and waders at the appropriate season. A few pairs of Little Terns attempt to breed annually in this area with varying success.

The beach running down the seaward side of the peninsula is wide and sandy and is a continuation of the beach which starts at Bridlington and sweeps in a long unbroken curve for 36 miles (57.5 km) to the tip of Spurn Point. On the west side is the River Humber and at low tide a large expanse of mud known as Kilnsea Clays is host to thousands of birds: Brent Geese, Common Shelducks, Eurasian Wigeons, Common Teals, Mallards and most of the commoner waders, particularly Red Knots and Dunlins, are usually to be seen here during the autumn and winter months. Seawatching from a hide behind the Warren Cottage, or from the Narrow Neck, can be good during the right weather conditions and at the appropriate season. Passage during the months of March, April, May and early June involves divers, gulls, terns and waders with a few shearwaters and skuas but in autumn, from July to November, the southward movements can be impressive. All the species mentioned in detail in the Flamborough chapters are involved but, interestingly, do not always coincide. Large movements off Flamborough are not always witnessed further south at Spurn and vice-versa. During the late autumn and winter, especially when gales from the northern quarter are whipping up the sea, divers and grebes are often evident and large movements of sea ducks, Kittiwakes and other gulls regularly occur.

Timing

During the winter months, Spurn can be a bleak and desolate place, often with little to interest the birdwatcher, but during the main periods of migration and sea movement it can be one of the most exciting places in the region under review. The success of visits during the winter months depends, as do those to most other coastal sites, on the weather conditions. The intending visitor must therefore have regard for this when planning a trip. Severe weather during the period December to March will often induce movement of seabirds, but the main periods for this group are late March to May and from July to November. The month of June can sometimes produce southern species such as Hobby, European Bee-eater, Golden Oriole and some rare warblers. Falls of passerines can occur at any time from late August to early November, the period October/November producing the eastern vagrants. Spectacular falls of thrushes also occur at this time. Rain following easterly winds produces the right conditions for these large falls when Ring Ouzels, Blackbirds, Fieldfares, Song Thrushes, Redwings and Common Starlings come in over the sea. Early morning is the best time to watch for passerine movement from the Narrow Neck. Seabird movements often occur early in the day, or sometimes in the evening during the autumn when large numbers of terns may pass along the coast.

Access

To reach Spurn Point, leave Hull on the A1033 and pass through Keyingham before bearing right in Patrington onto the B1445 for Easington where the road turns sharp right just through the village (straight on leads to the cliff top from where one can walk south to the Easington Lagoons, see below) and continues to Kilnsea. Pass the Crown and Anchor Inn, and after 0.5 miles (0.8 km) turn right at the junction (Caravan park on the left), and continue for another 1 mile (1.6 km) to reach the entrance gate to the reserve. A charge is made for cars (except on Fridays) which is usually collected near the observatory headquarters. No dogs are allowed on the Reserve. A road leads down the full length of the peninsula, except where the sea has broken through, but these stretches are maintained and are always passable. Look for the new Canal Scrape and hide on the right just before the entrance gate. The resident warden, or birdwatchers staying at the observatory, are usually around the headquarters at Warren Cottage during the migration periods and visitors should seek information at the shop.

Beacon Lane Ponds and Easington Lagoons can be reached either by walking north from Beacon Lane, or south from near the village of Easington. To reach Easington, drive north from Kilnsea for 2 miles (3.2 km) and just before entering the village, turn right and continue for about 500 yards (460 m) to park at the end of the lane near the cliff top. Walk south from here to the lagoons and the hides.

The Spurn Heritage Coast Project organises several bird walks during the summer and autumn including a visit to the Little Tern colony at Easington. For details contact Tim Collins, Spurn Heritage Coast Project, Easington, Hull HU12 0TG (Tel: 01964-650139). Total distance from Hull to Spurn Point is approximately 32 miles (51 km) on good but winding roads.

Calendar

Seawatching – winter (October to March): Includes the Humber estuary. Great Northern Diver, Great Crested Grebe, Red-necked Grebe, Shag, Brent Goose, Eurasian Wigeon, Common Teal, Mallard, Northern Pintail, Tufted Duck, Greater Scaup, Common Eider, Long-tailed Duck, Common Scoter, Common Goldeneye, Red-breasted Merganser, waders, Black-headed Gull, Common Gull, Herring Gull, Great Black-backed Gull, Kittiwake, Common Guillemot, Razorbill, Little Auk.

Seawatching – spring and autumn (March to May and late June to November): Includes several of the above. European Storm Petrel, Leach's Storm Petrel, Common Shelduck, Oystercatcher, Great Ringed Plover, European Golden Plover, Grey Plover, Northern Lapwing, Red Knot,

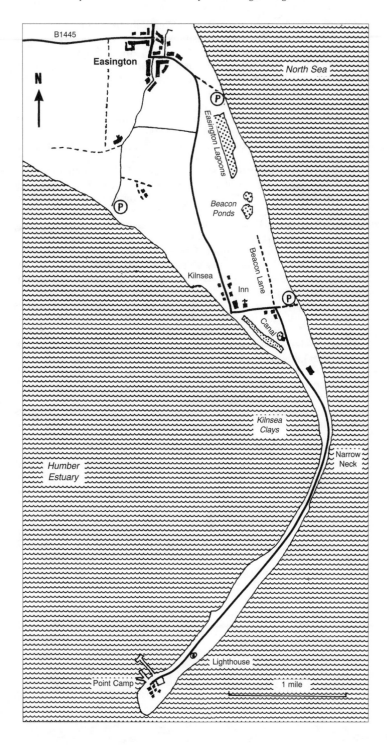

Sanderling, Dunlin, Ruff, Bar-tailed Godwit, Whimbrel, Eurasian Curlew, Spotted Redshank, Common Redshank, Common Greenshank, Common Sandpiper, Turnstone, Pomarine Skua, Arctic Skua, Long-tailed Skua, Great Skua, Sandwich Tern, Common Tern, Arctic Tern, Little Tern. Many of the waders are also present on Kilnsea Clays during the winter months.

Migrants along the Peninsula – spring and autumn migration periods (April to June and August to November): Marsh Harrier, Hen Harrier, Eurasian Sparrowhawk, Osprey, Common Kestrel, Merlin, Hobby, Wood Pigeon, Collared Dove, Turtle Dove, Common Cuckoo, Common Swift, Wryneck, Sky Lark, Sand Martin, Barn Swallow, House Martin, Richard's Pipit, Tawny Pipit (rare), Tree Pipit, Meadow Pipit, Yellow Wagtail, Grey Wagtail, Pied Wagtail, Wren, Hedge Accentor, Robin, Rufous Nightingale, Bluethroat, Black Redstart, Common Redstart, Whinchat, Common Stonechat, Northern Wheatear, Ring Ouzel, Blackbird, Fieldfare, Song Thrush, Redwing, Grasshopper Warbler, Sedge Warbler, Marsh Warbler, Reed Warbler, Icterine Warbler, Barred Warbler, Lesser Whitethroat, Common Whitethroat, Garden Warbler, Blackcap, Pallas's Leaf Warbler, Yellow-browed Warbler, Chiffchaff, Willow Warbler (other rare eastern *Phylloscopus* warblers are seen almost annually including Greenish Warbler, Arctic Warbler, Radde's Warbler, Dusky Warbler and Bonelli's Warbler), Goldcrest, Firecrest, Spotted Flycatcher, Red-breasted Flycatcher, Pied Flycatcher, Long-tailed Tit, Blue Tit, Great Tit, Eurasian Treecreeper, Red-backed Shrike, Great Grey Shrike, Woodchat Shrike, Eurasian Jackdaw, Rook, Carrion Crow (a few Hooded Crows in winter), Common Starling, House Sparrow, Tree Sparrow, Chaffinch, Brambling, Greenfinch, Goldfinch, Siskin, Linnet, Twite, Common Redpoll, Common Crossbill, Common Rosefinch, Bullfinch, Lapland Longspur, Snow Bunting, Yellowhammer, Reed Bunting, Corn Bunting (rare buntings have included Cirl, Rock, Ortolan and Rustic).

Spring and summer (April to July): Breeding along the peninsula: Mallard, Red-legged Partridge (occasional), Grey Partridge, Moorhen, Great Ringed Plover, Wood Pigeon, Little Tern (only odd pairs), Common Cuckoo (occasional), Sky Lark (few), Barn Swallow (usually around the observatory buildings), Wren (occasional), Hedge Accentor, Blackbird, Song Thrush, Sedge Warbler, Common Whitethroat, Willow Warbler (occasional), Blue Tit, Great Tit (occasional), Magpie, Carrion Crow, Common Starling, House Sparrow, Tree Sparrow, Greenfinch, Linnet, Yellowhammer, Reed Bunting, Corn Bunting. In addition, some movement over the sea is usually evident during June involving small numbers of Manx Shearwaters, waders, gulls and terns and there is always the chance of a southern rarity on the peninsula.

THE HUMBER ESTUARY

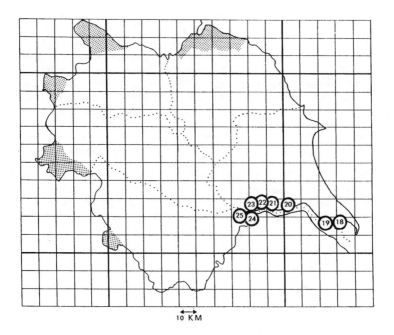

10 KM

18 WELWICK SALTING AND HAVERFIELD QUARRIES

OS Landranger
Map 113
Grimsby

Habitat

This site comprises the large raised Welwick saltmarsh and two small disused sand and gravel quarries near to the Humber shore. The land adjacent to the river embankment is mainly arable with some hedgerows and areas of rough ground. There are good patches of hawthorn and blackthorn along the embankment and also around the two quarry pools, which are largely overgrown with reeds, but each has a fairly extensive area of open water.

Species

Welwick Salting is a very important roosting site for waders during the autumn and winter months and is used mainly on low to medium range tides. On higher spring tides, some of the waders move to the south bank of the river but others roost in the adjoining fields, particularly near Outstray Farm, just to the south of the pools. The main species using this roost are European Golden Plovers and Northern Lapwings with several thousand of each, and Red Knots and Dunlins with about 10,000 of each in mid-winter.

During the autumn migration season from July to October, the quarry pools regularly attract passage waders and on one day in September 1992 there were 59 Common Greenshanks and 18 Spotted Redshanks there. Waterfowl along the estuary during the late autumn and winter months include a few Brent Geese, good numbers of Common

Barn Owl

74

Shelducks, Eurasian Wigeons, Common Teals, Mallards and Northern Pintails. The hedgerows and the bushes along the river embankment and around the pools are good for Common Whitethroats, Lesser Whitethroats, Willow Warblers, Linnets, Yellowhammers, Reed Buntings and Corn Buntings. The pools have breeding Sedge, Reed and occasional Grasshopper Warblers. Barn Owls are resident in the area and a solitary Short-eared Owl is regularly seen during the autumn and winter months. Eurasian Sparrowhawks may be seen around the hedgerows and Common Kestrels hunt over the open fields and along the shoreline. During the autumn and winter, a Merlin, Peregrine Falcon or lone Hen Harrier may be seen.

The pools have Mallards, Moorhens, Common Coots, Little Grebes and a pair of Mute Swans during the summer months. Wood Pigeons are common in the area and Stock Doves frequent the fields. Turtle Doves are breeding summer visitors. Black-headed Gulls are numerous throughout the year along the estuary and the larger gulls are also present in varying numbers. Small numbers of Common and Arctic Terns move along the Humber at times of spring and autumn passage, and during May, if the winds are easterly, Black Terns may also appear.

Timing

This site has something to offer the birdwatcher throughout the year. The best time for seeing the large flocks of waders is during the period November to February. Autumn is a good time for passage waders and migrant passerines. A visit to Haverfield Quarries during the late spring and summer months can be worthwhile for the breeding birds, particularly warblers, and also during the autumn for waders and migrant passerines.

Access

Travelling on the B1445 Patrington to Spurn road, turn south in the village of Welwick into Humber Lane. This narrow road continues for 2 miles (3.2 km) to the end of the tarmac where it bears right onto a wide unmade farm track. Just after the bend, a dirt track leads to the left and reaches the river embankment after 500 yards (460 m). This track is deeply rutted and can be impassable in the winter. It is better to park on the wider main track and walk to the embankment. From here, one can walk in both directions to view over the saltmarsh. To reach Haverfield Quarries, walk westwards along the embankment for about 0.75 miles (1.2 km), passing good areas of bushes before reaching the start of the reserve and the first pool on the left, at the end of which is a hide overlooking both pools. One should approach carefully as the waders are easily flushed.

The quarries are administered as a reserve by The South Holderness Countryside Society and the hide is open throughout the year.

Calendar

This includes the estuary, the adjoining fields and the quarry pools.

All year: Little Grebe, Mute Swan, Mallard, Eurasian Sparrowhawk, Common Kestrel, Red-legged Partridge, Grey Partridge, Common Pheasant, Moorhen, Common Coot, Oystercatcher, Northern Lapwing, Common Redshank, small numbers of non-breeding waders are present throughout the summer, Black-headed Gull, Stock Dove, Wood Pigeon, Collared Dove, Barn Owl, Sky Lark, Pied Wagtail, Wren, Hedge Accentor, Robin,

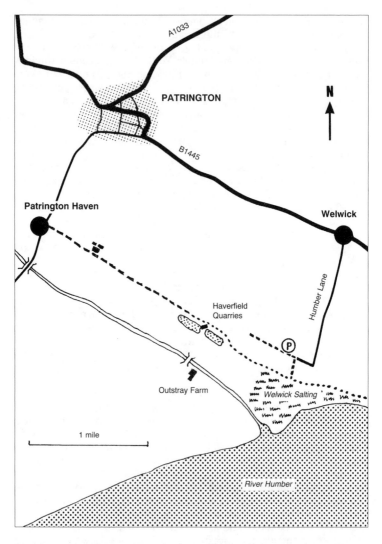

Blackbird, Mistle Thrush, Magpie, Eurasian Jackdaw, Rook, Carrion Crow, Common Starling, House Sparrow, Tree Sparrow, Chaffinch, Greenfinch, Goldfinch, Linnet, Yellowhammer, Reed Bunting, Corn Bunting.

Winter (October to March): Brent Goose, Common Shelduck, Eurasian Wigeon, Common Teal, Northern Pintail, Merlin, Peregrine Falcon, Hen Harrier, Great Ringed Plover, European Golden Plover, Grey Plover, Red Knot, Dunlin, Common Snipe, Bar-tailed Godwit, Eurasian Curlew, Turnstone, Common Gull, Herring Gull, Great Black-backed Gull, Short-eared Owl, Twite, Fieldfare, Redwing.

Spring and autumn passage (April to early June and July to October): Little Stint, Curlew Sandpiper, Ruff, Black-tailed Godwit, Whimbrel, Spotted Redshank, Common Greenshank, Green Sandpiper, Common Sandpiper,

Common Tern, Arctic Tern, Black Tern, Northern Wheatear, Whinchat, hirundines, warblers, Goldcrest (autumn).

Spring and summer (April to August): Turtle Dove, Common Cuckoo, Barn Swallow, Meadow Pipit, Yellow Wagtail, Sedge Warbler, Reed Warbler, Grasshopper Warbler, Common Whitethroat, Lesser Whitethroat, Willow Warbler.

19 CHERRY COBB SANDS AND STONE CREEK

OS Landranger
Map 113; Grimsby
and Cleethorpes

Habitat
Cherry Cobb Sands is the largest area of raised saltmarsh on the north bank of the River Humber. The adjacent area is flat agricultural land with hedgerows and drainage ditches. Stone Creek enters the estuary along a narrow muddy channel.

Species
The site has long been a favourite haunt for both birds and birdwatchers and Cherry Cobb is one of the most important autumn and winter wader roosts along the estuary. Some waders are present throughout the year, their numbers and species being augmented during the autumn by passage migrants and winter visitors. All the usual estuarine wader species are involved with an occasional rarity. There are also many Common Shelducks, and from October to March small numbers of Brent Geese and other waterfowl including Eurasian Wigeons, Common Teals, Mallards and Northern Pintails. The sands are very good for Grey Plovers and over 1,000 birds are often present during the winter months.

During late April and May, Great Ringed Plovers of the smaller and darker northern race *tundrae*, pass through in good numbers. At any time between August and March, but mainly from December to February, large flocks of waders can be seen including the following species with some regular maxima shown: Grey Plover (1,000), Red Knot (5,000), Dunlin (7,000), Bar-tailed Godwit (500), Eurasian Curlew (5,000) and Common Redshank (2,000). Up to 40 Common Greenshanks have been counted in September at which time other passage waders including Little Stints, Curlew Sandpipers, Ruffs and Whimbrels may be seen.

During the breeding season, the bushes and hedgerows around Stone Creek and the adjoining fields are good for Common Whitethroats, Sedge Warblers, Linnets, Yellowhammers, Reed Buntings and Corn Buntings. Sky Larks are common in the open fields where Northern Lapwings also nest.

At any time from September to March on high tides, the fields from Stone Creek eastwards to Sunk Island regularly hold large roosting assemblies of European Golden Plovers (up to 7,500), Northern Lapwings and Eurasian Curlews, particularly the last species. An occasional Hen

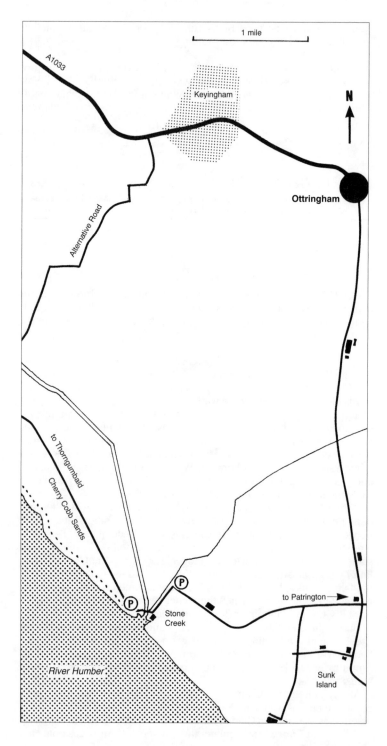

Harrier, Merlin or Peregrine Falcon may be seen over the estuary during the autumn and winter months. Common Kestrels are resident.

Timing
Being primarily a site for shorebirds and high-tide roosts, the best times to visit this area are during the spring and autumn migration seasons (April to early June and August to October) and through the winter for the roosting assemblies. Have regard for the state of the tides when planning a visit and endeavour to be there on a rising tide to witness the flocks of waders as they are displaced along the estuary or gather in the roosting fields.

Access
Travelling eastwards from Hull on the A1033, pass through the village of Thorngumbald and enter the adjacent village of Camerton (not marked on some maps). At the end of the houses, look for a very sharp right turn signed Paull 3. Take this road, and after only 200 yards (180 m), turn left onto a minor road signed Cherry Cobb Sands and Stone Creek (spelt Stoney Creek on the sign). This narrow winding road passes through arable land for 5.25 miles (8.4 km) to where Stone Creek enters the estuary. Park here in an obvious space beside the floodbank where the road bears left at the end of the tarmac.

One should walk westwards along the raised embankment to view over Cherry Cobb Sands and the estuary. On leaving the parking area continue along the short section of unmade road to cross a small bridge over Stone Creek and rejoin the tarmac. Continue to the left for about 400 yards (360 m) and park near another small bridge over the creek from where one can view the surrounding fields and the general area. From here, the road continues through flat agricultural land, passing Sunk Island Farm and back to the main road at Patrington after 7 miles (11.2 km) or Ottringham after 6 miles (9.6 km).

Calendar
The species list is almost the same as for Welwick Salting and Haverfield Quarries except for the breeding waterbirds associated with the quarry pools.

20 HUMBER BRIDGE COUNTRY PARK

OS Landranger
Map 106
Market Weighton

Habitat
This park, which was established in 1986, lies adjacent to the Humber Bridge and comprises large areas of woodland on the steeply sloping banks around disused chalk quarries which closed in 1960. There are exposed chalk cliffs, areas of open grassland and scrub, and three small ponds, two of which are seasonal. The complex abuts the north shore of the River Humber. It is managed by a team of Countryside Rangers who are available for guided walks or school parties.

Species

Most of the regular resident passerines can be found in the woods in addition to the summer visitors including Lesser Whitethroat, Garden Warbler, Blackcap, Chiffchaff, Willow Warbler and Spotted Flycatcher. Eurasian Sparrowhawks are resident. During the autumn, finches can be numerous as they flock and move along the estuary and Bullfinches are resident. The bushes and trees attract many migrant birds during the late summer and autumn. Warblers are much in evidence at this time, as well as wandering parties of titmice. Goldcrests can be numerous and there is always the chance of seeing one of the rare warblers in September and October. During the latter month, large flocks of Fieldfares and Redwings drop into the woodland, having crossed the North Sea to continue along the estuary.

The Humber shore is worth investigating, especially during the autumn when waders can be seen as they feed on the mud at low tide, or as they fly along the shoreline. The larger gulls are always present during the autumn and winter months and migrant Common and Arctic Terns pass through during the spring and early autumn.

Timing

A visit at any time of year could produce some birds of interest but the best time for seeing the highest number of species is from July to October when the breeding birds are dispersing and the migrants are moving through.

Access

Being situated alongside the Humber Bridge, this is a convenient place for a short stop, especially if *en route* to the east coast. Travel eastwards on the M62 to where it becomes the A63, and after 7 miles (11.2 km) leave the main road, signed Humber Bridge and Beverley, and follow the signs for Hessle Viewpoint and Humber Bridge Country Park. The Park is directly adjacent to the Humber Bridge. The large car parking area has an Information Centre, a café and toilet facilities, all of which are designed for the disabled. The Park is administered by The Humberside Leisure Services Countryside Department.

Calendar

All year: Eurasian Sparrowhawk, waders and gulls along the estuary, Wood Pigeon, Tawny Owl, Great Spotted Woodpecker, Pied Wagtail, Wren, Hedge Accentor, Robin, Blackbird, Song Thrush, Mistle Thrush, Long-tailed Tit, Marsh Tit, Blue Tit, Great Tit, Eurasian Treecreeper, Magpie, Eurasian Jackdaw, Carrion Crow, Common Starling, House Sparrow, Chaffinch, Greenfinch, Goldfinch, Linnet, Bullfinch, Yellowhammer.

Summer – Breeding: Common Cuckoo, Lesser Whitethroat, Garden Warbler, Blackcap, Chiffchaff, Willow Warbler, Spotted Flycatcher.

Spring and autumn passage (April to early June and July to October): Common and Arctic Terns along the estuary, Turtle Dove, Common Swift, Sky Lark, Sand Martin, Barn Swallow, House Martin, Meadow Pipit, Tree Pipit, Yellow Wagtail, Goldcrest.

Winter: Fieldfare, Redwing, Brambling, Siskin, Common Redpoll.

21 WELTON WATERS

Habitat

This complex, set close to the Humber shore, is certainly worth a visit. The lakes are surrounded by reeds and scrub and very good for breeding birds in consequence. The largest, eastern lake, is used by the Welton Sailing Club for water skiing and is much disturbed during the summer months. The western lake is used for angling but is the best for birds. A third lake to the east, included on the OS maps, is now almost completely overgrown with reeds. There is a smaller pool at the northwestern corner of the largest boating lake which is more secluded and easy to watch from a car parking area by the roadside.

Species

The diverse habitats at this site hold a wide variety of species throughout the year and it is a very good place during the late spring and summer for seeing the breeding waterbirds and passerines. Both Little and Great Crested Grebes nest and breeding waterfowl include Greylag Goose, Mallard, Northern Shoveler and Tufted Duck. Moorhens and Common Coots are resident and an occasional Water Rail may be heard, especially during the autumn and winter months, at which season visiting waterfowl include Eurasian Wigeons, Gadwalls, Common Teals, Northern Pintails, Common Pochards, Common Goldeneyes and Ruddy Ducks. Common Shelducks are present throughout the year. Eurasian Sparrowhawks and Common Kestrels are resident, and during the autumn and winter months an occasional Merlin, Peregrine Falcon or Hen Harrier may be seen.

This is a good area for Barn Owls and it is possible to see a solitary bird hunting along the field edges during the summer evenings. Short-eared Owl is also a frequent visitor during the autumn and winter. The fields have both Red-legged and Grey Partridges and Common Pheasants are numerous. Northern Lapwings breed in the area as well as being common during the winter when European Golden Plovers also frequent the ploughed land and the small airfield to the west. Black-headed Gulls are present throughout the year and the larger gulls are numerous during the winter. If the winds are from the east, and especially if accompanied by rain in late spring, mainly during May, Common, Arctic and Black Terns may pass through on migration. Stock Doves, Wood Pigeons and Collared Doves are all resident and common in the general area and Turtle Doves are breeding summer visitors. Look for Common Kingfisher on any of the three lakes. Common Cuckoos are relatively numerous during the summer, at which time the warblers are also well represented. Both Reed and Sedge Warblers breed around the lakes in addition to Common and Lesser Whitethroats, Blackcaps and Willow Warblers.

The rough ground is good for finches and buntings including Chaffinch, Greenfinch, Goldfinch, Linnet, Reed Bunting, Yellowhammer and Corn Bunting, particularly during the late summer and autumn when the weed seeds attract large flocks.

Timing

Welton Waters has something to offer the birdwatcher throughout the year, but a visit between April and September will produce the most species when the summer visitors are in residence and when the passage migrants are also moving through in the spring and early autumn. Winter can be good for waterfowl and also an occasional bird of prey.

Access

Travel east on the M62 to junction 38 where the main road becomes the A63. After 4 miles (6.4 km) take the turn off to Brough and bear left to cross the road bridge. After only a few yards look for a sign to the left reading 'Welton Water 1½' and 'Common Lane'. Turn left here and come to a 'T' junction after 175 yards (160 m). Turn right and pass over a manned railway crossing after 0.5 miles (0.8 km). Continue for a further 0.5 mile (0.8 km) and come to a small car parking area at the edge of the small northern pool where the road bears left to the Welton Sailing Club. A track leads straight on at this bend, between the two main lakes, and runs alongside areas of reeds and bushes, very good for passerines, particularly during the period April to June for breeding birds and from July to October for migrants. The track continues to the estuary floodbank along which one can walk in both directions. The lakes are best viewed from this elevated path, particularly as the light is from behind. The path to the west reaches Brough Haven after 1.5 miles (2.4 km) passing a small airfield and grassland which regularly attracts flocks of European Golden Plovers, Northern Lapwings and gulls during the autumn and winter. A small sheet of temporary floodwater often forms in this area and is attractive to gulls and waders (see map for site 22).

Calendar

All year: Little Grebe, Grey Heron, Mute Swan, Greylag Goose, Common Shelduck, Mallard, Tufted Duck, Eurasian Sparrowhawk, Common Kestrel, Red-legged Partridge, Grey Partridge, Common Pheasant, Moorhen, Common Coot, Northern Lapwing, Black-headed Gull, Stock Dove, Wood Pigeon, Collared Dove, Barn Owl, Common Kingfisher, Sky Lark, Pied Wagtail, Wren, Hedge Accentor, Robin, Blackbird, Mistle Thrush, Long-tailed Tit, Blue Tit, Great Tit, Magpie, Eurasian Jackdaw, Rook, Carrion Crow, Common Starling, House Sparrow, Tree Sparrow, Chaffinch, Greenfinch, Goldfinch, Linnet, Bullfinch, Yellowhammer, Reed Bunting, Corn Bunting.

Spring and autumn passage (April to early June and July to October): Garganey, Common Tern, Arctic Tern, Black Tern, Sand Martin, Common Redstart, Whinchat, Northern Wheatear.

Summer – breeding: Includes several species which also occur on passage in both spring and autumn. Great Crested Grebe, Northern Shoveler, Turtle Dove, Common Cuckoo, Barn Swallow, House Martin, Meadow Pipit, Yellow Wagtail, Song Thrush, Sedge Warbler, Reed Warbler, Lesser Whitethroat, Common Whitethroat, Blackcap, Willow Warbler.

Winter (October to March): Eurasian Wigeon, Gadwall, Common Teal, Northern Pintail, Common Pochard, Common Goldeneye, Ruddy Duck, Hen Harrier, Merlin, Peregrine Falcon, Water Rail, European Golden Plover, Northern Lapwing, Common Gull, Herring Gull, Great Black-backed Gull, Short-eared Owl, Fieldfare, Redwing, Twite.

In addition, most of the estuarine waders can be seen from the river-bank path, mainly during the autumn and winter months.

22 BROUGH HAVEN

OS Landranger Map 106
Market Weighton

Habitat

This locality, on the Upper Humber Estuary, comprises large areas of exposed low-tide mud which can be easily viewed from the raised flood-banks along the river. There are some small areas of reeds and scrub adjacent to a small car parking area and also near the Yawl Club (see 'Access' section below).

Species

The extensive areas of mud, particularly the raised mud bank to the west of the car park, attract large numbers of waders and Common Shelducks. Most of the usual estuarine waders can be seen here during the autumn and winter months as well as waterfowl including Eurasian Wigeons, Common Teals, Mallards and all the regular gulls. The small area of reeds with hawthorn and sallow scrub adjoining the car park has occasional Bearded Tits during the winter, and Reed and Sedge Warblers during the summer months. Greenfinches, Goldfinches and Linnets are numerous in this area and along the floodbanks. During the spring and autumn migration periods, Meadow Pipits, Yellow Wagtails, Whinchats and Northern Wheatears can also be seen here. Having such easy access, this is one of the best places along the estuary for watching waders at close quarters, especially from the car park and the floodbank to the west.

Common Shelduck

Timing

The best time to visit this area is from July through to April. The passage waders are in evidence from July and the winter populations are present from October to March. Waterfowl can also be seen at this time. It is best to be there on a rising tide when the birds are displaced and can be watched as they fly along the river to their high-tide roosting sites. April and May and again from August to October can be worthwhile for migrant passerines.

Access

To reach Brough Haven, leave the A63 (as for Welton Waters) and continue to Brough. Enter the village along Welton Road and look for Skillings Lane, 1 mile (1.6 km) from the main A63 road. Turn left here at traffic lights, signed Brough Haven, and having crossed the railway lines, come to a right bend into Saltgrounds Road after 530 yards (465 m). Pass the British Aerospace factory on the left, immediately after which turn left into a car park adjacent to the Humber shore. This parking area is run by the Parish Council and is signed 'Brough Haven Viewing Area'. Parking is free and limited to 3 hours. From here, walk eastwards along the riverbank footpath which passes behind the Aerospace works and continues past a small airfield and eventually to Welton Waters after about 1.5 miles (2.4 km).

To reach the riverbank footpath to the west, walk back to the road from the car park, turn left, and just before reaching the railway bridge, turn left again into a wide track which passes a large building signed 'Associated British Ports', before crossing a small bridge over a creek just before the Humber Yawl Club. Pass to the right of the club buildings and come to the embankment after about 100 yards (90 m). This path continues westwards, alongside the best area of mud bank, for just under 2 miles (3 km) to Crabley Creek. There is limited wildfowling along the

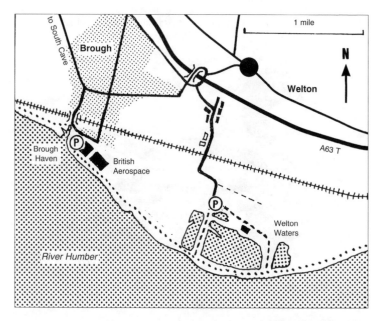

foreshore and wardens patrol the area during the shooting season. Please keep to the path along the top of the embankment and keep dogs on a lead at all times.

Calendar
The species list for Brough Haven is virtually the same as for the other estuarine localities (see Welwick Salting, site 18).

23 WHITTON SAND AND FAXFLEET PONDS

OS Landranger
Map 106
Market Weighton

Habitat
Whitton Sand is situated in the River Humber Estuary, 35 miles (56 km) west of Spurn Point. It is a raised sandbank, just under 2 miles (3.2 km) long, and has featured in historical writings for over 200 years. It is a very important roosting site for both waterfowl and waders, being completely covered only by very high tides of over 16 feet (5 m). On medium to normal tides, it is often the only exposed sandbank in the Upper Humber and attracts very many waterfowl and waders in consequence. Faxfleet Ponds are two large sheets of water surrounded by reeds, sallows and other lacustrine vegetation, lying to the north of, and adjacent to, the river floodbank. Extensive reedbeds also run along the estuary adjacent to the raised floodbank in the area of the car park and eastwards to Faxfleet Foreshore. The area of the estuary including Whitton Sand forms part of The Humber Wildfowl Refuge, created in 1955 and monitored by a warden during the autumn and winter months.

Species
This is an excellent place for birds, the most interesting aspect being the large assemblies of waterfowl and waders during the autumn and winter months. Whitton Sand is a traditional roosting site for Pink-footed Geese, which formerly occurred in much greater numbers when there were autumn and winter stubbles on the nearby Wolds. The annual winter population now reaches a maximum of around 2,000 birds, most of which fly to the Lincolnshire side of the river to feed.

Most of the usual passage waders can be seen from July to October and over 30 species have been recorded including Avocet, Kentish Plover, American Golden Plover and Semi-palmated Sandpiper. Many waders, and also some waterfowl, can be watched as they fly high inland along the estuary and continue their journey westwards. Waterfowl numbers in the general area can be spectacular during the winter months. Both Tundra and Whooper Swans call in from time to time and there is a resident flock of up to 200 Greylag Geese. A few Brent Geese wander along the estuary as far as Whitton Sand. Common Shelducks are numerous throughout the year, their numbers peaking in July and August when up to 1,200 may be present. Eurasian Wigeons are very common and, at any time from October to March, large flocks, frequently numbering several thousands can be seen. Common Teals often number around 2,000 birds during peak passage in September. Mallards regularly reach 3–4,000 birds and sometimes more. Up to 3,000 Northern Pintails can be seen during September and October and a few Northern Shovelers frequent the area for most of the year. Common Pochards, Tufted Ducks, Greater Scaups, Common Goldeneyes and Goosanders occur in varying numbers except during the summer months, and Common Scoters are often recorded during July and August as they fly westwards along the estuary, often at some height and usually in the evenings.

There is always the chance of seeing a solitary Marsh Harrier over the reeds during the late spring and autumn and also an occasional Hen Harrier during the autumn and winter months. It is not unusual to see a migrating Osprey in the area, usually during May or June. Single Merlins often hunt along the shore during the autumn and winter and, during most winters, a Peregrine Falcon harries the wader flocks. A roost of Black-headed Gulls on the sands in autumn regularly numbers up to 50,000 birds. Common Gulls are also present from the autumn onwards and can peak at similar numbers along with Herring and Great Black-backed Gulls which are common during the winter months. Up to 300 Lesser Black-backed Gulls attend the gull roost in both spring and autumn. An occasional Northern Gannet or Kittiwake is seen, usually on strong easterly winds, and a few Little Gulls pass through between May and August, mainly during July. Common and Sandwich Terns pass up river during the spring and autumn. A few Arctic and Black Terns may also be seen at these times.

The foreshore at Faxfleet, between the car park and Bowes Landing, is an excellent place for waders and also passerines; Rock Pipits occur here during the winter in most years and this is the best place to see small flocks of Twites during the spring. An occasional Lapland Longspur or Snow Bunting is seen here in addition to Sky Larks, Reed Buntings and small flocks of Corn Buntings. Faxfleet Ponds have breeding Little Grebes, Great Crested Grebes, a pair of Mute Swans, some Mallards, Tufted Ducks, Moorhens and Common Coots, in addition to good numbers of Sedge and Reed Warblers. Turtle Doves breed locally and Common Cuckoos are relatively numerous during the late spring and summer. Owls are well represented with Barn Owl, Tawny Owl and Little Owl as breeding residents. An occasional Short-eared Owl hunts over the area during the autumn and winter months. Sand Martins and Barn Swallows gather to roost in the reedbeds around Faxfleet Ponds or along the estuary during August and September each year, their numbers varying annually but often reaching a combined total of over 25,000. The area can be very interesting for other migrant passerines during the spring and autumn migration periods when Meadow Pipits, wagtails, Whinchats, Northern Wheatears and warblers pass through.

During the late summer, in July and August, post-breeding flocks of juvenile Common Starlings assemble to roost in the reedbeds around Faxfleet Ponds, their numbers often reaching 10,000. Small numbers of Bearded Tits are sometimes seen in the reeds at this locality during the late autumn and winter months.

One should look southwestwards from here, over the river to the large reedbeds of the RSPB Reserve at Blacktoft Sands where there is the chance of seeing a quartering Marsh Harrier during the summer and autumn. There are several wildfowling clubs along the estuary and this activity takes place along the foreshore during the autumn and winter months. There is a wardening scheme in operation and in no circumstances should one leave the top of the floodbank.

Timing

A visit at any time between July and May can be good for different groups of birds. During the period July to September, passage waders are present in large numbers. From September onwards, the winter wildfowl assemble and the winter wader flocks can be spectacular, often involving many thousands of birds. The Pink-footed Geese occur from late September to March and sometimes roost at night on Whitton Sand. Try to be in position at Bowes Landing, opposite the sandbank, at least one hour before a high tide, when all the waders will assemble on what will be the only available roosting site. On low tides, they may be scattered along the upper estuary when the roosting flocks are not so concentrated. The periods April/May and from July to September can be worthwhile for migrant passerines along the floodbanks and in the surrounding fields.

Access

To reach this site, travel east on the M62 and leave the motorway at junction 38. Take the B1230 which doubles back to the south west to Newport and Gilberdyke. Continue for 2.5 miles (4 km) and halfway between the two villages turn left just before the village of Scalby, to Faxfleet. The narrow road continues for 3.25 miles (5.2 km) to the small village of Faxfleet, having passed over a manned railway crossing. At the end of the village, where the road bears sharp right, drive straight ahead onto a small car parking area adjacent to the raised floodbank. Walk northeastwards along the top of the floodbank for 0.75 miles (1.2 km), passing Faxfleet Foreshore, to Bowes Landing which is the best place from which to watch over Whitton Sand. Market Weighton canal enters the estuary just under 0.5 miles (0.8 km) further east. The ponds lie 0.25 miles (0.4 km) to the west of the car park and are reached by walking along the floodbank from which they are easily viewed (see map for site 24).

Calendar

This includes the estuary, the ponds and the surrounding land.

Summer – breeding: Canada Goose, occasional Oystercatcher and Common Redshank, Turtle Dove, Common Cuckoo, Sky Lark, Barn Swallow, Meadow Pipit, Yellow Wagtail, Sedge Warbler, Reed Warbler, Lesser Whitethroat, Common Whitethroat, Reed Bunting.

All year: Little Grebe, Mute Swan, Greylag Goose, Canada Goose, Common Shelduck, Mallard, Northern Shoveler, Tufted Duck, Eurasian Sparrowhawk, Common Kestrel, Red-legged Partridge, Grey Partridge, Common Pheasant, Moorhen, Common Coot, Northern Lapwing, Black-headed Gull, Common Gull, Herring Gull, Great Black-backed Gull, Stock Dove, Wood Pigeon, Collared Dove, Barn Owl, Little Owl, Tawny Owl, Sky Lark, Pied Wagtail, Wren, Hedge Accentor, Robin, Blackbird, Song Thrush, Mistle Thrush, Blue Tit, Great Tit, Magpie, Eurasian Jackdaw, Rook, Carrion Crow, Common Starling, House Sparrow, Tree Sparrow, Chaffinch, Greenfinch, Goldfinch, Linnet, Yellowhammer, Reed Bunting, Corn Bunting.

Spring and autumn passage (April to early June and July to October): Common Scoter, Marsh Harrier, Little Ringed Plover, Great Ringed Plover, Little Stint, Curlew Sandpiper, Ruff, Black-tailed Godwit, Whimbrel, Spotted Redshank, Common Greenshank, Green Sandpiper, Wood Sandpiper (occasional), Common Sandpiper, Little Gull, Sandwich Tern, Common Tern, Arctic Tern, Black Tern, Sand Martin, Barn Swallow, House Martin, Meadow Pipit, Yellow Wagtail, Whinchat, Northern Wheatear, Spotted Flycatcher, Common Redpoll.

Winter (October to March): Includes some species which are present throughout the year. Great Cormorant, Grey Heron, Tundra Swan, Whooper Swan, Pink-footed Goose, Brent Goose, Eurasian Wigeon, Common Teal, Northern Pintail, Common Pochard, Greater Scaup, Common Goldeneye, Goosander, Hen Harrier, Merlin, Peregrine Falcon, Water Rail, European Golden Plover, Grey Plover, Red Knot (occasional), Sanderling (occasional), Dunlin, Bar-tailed Godwit, Eurasian Curlew, Common Redshank, Turnstone (few), Common Gull, Herring Gull, Great Black-backed Gull, Short-eared Owl, Rock Pipit, Fieldfare, Redwing, Twite, Lapland Longspur (occasional), Snow Bunting (occasional).

24 BLACKTOFT SANDS RSPB RESERVE

OS Landranger Map 112
Scunthorpe

Habitat

Blacktoft Sands is a reserve of national importance, leased by the RSPB from the British Transport Docks Board in 1973. It lies at the confluence of the rivers Ouse and Trent, some 38 miles (61 km) up the River Humber Estuary from Spurn Point. Being one of the largest areas of brackish reedswamp is Britain, the Reserve is a prime example of this rare habitat. The *Phragmites* reeds reach a height of up to 10 feet (3.5 m) in places and are home to one of the largest northerly breeding colonies of Reed Warblers in England. The outer edges of the Reserve, adjacent to the two rivers, form a saltmarsh with an area of low-lying mud at their junction. The Reserve is regularly inundated on high tides along a series of creeks. Six shallow lagoons have been created and now form an important habitat for passage waterfowl and waders, as well as being attractive to many passerines. There are six observation hides overlooking these, two of which are two-storey, affording open views over the extensive reedbeds to the River Ouse.

Species

Between 170 and 180 species are recorded annually within the Reserve boundaries, waterfowl and waders being very well represented. The breeding population of Sedge and Reed Warblers regularly numbers up to 80 and 350 pairs respectively. The Reserve is well known for its breeding and wintering population of Bearded Tits and around 100 pairs normally breed each year. The autumn numbers, which sometimes indulge in spectacular eruptive movements during September and October, often reach up to 150 birds. Large gatherings are sometimes present during the winter months, their numbers often being affected and reduced by the severity of the weather.

Numbers of Little Grebes increase during March and April with a breeding population of around ten pairs. Great Cormorants are in evidence throughout the year and an occasional Great Bittern is seen, usually during the winter months. Grey Herons are normally present, the largest numbers being seen during July and August. An occasional Little Egret and Eurasian Spoonbill has been recorded in recent years. One or two pairs of Mute Swans nest on the Reserve and a few Tundra and Whooper Swans may drop in or pass over during the autumn and winter months. Skeins of Pink-footed Geese are often seen during this same period mainly in flight over the area *en route* to their roost on Whitton Sand or to their feeding grounds in Lincolnshire. Small numbers of other grey geese are seen from time to time and also some Barnacle and Brent Geese. A few pairs of Canada Geese and Greylag Geese now breed. Common Shelducks are resident and up to ten pairs have bred annually in recent years.

Other waterfowl are a feature of the area in autumn and winter and include the following species with some recent maxima and peak months of occurrence shown in brackets: Eurasian Wigeon (between 1,000 and 2,000 October to February), Gadwall (small numbers only; breeds), Common Teal (between 500 and 1,000 September to February; breeds), Northern Shoveler (small numbers throughout the year; breeds), Common Pochard (100 to 300 October; breeds), Tufted Duck (small numbers October; breeds), Common Goldeneye (small numbers October), Goosander (small numbers throughout the winter). In addition, an occasional Garganey is seen during the spring, and Greater Scaup, Common Scoter, Smew, Red-breasted Merganser are sometimes seen during the winter. Blue-winged Teal has occurred on three occasions (September, October and November) and a pair of Ruddy Ducks has nested in recent years.

Blacktoft Sands is one area where there is a good chance of seeing Marsh Harrier; several birds move through between early April and early June, and from late July to early October, with as many as 50 individuals being involved annually and an occasional pair staying throughout the summer. A few Hen Harriers move through between September and April, some staying throughout the winter when they roost in the reedbeds. An occasional Montagu's Harrier passes through on migration, usually during the late spring. Eurasian Sparrowhawks and Common Kestrels are local residents and often seen about the Reserve. During the spring, a passing Osprey is possible, one or two Merlins are in the area during the autumn and winter months and Hobbies are now recorded annually during the spring and autumn. There is also a chance of seeing Peregrine Falcon during the winter.

Red-legged Partridge, Grey Partridge and Common Pheasant are common breeding species. This is perhaps the best place in the region to see, or hear, Water Rails, especially during the winter months when good numbers are present in the reedbeds; a few pairs breed annually. Both Moorhens and Common Coots are numerous and resident breeding species.

Waders are well represented and Blacktoft is one of the best places to see a wide selection of this group. Most of the usual species pass through, mainly in the autumn with some spending the winter here; several others nest on or near the Reserve (see the Calendar section for list of species involved). Spectacular flocks of European Golden Plovers regularly number up to 1,000 birds and more during the winter months when Northern Lapwings also congregate in the area, their flocks sometimes numbering between 2,000 and 3,000 birds. Dunlins are common, and are present throughout the year with peak numbers during the autumn and winter when gatherings of around 500 birds may occur. A few Black-tailed Godwits pass through in spring and autumn as do Bar-tailed Godwits, Spotted Redshanks and Common Greenshanks. Some rare waders in recent years have been Black-winged Stilt, Avocet, Red-necked Stint, Temminck's Stint, Baird's Sandpiper, Pectoral Sandpiper, Sharp-tailed Sandpiper, Broad-billed Sandpiper and Hudsonian Godwit.

Several seabirds find their way along the estuary, especially during the autumn and winter months, and are recorded at Blacktoft. These have included Fulmar, Northern Gannet, Great Skua, Pomarine Skua, Arctic Skua, Kittiwake (almost annual), Sandwich Tern, Little Tern, Little Auk and Common Guillemot. Gulls are ever present including the five regular species in addition to which Mediterranean, Little and Glaucous have occurred. Spring passage of Common, Arctic and Black Terns varies annually, depending on the winds and weather during the peak migration period in May.

Turtle Doves can be seen during the summer months and one or two pairs breed locally. Although five species of owls are resident in the area and occur on the Reserve almost annually, only the Short-eared is at all regular; a pair occasionally breeds on the Reserve. There is also a chance of seeing a lone Barn Owl as it hunts over the area in the early mornings or at dusk. Little and Tawny Owls visit the Reserve from local breeding sites and an occasional Long-eared Owl is seen, usually during the autumn. Varying numbers of Sand Martins and Barn Swallows roost in the reedbeds during August and September. Tree Pipits and Meadow Pipits

Short-eared Owls

90

pass through on spring and autumn migration, Meadow Pipits also being a common breeding species. Both Water Pipit and Rock Pipit occur regularly during the winter. Good numbers of Yellow Wagtails occur in both spring and autumn and a roost holds up to 50 or 60 birds during August and early September; a few pairs of Grasshopper Warblers nest annually. Reed Buntings are common with up to 100 pairs breeding each year and large numbers are also present throughout the winter months.

Timing

The periods of spring and autumn migration, April to early June and August to October, are the best times to visit Blacktoft Sands. During the spring, waterfowl and waders move through in good numbers, the migrant passerines are on the move and the summer visitors are arriving and settling in to sing and take territory. Autumn is particularly good for waders and hirundines. During the winter months, unless frozen off, the waterfowl numbers can be high. Most of the hides face north and the light is consequently good for viewing at any time of day.

Access

To reach Blacktoft Sands, leave the M62 motorway at junction 36 onto the A614 signed for Goole 1 mile (1.6 km). On entering the outskirts of the town, turn right at traffic lights for the A161, signed 'Old Goole, Swinefleet, RSPB Blacktoft'. Follow the signs for Reedness and pass through the village of Swinefleet after 3 miles (4.8 km). Continue through Reedness, Whitgift and Ousefleet before coming to the Reserve entrance on the left 1.5 miles (2.4 km) beyond Ousefleet. Park and walk the short distance to the reception area (toilets) where information about the Reserve is available. After passing beyond the reception area, the path continues over the top of a flood embankment and leads straight on through the reeds. After only a few yards, paths to both left and right lead to the hides. Another path leads westwards along the bottom of the floodbank to reach the Ousefleet Hide after about 700 yards (640 m). Please keep to the low pathways on the Reserve side of the floodbank and do not walk along the top.

The Reserve is open throughout the year except on Tuesdays and at Christmas, from 9 am until 9 pm between May and August inclusive and from 9 am until dusk between September and April. An entrance charge is made for non RSPB members (£2.50 in 1993).

Calendar

All year: Includes several species which also occur on passage in both spring and autumn. Little Grebe, Great Crested Grebe (few), Great Cormorant, Grey Heron, Mute Swan, Greylag Goose, Canada Goose, Common Shelduck, Gadwall, Common Teal, Mallard, Northern Shoveler, Common Pochard, Tufted Duck, Eurasian Sparrowhawk, Common Kestrel, Red-legged Partridge, Grey Partridge, Common Pheasant, Water Rail, Moorhen, Common Coot, Northern Lapwing, Dunlin, Common Redshank, Black-headed Gull, Common Gull, Lesser Black-backed Gull, Stock Dove, Wood Pigeon, Collared Dove, Barn Owl, Little Owl, Tawny Owl, Short-eared Owl, Common Kingfisher (scarce), Sky Lark, Meadow Pipit, Pied Wagtail, Wren, Hedge Accentor, Blackbird, Song Thrush (scarce), Bearded Tit, Magpie, Eurasian Jackdaw, Rook, Carrion Crow, Common Starling, House Sparrow, Chaffinch, Goldfinch (scarce in winter), Linnet, Yellowhammer, Reed Bunting, Corn Bunting.

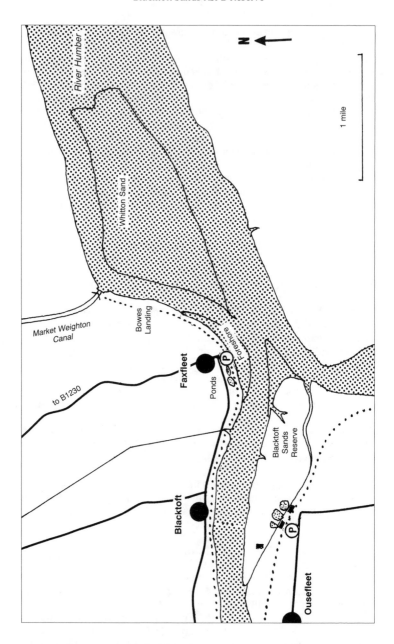

Winter (October to March): Great Bittern (rare), Tundra Swan (occasional), Whooper Swan, Eurasian Wigeon, Northern Pintail, Common Scoter, Common Goldeneye, Smew (rare), Red-breasted Merganser, Goosander, Hen Harrier, Merlin, Peregrine Falcon, European Golden Plover, Grey Plover, Jack Snipe, Common Snipe, Glaucous Gull (scarce), Water Pipit, Rock Pipit, Robin, Common Stonechat, Fieldfare, Redwing, Mistle Thrush, Blue Tit, Great Tit, Tree Sparrow (scarce), Brambling,

Greenfinch, Siskin, Common Redpoll, Bullfinch (scarce), Snow Bunting (sporadic).

Spring and autumn passage (late March to early June and August to October): Garganey (scarce), Marsh Harrier, Montagu's Harrier (occasional), Osprey (occasional), Hobby, Oystercatcher, Great Ringed Plover, Red Knot, Sanderling, Little Stint, Temminck's Stint (rare), Curlew Sandpiper, Ruff (also small numbers in summer and winter), Black-tailed Godwit, Bar-tailed Godwit, Whimbrel, Eurasian Curlew, Spotted Redshank, Common Greenshank, Green Sandpiper, Wood Sandpiper, Common Sandpiper, Little Gull, Kittiwake (usually spring), Common Tern, Arctic Tern, Black Tern, Long-eared Owl, Tree Pipit, Yellow Wagtail, Grey Wagtail (usually autumn), Whinchat, Northern Wheatear, Lesser Whitethroat, Common Whitethroat, Chiffchaff, Willow Warbler, Goldcrest (autumn), Twite.

Spring and summer (April to September): Ruddy Duck, Little Ringed Plover, Turtle Dove, Common Cuckoo, Common Swift, Sand Martin, Barn Swallow, House Martin, Grasshopper Warbler, Sedge Warbler, Reed Warbler.

25 SWINEFLEET PEA FIELDS

OS Landranger Map 112
Scunthorpe

Habitat

This very flat area of intensive agriculture is typical of the low-lying featureless landscape of the region. Interlaced with drainage ditches and with some scattered farms, it is regularly put down to pea cropping and has become a popular place for migrating Dotterels in the spring. The birds usually feed or rest in the pea fields or amongst young corn where they are often very difficult to see especially if they are sitting down, which they often do. Numbers vary annually and in some years very few birds pass through the area. In 1984, the flock peaked at 39 birds on 12th May but numbers have been lower since then.

Timing

It is certainly worth calling at this site if *en route* to Blacktoft Sands Reserve, at any time between mid-April and the end of May.

Access

Travelling on the M62, leave the motorway at junction 36 as for Blacktoft Sands (site 24) and continue to Swinefleet. Instead of bearing left onto the minor road to Reedness, Whitgift and Blacktoft, keep right on the A161, signed for Eastoft and Crowle. On leaving Swinefleet, the flat open fields appear on each side of the road. Proceed past a sign on the right reading 'Peat Works' after which the fields on each side for the next 2 miles (3.6 km) should be searched for Dotterels. There are several side roads which should also be checked.

THE NORTH YORK MOORS AND THE HAMBLETON HILLS

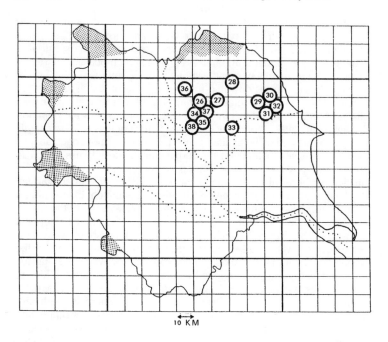

10 KM

Habitat

The gardens and most of the parkland of Duncombe Park, the ancestral home of Lord and Lady Feversham, became a National Nature Reserve in 1994. It is set in rolling farmed countryside on the edge of the North York Moors National Park. There are large areas of ancient woodland, mainly beech, lime, oak and ash which contain some of the tallest hardwoods in the country and along with the younger plantations of conifers, provide ideal habitat for many species of bird. The River Rye winds its way through the estate, being very shallow and often dry in parts during the summer.

Species

On leaving the Parklands Centre (see Access section), the recommended River Walk passes in front of the main house and alongside a large area of meadowland where Eurasian Curlews breed during the spring and summer. Grey Partridges are often seen here and an occasional Yellow Wagtail occurs, mainly during the spring and late summer.

The path then drops downhill through an area of young larch, silver birch and beech where titmice including Coal, Blue and Great can be seen all year round and warblers in spring and summer. Wrens are common throughout the area. Wood Pigeons breed in the conifers and are a familiar sight. At the end of the plantation, the path enters a more open area by the River Wye with mature mixed woodland on the steep banks to the left. Look out for Stock Doves here. During the spring and early summer, the smaller songbirds will include Willow Warbler, Chiffchaff, Garden Warbler, Blackcap, Robin, Hedge Accentor, Chaffinch, Greenfinch, Blackbird and Song Thrush. Mistle Thrushes can be seen, especially early in the spring, and Eurasian Jays are heard regularly, if not seen. Take time to stop at a bridge over the river in this area where Common Kingfisher may be seen flying along the watercourse. Return to the path and continue alongside the woodland. Great Spotted Woodpecker can occur anywhere along the route and, with luck, Lesser Spotted Woodpecker may be located high in the branches, but this species is rare. Green Woodpecker prefers the more open parkland. After crossing an area of open meadowland, the path joins the riverside and runs along the tree-lined banks. Look out for Dipper and Grey Wagtail near a waterfall on this stretch where Common Sandpiper may also be seen. Both Pied and Spotted Flycatchers can be found in the riverside trees here. Listen for the songs of Wood Warblers, especially near the beech trees on the slopes to the left. Although difficult to locate during the day unless accidentally flushed, Woodcocks breed here and are best seen during the evenings when they display over the woods and along the open rides during April and May. An occasional Goosander frequents the river during the winter months at which period the immigrant Fieldfares and Redwings will be in evidence, particularly during October and November. Bramblings should be looked for beneath the beech trees at this time when beechmast is their favourite food. Winter flocks of Siskins and Common Redpolls may be encountered in the alders along the river course. Common Kestrel and Eurasian Sparrowhawk are present throughout the year, the latter being most in evidence during the early spring when displaying over the woods. Both Tawny and Little Owls occur, the Little Owl being most evident because it often hunts during the daytime.

Common Swifts are regularly overhead during the summer months and Barn Swallows and House Martins feed over the area. Small numbers of Sand Martins nest in the sandbanks along the river. Duncombe is one of the few places where the elusive Hawfinch may be found. Keep a look out for them as they fly over the woodland uttering their lout Robin-like 'tick' calls.

Timing

April, May and early June is the best period to undertake the River Walk when the resident and migrant songbirds are most in evidence. It is advisable to be there as early as possible in the morning or during the evening, when their song is at its best. Visits during the winter months can of interest for the resident woodland species and winter visitors which are easy to see at this time.

Access

Duncombe Park lies on the southern edge of the town of Helmsley on the A170 Thirsk to Scarborough road. On entering Helmsley from Thirsk, cross over a bridge as one enters the town and after 100 yards (90 m), turn left to the estate entrance. The Park is open daily from 1 April to 31 October inclusive. The entry fee to the Park only, which includes access to the Parkland Centre (shop, restaurant and toilets) costs £1.50 per person at the time of writing. Details of admission charges to the House and Gardens can be obtained at the Park entrance kiosk. There is ample car parking space. Dogs are permitted but only if kept strictly under control on a lead.

Information leaflets with sketch maps are available at the Centre, showing the two major walks, The River Walk (see above) and The Country Walk, both of which are approximately 2.25 miles (3.6 km) long and clearly waymarked. The first of these is recommended for the best birdwatching, passing through and alongside the mature mixed woodland and also through the meadows by the River Rye. This route takes about two hours to complete at a leisurely pace. It is an ideal walk for family birdwatchers being mostly on level ground and not too demanding. Guided walks are available on request at the Parkland Centre.

Calendar

All year: Woodcock, Eurasian Sparrowhawk, Common Kestrel, Grey Partridge, Common Pheasant, Stock Dove, Wood Pigeon, Collared Dove, Little Owl, Tawny Owl, Great Spotted, Lesser Spotted (scarce) and Green Woodpeckers, Dipper, Wren, Hedge Accentor, Robin, Blackbird, Song Thrush (scarce in winter), Mistle Thrush, Goldcrest, Long-tailed, Marsh, Coal, Blue and Great Tits, European Nuthatch, Eurasian Treecreeper, Eurasian Jay, Magpie, Eurasian Jackdaw, Rook, Carrion Crow, Common Starling, House Sparrow, Chaffinch, Greenfinch, Bullfinch, Hawfinch, Common Redpoll.

Spring and summer (April to early August): Eurasian Curlew (meadows), Common Sandpiper, Common Cuckoo, Common Swift, Sky Lark, Barn Swallow, House Martin, Sand Martin, Yellow Wagtail, Grey Wagtail, Pied Wagtail, Common Redstart, Garden Warbler, Blackcap, Wood Warbler, Chiffchaff, Pied Flycatcher, Spotted Flycatcher, Goldfinch, Linnet.

Winter (October to March): Goosander (occasional on river), Fieldfare, Redwing, Brambling, Siskin.

Habitat

Bransdale has a very wide variety of habitats including wooded slopes and gullies with streams, open parkland with mature deciduous trees, conifer plantations, open pasture with dry-stone walls and open heather moorland. The lower parts of the valley are mainly sheep-grazing land with an ample scattering of deciduous trees and conifer plantations. As one reaches the high ground, broken pastureland gives way to heather moor, finally dropping down at the head of the dale into a large area of open parkland with mature deciduous trees along the Hodge Beck which runs along the length of the dale to join the River Dove 2 miles (3.2 km) south of Kirkbymoorside.

Species

The very varied habitats make Bransdale one of the most interesting areas for birds on the North York Moors. The specialities are Red Grouse and Ring Ouzel but there is much more of interest for the birdwatcher. Red Grouse are easy to see on the open moorland, but Ring Ouzels are very shy and are best seen as they feed on the broken sheep pasture and around the dry-stone walls. The wooded gullies and stream sites have breeding warblers, Common Redstarts and the usual small passerine species associated with this habitat including Hedge Accentor, Robin, Blackbird, Song Thrush, Goldcrest, Spotted Flycatcher, titmice and Chaffinches.

The open parkland at the head of the valley is good for Green and Great Spotted Woodpeckers, Stock Doves, Mistle Thrushes and Eurasian Treecreepers. During the winter months flocks of Fieldfares and some Redwings are present along the valley. Wood Pigeons are numerous throughout the year.

The broken pastureland bordering the moorland areas is the breeding ground for many pairs of Northern Lapwings as well as European Golden Plovers, Common Snipe, Eurasian Curlews and Common Redshanks which all breed in the general area of the high ground. Meadow Pipit is a common bird during the summer months on the open moorland and adjacent rough grazing land and Tree Pipits frequent the wooded slopes. Small numbers of Sky Larks, Pied Wagtails, Whinchats and Northern Wheatears breed.

Birds of prey are well represented and Bransdale is a traditional wintering area for Rough-legged Buzzards which are regular visitors, more so in some years than others. An occasional Common Buzzard, Hen Harrier, Merlin or Peregrine Falcon can be seen and Common Kestrel is present throughout the year. The extensive plantations of conifers along the valley sides hold several pairs of Eurasian Sparrowhawks and a few Northern Goshawks. Both Little and Tawny Owls are present in the dale and there is always the chance of seeing Short-eared Owl.

Winter flocks of Chaffinches, Bramblings, Greenfinches and Yellowhammers are sometimes present near Breck House Farm at the head of the dale after the first road-gate, and often near the farms lower down the valley nearer Carlton. During periods of severe weather, Snow Buntings are a possibility along the moorland stretches.

Timing

The very varied habitats along the dale make a visit at any time of year worthwhile. The best time for Red Grouse and Ring Ouzels is during April and May; Red Grouse are present throughout the year but are more obvious during the early spring when displaying; Ring Ouzels can be very secretive once settled down to nest and are best seen as they feed out on the broken grazing land and dry-stone wall areas. Autumn and winter are the best periods to see birds of prey.

Access

Starting at Helmsley market place, take the A170 Scarborough road and after 500 yards (460 m) turn left to Carlton, opposite a garage. After 2.5 miles (4 km) a strip of woodland on the left with pines and beech is worth checking for warblers and other small passerines; there are forestry rides along which to walk. Another 1 mile (1.6 km) further on brings you to an open area on the left signed 'Forestry Commission – Cow House Bank Viewpoint'. Park here and investigate the woodland for passerines and scan over the valley to the heather moors and ridges for birds of prey. Continue down a steep wooded incline before coming out into open pasture. A high ridge on the right should be checked for soaring raptors. Park at a small bridge over a stream a little further on and look for woodland species.

A large conifer plantation on the left starting at a small church and a phone box continues along the roadside for some distance. Stop at the end of this roadside belt of trees and look over the extensive plantations in the valley to the left of the road. This is a good site for Eurasian Sparrowhawks and Northern Goshawks, especially during the spring when the former are displaying. Wood Pigeons are numerous in this area. The first heather moor starts at this point and an area of open grazing land on the left is very good for breeding Northern Lapwings. The stone walls and pasture in this area, opposite a small red-roofed hut, are favoured by Ring Ouzels. Flocks of Mistle Thrushes gather here during late summer and autumn to feed on the rowan berries. Winter flocks of Fieldfares also use this area for feeding. A gully on the left with silver birch trees should be checked for Common Redstarts in the summer, and the adjacent fields around Bonfield Gill (look for signed gate on left) are worth a stop for thrushes in winter.

After a stretch of open moor where Red Grouse are always evident, the road drops down a steep hill with a larch plantation on the right before entering the large area of open parkland at the head of the dale. There are two gates across the road here by Breck House farm. The road now drops down to the Hodge Beck and a cattle grid and passes through parkland with mature deciduous trees along the watercourse, good for Green and Great Spotted Woodpeckers, Eurasian Treecreepers and Common Redstarts.

A sign for St. Nicholas Church and Bransdale Hall marks the head of the dale at Cockayne. After crossing a second bridge and cattle grid, the road now climbs up a steep hill onto the high ground to come down the valley on the eastern side. The extensive conifer plantations on the left should be checked for raptors. The stretch of road between here and the end of the heather moor towards Fadmoor is very good for Red Grouse, European Golden Plover, Northern Lapwing, Common Snipe and Eurasian Curlew, particularly during mid May when most will have chicks. Both Red-legged and Grey Partridges occur in the marginal pasture land.

If entering the dale from the direction of Scarborough, turn right at a roundabout into Kirkbymoorside and continue through the town,

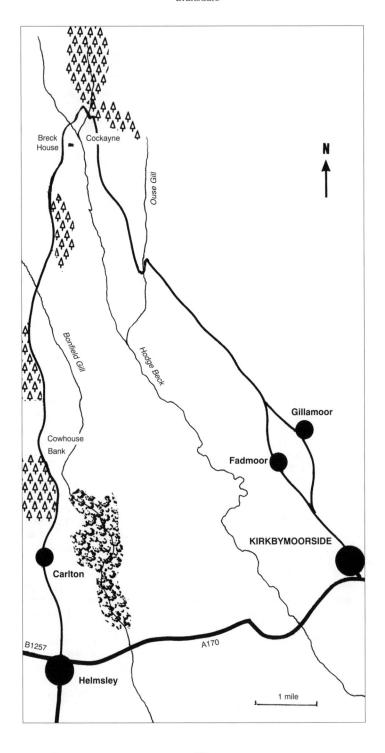

Bransdale

bearing left at the top of the main street, following signs to Fadmoor and Bransdale bearing left at a junction after 1.5 miles (2.4 km).

Calendar

Autumn and winter (September to March): Hen Harrier, Northern Goshawk, Eurasian Sparrowhawk, Rough-legged Buzzard, Common Buzzard, Common Kestrel, Merlin, Peregrine Falcon, Red Grouse, Fieldfare, Redwing, Chaffinch, Brambling, Greenfinch, Yellowhammer.

Spring and summer (April to August): Includes several resident species which are present through the year. Northern Goshawk, Eurasian Sparrowhawk, Common Kestrel, Red Grouse, Red-legged Partridge, Grey Partridge, Common Pheasant, European Golden Plover, Northern Lapwing, Common Snipe, Eurasian Curlew, Common Redshank, Stock Dove, Wood Pigeon, Common Cuckoo, Little Owl, Tawny Owl, Common Swift, Green Woodpecker, Great Spotted Woodpecker, Sky Lark, Barn Swallow, House Martin, Tree Pipit, Meadow Pipit, Pied Wagtail, Wren, Common Redstart, Whinchat, Northern Wheatear, Ring Ouzel, Blackbird, Song Thrush, Mistle Thrush, Lesser Whitethroat, Common Whitethroat, Garden Warbler, Blackcap, Chiffchaff, Willow Warbler, Goldcrest, Spotted Flycatcher, Long-tailed Tit, Coal Tit, Blue Tit, Great Tit, Eurasian Treecreeper, Magpie, Eurasian Jackdaw, Rook, Carrion Crow, Common Starling, Chaffinch, Greenfinch, Goldfinch, Siskin, Linnet, Common Redpoll, Common Crossbill, Bullfinch.

28 ROSEDALE AND BLAKEY RIDGE INCLUDING CROPTON FOREST AND ROSEDALE MOOR

OS Landranger
Map 100
Malton and Pickering

Habitat

Rosedale is typical of most of the major valleys cut into the southern part of the North York Moors; sheep grazing land with plenty of scattered deciduous trees at the lower end, eventually giving way to wooded ravines and gullies at the head of the valley. Cropton Forest is a large coniferous area on the east side, extending northwards to the edge of the open moorland. Rosedale Moor extends northwards above Rosedale Abbey while on the west side is the wide expanse of Spaunton Moor, both areas of 'managed' heather moorland.

Species

This valley has most of the species listed in the chapter on Bransdale with the addition of European Nightjar. Cropton Forest is one of the best areas for this species in Yorkshire and any fairly open area along the forest edges, and where recent felling and replanting has taken place, should produce singing males at dusk during May and June. A campsite in Cropton Forest at Spiers House is ideally suited for staying in the area and thereby being around at dusk. The extensive plantations of conifers hold many Goldcrests and a few pairs of Siskins and Common Crossbills which all breed.

Beyond Cropton is the picturesque village of Rosedale Abbey which has a caravan park and a campsite by the river where Grey Wagtails and Dippers can be seen. A minor road running eastwards from the village leads onto Rosedale Moor where Dotterels often occur on passage in the spring. Birds of prey during the winter months and during migration in both spring and autumn regularly include Rough-legged Buzzard, Common Buzzard and Hen Harrier with an occasional Marsh Harrier. During the summer months, Red Grouse, European Golden Plover, Eurasian Curlew, Common Redshank, Common Snipe, Northern Wheatear, Meadow Pipit, Whinchat and Ring Ouzel are typical breeding birds of the open moorland and there is the chance of Short-eared Owl and Merlin at this time.

Timing

The best time to visit Rosedale is during late April, May and early June, when passage Dotterels are most likely to be present and when the woodland passerines are in full song. European Nightjars are also more conspicuous at this time. Visits during the autumn and winter months can be worthwhile for occasional birds of prey on the moors and flocks of Common Crossbills around the coniferous areas in addition to flocks of winter thrushes, Goldcrests, titmice and finches.

Access

Leave the main A170 Thirsk to Scarborough road at the village of Wrelton 5 miles (8 km) east of Kirkbymoorside, and proceed into Main Street, signed 'Cropton, Hartoft and Rosedale'. After passing through the village of Cropton, look for a sign on the left reading 'Forestry Commission – North Riding Forest Park' which marks the start of the extensive Cropton Forest. Just beyond this sign, a minor road runs off to the right and leads for 0.75 miles (1.2 km) to Spiers House Campsite. This road is worth investigating, even if not intending to stay at the campsite, as it is good for several species of woodland passerines including possible Common Crossbills and for European Nightjars at dusk. The Forestry Commission organises guided walks during the summer from Spiers House campsite (and also from Dalby and Wykeham Forests) to look for birds including European Nightjars. Details are available from The Forestry Commission, Forest Enterprise Office, 42 Eastgate, Pickering YO18 7DU (Tel: 01751-72771).

About 1 mile (1.6 km) further along the main road is a dip in the road at a bridge just before reaching Hartoft End, where one can park and take a public footpath along the riverbank, downstream from the bridge. This track passes through deciduous woodland, good for passerines. The village of Rosedale Abbey is reached after a further 3 miles (4.8 km). The caravan park and campsite is alongside the river opposite The Coach House Inn.

To reach Rosedale Moor, take a road to the east out of the village by the side of The Milburn Arms, and continue for 2.5 miles (4 km) to where the Lyke Wake Walk crosses the road in the area of Shunner Howe. Park here and investigate the area on foot, proceeding initially westwards, looking to the north, particularly for Dotterels during the spring.

A recommended route back to the main A170 Scarborough road after the above detour is to take the road to Castleton, passing Low Bell End

Farm to reach a cattle grid after about 2 miles (3.2 km) at the start of the open heather moor. Continue along the moorland road for 3 miles (4.8 km) to a 'T' junction and turn left signed 'Farndale, Hutton-le-Hole and Kirkbymoorside'. This road runs south along Blakey Ridge, the watershed between Rosedale on the left and Farndale on the right, passing through the picturesque village of Hutton-le-Hole after 8 miles (12.8 km) and finally to Keldholme to rejoin the A170 main road. The stream running through Hutton-le-Hole is worth checking for Grey Wagtails and Dippers. Total distance from Wrelton to the head of the dale and back down Blakey Ridge to Keldholme is 25 miles (40 km) not including the detour to Rosedale Moor which is 5 miles (8 km).

Calendar

Autumn and winter (September to March): Hen Harrier, Eurasian Sparrow-hawk, Rough-legged Buzzard, Common Buzzard, Common Kestrel, Merlin, Peregrine Falcon, Red Grouse, Fieldfare, Redwing, Goldcrest, Chaffinch, Brambling, Greenfinch, Siskin, Common Crossbill, Yellowhammer.

Spring and summer (April to August): Includes several resident species which are present throughout the year. Eurasian Sparrowhawk, Common Kestrel, Red Grouse, Common Pheasant, Dotterel (spring passage), European Golden Plover, Northern Lapwing, Common Snipe, Eurasian Curlew, Common Redshank, Stock Dove, Wood Pigeon, Common Cuckoo, Little Owl, Tawny Owl, Short-eared Owl (scarce), European Nightjar, Common Swift, Green Woodpecker, Great Spotted Wood-pecker, Sky Lark, Barn Swallow, House Martin, Tree Pipit, Meadow Pipit, Grey Wagtail, Pied Wagtail, Wren, Common Redstart, Whinchat, North-ern Wheatear, Ring Ouzel, Blackbird, Song Thrush, Mistle Thrush, Lesser Whitethroat, Common Whitethroat, Garden Warbler, Blackcap, Chif-fchaff, Willow Warbler, Goldcrest, Spotted Flycatcher, Long-tailed Tit, Coal Tit, Blue Tit, Great Tit, Eurasian Treecreeper, Eurasian Jay, Magpie, Eurasian Jackdaw, Rook, Carrion Crow, Common Starling, Chaffinch, Greenfinch, Goldfinch, Siskin, Linnet, Common Redpoll, Common Cross-bill, Bullfinch.

29 DALBY AND STAINDALE FORESTS

OS Landranger
Maps 100/101
Malton and
Pickering/Scarborough

Habitat

This extensive area of the North York Moors National Park comprises large tracts of conifers, which, as areas are felled, are being replanted with, in order of abundance, sitka spruce, hybrid larch and Douglas fir. The valley bottom is lined with mature alders, and the slopes are clad with silver birch and some beech, as well as the numerous conifers.

Approaching from the west, the forest road runs north along the valley of Dalby Beck and then east alongside Staindale Beck for much of the way. A lake has been man made at High Staindale after which the road climbs uphill to the top of the surrounding hills and then turns eastwards before dropping down to Bickley, at the end of the Dalby Forest Drive. The whole area is very well managed by the Forestry Commission and includes several car parking areas with picnic tables, toilet facilities, a visitor centre and maps showing the numerous walks through the forest and onto the adjoining moorland.

Species

The vast stretches of conifers hold Common Crossbills, Goldcrests and Siskins during the summer months as well as the more usual warblers, titmice and finches. Eurasian Sparrowhawks, Wood Pigeons and Eurasian Jays are resident and can usually be seen. The area around Staindale Lake is good for several species, especially where a feeding station in the car park regularly attracts Coal, Blue, Great and Marsh Tits, European Nuthatches, Eurasian Jays, Greenfinches, Chaffinches, Hedge Accentors, Robins and Wrens. The lake usually has a few Canada Geese, Mallards, Tufted Ducks, Moorhens and Common Coots. The beckside alders attract flocks of Siskins and Common Redpolls during the autumn and winter months when immigrant thrushes are often present in good numbers.

Siskins and Common Redpolls

This eastern part of the North York Moors is one of the best places for European Nightjars where any area of recently felled and open ground is worth checking for this species at dusk during the late spring and summer. Tree Pipits, Common Redstarts and a few pairs of Wood Warblers breed in and around the oakwoods in Low Staindale where it is also worthwhile searching for Pied Flycatchers. The areas of heather moorland around The National Trust Bridestones Reserve are not 'managed' but a few pairs of Red Grouse still breed there. Whinchats nest on the bracken-covered slopes. Check along Staindale Beck for Common Sandpipers, Common Kingfishers, Grey Wagtails and Dippers. Both Green and Great Spotted Woodpeckers may be seen or heard anywhere in the area.

Timing

As recommended for Bransdale and Rosedale, the best time to visit this area is during late April, May and early June when the passerines are in song and the other breeding species are displaying and more in evidence. Visits during the autumn and winter months can be worthwhile for the occasional bird of prey, large flocks of Wood Pigeons and winter thrushes as well as Siskins, Common Redpolls, titmice, Common Crossbills and finches.

Access

Travelling eastwards along the main A170 Thirsk to Scarborough road, pass through the town of Pickering and come to the village of Thornton-le-Dale. On entering the village, look for a garage on the left, just after which is a minor crossroads signed Whitby/Malton and Dalby Forest Drive. Turn sharp left into the narrow road, opposite the small and fenced village green, proceed for 1 mile (1.6 km) and turn right, signed 'Lower Dalby Forest Drive 2 miles'. A charge is made for each car at a toll booth on entering the forest (£2 in 1993). Shortly after the toll booth, look for Haygate Picnic Site on the right from where one can get uninterrupted views over the forest. It is worth checking here in spring for displaying *Accipiters*. After a further 2 miles (3.2 km), in Dalby village, there is a visitor centre, car parks, toilets and the starting point for several walks, details of which can be obtained at the centre. The road now runs alongside the alder-lined Staindale Beck where there are several places to stop and look for birds.

About 2 miles (3.2 km) from the visitor centre is Staindale car park and information board. Park on the left, adjacent to a small grassy area across which a path leads to the National Trust Bridestones Reserve. At the entrance to the Reserve, the path offers three alternatives; one runs along the bottom of a hillside covered by mixed woodland before turning right and entering the Reserve via Dovedale, which has a hanging oakwood on its eastern side. This path passes along the valley bottom before rising up Needle Point to the moortop. The second path runs diagonally upwards through mixed woodland to the escarpment edge along which The Bridestones stand as outcrops of weathered rock, and the third path climbs steeply upwards along the edge of Jonathan Gill to the moor top, where it becomes a sandy track beside the adjoining Forestry Commission conifer plantation on the eastern boundary of the Reserve from where several paths cross the moor to the western escarpment.

Returning to the car park, continue along the forest drive, passing Staindale Lake on the right and just after a sharp right hairpin bend is the Staindale Lake car park from where a path leads the short distance to the lakeside picnic tables. A feeding station in the car park attracts lots of birds and is well worth investigation. After leaving the car park, the road now climbs to the hilltop through open sheep pasture on the right with conifers on the left. Turn left onto a forest track to Crosscliffe Viewpoint (signed '¾ mile'), park the car and walk for 1.3 miles (2 km) through the forest to the viewpoint overlooking Thompson's Rigg with the conical hill of Blakey Topping, and the forestry plantations on Allerston High Moor and Langdale Forest. Return to the tarmac forest drive and continue to a 'T' junction at the end of the Dalby Forest Drive. Turn right here for Langdale End and Hackness. From here, the road continues through open sheep pasture with a few farms and the small village of Langdale End before reaching Hackness where there is a choice of turning left to Scalby and Scarborough, or right to Forge Valley (see site 29) to join the main A170 road at East Ayton.

Total distance from Thornton-le-Dale to Hackness is 21 miles (33.5 km).

Calendar

Autumn and winter (September to March): Includes several resident species which are present through the year. Grey Heron, Eurasian Sparrowhawk, Northern Goshawk (occasional), Common Kestrel, Common Pheasant, Stock Dove, Wood Pigeon, Tawny Owl, Common Kingfisher, Green Woodpecker, Great Spotted Woodpecker, Grey Wagtail, Pied Wagtail, Dipper, Wren, Hedge Accentor, Robin, Blackbird, Fieldfare, Redwing, Mistle Thrush, Goldcrest, Long-tailed Tit, Marsh Tit, Coal Tit, Blue Tit, Great Tit, European Nuthatch, Eurasian Treecreeper, Eurasian Jay, Magpie, Eurasian Jackdaw, Rook, Carrion Crow, Common Starling, Chaffinch, Brambling, Greenfinch, Siskin, Common Redpoll, Common Crossbill, Bullfinch, Yellowhammer.

Spring and summer (April to August): Common Sandpiper, European Nightjar, Barn Swallow, House Martin, Tree Pipit, Common Redstart, Whinchat, Song Thrush, Lesser Whitethroat, Common Whitethroat, Garden Warbler, Blackcap, Wood Warbler, Chiffchaff, Willow Warbler, Spotted Flycatcher, Goldfinch.

30 WYKEHAM FOREST AND TROUTSDALE

OS Landranger Map 101
Scarborough

Habitat

Wykeham Forest is an extensive area of conifers in blocks of varying age and species including Sitka spruce, hybrid larch and Douglas fir. The valley of Troutsdale, which runs along the northwestern boundary, is mainly sheep pasture with plenty of deciduous timber. The River Derwent flows southeastwards along the northern edge of the forest.

Species

This forest is similar in character to the others in this part of the North York Moors National Park and has more or less the same bird species list (see chapter on Dalby and Staindale Forests). It is good for European Nightjars, having large open areas of recently felled timber which hold several pairs during the summer months. Recent observations have shown that the nightjars enter the villages in the valleys at night to hawk for insects around the lights. The Forestry Commission has provided a viewing area near High Wood Brow car park, intended primarily to enable birdwatchers to look over the valley towards the eastern sector of Dalby Forest for Honey-buzzards, a few pairs of which are now attempting to breed in the general area and are being monitored by the Forest Rangers. The birds are very elusive but, with patience, it is possible to obtain occasional views as they soar over the valley. In no circumstances should one enter the forests to search for these rare birds.

Having driven down into Troutsdale, one should stop at the bridge over the River Derwent at Hilla Green and walk along the riverside footpaths to look for Dippers, Grey Wagtails and Common Kingfishers.

Timing

The best time to visit the forest, particularly for Honey-buzzards and European Nightjars, is during late May and June. Visits during the late autumn and winter months will provide relatively few birds but there is a chance of seeing Common Crossbills, an occasional Hen Harrier or Northern Goshawk at this time.

Access

Travelling eastwards on the A170 Pickering to Scarborough road, come to the village of Wykeham, 10 miles (16 km) east of Pickering, and turn left between The Downe Arms public house and the church, signed 'North Moor 2'. Reach North Moor (Foresters' houses) and continue through the forest for 1 mile (1.6 km) to an open area of cleared trees on the right which is good for European Nightjars, as is a second similar area some 0.5 miles (0.8 km) further along the road. Just 0.5 miles (0.8 km) beyond this second area is a crossroads and a car park signed 'High Wood Brow' from where there are excellent views over Troutsdale and beyond. The viewing area is off to the right of the track which leads to the left near the car park. It is permitted to drive along any of the ungated tracks which intersect large areas of forest. From the High Wood Brow car park, continue down the steep hill to join the main Troutsdale road after about 1 mile (1.6 km) and turn right to Hackness. Stop near the bridge at Hilla Green after 0.5 miles (0.8 km) from where a public footpath runs along the right bank of the river. After the bridge, the road continues for 0.5 miles (0.8 km) to a 'T' junction. Turn right here signed Hackness and Scarborough and enter Hackness after 0.5 miles (0.8 km), after which one should bear right and drive along Forge Valley to join the main A170 Scarborough road at East Ayton.

Calendar

Same as for Dalby and Staindale Forests (see that chapter), with the addition of Honey-buzzard during the summer.

31 BROMPTON POND
OS Landranger Map 101
Scarborough

Habitat and Species

This large pond, behind and adjacent to the village of Brompton, is certainly worth a visit if in the area. Being only 200 yards (180 m) from the main A170 Scarborough to Pickering road, it can be included with one of the forest drives.

The pond is bordered by grazing land, with willows and other trees and bushes along its margins. A minor access road runs past the northern end between the water and the churchyard. Several species of waterbirds favour the pond and some can be seen at close range from the road as they feed just over the wall. Mute Swans regularly breed and Mallards, Little Grebes, Moorhens and Common Coots are resident. Tufted Ducks are usually present and Common Pochards and Common Goldeneyes use the water in winter when Common Teals may also be present. The surrounding trees and those in the churchyard attract many species of song birds, especially during the spring and early summer.

Timing

A visit at any time of the year can be of interest for waterbirds but spring and early summer are best for the most species when the summer visitors are present and the resident passerines are in song.

Access

Approaching from Scarborough, travel along the A170 Pickering road for 7.5 miles (12 km) to the village of Brompton by Sawdon and come to the Cayley Arms, a large public house on the left. Immediately past the pub, turn left into Cayley Lane. Proceed downhill for 150 yards (135 m) and turn right into Church Lane to reach the pond on the left after 50 yards (45 m). Park on the narrow grass verge and look over the stone wall to view the water and surrounding area. A public footpath leads along the right side of the pond. The trees and shrubs on the opposite side of the road above a high wall in the churchyard can also be viewed from the road. On leaving the pond, continue along the narrow road for 350 yards (320 m) and bear right at some houses into West Brow on the western edge of the village, rejoining the main A170 road after 200 yards (180 m).

Calendar

All year: Little Grebe, Mute Swan, Mallard (including several feral types), Tufted Duck, Moorhen, Common Coot, Wood Pigeon, Collared Dove, Tawny Owl, Pied Wagtail, Wren, Hedge Accentor, Robin, Blackbird, Mistle Thrush, Blue Tit, Great Tit, Magpie, Eurasian Jackdaw, Rook, Carrion Crow, Common Starling, House Sparrow, Greenfinch, Chaffinch, Yellowhammer.

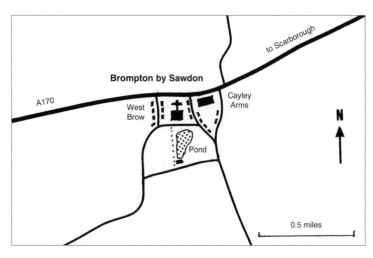

Winter (October to March): Common Teal, Common Pochard, Common Goldeneye, Black-headed Gull, Common Gull, Common Kingfisher (occasional), Fieldfare, Redwing.

Spring and Summer (April to August): Northern Lapwing, Common Cuckoo, Common Swift, Sand Martin, Barn Swallow, House Martin, Song Thrush, Blackcap, Willow Warbler, Spotted Flycatcher, Goldfinch.

32 FORGE VALLEY

OS Landranger Map 101
Scarborough

Habitat

This well-wooded valley, cut by meltwater from the old Hackness Lake at the end of the last ice age, is an excellent place to visit for woodland birds. The River Derwent runs along the valley on its journey southwards, 10 miles (16 km) from its source on the North York Moors. The valley road runs north from the village of East Ayton towards Hackness but a recommended route turns off at the end of the valley onto the road to Scalby and passes along the lower edge of Raincliffe Woods and finally alongside Throxenby Mere, coming out on the A171 main Scarborough to Whitby road. Total distance from East Ayton to the A171 is approximately 6 miles (9.6 km).

Species

The high and mature deciduous timber is home to Eurasian Sparrowhawks, Stock Doves, Wood Pigeons, Tawny Owls, Great Spotted Woodpeckers, European Nuthatches, Eurasian Jays and Carrion Crows throughout the year. There is a small colony of nesting Grey Herons in the area and these birds are often seen along the valley. A parking area, where several feeding tables are kept permanently supplied with food by interested local people, attracts many birds, particularly during the winter months, including Great Spotted Woodpecker, Hedge Accentor, Robin, Blackbird, Song Thrush, Long-tailed Tit, Marsh Tit, Coal Tit, Blue Tit, Great Tit, European Nuthatch, Eurasian Jay, Eurasian Treecreeper and Chaffinch. All can be watched at close range from one's car and titmice and Chaffinches will take food from the hand held out of the window.

During the summer months large numbers of migrants arrive to breed along the valley; Common Cuckoo, Common Redstart, Lesser Whitethroat, Common Whitethroat, Garden Warbler, Blackcap, Wood Warbler, Chiffchaff, Willow Warbler and Spotted Flycatcher are all present in addition to the resident passerines. The river attracts Common Kingfisher, Dipper, Grey Wagtail and Pied Wagtail. Throxenby Mere has its resident Mallards, Moorhens and Common Coots with an occasional Great Cormorant during the winter months.

Timing

A visit any time of year can be worthwhile but spring and early summer (April to mid-June) is perhaps the most attractive time to drive along the

Chaffinches

valley when the birds are in full song. The feeding area is very good during the winter months.

Access
Forge Valley is reached from the village of East Ayton on the A170 main
Scarborough to Pickering road, 4 miles (6.4 km) west of Scarborough.
Turn right in the village at a sign for Forge Valley and Hackness, into
Castlegate. The road runs along the bottom of the valley with the river on
the left. There are several parking areas and paths into the woods; the first
one is a little under 1 mile (1.5 km) along the valley on the right; park here
and walk into the wood on an obvious pathway. A similar distance further along brings you to another parking area signed 'Old Man's Mouth
Picnic Site' on the left by the river. Drive down the short, steep entrance
track to park, and walk across a footbridge over the river and into the
woods which are good for Wood Warblers. Return to the car park, drive
for 350 yards (320 m) along the road and look for the feeding area on the
left signed 'Birdwatchers Car Park'. Park close to the feeding tables and
watch the birds from the car.
    Another 350 yards (320 m) past the feeding area is the right turn-off to
Scalby signed 'Raincliffe Woods and Lady Edith's Drive'. Follow this road,
along which there are three parking areas with paths leading into the
woods, the last one being signed 'Sawmill Bank Picnic Site' after 0.5 miles
(0.8 km). Throxenby Mere is a further 1.5 miles (2.4 km) along the road
on the right. Keep right at a junction and follow the side of the mere to
park at the far end. Paths lead into the woods from here. Continue along
Lady Edith's Drive to come out on the main A171 Scarborough to Whitby
road, 2 miles (3.2 km) from the town centre.

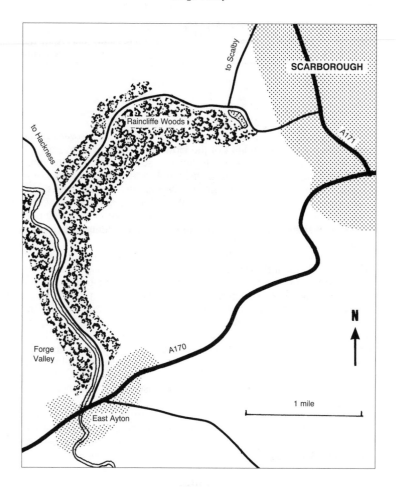

Calendar

All year: Grey Heron, Mallard, Tufted Duck (occasional), Moorhen, Common Coot (Throxenby Mere), Eurasian Sparrowhawk, Common Kestrel, Common Pheasant, Northern Lapwing, Stock Dove, Wood Pigeon, Collared Dove, Tawny Owl, Common Kingfisher, Great Spotted Woodpecker, Grey Wagtail, Pied Wagtail, Wren, Robin, Blackbird, Song Thrush, Mistle Thrush, Goldcrest, Long-tailed Tit, Marsh Tit, Coal Tit, Blue Tit, Great Tit, European Nuthatch, Eurasian Treecreeper, Eurasian Jay, Magpie, Eurasian Jackdaw, Rook, Carrion Crow, Common Starling, House Sparrow, Chaffinch, Greenfinch, Common Redpoll, Yellowhammer, Reed Bunting.

Summer (April to August): Common Cuckoo, Barn Swallow, Common Redstart, Lesser Whitethroat, Common Whitethroat, Garden Warbler, Blackcap, Wood Warbler, Chiffchaff, Willow Warbler, Spotted Flycatcher.

Winter (October to March): Great Cormorant (Throxenby Mere), Fieldfare, Redwing, Siskin, Brambling.

33 CASTLE HOWARD LAKE

OS Landranger Map 100
Malton and Pickering

Habitat and Species

The lake is situated in the splendid grounds of the Castle Howard Estate amidst the rolling pastureland of the Howardian Hills, with avenues of large deciduous trees and much other scattered timber. The main lakeshore is varied in character, having ample tree cover along the north-western corner, large areas of waterside vegetation along the edges adjacent to the roadside and there is a small reedbed near the house. Good areas of mud are often exposed at the northwestern corner during periods of dry weather which regularly attract passage waders at the appropriate season.

Great Crested and Little Grebes breed, as do Greylag and Canada Geese, Moorhens and Common Coots. Flocks of Greylag Geese often reach 150 birds during the winter months and sometimes attract individuals of other species of grey geese. Grey Herons often frequent the shoreline. During times of spring and autumn passage, in addition to the waders, Common, Arctic and Black Terns may occur on easterly winds, and the occasional Osprey passes through during April or May. Large assemblies of Common Swifts and hirundines regularly feed over the lakes at this time and also during the autumn. The reedbed holds a few pairs of Reed Warblers and Sedge Warblers, the latter being fairly common around the lake. Both Green and Great Spotted Woodpeckers are resident in the grounds and Hawfinch is a possibility.

In winter, good numbers of both diving and surface-feeding ducks assemble, and an occasional diver or rarer grebe has been recorded. Gatherings of gulls which roost on the main lake, often number several thousands, consisting mainly of Black-headed and Common.

Timing

Visits at any time from late July to May can be worthwhile but periods of easterly winds in spring are best for passage waders and terns. Feeding assemblies of Common Swifts and hirundines are most spectacular during cold overcast conditions in May and September. During the summer months, the lakeside footpath can be busy with families and anglers but most species are little affected.

Access

To reach the lake, leave York on the main A64 York to Scarborough road and after 11 miles (17.6 km) look for a turning to the left, signed 'Castle Howard'. Continue for 4 miles (6.4 km) passing a large ornate column on the left, and after passing through two stone archways, proceed straight on to reach the lakeside car parking area shortly after a large obelisk at a minor crossroads. Walk across the road from the car parking area, through a gate, and along the footpath which borders the north eastern edge of the lakeshore. Approaching on the A643 from the east, look for the Castle Howard sign on the right about 5 miles (8 km) west of Malton. This road brings you to the lake after 3 miles (4.8 km).

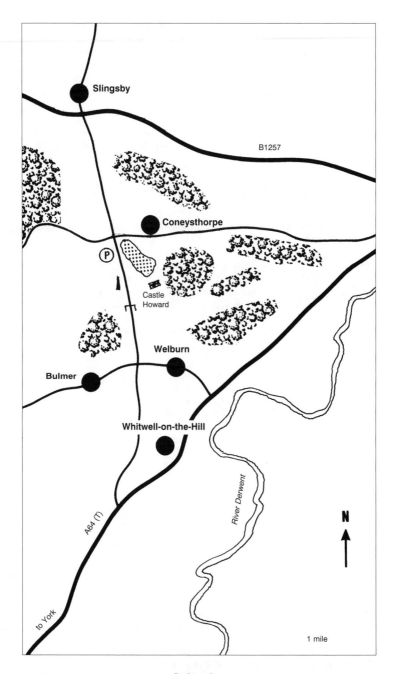

Calendar

Winter (October to March): Occasional divers and rarer grebes, Whooper and Tundra Swans (occasional), Greylag and Canada Geese, Eurasian Wigeon, Common Teal, Mallard, Northern Pintail, Northern Shoveler,

Common Pochard, Tufted Duck, Common Goldeneye, Goosander, occasional birds of prey, Moorhen, Common Coot, Northern Lapwing, Black-headed Gull, Common Gull, Herring Gull, Great Black-backed Gull, Stock Dove, Wood Pigeon, Little Owl, Tawny Owl, Green Woodpecker, Great Spotted Woodpecker, Pied Wagtail, Fieldfare, Redwing, titmice, Common Starling, Chaffinch, Brambling, Greenfinch, Siskin, Common Redpoll, Hawfinch, Yellowhammer, Reed Bunting.

Spring and autumn passage (April to early June and August to October): Waterfowl, Osprey, waders, terns, Common Swift, hirundines, Yellow Wagtail, warblers.

Spring and summer (April to August – breeding): Great Crested Grebe, Little Grebe, Mute Swan, Greylag Goose, Canada Goose, Mallard, Tufted Duck, Eurasian Sparrowhawk, Common Kestrel, Moorhen, Common Coot, Northern Lapwing, Stock Dove, Wood Pigeon, Common Cuckoo, Little Owl, Tawny Owl, Green Woodpecker, Great Spotted Woodpecker, Sky Lark, Barn Swallow, House Martin, Yellow Wagtail, Pied Wagtail, Wren, Hedge Accentor, Robin, Common Redstart, Blackbird, Song Thrush, Mistle Thrush, Sedge Warbler, Reed Warbler, Common Whitethroat, Garden Warbler, Blackcap, Chiffchaff, Willow Warbler, Long-tailed Tit, Marsh Tit, Blue Tit, Great Tit, Eurasian Jay, Magpie, Eurasian Jackdaw, Rook, Carrion Crow, Common Starling, Tree Sparrow, Chaffinch, Greenfinch, Goldfinch, Linnet, Yellowhammer, Corn Bunting, Reed Bunting.

34 SUTTON BANK AND GARBUTT WOOD

OS Landranger Map 100
Malton and Pickering

Habitat

This area lies on the west-facing slopes of the Hambleton Hills, just 5 miles (8 km) east of Thirsk and 6 miles (9.6 km) west of Helmsley. The most impressive features are the precipitous cliffs which dominate the landscape and overlook the boulder-strewn wooded slopes of the escarpment. Garbutt Wood, situated on the slopes above Lake Gormire, is predominately birch with some oak and sycamore and there are areas of scattered scrub of birch, hazel, sallow, bramble, rosebay willowherb, and large stands of bracken. The upper slopes of the wood are dominated by the 50' to 70' (15 m to 21 m) sheer sandstone face of the Whitestone Cliff.

The southern part of the escarpment is overlooked by the impressive cliffs of Roulston Scar which are seen to advantage on the right as one ascends Sutton Bank. The famous 'White Horse', cut into the hillside above the village of Kilburn, is a popular tourist attraction. There are large stands of conifers adjacent to the car park at the top of Sutton Bank and also along the main road to Helmsley. The lake, set in a basin, is deep, with very little emergent vegetation and surrounded by trees.

Species

The woodland along the slopes, particularly that in Garbutt Wood, holds most of the common resident species and also several summer visitors. Willow Warblers are common along the woodland edges and amongst the scrub where Tree Pipits and Common Whitethroats can also be found. The more mature parts of the woods hold a few pairs of Common Redstarts, Spotted Flycatchers, Blackcaps and Wood Warblers as well as all three species of woodpeckers. Chaffinches are particularly numerous throughout the area and Yellowhammers are fairly common. The titmice are well represented with Long-tailed, Marsh, Willow, Coal, Blue and Great all nesting in the area.

The woods are host to Eurasian Sparrowhawks and Wood Pigeons throughout the year and the cliffs along the escarpment are home to several pairs of Eurasian Jackdaws, Stock Doves and House Martins and also a pair of Common Kestrels. One of the most surprising breeding birds is the Fulmar, a few pairs having frequented the main cliff at Roulston Scar which faces west and is 25 miles (40 km) from the sea, since the mid 1960s.

Lake Gormire is strangely not very attractive to waterbirds. It is well stocked with fish and there are small areas of waterside vegetation, but it is deep and surrounded by trees, which is doubtless the cause. Both Little and Great Crested Grebes, however, attempt to breed annually and there are usually a few Tufted Ducks present. During the winter months, Goosanders sometimes drop in. It is always worth keeping an eye out for passing birds of prey which may be seen as they drift along the slopes, particularly if the wind is in the west during the spring and autumn migration seasons (see 'Calendar' section below).

Timing

Visits during the spring and autumn can be equally rewarding. The song birds along the wooded slopes are best seen during late April, May and June when both the residents and the summer visitors are present. Autumn can be very pleasant and there is always the chance of seeing a migrant bird of prey at this time. Some raptors are known to drift south along the west-facing slopes and the area would certainly be worth investigating for this group during August and September. A few also pass during May and June and the existing records suggest that regular watching would produce results.

Access

Leave Thirsk on the A170 and, after 5 miles (8 km), come to the steep hill at Sutton Bank (gradient 1 in 4). Continue to the top where there is a large car parking area, with an information centre and toilets, on the left at Coopers Cross. To reach Garbutt Wood from here, walk back to the main road at the top of Sutton Bank where there is a finger sign reading 'Sneck Yate 3'. Take this footpath which runs north along the top of the escarpment and forms part of the Cleveland Way. After about 500 yards (460 m), look for a Yorkshire Wildlife Trust sign at a junction and follow the narrow path which drops steeply down to the left and leads to Garbutt Wood and eventually down to Lake Gormire. An easier way to reach the lake and woods is along a public bridleway at the bottom of Sutton Bank. One can drive along this track for 0.5 miles (0.8 km) to a farm, where a small charge is made for each car. Pass the farm and drive to the right of the farm buildings to a wide grassy parking area just before a gate to the lake. Walk from here, through the gate, and along the path which runs

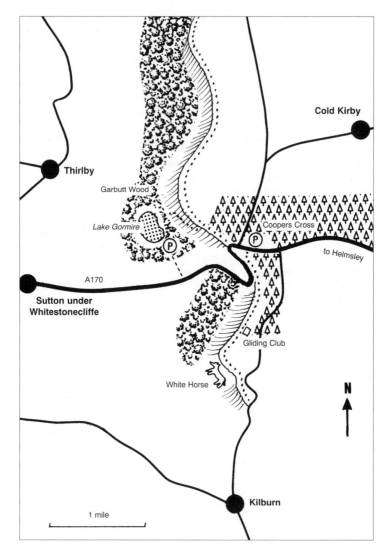

alongside the lake, and after about 400 yards (360 m) a path leads up the bank into the wood below Whitestone Cliff. The bridleway is signed on the left as one approaches Sutton Bank from Thirsk, just before the red sign 'Gradient 1 in 4'.

To reach the Fulmar cliff at Roulston Scar, cross the road from the Coopers Cross car park and follow a path which runs south along the top of the impressive escarpment, passing the Gliding Club, and coming eventually to the 'White Horse' after 1 mile (1.6 km). One can drive to the 'White Horse' from the village of Kilburn.

Calendar

This includes the wooded slopes, the conifer plantations, the cliffs and Lake Gormire.

All year: Little Grebe, Mallard, Tufted Duck, Eurasian Sparrowhawk, Common Kestrel, Common Coot, Common Pheasant, Stock Dove, Wood Pigeon, Tawny Owl, Green Woodpecker, Great Spotted Woodpecker, Lesser Spotted Woodpecker, Wren, Hedge Accentor, Robin, Blackbird, Mistle Thrush, Goldcrest, Long-tailed Tit, Marsh Tit, Willow Tit, Coal Tit, Blue Tit, Great Tit, Eurasian Treecreeper, Eurasian Jay, Magpie, Eurasian Jackdaw, Rook, Carrion Crow, Common Starling, Chaffinch, Greenfinch, Common Redpoll, Bullfinch, Yellowhammer.

Spring and summer (April to August): Fulmar, Great Crested Grebe, Turtle Dove, Common Cuckoo, Barn Swallow, House Martin, Tree Pipit, Common Redstart, Song Thrush, Common Whitethroat, Blackcap, Wood Warbler, Willow Warbler, Spotted Flycatcher, Goldfinch, Linnet.

Passage: Occasional birds of prey pass along the escarpment during both the spring and autumn migration seasons and species recorded in recent years have been Honey-buzzard, Black Kite, Hen Harrier, Northern Goshawk, Merlin, Hobby and Peregrine Falcon (the last named species may also occur during the winter months).

Winter (October to March): Goosander (occasional on the lake), Fieldfare, Redwing, Siskin.

35 WASS BANK WOODS

OS Landranger Map 100
Malton and Pickering

Habitat

This area, lying some 8 miles (12.8 km) east of Thirsk, comprises a large expanse of both coniferous and deciduous woodland on the south-facing slopes of the Hambleton Hills above the village of Wass. The lower ground is mainly sheep pasture surrounding the impressive ruins of Byland Abbey.

Species

Situated in a very picturesque part of Yorkshire, this site is well worth a visit during the late spring and summer for woodland birds, and most of those associated with the hillside deciduous habitat can be found here. The large conifer plantations have breeding Eurasian Sparrowhawks and many Wood Pigeons but birds can be sparse in this alien monoculture. Some pairs of Siskins have settled in the forests and now breed there. Green Woodpeckers can be found in the more open areas along the hillsides and Great Spotted Woodpeckers can be found throughout.

During the summer months, the recommended walk through Elm Hag wood, starting in the village of Wass (see 'Access' section below) should produce most of the common resident passerines in addition to the summer migrants which include Garden Warbler, Blackcap, Wood Warbler,

Chiffchaff, Willow Warbler, Spotted Flycatcher and Common Redstart. European Nuthatches and Eurasian Treecreepers are relatively common and the former should certainly be found. An occasional Grey Wagtail frequents a small pond in this wood. One should look out for the occasional birds of prey, particularly during the autumn, when some migrate along the hills; Hen Harrier, Northern Goshawk and Hobby have been seen in recent years.

Timing

The best time to visit this site is during late April, May and June when the summer migrants augment the resident species. An early morning visit to hear the dawn chorus is worthwhile if staying nearby. Visits during the autumn and winter months should provide most of the resident species in addition to wandering flocks of Fieldfares and Redwings; the woodpeckers, titmice and Wood Nuthatches are often easier to see at this time.

Access

There are several public bridleways and footpaths in this general area, many of which pass through good bird habitat and may be investigated by those touring the region. A recommended walk however, passes through excellent deciduous woodland with many old beeches and oaks, starting in the village of Wass. Travelling eastwards from Thirsk along the A170 Helmsley road, climb the steep gradient of Sutton Bank after 5 miles (8 km). After a further 3.5 miles (5.6 km) look for a minor road to the right signed 'Wass Bank'. Proceed down the very steep hill (gradient 1 in 4), and after 1 mile (1.6 km) look for a forestry car parking area on the left where it is worth stopping to investigate the mature conifer woods before reaching Wass.

Continuing down the hill for a further 0.5 mile (0.8 km), and about 200 yards (180 m) before reaching the main village junction at the Wombwell Arms public house, look for the village hall parking area on the left where it is permitted to leave one's car. Walk from here to the junction and turn right onto a track signed No Through Road. After passing some houses, this track climbs steadily uphill into a stretch of very good deciduous woodland known as Elm Hag. Stop at a small pond in the wood on

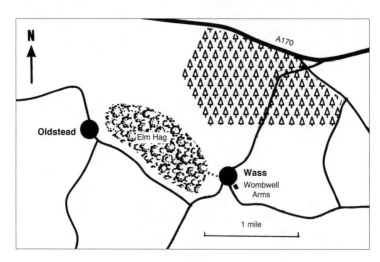

the right of the track to view the general area for most of the song birds. About 300 yards (275 m) further along, the recommended walk ends where the main track bears right to a farm and another bears left through a metal gate and along a private forestry road. It is perhaps better to return from here along the woodland track back to Wass as this is certainly the best part for birds. For those wishing to walk further however, the footpath continues straight on over a stile marked with a wooden finger sign reading 'Cam Farm and Observatory'. The 'Observatory' is an old stone tower just over 0.5 miles (0.8 km) further along the ridge from where the path continues to the village of Oldstead, some 2 miles (3.2 km) west of Wass.

Calendar

All year: Eurasian Sparrowhawk, Common Kestrel, Common Pheasant, Moorhen (regularly on the pond in the wood), Wood Pigeon, Collared Dove (in the village), Turtle Dove, Tawny Owl, Green Woodpecker, Great Spotted Woodpecker, Grey Wagtail (woodland pond), Pied Wagtail, Wren, Hedge Accentor, Robin, Blackbird, Mistle Thrush, Long-tailed Tit, Marsh Tit, Willow Tit, Coal Tit, Great Tit, European Nuthatch, Eurasian Treecreeper, Eurasian Jay, Magpie, Eurasian Jackdaw, Rook, Carrion Crow, Common Starling, House Sparrow, Chaffinch, Greenfinch, Bullfinch.

Spring and summer (April to August): Common Cuckoo, Common Swift (feeding overhead), House Martin, Barn Swallow, Common Redstart, Song Thrush, Garden Warbler, Blackcap, Wood Warbler, Chiffchaff, Willow Warbler, Spotted Flycatcher, Goldfinch, Siskin.

36 CLEVELAND FOREST (OVER SILTON PICNIC SITE) AND THE NORTHERN HAMBLETON HILLS

OS Landranger
Map 99
Northallerton
and Ripon

Habitat

This large area of conifers on the western slopes of the Hambleton Hills below the open heather moors consists of spruce, larch and Scots pine. There is an open scrubby area near the picnic site car park with silver birches and an alder-lined stream. The wide track through the forest has some open forest edges and eventually leads onto the heather moor. The minor approach road is lined with stretches of hedgerow and some large trees.

Species

The species found in this large coniferous forest are relatively few with Robin, Wren, Goldcrest and Chaffinch being by far the most numerous during the spring and summer months. Coal Tits are present in small numbers. Although sporadic in their occurrence, Common Crossbills could occur and should be looked for in early spring and again in summer. A few pairs of Siskins breed in the forest. Eurasian Sparrowhawks display over the trees during the early spring and Common Kestrel can be seen over the adjacent open country. Wood Pigeons are common throughout the year.

The trees and hedgerows along the approach road, the forest edges and the open area near the picnic site car park have Mistle Thrushes, Song Thrushes, Blackbirds, Willow Warblers, Chiffchaffs, Common Whitethroats, Blackcaps, Spotted Flycatchers, Blue and Great Tits, Chaffinches and Greenfinches during the spring and summer months and into the autumn. Tawny Owl, Green Woodpecker and Great Spotted Woodpecker may be seen or heard in the more open parkland habitat adjacent to the forest.

As one leaves the forest to come out onto the open heather moor, Northern Lapwing, Eurasian Curlew, Red Grouse and Meadow Pipit are familiar breeding birds and Common Cuckoo can often be seen at the forest edge.

Timing

April, May and June are the best months to visit this site when the resident and migrant songbirds are most noticeable. Late summer and autumn can be interesting when the young birds are in evidence. Flocks of Common Redpolls and Siskins are a possibility in the alders near the picnic site during the winter. One should always keep an eye out for birds of prey in the general area, a few of which are known to drift south along the west-facing scarp of the hills during the autumn.

Access

To reach this site, travel north on the A19, and after by-passing Thirsk, look for the southern turn-off to Over Silton on the right, 5.5 miles (9 km) north of Thirsk. This narrow winding road passes through some fine avenues of old trees and continues for 2.5 miles (4 km) to a 'T' junction at the eastern edge of the village. Turn right here for Nether Silton and continue for 0.7 miles (1 km), passing an old church and cemetery set back in the fields to the left, and look for a minor no-through-road (sharp left turn) just before a stone house. This straight approach road runs through open grazing land with a few isolated houses, overlooked by the western slopes of the northern end of the Hambleton Hills. After 0.8 miles (1.2 km) come to the Cleveland Forest Silton Picnic Site on the left. Park here and walk down a short set of steps with hand rails into a gully to cross a stream and follow a track alongside the forest with the alder-lined stream and open scrubby area with silver birch on the right.

On returning to the car park, one can walk north along the main forest track, which climbs steadily uphill for 1 mile (1.6 km) to the open heather moor under the northern slopes of the peak of Black Hambleton, which stands at around 1300 feet (400 m) above sea level, and joins the Osmotherly/Hawnby minor road. Even during the winter months, this is a most pleasant walk if one has the time. If travelling south on the A19, look for the northern turn-off to Over Silton on the left, 2 miles (3.2 km) after passing the A684 Northallerton road. Enter the village and bear right, signed Nether Silton, Kepwick and Borrowby, to pass the old church and come to the forest road as above.

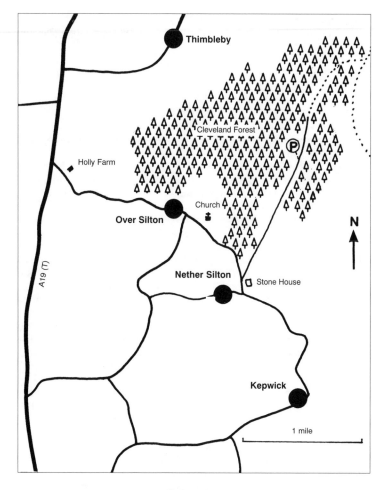

Calendar

All year: Eurasian Sparrowhawk, Common Kestrel, Common Pheasant, Stock Dove, Wood Pigeon, Tawny Owl, Green Woodpecker, Great Spotted Woodpecker, Wren, Hedge Accentor, Robin, Blackbird, Mistle Thrush, Goldcrest, Coal Tit, Blue Tit, Great Tit, Eurasian Jay, Magpie, Eurasian Jackdaw, Rook, Carrion Crow, Common Starling, Chaffinch, Greenfinch, Common Redpoll, Siskin, Common Crossbill (sporadic).

Spring and summer (April to September): Red Grouse, Northern Lapwing, Eurasian Curlew, Common Cuckoo, Sky Lark, Tree Pipit, Meadow Pipit, Song Thrush, Common Whitethroat, Blackcap, Chiffchaff, Willow Warbler, Spotted Flycatcher.

Habitat

Nettle Dale is a small valley running for 1 mile (1.6 km) along a tributary of the River Rye some 3 miles (4.8 km) west of the town of Helmsley. The northern side of the valley is clothed with conifers, and the southern slopes with good open deciduous trees, mainly oaks. There are four fish ponds along the wide valley floor and the tributary stream is lined with alders.

Rievaulx Abbey is set below a wooded hillside beside the River Rye, just 1 mile (1.6 km) east of the Nettle Dale car park.

Species

Apart from the small numbers of Mallards, Tufted Ducks and Moorhens which frequent the fish ponds, the species in this area are the same as those at Wass (see site 35). The hanging oak woodland on the left as one passes up the valley has Wood Warblers in summer as well as Blackcaps, Chiffchaffs, Willow Warblers, Common Redstarts and Spotted Flycatchers. Most of the common resident passerines can be found. Until recently, Pied Flycatchers nested in boxes provided by the Forestry Commission but these were vandalised and have fallen into disrepair, since when the species no longer breeds in the valley. If this nest box scheme is renewed, they will certainly nest here again. Both Green and Great Spotted Woodpeckers reside here and European Nuthatches can be seen.

It is worth stopping at the bridge over the River Rye near Ashberry House, *en route* to Rievaulx Abbey, to look for Dippers and Grey Wagtails. The Abbey grounds and the adjacent woods are worth investigating for birds.

Access

To reach Nettle Dale, leave Thirsk on the A170 Helmsley road and after climbing Sutton Bank, continue for a further 1 mile (1.6 km) and take a road to the left signed 'Scawton and Rievaulx'. After 2.75 miles (3.4 km) having passed through the village of Scawton, look for a car parking area on the left, just before the road bears right to Ashberry. Park here and walk past the fish ponds for 0.5 miles (0.8 km) to where a path leads to Old Byland and another heads north and circles back to the Ashberry road just over 0.5 miles (1 km) north of Ashberry House. On leaving the Nettle Dale car park, drive for 0.5 miles (0.8 km) to Ashberry House and keep right to cross the river bridge, immediately after which turn left to Rievaulx.

Timing

This area is mainly a spring and summer site. The walk along Nettle Dale is very pleasant at this time, especially in the early morning or in the evening when there are fewer people about.

Calendar

All Year: Mallard, Tufted Duck, Eurasian Sparrowhawk, Common Kestrel, Common Pheasant, Moorhen, Wood Pigeon, Tawny Owl, Green Woodpecker, Great Spotted Woodpecker, Grey Wagtail, Pied Wagtail, Wren, Hedge Accentor, Robin, Blackbird, Mistle Thrush, Long-tailed Tit, Marsh

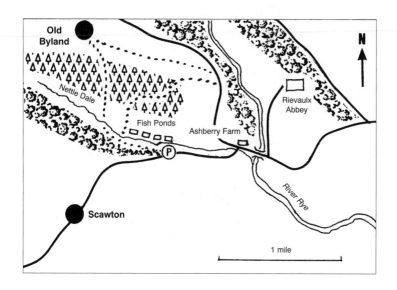

Tit, Coal Tit, Blue Tit, Great Tit, European Nuthatch, Eurasian Treecreeper, Eurasian Jay, Magpie, Eurasian Jackdaw, Rook, Carrion Crow, Common Starling, House Sparrow, Chaffinch, Greenfinch, Bullfinch, Siskin.

Spring and Summer: Common Cuckoo, Barn Swallow, House Martin, Common Redstart, Song Thrush, Garden Warbler, Blackcap, Wood Warbler, Chiffchaff, Willow Warbler, Spotted Flycatcher, Goldfinch.

38 NEWBURGH PRIORY LAKE

OS Landranger Map 100
Malton and Pickering

Habitat and Species

This lake is just 0.5 miles (0.8 km) south of the village of Coxwold and 7 miles (11.2 km) southeast of Thirsk. It is worth a look if one is in the area and can be combined with visits to Garbutt Wood on Sutton Bank and the woodland walks at Wass and Nettle Dale (see sites 31, 32 and 33). The lake is adjacent to Newburgh Priory and the priory lawns abut the southern shore. Agricultural land and large deciduous trees border the north and east shores and the road runs along the western edge. One can view the lake and the surrounding area from a convenient layby.

A pair of Mute Swans regularly breeds on the lake and there is a resident population of Mallards including several feral types. Moorhens and Common Coots breed, along with a few Tufted Ducks. An occasional migrant Osprey has called in here, sometimes staying for several days, in the late spring of several recent years. During the winter months, waterfowl include Common Teals, Common Pochards, Common Goldeneyes and occasional Goosanders in addition to the resident species. Black-headed Gulls are sometimes numerous at this season. The lake is a good place to see early Sand Martins and Barn Swallows which feed over the water on arrival. Titmice and finches can be seen around the lake or along the road-side hedgerows and bushes, where Yellowhammers are also resident.

Timing
April, May and early June is a good time to visit this area when the resident birds are in territory and the migrants are settled in and singing. Visits at any time during the winter months will produce some waterfowl which can be seen at fairly close range.

Access
Starting from Thirsk, take the A19 York road and after 3 miles (4.8 km), fork left for Coxwold and reach the village after 4.5 miles (7.2 km). Follow the signs for Oulston and Easingwold to come to the lake after 0.5 miles (0.8 km). Park in the layby to view the lake. It is worth walking along the road to look for small birds in the adjacent fields and near the Priory gates.

Calendar
Spring and summer (April to August): Includes several resident species which can be seen throughout the year. Little Grebe, Mute Swan, Mallard, Tufted Duck, Osprey (occasional on spring passage), Common Pheasant, Moorhen, Common Coot, Stock Dove, Wood Pigeon, Collared Dove, Common Swift, Sand Martin (passage), Barn Swallow, House Martin, Pied Wagtail, Wren, Hedge Accentor, Robin, Blackbird, Song Thrush, Mistle Thrush, Willow Warbler, Spotted Flycatcher, Long-tailed Tit, Blue Tit, Great Tit, Magpie, Eurasian Jackdaw, Rook, Carrion Crow, Common Starling, House Sparrow, Chaffinch, Greenfinch, Goldfinch, Bullfinch, Yellowhammer.

Winter (October to March): Common Teal, Common Pochard, Common Goldeneye, Goosander (occasional), Black-headed Gull, Common Gull, Coal Tit, Fieldfare, Redwing, Siskin, Common Redpoll.

THE NORTHWESTERN DALES AND THE RICHMOND AREA

39 Swaledale, Stonesdale Moor and Arkengarthdale
40 Hudswell Woods and Marske Bridge, Richmond
41 Thornton Steward Reservoir
42 Bolton-on-Swale Lake, Scorton Tip and Great Langton

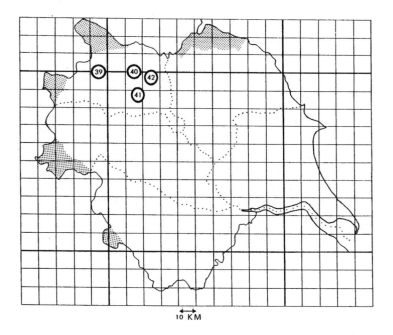

10 KM

39 SWALEDALE, STONES-DALE MOOR AND ARKENGARTHDALE

OS Landranger
Maps 91 and 98
Appleby and
Westmoreland/
Wensleydale

Habitat

There are many roads in this part of the Yorkshire Dales which run through beautiful scenery and which have good areas for the birds of the region. The following route, however, is recommended, being most representative of this part of Yorkshire and embracing most of the special habitats associated with the 'northern' species.

Swaledale is typical of all the dales, being composed of fellside sheep pasture giving way to barren *Juncus* and heather moorland on the tops, interlaced with dry-stone walls and with many scattered deciduous trees, mainly ash, oak and sycamore. There are also some small stands of larch. From the town of Reeth, the road runs alongside the River Swale for most of the way to the village of Keld where the route turns north to leave the dale. The river valley is lined with alders and there are wide flat areas of floodplain in some parts. Towards the villages of Gunnerside and Thwaite there are many small waterfalls along the young River Swale and along the Muker Beck where the scenery is spectacular.

Turning north at the village of Keld, and climbing onto the higher ground, the character of the landscape changes and the area becomes open barren *Juncus* moor grazed by sheep and relieved only by gullies and streams. Turning eastwards at Tan Hill, the site of the highest public house in England at a height of 1,732 feet (528 m) above sea level, the road passes through heather moor for five miles before dropping down into the hill pastureland of Arkengarthdale and finally back to Reeth.

Species

The upland areas have only a limited number of species but those that do occur are one of the attractions of this route in spring and summer, especially European Golden Plover, Dunlin, Black Grouse, Red Grouse, Peregrine Falcon, Short-eared Owl, Grey Wagtail, Dipper and Ring Ouzel. During late April, May and June, this drive will provide the birdwatcher with the chance of seeing most if not all of those species. Grey Herons are often along the valleys and a few Mallards frequent the river. Goosanders breed in the area and can be seen either on or flying up and down the river course. Birds of prey favour the upland areas and Eurasian Sparrowhawk, Common Kestrel and Peregrine Falcon are resident species. During the autumn and winter months, a lone Hen Harrier, Common Buzzard or Rough-legged Buzzard may be seen hunting over the moors. Merlin is a possibility during the summer and autumn. In addition to the Red and Black Grouse, Grey Partridges occur and Common Pheasants are numerous.

During the spring and early summer, waders return to the valleys and moors to breed and these include Oystercatcher, European Golden Plover, Northern Lapwing, Dunlin, Common Snipe, Eurasian Curlew, Common Redshank and Common Sandpiper. Black-headed and Lesser Black-backed Gulls are usually in evidence during the summer from

Peregrine Falcon

nearby breeding colonies. Stock Doves and Wood Pigeons can be seen at any time of year. Common Cuckoo can be seen or heard in spring and early summer and a few Short-eared Owls breed on the moors. The villages have their summer populations of Common Swifts, Barn Swallows and House Martins as well as the typical garden species including Wrens, Hedge Accentors, Robins, Blackbirds, Song Thrushes, Blue and Great Tits, Chaffinches, Greenfinches and Common Starlings. Meadow Pipits are very common on the moorland and all three species of wagtails are present in the area; any stretch of river or beck should produce Grey and Pied Wagtails and Yellow Wagtails breed along the valleys. Common Redstarts and a few Pied Flycatchers nest in the woods on the hillsides. Whinchats and Northern Wheatears breed in the marginal upland areas where any gullies or rocky outcrops may also hold a pair of Ring Ouzels. The riverside trees are host to several species during the summer when warblers and finches can be seen.

Corvids are common all over the area, especially Eurasian Jackdaws which frequent any exposed crags in large numbers. Carrion Crows are familiar birds of the barren uplands and a solitary Common Raven is always a possibility during the autumn and winter months.

Timing

The best time to undertake this drive is during March, April, May and June when the Red and Black Grouse are most in evidence and the breeding waders are back in the area and displaying. The migrant passerines are in their territories from late April and early May. Visits during the winter months, if the weather permits, will produce Red Grouse and an occasional Peregrine Falcon, Common Buzzard or Rough-legged Buzzard, but otherwise, birds can be very thin on the ground. Post-breeding Northern Lapwings and Eurasian Curlews start flocking and preparing to leave the high ground as early as late June and during July, after which time the upland area can be relatively devoid of birds.

Access

Starting at the town of Reeth which lies 10 miles (16 km) west of Richmond on the B6270 road to Kirkby Stephen, this route proceeds initially westwards for 13 miles (20.8 km) to the village of Keld. The road runs along the valley of the River Swale and 2 miles (3.2 km) from Reeth, shortly after passing through Healaugh look for a parking space on the left beside the river. This is a good place to stop for riverside birds and to search the alders for passerines. Just after the village of Low Row the road runs alongside the tree-lined river for about 1 mile (1.6 km). The trees and scrub along this section and also Rowlett Wood on the steep hillside to the right of the road are good for birds; there are several places to stop.

Enter the village of Gunnerside where the road turns sharp left and runs alongside a beck before coming to a bridge over the River Swale. Before crossing the bridge, park on the left and view the river and the wooded crag downstream. Continue over the bridge and come to the village of Muker, where the road leaves the River Swale and runs alongside Muker Beck. It is worth stopping to look at the riverside alders anywhere in this area. The road crosses Muker Beck three times along this stretch. Just after by-passing Keld, look to the right where there are several waterfalls and the rocky gully of Kisdon Force, shortly after which is a road marked 'Unsuitable for coaches and heavy goods vehicles' and signed for West Stonesdale and Tan Hill. This is the road you need to take but before doing so it is worth continuing for a couple of miles (3.2 km) along the main road which runs alongside limestone crags and the River Swale. This short detour can be good for birds and is scenically impressive. Return to the West Stonesdale turn-off and stop at the river bridge to look for Dipper and Grey Wagtail and also to scan the ridges for birds of prey.

Continue through the tiny village of West Stonesdale beyond which the narrow winding road climbs steeply uphill to the wild and barren unfenced Stonesdale Moor. After 1.5 miles (2.4 km), look for an open grassy parking area on the left beside a stream and near a small bridge. This is the place to look for Black Grouse in April and May. The area is mainly *Juncus* moor, grazed by sheep and is often snowbound in the winter. Continue along the road and after climbing a steep winding hill look for another parking place on the left, 1 mile (1.6 km) from the bridge. This affords good views over the wide valley and may also produce Black Grouse. Tan Hill is reached after a further 1 mile (1.6 km). Turn right at the 'T' junction and proceed eastwards, passing through heather moor for 5 miles (8 km), which is very good for Red Grouse and also Peregrine Falcon and Raven in the winter months. After this upland stretch, the road drops steadily down through Arkengarthdale and finally returns to Reeth. Total distance of this circular route from Reeth and back is 30 miles (48 km). Do not walk over the moorland except along recognised pathways.

Calendar

Spring and summer (April to August): Goosander, Black Grouse, Oyster-catcher, European Golden Plover, Northern Lapwing, Dunlin, Common Snipe, Eurasian Curlew, Common Redshank, Common Sandpiper, Black-headed Gull, Lesser Black-backed Gull, Common Cuckoo, Short-eared Owl, Common Swift, Sky Lark, Sand Martin, Barn Swallow, House Martin, Yellow Wagtail, Grey Wagtail, Common Redstart, Whinchat, Northern

Wheatear, Ring Ouzel, Song Thrush, Common Whitethroat, Blackcap, Willow Warbler, Spotted Flycatcher, Pied Flycatcher (scarce), Goldfinch, Linnet, Reed Bunting.

Autumn and winter (September to March): Hen Harrier, Common Buzzard, Rough-legged Buzzard (sporadic), Merlin, Fieldfare, Redwing, Common Raven (scarce).

All Year: Grey Heron, Mallard, Eurasian Sparrowhawk, Peregrine Falcon, Common Kestrel, Red Grouse, Grey Partridge, Common Pheasant, Stock Dove, Wood Pigeon, Great Spotted Woodpecker, Pied Wagtail, Dipper, Wren, Hedge Accentor, Robin, Blackbird, Mistle Thrush, Blue Tit, Great Tit, Magpie, Eurasian Jackdaw, Rook, Carrion Crow, Common Starling, House Sparrow, Chaffinch, Greenfinch, Common Redpoll, Yellowhammer.

40 HUDSWELL WOODS AND MARSKE BRIDGE, RICHMOND

OS Landranger
Map 92
Barnard Castle

Habitat

Hudswell Woods, which comprises Calfhall, Round Howe and Billy Bank Woods, are situated on the west side of Richmond alongside the River Swale and are owned by The National Trust. High and steeply sloping hillsides clothed in mature deciduous trees and understorey form the main part of the area. A unique conical hill known locally as the Camel's Hump is similarly garbed. The woodland contains much old and dead timber and is one of the best examples of this type of habitat. Open areas of grassland run alongside the river downstream from the Camel's Hump and are backed by a tree-covered limestone crag. The river is fairly wide, shallow and stony and the banks are lined with alder trees. The main road runs westwards from here to Marske Bridge, and beyond to the towns of Reeth or Leyburn, and is an extremely pleasant and scenic drive, passing through good areas of woodland and pastureland along the valley of the River Swale.

Species

The main attraction is the large area of mature timber at the Round Howe and most of the species associated with this habitat can be seen here. Eurasian Sparrowhawks and Common Kestrels are usually around throughout the year. Both Stock Doves and Wood Pigeons are resident and Collared Doves are common in the adjacent built-up area across the river. Tawny Owls breed as do Green, Great Spotted and Lesser Spotted Woodpeckers. Small woodland passerines including Common Redstart, Lesser and Common Whitethroat, Garden Warbler, Blackcap, Wood Warbler, Chiffchaff, Willow Warbler, Spotted and Pied Flycatchers, most of the titmice, European Nuthatch and Eurasian Treecreeper can all be seen on a walk around the Camel's Hump. The alder trees along the riverbanks attract Siskins and Common Redpolls during the autumn and winter months. Grey and Pied Wagtails frequent the river and Common Kingfisher is a possibility. Common Sandpiper and Dipper should be looked for from the footbridge over the river at the Round Howe site and also from Marske Bridge. Goosanders regularly fly up and down the river course during the spring and breed in the area. Common Swifts are always overhead during the summer as they hawk for insects along the valley.

Timing
Between late April and mid-June is the best time to visit when the passerines are in full song. Visits during the autumn and winter can be rewarding when the resident woodland birds are easy to see and the winter visitors are in the area.

Access
Leave Richmond on the A6108 Leyburn/Reeth Road at a roundabout in the town centre. After exactly 1 mile (1.6 km) just beyond a cemetery (large green gates on the right), look for the Round Howe sign at a wide entrance on the left. Drop down a steep incline and bear right into the car park (voluntary contributions) and picnic area by the river (toilet facilities). To reach the woods, walk across the footbridge over the river from where several paths lead in both directions along the river bank and into the woods. Initially, turn left and after about 20 yards (18 m) a wide grassy track leads off to the right and circles the Camel's Hump, an obvious wooded hill with a fence around the base. The woodland on this hill and on the enclosing slopes to the right holds all the woodland species. The track, which can be very muddy in wet weather, rejoins the riverside, 200 yards (180 m) downstream. Continue to an open area of grassland and investigate the tree-covered limestone crag on the right. Upstream from the footbridge are two obvious paths, one along the riverbank and the other leading up into the wooded hillside. A path leads upstream from the car park alongside the river beyond the picnic tables.

On leaving the site, turn left onto the Reeth road which runs partway along the valley of the River Swale and after 1 mile (1.6 km) passes the very scenic Whitcliffe Woods and Whitcliffe Scar, a long limestone ridge on the right. There is a large parking area on the left below a high crag with wooded slopes 3.5 miles (5.6 km) from the Round Howe site where it is worth stopping to look for birds. Shortly after leaving this layby, take a right turning to Marske and park just over the river bridge which is a good place to look for Dippers and Grey Wagtails. Continuing towards Marske and after only 450 yards (405 m) park on the left in a wide gateway and walk along the bridleway which passes through good open deciduous woodland by the river. Return over the bridge to the main road which continues to the towns of Reeth or Leyburn.

Calendar
Spring and summer (April to August): Common Sandpiper, Turtle Dove, Common Cuckoo, Common Swift, Sand Martin, Barn Swallow, House Martin, Common Redstart, Lesser Whitethroat, Common Whitethroat, Garden Warbler, Blackcap, Wood Warbler, Chiffchaff, Willow Warbler, Spotted Flycatcher, Pied Flycatcher.

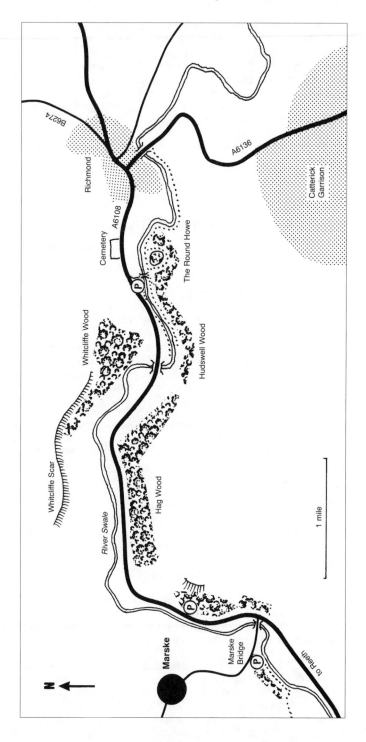

All year: Goosander, Eurasian Sparrowhawk, Common Kestrel, Stock Dove, Wood Pigeon, Collared Dove, Tawny Owl, Common Kingfisher, Green Woodpecker, Great Spotted Woodpecker, Lesser Spotted Woodpecker, Grey Wagtail, Pied Wagtail, Dipper, Wren, Hedge Accentor, Robin, Blackbird, Song Thrush, Mistle Thrush, Goldcrest, Long-tailed Tit, Marsh Tit, Coal Tit, Blue Tit, Great Tit, European Nuthatch, Eurasian Treecreeper, Eurasian Jay, Magpie, Eurasian Jackdaw, Rook, Carrion Crow, Chaffinch, Greenfinch, Goldfinch, Common Redpoll, Bullfinch, Yellowhammer.

Winter (October to March): Fieldfare, Redwing, Brambling, Siskin.

41 THORNTON STEWARD RESERVOIR

**OS Landranger Map 99
Northallerton and Ripon**

Habitat and Species

This small barren reservoir is worth a short visit if in the area. Lying 4 miles (6.4 km) to the east of Leyburn, it can be included with a visit to the nearby Hudswell Woods and Bolton-on-Swale Lake (see sites 40 and 42). The grassy banks are bare and open with little cover and there is virtually no emergent vegetation. It is used for boating and angling and much disturbed in consequence. Visits during the spring and autumn migration seasons, however, will produce several interesting birds. Waders move through in small numbers and include most of the common passage species. Some waterfowl are evident at this time as well as migrant passerines including hirundines, wagtails, pipits and Northern Wheatears. During the winter months Great Cormorants are sometimes present as well as occasional Whooper Swans, Greylag and Canada Geese and several species of ducks.

Access

Leave Masham on the A6108 Leyburn road passing Jervaulx Abbey on the right before entering the village of East Witton after 7 miles (11.2 km). Shortly after leaving East Witton, the road crosses a bridge at the Cover-bridge Inn, immediately after which, take the first right signed 'Spennithorne 1¾'. Pass over a narrow humpbacked bridge and turn right immediately, signed 'Thornton Steward 2½'. Follow the narrow winding road for 1.5 miles (2.4 km) and fork right to Thornton Steward. Pass the village and almost immediately turn left to reach the reservoir car park after about 0.5 miles (0.8 km). Cross over a stile in the corner of the parking area and watch the water and the surrounding banks from the track.

Calendar

Winter (October to March): Little and Great Crested Grebes, Great Cormorant, Grey Heron, Whooper Swan, Greylag Goose, Canada Goose, Eurasian Wigeon, Common Teal, Mallard, Common Pochard, Tufted Duck, Common Goldeneye, Moorhen, Common Coot, Northern Lapwing, gulls, Sky Lark, Pied Wagtail, finches, winter thrushes.

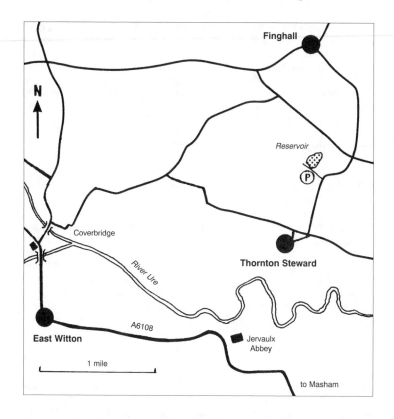

Spring and autumn passage (late March to early June and late August to October): Oystercatcher, waders (including most of the common passage species in small numbers), terns (occasional on easterly winds during April and May), Sand Martin, Barn Swallow, House Martin, Meadow Pipit, Yellow Wagtail, Northern Wheatear.

42 BOLTON-ON-SWALE LAKE, SCORTON TIP AND GREAT LANGTON

OS Landranger Map 93 Middlesbrough and Darlington

Habitat and Species

Bolton-on-Swale Lake is an extensive area of restored gravel workings administered by the Yorkshire Wildlife Trust. The large sheet of open water is surrounded by grassy banks on the east side and by a large open grass field on the west, favoured by Eurasian Wigeons during the winter months. Islands at the northern end afford shelter for waterfowl, and the short grassland at the southern end is frequented by breeding Northern Lapwings and Oystercatchers as well as by large flocks of Eurasian Wigeons and Eurasian Curlews during the winter months. An assembly of Greylag Geese is resident with numbers rising sharply during the winter and attracting small numbers of other species of geese. Diving ducks are numerous including good numbers of Common Pochards, Tufted Ducks and Common Goldeneyes; Ring-necked Duck has occurred. Small herds of Tundra and Whooper Swans may drop in during the winter months.

During the period of spring passage, Common, Arctic and Black Terns regularly occur on easterly winds and the short turf is favoured by migrant pipits, wagtails and Northern Wheatears during this time. Migrant waders occur around the margins in both spring and autumn. Up to 50 Great Cormorants winter here and large numbers of gulls roost on the water, often including those that have spent the day at nearby Scorton rubbish tip. This tip is about 1 mile (1.6 km) from the lake and attracts large numbers of gulls during the winter months including an occasional Iceland or Glaucous Gull. The tip area has also had Franklin's Gull, the *kumlieni* race of Iceland Gull and several Yellow-legged Gulls in recent years.

The Bolton-on-Swale flock of Greylag Geese usually feeds by day around the nearby village of Great Langton where a pool also holds a small regular wintering flock of Tundra and Whooper Swans. During the spring, gatherings of Grey Herons can be seen standing in the fields beyond the pool.

Timing

The best time to visit Bolton-on-Swale Lake is during April and May, July to September and through the winter months, although the summer can be good for breeding waterfowl and the lacustrine passerines. Migrant waders and passerines are evident during the spring and again during the autumn. Waterfowl and some waders occur in good numbers during the winter. The track runs along the eastern side of the lake and the lighting can be difficult for viewing in the winter when the sun is low in the sky. Winter is the best time to visit the nearby Great Langton area when the wild swans are present. The public amenity tip is worth a visit during the late summer as gulls assemble by then and an occasional Yellow-legged Gull is sometimes present at this time. The other gulls are in evidence at any time from July through to April.

Access

Travelling north on the A1 motorway, turn left for Catterick and Richmond, 6 miles (9.6 km) north of Leeming Bar. Proceed through the village of Catterick and pass the racecourse on the left just before a bridge over the River Swale. Continue over the bridge for 0.5 miles (0.8 km) and turn right opposite a garage showroom onto the B6271 road signed 'Scorton; Northallerton; Teeside'. After 1.25 miles (2 km) a line of poplar trees on the right, just after a working gravel pit, identifies the entrance which has a small wooden finger sign engraved 'Coast to Coast'. Drive along the unmade track to reach the water on the right after 0.5 miles (0.8 km). View from the track and do not trespass to the water's edge. The track eventually returns to the B6271 after a further 0.5 miles (0.8 km).

Approaching from the north on the A1 motorway, bear left 3 miles (4.8 km) south of Scotch Corner onto the A6136 Catterick road and pass the

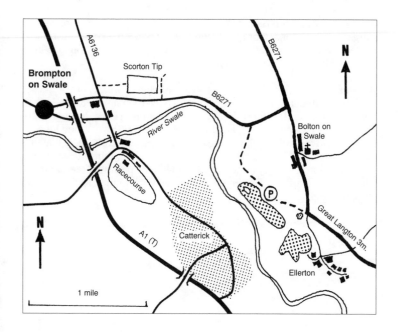

Tudor Hotel on the left, shortly after which is the B6271 just after 'Catterick Caravans'.

To reach the tip, signed 'Catterick Bridge Waste Disposal Site', turn into a wide tarmac entrance immediately opposite 'Catterick Caravans' and drive the short distance to the gate. Ask for permission to enter on foot and view the tipping area for gulls although the adjacent grass field on the right between the main road and the tip gate, which is subject to flash flooding during periods of heavy rain and also in the winter, is often better for watching the gulls bathing and loafing.

Great Langton is reached by continuing from Bolton-on-Swale Lake along the B6271 towards Northallerton. After 3 miles (4.8 km), just before entering the village of Great Langton, turn right for Kirkby Fleetham and immediately cross the River Swale on a narrow metal bridge. Continue for about 0.25 miles (0.4 km) and then park carefully on the roadside, to view the pool and surrounding fields on the right.

Calendar

This includes all three sites.

Spring and summer (April to August): Common Shelduck, Northern Shoveler, Ruddy Duck, Oystercatcher, Great Ringed Plover, Little Ringed Plover, Common Sandpiper, Turtle Dove, Common Cuckoo, Common Swift, Sand Martin, Barn Swallow, House Martin, Sedge Warbler, Willow Warbler.

Winter (October to March): Great Cormorant, Grey Heron, Tundra and Whooper Swans, Eurasian Wigeon, Gadwall, Common Teal, Northern Pintail, Common Pochard, Common Goldeneye, occasional Merlin, European Golden Plover, Common Snipe, Eurasian Curlew, Common Gull, Herring Gull, Great Black-backed Gull, Fieldfare, Redwing, Brambling, Common Redpoll.

Spring and autumn passage (April to early June and July to September): Garganey, occasional Hobby, waders, Lesser Black-backed Gull, Yellow-legged Gull (July/August), terns, Meadow Pipit, Yellow Wagtail, Pied Wagtail, Northern Wheatear, warblers.

All year: Little Grebe, Great Crested Grebe, Mute Swan, Greylag Goose, Mallard, Tufted Duck, Eurasian Sparrowhawk, Common Kestrel, Red-legged Partridge, Grey Partridge, Moorhen, Common Coot, Northern Lapwing, Common Redshank, Black-headed Gull, Stock Dove, Wood Pigeon, Collared Dove, Little Owl, Common Kingfisher, Sky Lark, Pied Wagtail, Blackbird, Mistle Thrush, Blue Tit, Great Tit, Magpie, Eurasian Jackdaw, Rook, Carrion Crow, Common Starling, House Sparrow, Tree Sparrow, Chaffinch, Greenfinch, Goldfinch, Linnet, Yellowhammer, Reed Bunting, Corn Bunting.

THE SETTLE AREA
AND UPPER WHARFEDALE

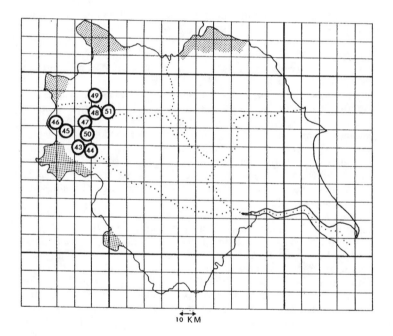

10 KM

43 RIBBLE VALLEY FLOODS

Habitat

This area of low-lying land alongside the River Ribble, just 3 miles (4.8 km) south of Settle, is subject to flooding at any time of the year after heavy rains and particularly during the winter after periods of thawing. It comprises rough grazing and meadowland dissected by dykes and dry-stone walls, with a few hawthorn hedges and scattered willows and alders. It is an important flyway for birds crossing the Pennines on migration from either the east or west.

Species

The number of birds at this site depends mainly on the presence or absence of floodwater and also disturbance from shooters or fishermen along the riverbanks. Several species of waterfowl and waders breed in the damp meadows and also along the river. These include Mute Swan, Common Shelduck, Mallard, Goosander, Oystercatcher, Northern Lapwing, Common Snipe, Eurasian Curlew, Common Redshank and Common Sandpiper, in addition to Moorhens and Common Coots. Small numbers of Canada Geese are often present. Eurasian Sparrowhawk and Common Kestrel are resident species in the area. During periods of spring and autumn migration, especially if these coincide with cool, damp weather, many Common Swifts, Sand Martins, Barn Swallows and House Martins feed low over the wet meadows. Meadow Pipits, Yellow Wagtails and Pied Wagtails pass through on migration and some stay to breed. Sand Martins, Sedge Warblers, Magpies, Eurasian Jackdaws, Rooks, Carrion Crows, Greenfinches, Goldfinches, Linnets and Reed Buntings also nest in the area.

Many waders frequent the wet meadows whilst on migration at both seasons and 30 different species have been recorded here. Waterfowl pass through also, and include a few Northern Pintails, Northern Shovelers and Common Teals. Grey Herons are usually present, mainly during the autumn, at which time an occasional Merlin, Peregrine Falcon, Short-eared Owl or Common Kingfisher is likely to be seen. The winter months are good, especially if there is adequate floodwater which may attract Little Grebe, Great Cormorant, Whooper Swan, Pink-footed Goose, Canada Goose, Eurasian Wigeon, Common Teal, Tufted Duck, Common Goldeneye and Goosander as well as some birds of prey including Hen Harrier and Peregrine Falcon. Water Rail may occur and Jack Snipe is usually present. An occasional Water Pipit is recorded in most winters at which season Dippers can be seen along the beck. Several unusual species have occurred on the floods over the years including Black-throated Diver, Slavonian Grebe, White-fronted Goose, Green-winged Teal, Garganey, Greater Scaup, Smew, Osprey, Common Quail and Spotted Crake.

Timing

The success of a visit to this site depends to some extent on the state of the floodwater. This is usually good during the period March to May which is perhaps the best time to visit, particularly during March and early April if snow on the surrounding hills has held back migrant waders and some passerines from continuing their journey to the high breeding grounds. At such times large concentrations of waterfowl, up to 100 Oystercatchers, 4,000 Northern Lapwings, 500 European Golden Plovers and 1,000 Eurasian Curlews have been recorded. Many Meadow Pipits also assemble at such times. During exceptionally dry winters, there may be no standing water along the valley.

Access

Leave Settle on the A65 Skipton road and after 4 miles (6.4 km) enter the village of Long Preston. Turn right here onto the B6478 Slaidburn road and come to Cow Bridge after about 1 mile (1.6 km). Just before reaching the bridge, there is limited parking on the roadside at the junction with Flat Lane. Walk over the bridge and take a footpath to the right through a gate between the River Ribble and a dyke. Continue to where Wigglesworth Beck enters the river and bear left alongside the beck to the rear of Wigglesworth Hall, passing Rookery Wood, before crossing over the beck. The path now turns north and climbs uphill passing over two stiles to join a rough track. View the floods from an elevated position near a wall-stile. Return via the same route. The track is usually wet and muddy so wellingtons or strong boots are recommended. A telescope is essential for viewing the flooded areas on both sides of the River Ribble. Do not walk along the riverside on the floodbanks as this is private land and disturbs the birds in any case. Total distance of the walk from the bridge to the viewpoint and back is 3.5 miles (5.6 km).

Calendar

Summer (April to August): Includes several resident species which may also occur in winter and on passage in both spring and autumn. Mute Swan, Common Shelduck, Mallard, Goosander, Eurasian Sparrowhawk, Common Kestrel, Grey Partridge, Moorhen, Common Coot, Oystercatcher, Northern Lapwing, Common Snipe, Eurasian Curlew, Common Redshank, Common Sandpiper, Common Swift, Sky Lark, Sand Martin, Barn Swallow, House Martin, Meadow Pipit, Yellow Wagtail, Grey Wagtail, Pied Wagtail, Dipper, Sedge Warbler, Greenfinch, Goldfinch, Linnet, Reed Bunting.

Spring and autumn passage (March to May and August to October): Common Teal, Northern Pintail, Northern Shoveler, Great Ringed Plover, European Golden Plover, Common Greenshank, Dunlin, Ruff, Whimbrel, gulls, Short-eared Owl, Whinchat, Northern Wheatear.

Winter (October to March): Little Grebe, Great Cormorant, Grey Heron, Whooper Swan, Canada Goose, Pink-footed Goose, Eurasian Wigeon, Common Teal, Tufted Duck, Common Goldeneye, Goosander, Hen Harrier, Peregrine Falcon, Water Rail, Northern Lapwing, Jack Snipe, Common Redshank, Green Sandpiper, Little Owl, Short-eared Owl, Common Kingfisher, Water Pipit, Dipper, Fieldfare, Redwing, Magpie, Eurasian Jackdaw, Rook, Carrion Crow, Siskin, Common Redpoll.

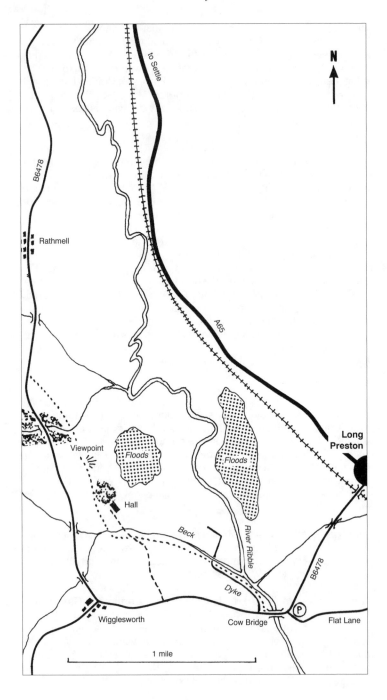

Habitat

This area of open floodwater is set in grazing land adjacent to the A65 Skipton to Settle road. There is little emergent vegetation save for small areas of *Juncus* rush, and the birds are easy to see in consequence. The water level varies according to the rainfall but rarely dries out completely. The Flash is strategically placed for migrants, being situated along the flyway through the Aire Gap and thus attracting birds as they pass across the country in either direction.

Species

Although mainly a site for passage migrants, a few species breed around the edges and in the adjacent fields. An occasional pair of Great Ringed Plovers stays to nest and Little Grebe, Mallard, Northern Shoveler, Moorhen, Common Coot, Oystercatcher, Northern Lapwing, Common Snipe, Eurasian Curlew, Common Redshank, Sky Lark, Meadow Pipit, Yellow Wagtail and Pied Wagtail all breed annually with varying success.

During the spring and autumn migration periods, from late March to early June and from July to September, several waders occur and apart from the commoner species, some less usual ones in recent years have been Grey Plover, Red Knot, Sanderling, Little Stint, Bar-tailed and Black-tailed Godwits, Spotted Redshank and Turnstone. Several species of waterfowl pass through at both seasons with Common Shelduck, Eurasian Wigeon, Gadwall, Northern Pintail, an occasional Garganey, Northern Shoveler and Tufted Duck occurring in small numbers each year. Several of these species are present during the winter months in addition to an occasional Tundra Swan, a few Whooper Swans, Common Pochard and Common Goldeneye. Rarer ones have included White-fronted Goose, Ring-necked Duck and Greater Scaup. Common and Black Terns sometimes pass through on easterly winds in May and both Mediterranean and Little Gulls have occurred. The edges of the flash attract many migrant pipits and wagtails during April and May and hirundines feed over the water whilst on migration.

Timing

This interesting area of shallow water is certainly worth a visit, particularly during the spring and early summer for the largest number of species. The autumn and winter periods can also be good but the birds are often disturbed by wildfowlers.

Access

The Flash lies between the villages of Hellifield and Long Preston on the A65 Skipton to Settle road, some 9 miles (14.4 km) west of Skipton and 5 miles (8 km) southeast of Settle. Approaching from Skipton, pass through the village of Hellifield, and after a loop layby on the left, look for a line of large sycamore trees which straddle the road after 100 yards (90 m). Park on the right in a small layby underneath the trees and view from here. A telescope is essential. Alternatively one can park in another small layby on the left about another 100 yards (90 m) further along the road, and walk back to view the Flash. The road is extremely busy with

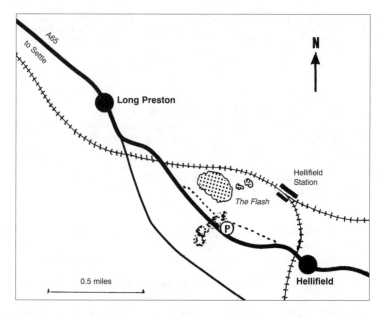

fast-moving traffic and one should take care when parking and walking
along the verges. A public footpath runs across the fields from Hellifield
towards Long Preston passing between the main road and the Flash. This
path runs beneath the line of trees referred to above, about 50 yards
(45 m) from the road and is identified by a stile in the stone wall. It is
possible to watch from here without disturbing the birds. Do not proceed
to the water's edge.

Calendar

All year: Grey Heron, Mute Swan, Canada Goose, Mallard, Eurasian Spar-
rowhawk, Common Kestrel, Northern Lapwing, Common Redshank,
Black-headed Gull, Little Owl, Eurasian Jackdaw, Magpie, Rook, Carrion
Crow, Common Starling.

Summer (April to August – breeding): Little Grebe, Common Shelduck,
Northern Shoveler, Moorhen, Common Coot, Oystercatcher, Great
Ringed Plover (occasional), Eurasian Curlew, Common Snipe, Sky Lark,
Meadow Pipit, Yellow Wagtail, Pied Wagtail.

Spring and autumn passage (March to early June and July to September):
Garganey (occasional), Dunlin, Ruff, Whimbrel, Common Greenshank,
Wood Sandpiper, Common Sandpiper, any of the other regular passage
waders are a possibility, Common Gull, Lesser Black-backed Gull, Common Swift, Sand Martin, Barn Swallow, House Martin, Northern Wheatear.

Winter (October to March): Tundra Swan (occasional), Whooper Swan,
Eurasian Wigeon, Common Teal, Northern Pintail, Common Pochard,
Tufted Duck, Common Goldeneye, Merlin, Jack Snipe, Green Sandpiper,
Common Gull, Herring Gull, Great Black-backed Gull, Fieldfare, Red-
wing, Twite (occasional).

45 CLAPHAM WOODS AND THWAITE SCAR

OS Landranger Map 98
Wensleydale

Habitat

Clapham Woods are part of an old estate and are set in a narrow valley running north from the picturesque village of that name, through which runs the Clapham Beck. The woods include several exotic plants including rhododendrons which were introduced by the botanist Reginald Farrer during the early 1900s and also an artificial lake.

The wooded valley is bordered on both sides by open sheep pasture with dry-stone walls and limestone scree and outcrops, and is dominated on the eastern side by the impressive limestone ridge of Thwaite Scar. Permissive footpaths run along both sides of the valley and continue beyond the woodland to Trow Gill, 2 miles (3.2 km) beyond which lies the lofty Ingleborough, standing at a height of 2,373 feet (723 m) above sea level.

Species

Clapham, with its beck running through the middle of the village and an abundance of old timber and bushes along its course and amongst the buildings, is host to several breeding species of birds during the summer months. Wood Pigeons, Collared Doves, Chaffinches, Greenfinches and Goldfinches nest in the trees around the village, Common Swifts, Barn Swallows and House Martins breed in or on the stone buildings, and Dippers, Grey Wagtails and Pied Wagtails can be seen along the beck and waterfall near the church. The lake is not very suitable for waterfowl but a few pairs of Mallards, Moorhens and Common Coots breed there and Common Sandpipers are usually in evidence during the summer. Most of the common passerines nest in and around the village as well as in the woods along the valley, where, in addition, are Eurasian Sparrowhawk, Common Pheasant, Woodcock, Tawny Owl, Common Cuckoo, Great Spotted Woodpecker, Garden Warbler, Blackcap, Wood Warbler, Chiffchaff, Willow Warbler, Goldcrest, Long-tailed Tit, Marsh Tit, Coal Tit, European Nuthatch, Eurasian Treecreeper, Eurasian Jay, Common Redpoll and Bullfinch.

As the woodland gives way to the more open and barren rocky gully with scattered trees towards Ingleborough Cave and Trow Gill, Common Kestrel, Little Owl, Stock Dove, Green Woodpecker, Sky Lark, Common Redstart, Yellow Wagtail and Tree Pipit can be seen. The scree slopes, dry-stone walls, limestone outcrops and the sheep pasture along the eastern side of the valley below Thwaite Scar are good for Eurasian Curlews, Northern Lapwings, Common Redshanks, Grey Partridges, Pied Wagtails, Northern Wheatears and Ring Ouzels. During the spring and through to the autumn, Black-headed and Lesser Black-backed Gulls are usually around the area from their breeding colonies on the nearby Bowland moors and Common Gulls are numerous in winter. A solitary Grey Heron may be seen passing overhead at any time of year and Carrion Crows are common in the upland sheep pasture where an occasional Common Raven is seen during the winter months.

Timing

During the summer months and on fine days in the spring and autumn, the village of Clapham can be exceptionally crowded with tourists when the otherwise tranquil character of the area is somewhat changed. The path along the valley is popular with hikers on their way to the slopes of Ingleborough. If staying in the area, one should try to arrive early and walk through the woods and the gully before the tourists arrive in force. Parking may be difficult later in the day. The woods are very rich in song birds and the period from mid-May to early June is the best time to visit. It is worth arriving early for the dawn chorus.

Access

Clapham lies 6 miles (9.6 km) northwest of Settle and is bypassed by the A65 road to Kendal. Approaching from Settle, turn right into the village and proceed to the official National Park car park on the right off the main street (pay machines). From here, walk right to the church from where footpaths lead through the woods and eventually onto the higher ground. Paths lead along both sides of the valley and one can undertake the whole or part of the circular route depending on the time available and the preference for woodland birds or the upland specialities.

For an early morning visit, it is perhaps better to start by taking the route along the eastern side as the light is better for viewing the hillsides and the wooded valley. This eastern path, signed 'Austick', leads from the right of the church and passes through two tunnels before coming to a junction where one should keep left onto Long Lane, signed Selside. From here, the track climbs a steep incline and passes alongside open sheep pasture with dry-stone walls, limestone scree and outcrops which is a very good area for the upland birds. After about 1.5 miles (2.4 km) from the start, a wooden stile over the stone wall on the left marks the northern end of the circular route. Cross over the stile and walk down a steep stony field to cross another stile (visible from the top track) and join the western path just south of the narrow rocky gorge of Trow Gill, back to the village. The path now proceeds south through a wide rocky gully, passing the entrance to Ingleborough Cave on the right, and comes to the start of the woodland after about 0.75 miles (1.2 km). Proceed through a gate, from where the path leads through good deciduous woodland all the way back to the village, passing the artificial lake towards the lower end. Total distance from the church to Trow Gill and back is about 3 miles (4.8 km).

A shorter route of about 1.5 miles (2.4 km) is recommended for those with limited time. Start by taking the western woodland path and on coming to a gate at the far end of the woods, turn right and drop down to the beck where the path crosses over a narrow wooden bridge and cuts uphill across sheep pasture to join the eastern track back to the village. If undertaking this shorter route along the eastern side, look for the cross track on the left, through a gate in the stone wall, a little way beyond the top of the steep rise after the Selside junction. The path across the field is not obvious but runs alongside a stone wall bordering woodland.

The walk along the valley is on permissive footpaths and a charge of 20 pence per person is made to enter the woodland section, payable in the village at the start of the western footpath.

Calendar

This includes the wooded valley and the open higher ground.

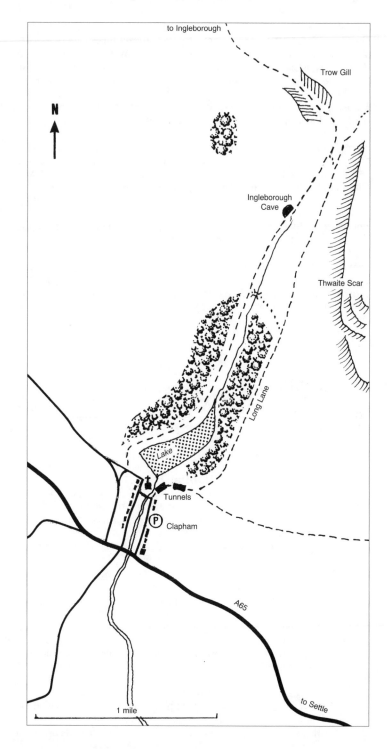

All year: Grey Heron, Mallard, Eurasian Sparrowhawk, Common Kestrel, Grey Partridge, Common Pheasant, Moorhen, Common Coot, Stock Dove, Wood Pigeon, Collared Dove, Little Owl, Tawny Owl, Great Spotted Woodpecker, Green Woodpecker, Dipper, Wren, Hedge Accentor, Robin, Blackbird, Song Thrush, Mistle Thrush, Goldcrest, Long-tailed Tit, Marsh Tit, Coal Tit, Blue Tit, Great Tit, European Nuthatch, Eurasian Treecreeper, Eurasian Jay, Magpie, Eurasian Jackdaw, Rook, Carrion Crow, Common Starling, House Sparrow, Chaffinch, Greenfinch, Bullfinch.

Spring and summer (April to early August): Northern Lapwing, Common Snipe, Woodcock, Eurasian Curlew, Common Redshank, Common Sandpiper, Black-headed Gull, Lesser Black-backed Gull, Common Cuckoo, Common Swift, Sky Lark, Barn Swallow, House Martin, Tree Pipit, Grey Wagtail, Pied Wagtail, Meadow Pipit (also many on passage in spring), Yellow Wagtail, Common Redstart, Northern Wheatear, Ring Ouzel, Garden Warbler, Blackcap, Wood Warbler, Chiffchaff, Willow Warbler, Spotted Flycatcher, Goldfinch, Common Redpoll.

Winter (October to March): Common Buzzard (occasional), Peregrine Falcon (occasional), Common Gull (also on passage in the spring), Common Kingfisher (scarce), Fieldfare, Redwing, Common Raven (occasional on the high ground), Brambling, Siskin.

46 INGLETON WATERFALLS WALK

OS Landranger Map 98
Wensleydale

Habitat

This site is described as 'The finest waterfall walk in England' and comprises 4.5 miles (7.2 km) of very well maintained paths alongside the rivers Twiss and Doe above the village of Ingleton. It is administered by The Ingleton Scenery Company and has been enjoyed by the public since 1885. The ghyll, through which runs the River Twiss, is thickly wooded with deciduous trees and continues for 1.5 miles (2.4 km) before reaching high ground, where it gives way to open sheep pasture with drystone walls where the path turns eastwards for 1 mile (1.6 km) before joining the valley of the River Doe. This ghyll is quite different from that of the River Twiss, having deep gorges and areas of more open oak woodland, eventually opening onto sheep pasture with large crags of limestone, part of a former quarry, before returning to the village of Ingleton. The several waterfalls along the route are most spectacular during the winter months or after heavy rain in the surrounding hill country.

Species

Most of the small birds associated with deciduous woodland can be found at this site during the spring and early summer but it is particularly good for the woodland specialities including Common Redstart, Pied

Flycatcher, Wood Warbler and European Nuthatch. Common birds along the whole route include Wood Pigeon, Blackbird, Song Thrush, Robin, Wren and Chaffinch with Willow Warbler, Chiffchaff, Blackcap, Garden Warbler, Great and Blue Tits being well represented. The rivers are host to several pairs of Grey Wagtails with fewer pairs of Pied Wagtails in the more open areas. Dippers are easily seen, particularly in the vicinity of the waterfalls. European Nuthatches are fairly common and Eurasian Treecreepers should be looked for along the River Twiss section. Both Green and Great Spotted Woodpeckers occur, the Green usually in the higher, more open woodland. Beyond the first stretch of woodland, where the route passes through an open valley of sheep pasture, Mistle Thrush can be found along with Common Kestrel, Stock Dove, Common Cuckoo, Eurasian Jackdaw, a few Carrion Crows and, with luck, Common Buzzard, Peregrine Falcon and Common Raven, all of which breed in the vicinity. Northern Lapwings and Eurasian Curlews nest here and can be seen in the pastureland where Sky Larks, Northern Wheatears and Meadow Pipits also occur. During the summer, Sand Martins are usually flying around the area of Thornton Force, a large waterfall at the head of Twiss Ghyll, and Common Swifts and Barn Swallows are regularly overhead at this time. Look out for Goosanders along this part of the river.

The oak woodland along the River Doe is good for Pied and Spotted Flycatchers, Common Redstarts and Great Spotted Woodpeckers and the first waterfall to the left as one enters the Doe Ghyll is very good for Dippers and Grey Wagtails. The large limestone crags on the right as one nears the village of Ingleton are home to many Eurasian Jackdaws.

This walk is thoroughly recommended, being very rich in birdlife, scenically impressive and botanically interesting.

Timing

The most productive time to visit is during late April, May and early June when all the resident species and summer visitors are in song and much in evidence. Try to be there as early as possible in the morning when the song is at its best. Although recommended primarily as a spring site, a visit during the autumn and winter months, if the weather is fine, can be very rewarding, not least for the more spectacular condition of the waterfalls. Birds will certainly be less in evidence at this time but the resident species including woodpeckers, wrens, titmice, thrushes, wagtails, finches, European Nuthatches, Eurasian Treecreepers and Dippers will be seen in addition to the winter visitors such as Redwings and Fieldfares. There is perhaps more chance of seeing Common Buzzard, Common Raven and Peregrine Falcon at this time.

Access

This site lies some 25 miles (40 km) northwest of the town of Skipton on the A65. The Waterfalls Walk is well signed on reaching Ingleton and there are several signs within the village directing one to the car parking area which has toilets and several picnic tables. Admission is £4 per car with up to four occupants, £1.50 for pedestrian adults and 50 pence for children (at the time of writing). There is a cafe adjacent to the car park and a snack cabin at the head of Twiss Ghyll after 1.5 miles (2.4 km) which is open daily from Easter to late September and at the weekends during the winter months, except during extremely inclement weather. Hardcore and concrete paths with concrete steps, often steep, run along both wooded ghylls. The walk is strenuous and takes about three hours to complete at a leisurely pace.

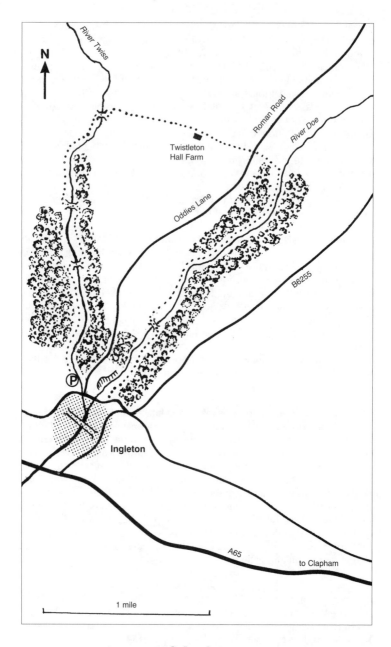

Calendar

All year: Eurasian Sparrowhawk, Common Buzzard, Peregrine Falcon, Common Kestrel, Common Pheasant, Stock Dove, Wood Pigeon, Collared Dove (in the village), Tawny Owl, Great Spotted Woodpecker, Green Woodpecker, Dipper, Wren, Hedge Accentor, Robin, Blackbird, Song Thrush, Mistle Thrush, Goldcrest, Long-tailed Tit, Blue Tit, Great Tit, European Nuthatch, Eurasian Treecreeper, Eurasian Jay, Magpie,

Eurasian Jackdaw, Rook, Carrion Crow, Common Raven (high ground – scarce), Common Starling, House Sparrow (in the village), Chaffinch, Greenfinch, Goldfinch.

Spring and summer (April to early August): Goosander (occasional), Northern Lapwing (high ground), Eurasian Curlew (high ground), Black-headed Gull (overhead), Common Cuckoo, Common Swift (overhead), Sky Lark (high ground), Barn Swallow, House Martin (in the village), Sand Martin, Meadow Pipit, Common Redstart, Northern Wheatear, Garden Warbler, Blackcap, Wood Warbler, Chiffchaff, Willow Warbler, Spotted Flycatcher, Pied Flycatcher, Goldfinch, Common Redpoll.

Winter (October to March): Fieldfare, Redwing, Siskin.

47 LITTONDALE, SILVERDALE AND PEN-Y-GHENT

OS Landranger Map 98
Wensleydale

Habitat

Littondale is the valley of the River Skirfare, a tributary of the River Wharfe, which runs in a southeasterly direction to join the Wharfe 2 miles (3.2 km) south of the village of Kettlewell.

The valley floor is sheep-grazing land with dry-stone walls and some small stands of deciduous timber. The hillside to the north of the road is an impressive high and barren scree slope with a long limestone crag running for most of its length near the summit. At the top of the dale is the small village of Halton Gill where the road turns south westwards to join the B6469 road at Stainforth, 3 miles (4.8 km) north of Settle. The 8-mile (12.8-km) stretch of upland road from Halton Gill passes through sheep pasture with exposed limestone pavements and outcrops and is laced with dry-stone walls. The peaks of Fountains Fell on the left and Pen-y-Ghent on the right dominate this final section before the road drops down through Silverdale into the Ribble Valley.

Species

Typical breeding birds of the riverside meadows along the valley bottom are Oystercatchers, Northern Lapwings and Common Redshanks with Common Sandpipers, Sand Martins, Grey Wagtails and Dippers along the shallow, stony river. Pied Wagtails and Northern Wheatears are common along the roadside dry-stone walls and a few pairs of Yellow Wagtails breed in the meadows. The open sheep pasture on the high ground is favoured by feeding Eurasian Jackdaws and Rooks. Common Raven is always a possibility, usually flying over, to and from the heights of Fountains Fell and Pen-y-Ghent. Eurasian Curlews, Northern Lapwings, Common Snipe, Sky Larks and Meadow Pipits are regular breeding birds on the high ground. Northern Wheatears and Ring Ouzels can also be found around the rocky outcrops and limestone pavement areas.

The deciduous trees along the river and around the farms are host to Wrens, Hedge Accentors, Robins, Common Redstarts, Willow Warblers, Spotted Flycatchers, Chaffinches, Greenfinches and Goldfinches. Barn Swallows, House Martins and Common Starlings breed around the farm buildings. Small parties of Twites can often be seen along the road from the second cattle grid during the spring and summer.

Timing

The best time to undertake this drive is during March, April and May, or during the autumn from August to October. Birds can be sparse on the high ground during the summer months with a limited number of species in evidence. Northern Wheatears and Ring Ouzels are best seen during the period of their first arrival in late March and April before settling in to nest, after which they become very elusive. Most of the other species are also more conspicuous at this time when displaying. Visits during the autumn can produce occasional birds of prey, including Hen Harrier, Common Buzzard, Peregrine Falcon and Merlin.

Access

To reach Littondale, drive north from Grassington, passing the spectac-ular Kilnsey Crag on the left after 3 miles (4.8 km). It is worth a stop here to look for migrant Northern Wheatears, Meadow Pipits and Yellow Wag-tails along the stream during the late spring. The crag usually has a breed-ing pair of Common Kestrels, a few Stock Doves, Eurasian Jackdaws and some pairs of Common Swifts and House Martins. One mile (1.6 km) beyond the crag, bear left for Arncliffe (signed 3 miles). Take a right-hand bend in Arncliffe village and follow signs for Halton Gill (signed '4½ miles'). The road turns sharp left at Halton Gill and crosses a bridge over the river. Stop here to look for Grey Wagtails and Dippers. Continue up a steep incline, passing areas of good limestone pavement amongst the sheep pasture, and stop at the second cattle grid. This is a good place to see, or initially hear, Common Ravens which frequent the area. The road drops steadily down from here, passing Pen-y-Ghent, an obvious hill on the right which stands at 2,273 feet (692 m) above sea level. A foot-path leads from the main road to the summit of Pen-y-Ghent where the more energetic birdwatcher has the chance to see small trips of Dotterels in the spring. Some pairs of European Golden Plovers, Dunlins and Red Grouse nest on this high ground and also on Plover Hill to the north. Dis-tance from the road to the summit of Pen-y-Ghent is approximately 1 mile (1.6 km). The road finally drops down through Silverdale into the village of Stainforth before joining the main B6469 road for Settle. Total distance from Skirfare Bridge to Stainforth is 17 miles (27.2 km).

Calendar

Spring and early summer (April to early June): Includes several resident species which are present throughout the year. Common Kestrel, Com-mon Pheasant, Oystercatcher, Northern Lapwing, Common Snipe, Eurasian Curlew, Common Sandpiper, European Golden Plover, Dunlin, Black-headed Gull, Lesser Black-backed Gull (non-breeders), Stock Dove, Wood Pigeon, Common Cuckoo, Little Owl, Tawny Owl, Common Swift, Sky Lark, Sand Martin (occasional along river), Barn Swallow,

House Martin, Meadow Pipit, Yellow Wagtail (scarce), Grey Wagtail, Pied Wagtail, Wren, Hedge Accentor, Robin, Common Redstart, Northern Wheatear, Ring Ouzel, Blackbird, Song Thrush, Mistle Thrush, Willow Warbler, Spotted Flycatcher, Blue Tit, Great Tit, Magpie, Eurasian Jackdaw, Rook, Carrion Crow, Common Raven, Common Starling, House Sparrow, Chaffinch, Greenfinch, Twite.

Autumn and winter (September to March): Hen Harrier, Common Buzzard, Common Kestrel, Merlin, Peregrine Falcon, Twite (lower ground along the roadsides in September), in addition to some of the above on autumn passage.

48 LANGSTROTHDALE, UPPER WHARFEDALE

OS Landranger Map 98
Wensleydale

Habitat

Running northwestwards from the village of Buckden in Upper Wharfedale, this recommended route passes through one of the most attractive dales in the region and is part of the extensive Langstrothdale Chase. The valley is wide and composed mainly of sheep pasture with dry-stone walls, scattered deciduous trees and some stands of hanging oak woodland on the limestone scree slopes. The young River Wharfe tumbles southeastwards along a rocky watercourse and runs alongside the road for much of the way from the village of Beckermonds, the end of the recommended drive, to Buckden, thence southwards to Addingham where it turns eastwards to join the River Ouse near Cawood.

Species

The main attractions of this route are the birds associated with upland streams and rivers and this is perhaps the best place in the region to see Dippers and Grey Wagtails. A few Mallards frequent the river and it is possible to see Goosanders flying along the valley during the spring and early summer. Oystercatchers, Northern Lapwings, Eurasian Curlews, Common Redshanks and Common Sandpipers all breed in the area and can be seen along the river or in the adjacent fields. Common Snipe display over the area. Black-headed Gulls are a feature of the rivercourse and regularly attend the parked cars in search of scraps. Dippers, Grey Wagtails, Pied Wagtails and Common Sandpipers are very familiar birds of the shallow stony river and can be seen to advantage from the roadside. A few Yellow Wagtails nest in the pastures.

The larger stands of mature timber around the farmsteads have their breeding Common Redstarts and Spotted Flycatchers as well as Blue and Great Tits, Mistle Thrushes, Chaffinches and most of the other common garden birds, Eurasian Jackdaws are very common all along the valley and Rooks and Carrion Crows can always be seen.

dines

Dipper

Timing

This is primarily a spring and summer site and the best time to undertake the drive is during April, May and June. It is a very popular route for tourists, especially at weekends, and one should endeavour to avoid those times if possible. Birds can be sparse during the winter months.

Access

This recommended route follows the infant River Wharfe for 5 miles (8 km) and travels upstream from the village of Buckden to Beckermonds. Drive north from Grassington on the B6160 and come to Buckden after 9 miles (14.4 km). After passing The Buck Inn on the right, proceed for 200 yards (180 m) and take a minor road to the left at the village green signed 'Hubberholme and Hawes'. After 1 mile (1.6 km) keep left in Hubberholme and after a further 1 mile (1.6 km), cross a cattle grid at Raisgill, beyond which the river is adjacent to the road and an excellent place to see Common Sandpipers, Dippers and Grey Wagtails. There are plenty of parking places on the grassy verges. Just over 1 mile (1.6 km) beyond the cattle grid, the road crosses over a green trellis bridge at Deepdale where one should stop to view the river and the surrounding trees. The stretch of river from the bridge for the next 0.5 miles (0.8 km) or so is the best place to see Dippers. Continue for 1.25 miles (2 km) and come to a minor road on the left signed 'Greenfields: No through road for motor vehicles', beyond which the minor road through Beckermonds is gated and not recommended. This junction marks the end of the suggested drive and one can either return down the valley or continue for 7 miles (11.2 km) to Hawes in Wensleydale.

Calendar

Spring and summer (late March to August): Mallard, Goosander, Common Pheasant, Oystercatcher, Northern Lapwing, Common Snipe, Eurasian Curlew, Common Redshank, Common Sandpiper, Black-headed Gull, Lesser Black-backed Gull (passage birds), Stock Dove, Wood Pigeon, Common Cuckoo, Little Owl, Common Swift, Green Woodpecker, Great

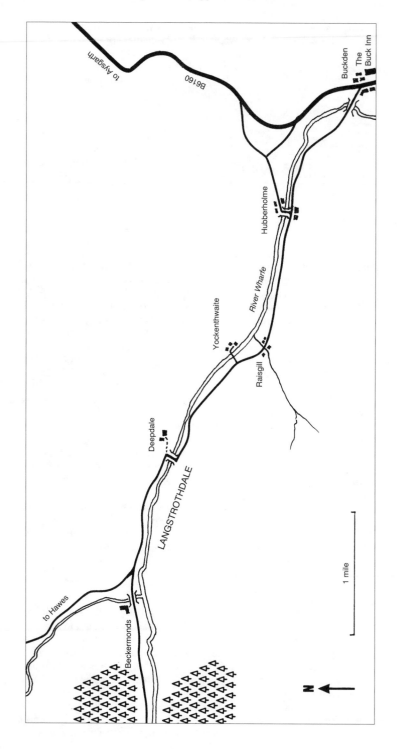

Spotted Woodpecker, Sky Lark, Barn Swallow, House Martin, Meadow Pipit, Yellow Wagtail, Grey Wagtail, Pied Wagtail, Dipper, Wren, Hedge Accentor, Robin, Common Redstart, Whinchat, Northern Wheatear, Ring Ouzel, Blackbird, Song Thrush, Mistle Thrush, Willow Warbler, Spotted Flycatcher, Blue Tit, Great Tit, Magpie, Eurasian Jackdaw, Rook, Carrion Crow, Common Starling, House Sparrow, Chaffinch, Greenfinch, Linnet.

49 SEMER WATER

OS Landranger Map 98
Wensleydale

Habitat

Semer Water is the second largest natural lake in Yorkshire (after Hornsea Mere). It is of glacial origin, the water being retained by a terminal moraine on the northeast corner lying at an altitude of 830 feet (250 m) above sea level, and reaching a maximum depth of around 33 feet (10 m). It is fed by Crooks Beck which enters at the southwestern corner. This part of the lake and some of the adjoining land, comprising 53 acres (21 ha), is owned by The Yorkshire Wildlife Trust and is an area of alluvial silt marshland and fell-side sheep pasture with limestone outcrops. The marshy area is very wet for much of the year, especially during periods of heavy rainfall and at any time during the winter months when it is often completely flooded and becomes an extension of the lake. The Reserve is botanically rich as well as being good for lacustrine birds in the summer and during both migration seasons.

Species

There is no great abundance of birds here during the breeding season but a good variety of species associated with the marshy lakeside habitat can be found. A pair or two of Great Crested Grebes and some pairs of Common Coots breed annually and there is a small flock of Canada Geese, some of which rear young. A solitary Grey Heron is often in the marsh. Mallards are common and an occasional Eurasian Wigeon sometimes lingers into the summer; the species may breed here. A few Tufted Ducks and Goosanders frequent the southwestern end of the lake where Crooks Beck enters through the marsh. Oystercatchers, Northern Lapwings, Common Snipe, Eurasian Curlews and Common Redshanks all breed in the area and an occasional Dunlin may be seen feeding around the edges during the summer. Any of the usual passage waders are a possibility during the spring and autumn migration seasons, but only in small numbers and away from the disturbed shoreline along the roadside. Black-headed Gulls are always around, their numbers increasing during late summer when juveniles from the nearby moorland colonies assemble at the lake.

During periods of easterly winds in May, especially with rain, Common, Arctic or Black Terns may drop in to feed for short periods whilst on passage. Meadow Pipits are common breeding birds and a few pairs of Yellow Wagtails can be found.

During the winter months, Whooper Swans often call in for variable lengths of time and some Common Teals, Eurasian Wigeons, Common Pochards, Tufted Ducks and Common Goldeneyes are normally present.

Timing
A visit at any time of year could prove worthwhile but May and June are perhaps the best for seeing most species. August and September will produce migrant waterfowl, waders and passerines and a winter visit should be good for waterfowl and perhaps an occasional bird of prey.

Access
Semer Water lies 12 miles (19 km) west of Leyburn off the A684 Sedbergh road. Travelling from the east, turn left signed 'Semer Water 3', just before entering the village of Bainbridge. This minor road continues for 5 miles (8 km) straight to the small village of Stalling Busk, from where a path leads past a ruined church to the Reserve. This path is steep and rocky and some may find it difficult. A second, and recommended access road, leads from the centre of Bainbridge, signed Countersett and Semer Water. Taking this second road, continue for just over 2 miles (3.2 km) to Countersett and turn left signed Stalling Busk. Proceed down a steep hill and cross a narrow bridge over the River Bain immediately after which is the lake shore on the right. Park further along the road by the lake shore and walk for about 200 yards (180 m) to where a stream passes under the road at Low Blean Farm. Look for a wooden finger sign reading 'Stalling Busk 1', at a stile over a stone wall on the right. This path crosses two grass fields before continuing along the lake shore to the YWT Reserve and eventually to Stalling Busk.

Calendar
Spring and summer (April to August): Includes several resident species which are present throughout the year. Great Crested Grebe, Grey Heron,

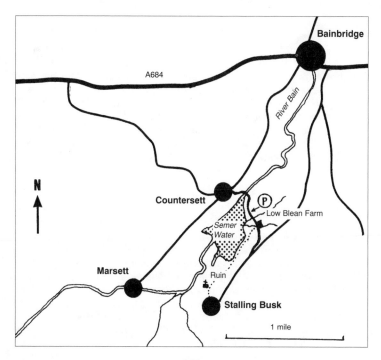

Canada Goose, Mallard, Goosander, Common Kestrel, Common Pheasant, Moorhen, Common Coot, Oystercatcher, Northern Lapwing, Dunlin, Common Snipe, Eurasian Curlew, Common Redshank, Common Sandpiper, Black-headed Gull, Stock Dove, Wood Pigeon, Common Cuckoo, Sky Lark, Sand Martin, Barn Swallow, House Martin, Meadow Pipit (also on passage), Yellow Wagtail, Pied Wagtail, Wren, Hedge Accentor, Robin, Blackbird, Mistle Thrush, Willow Warbler, Blue Tit, Great Tit, Magpie, Eurasian Jackdaw, Rook, Carrion Crow, Common Starling, House Sparrow, Chaffinch, Greenfinch, Goldfinch, Linnet.

Spring and autumn passage (April to June and July to September): Northern Shoveler, any of the usual passage waders, Common Tern, Arctic Tern, Black Tern, hirundines.

Winter (October to March): Whooper Swan, any of the grey geese in small numbers, Eurasian Wigeon (occasionally in summer also), Common Teal, Common Pochard, Common Goldeneye, Hen Harrier, Common Gull, Herring Gull, Great Black-backed Gull, Fieldfare, Redwing.

50 MALHAM TARN AND WOODS

OS Landranger Map 98
Wensleydale

Habitat

Malham Tarn and the surrounding area is a National Nature Reserve owned by the National Trust and jointly managed by them and the Field Studies Council. It comprises a large and open sheet of water between Settle and Grassington, lying at an altitude of 1200 feet (365 m) above sea level and is surrounded in the main by open sheep grazing land with a large area of mature woodland on the north side, known as Tarn Woods. Three miles to the northwest is Fountains Fell which reaches a height of 2191 feet (670 m) above sea level. The general area is almost exclusively upland pasture with many dry-stone walls and much exposed limestone.

Species

Up to eight pairs of Great Crested Grebes and an occasional pair of Little Grebes breed annually at the tarn along with Mallards, Tufted Ducks and Common Coots. A Red-necked Grebe stayed for a month during July and August 1989. Great Cormorants call in occasionally and a few Grey Herons are usually present. The Tarn attracts good numbers of waterfowl during the autumn and winter months, including occasional parties of Whooper Swans. Eurasian Wigeons are regular visitors and gatherings of up to 30 birds occur in most winters. Common Teals (up to 30) and Mallards (up to 100) are also present at this time. Flocks of Common Pochards usually number around 250 to 350 birds; an exceptional 458 were present in January 1980. Tufted Duck numbers reach up to 100 birds, and a few Common Goldeneyes (up to 15) spend the winter here.

Common Scoters may drop in from time to time, usually during the late summer or winter. Goosanders are present throughout the year with peak numbers during the early spring when around 20 birds may occur.

Occasional birds of prey hunt over the area during the winter months when a solitary Hen Harrier, Common Buzzard or Peregrine Falcon may be seen. Eurasian Sparrowhawks, Common Kestrels and a few pairs of Merlins breed locally. Moorhens are scarce and only one or two pairs are resident at the Tarn. Flocks of Common Coots regularly number between 500 and 700 birds during the autumn and winter (950 on 3rd January 1976). Oystercatchers, Common Snipe, Northern Lapwings, Common Redshanks, Eurasian Curlews and Common Sandpipers nest in the area and some passage waders are usually to be seen at the appropriate season. European Golden Plovers and Dunlins breed on the nearby Fountains Fell. A large gull roost builds up during late autumn, consisting mainly of Black-headed and Common Gulls. Lesser Black-backed Gulls pass through in good numbers in both spring and autumn with some non-breeders being present throughout the summer. A few Common and Black Terns may pass through during the spring on easterly winds.

Both Little and Tawny Owls breed in the vicinity and an occasional pair of Short-eared Owls sometimes stays to nest. Great Spotted Woodpecker is a regular visitor to Tarn Woods but does not breed. Several pairs of Pied Wagtails, Meadow Pipits and Northern Wheatears nest around the tarn and a few pairs of Common Redstarts, Garden Warblers, Blackcaps, Wood Warblers (usually at least one pair), Willow Warblers, Spotted Flycatchers, Pied Flycatchers and European Nuthatches breed in Tarn Woods. Common Raven is always a possibility, mainly during the winter months. Twites often occur in good numbers around the tarn or along the approach roads during the autumn when flocks of around 100 are often seen. Snow Buntings are seen during most winters, mainly singly, but more on occasions; separate parties of ten and 20 birds in December 1974.

Timing

A visit at any time of year can be worthwhile, but March to May and August to October are perhaps the best for numbers of species. Winter can be good for waterfowl, raptors and possible Snow Buntings. Viewing the Tarn from the south shore is always best as the light is from behind.

Access

The Tarn can be reached from Settle, or from the village of Arncliffe in Littondale. Approaching from Settle, proceed north on the B6479 for 1 mile (1.6 km) and turn right into the village of Langcliffe. Follow the road signed 'Malham 7½'. This road is steep and narrow as it climbs up onto the high ground, passing through limestone pavements and outcrops. After 3 miles (4.8 km) turn right for Malham and fork right again after 1.5 miles (2.4 km) at the junction for Arncliffe and proceed straight over the crossroads to reach the Tarn after a further 1.5 miles (2.4 km). Park on the roadside and walk the short distance to the south side of the Tarn. (Do not park off the roadside as this has caused severe erosion in the past.)

Approaching from Arncliffe, leave the village on the road signed 'Malham 9¼' and continue for 5 miles (8 km) to a gateway signed for Malham Tarn Field Centre. Park near here on the roadside and follow a bridleway to Tarn Woods and a hide overlooking the Tarn after about 0.5 miles (0.8 km). To reach the south side of the Tarn by car, continue along the road

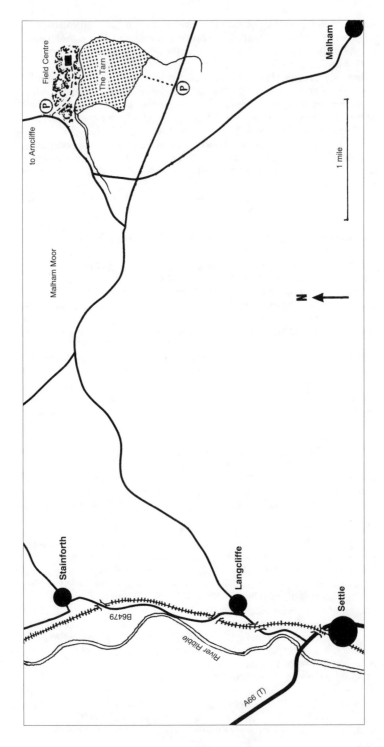

past the Field Centre sign and turn sharp left after about 1 mile (1.6 km) to reach the roadside parking area after a further 0.5 miles (0.8 km).

Calendar

Spring and Summer (April to August): Includes several resident species which are present throughout the year. Little Grebe, Great Crested Grebe, Grey Heron, Canada Goose, Common Teal, Mallard, Tufted Duck, Goosander, Eurasian Sparrowhawk, Common Kestrel, Common Pheasant, Moorhen (scarce), Common Coot, Oystercatcher, Northern Lapwing, Common Snipe, Eurasian Curlew, Common Redshank, Common Sandpiper, Black-headed Gull, Lesser Black-backed Gull, Stock Dove, Wood Pigeon, Common Cuckoo, Little Owl, Tawny Owl, Short-eared Owl (occasional), Common Swift, Great Spotted Woodpecker, Sky Lark, Sand Martin, Barn Swallow, House Martin, Meadow Pipit, Yellow Wagtail, Pied Wagtail, Wren, Hedge Accentor, Robin, Common Redstart, Northern Wheatear, Ring Ouzel (Fountains Fell), Blackbird, Song Thrush, Mistle Thrush, Garden Warbler, Blackcap, Wood Warbler (only an odd pair), Willow Warbler, Goldcrest, Spotted Flycatcher, Pied Flycatcher, Coal Tit, Blue Tit, Great Tit, European Nuthatch, Eurasian Treecreeper, Magpie, Eurasian Jackdaw, Rook, Carrion Crow, Common Raven (high ground), Common Starling, Chaffinch, Greenfinch, Goldfinch, Twite, Common Redpoll, Reed Bunting (scarce; irregular breeder). Several species which are normally classed as resident may leave the high ground in winter and return in spring to breed.

Winter (October to March): Whooper Swan, Eurasian Wigeon, Common Teal, Mallard, Common Pochard (non-breeders in summer also), Tufted Duck, Common Goldeneye, Goosander, Hen Harrier, Common Buzzard (scarce), Peregrine Falcon, Common Coot, Common Gull, Herring Gull, Great Black-backed Gull, Fieldfare, Redwing, Brambling, Siskin, Snow Bunting.

Spring and autumn passage (March to May and July to October): Northern Shoveler (scarce), Common Scoter (occasional), Red-breasted Merganser (occasional), Merlin, Great Ringed Plover, European Golden Plover, Dunlin, any of the other passage waders are a possibility, Common Gull, Lesser Black-backed Gull, Kittiwake (after gales), Common Tern, Black Tern (occasional), Short-eared Owl, Chiffchaff (Tarn Woods).

51 COVERDALE

OS Landranger Map 98
Wensleydale

Habitat and Species

This attractive dale, which connects Wharfedale with Wensleydale, is similar in character to most of the others in the region, with sheep pasture enclosed by dry-stone walls, some scattered deciduous timber and extensive areas of *Juncus* moorland on the higher ground. Towards its northern end, the valley becomes wider and is mainly pastureland with trees, hedgerows and several farmsteads and villages.

A few Red Grouse may be seen on the high ground along with European Golden Plover, Northern Lapwing, Eurasian Curlew, Common Redshank and Common Snipe. During the autumn and winter, it is possible to see a solitary Common Buzzard, Hen Harrier, Merlin, Peregrine Falcon or Common Raven, usually along the upland stretch of road from the first cattle grid to Woodale. This is a very good route in the spring for Ring Ouzels and Northern Wheatears. Flocks of Fieldfares frequent the valley during the late winter and early spring before departing northwards. One mile (1.6 km) before reaching Middleham, look for Pinker's Pond on the left. This large sheet of shallow water attracts Mallards, Common Teals and other waterfowl on occasions as well as waders including Northern Lapwing and Common Redshank which breed, and Common Snipe during the autumn. During prolonged periods of very dry weather, the water level may drop considerably, exposing mud which is good for migrant waders in late summer and autumn.

Timing

Late March, April, May and June are good months for migrants, and a visit at any time from September to March could produce birds of prey and Common Raven on the high ground.

Access

To reach Coverdale, leave Skipton for Grassington and continue on the B6160 to Kettlewell. Cross over the bridge here and turn right in front of the Bluebell Hotel, signed 'Leyburn: Coverdale: Gradient 25%', and proceed through the narrow village street to a crossroads. Continue straight on, signed 'Leyburn: Gradient 1 in 4', from where the road climbs steeply uphill to a cattle grid after 2.5 miles (4 km). The road now passes under the western slopes of Little Whernside, the summit of which stands at 1984 feet (605 m) above sea level. The next 2 miles (3.6 km) is the best stretch along which to see birds of prey and Common Raven during the winter and Ring Ouzels and Northern Wheatears in spring. After passing through the tiny village of Woodale, the road drops steadily down into the wider valley, passing through the villages of Horsehouse and Carlton before coming to Pinker's Pond on the left after 14.5 miles (23.2 km) from Kettlewell and just 1 mile (1.6 km) before reaching Middleham.

Calendar

This includes both the upland and lowland valley areas.

Spring and summer (late March to August): Eurasian Sparrowhawk, Common Kestrel, Oystercatcher, European Golden Plover, Northern Lapwing, Common Snipe, Eurasian Curlew, Common Redshank, Common Sandpiper, Black-headed Gull, Stock Dove, Wood Pigeon, Common Swift (from mid-April), Sky Lark, Barn Swallow, House Martin, Meadow Pipit, Yellow Wagtail, Grey Wagtail, Pied Wagtail, Wren, Hedge Accentor, Robin, Common Redstart, Whinchat, Northern Wheatear, Ring Ouzel, Blackbird, Song Thrush, Mistle Thrush, Willow Warbler, Spotted Flycatcher, Blue Tit, Great Tit, Magpie, Eurasian Jackdaw, Rook, Carrion Crow, Common Starling, House Sparrow, Chaffinch, Greenfinch, Goldfinch, Linnet, Common Redpoll, Yellowhammer.

Autumn and winter (September to March): Hen Harrier, Common Buzzard, Merlin, Peregrine Falcon, Fieldfare, Redwing, Common Raven, and most of the resident species listed above.

UPPER NIDDERDALE AND THE MASHAM AREA

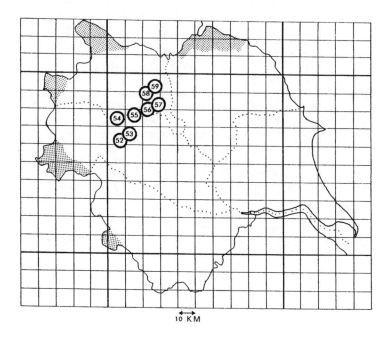

10 KM

Habitat

This recently enlarged and modernised reservoir is set in high ground consisting of heather moor and sheep grazing pastureland. The edges are largely devoid of vegetation and offer little food or shelter for surface-feeding ducks and other waterbirds. Some newly planted deciduous trees along the approach road will be suitable for passerines in due course.

Species

Being largely open and exposed, the reservoir is not a particularly good site for waterfowl. An occasional pair of Eurasian Wigeons and a few pairs of Common Teals breed in the adjacent area and appear with their young on the water in early summer. Several pairs of Great Ringed Plovers nest annually around the edges. Some diving ducks are usually present, but only in small numbers and mainly during the autumn and winter.

The edges of the reservoir and the adjacent moorland are worth investigating during the summer for breeding Oystercatchers, Great Ringed Plovers, European Golden Plovers, Northern Lapwings, Common Snipe, Eurasian Curlews and Common Redshanks. Some birds of prey may be seen during the autumn and winter months including Hen Harrier, Common Buzzard, Merlin and Peregrine Falcon. Red Grouse are present on the heather throughout the year. Short-eared Owls often hunt the area during autumn and winter and can often be seen from the car park. Meadow Pipits, occasional Yellow Wagtails, Pied Wagtails, Whinchats, Northern Wheatears and Ring Ouzels all breed in the area and Common Stonechat is a possibility. Both Horned Lark and Snow Bunting have occurred in recent years.

Timing

April, May and June is the best period to visit this site for the most species, the autumn and winter months may produce the occasional bird of prey and some waterfowl.

Access

Grimwith Reservoir lies to the north of the B6265 Grassington to Pateley Bridge road. Approaching from Grassington, continue for 5 miles (8 km) and after passing through the village of Hebden, the road drops down a steep incline to a sharp left-hand bend over a bridge. Just after the bridge, look for the reservoir road on the left (signed) and drive to the car parking area overlooking the water (pay machine and toilet facilities). From here, a well marked footpath circles the reservoir and this walk is the best way to see most of the moorland species.

Approaching from Pateley Bridge, leave the town on the B6265 Grassington road and climb the steep Greenhow Hill. The reservoir entrance is on the right just after Stump Cross Caverns, 6 miles (9.6 km) from Pateley Bridge.

Calendar

Spring and Summer (April to August): Common Teal, Mallard, Eurasian Wigeon (rare), Common Kestrel, Moorhen, Common Coot, Oystercatcher,

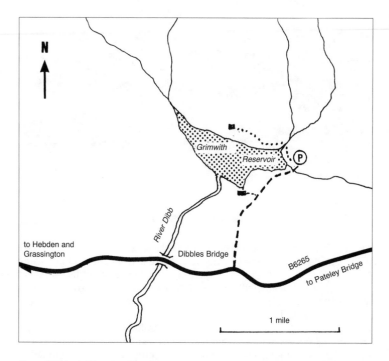

Great Ringed Plover, European Golden Plover, Northern Lapwing, Common Snipe, Eurasian Curlew, Common Redshank, Common Sandpiper, Little Owl, Short-eared Owl (scarce), Sky Lark, Meadow Pipit, Pied Wagtail, Ring Ouzel, Whinchat, Northern Wheatear, Chaffinch, Linnet.

Autumn and winter (September to March): Common Pochard, Tufted Duck, Common Goldeneye, Hen Harrier, Common Buzzard, Merlin, Peregrine Falcon, Short-eared Owl, Fieldfare, Redwing, Horned Lark (occasional), Snow Bunting (occasional).

53 GOUTHWAITE RESERVOIR

OS Landranger Map 99
Northallerton and Ripon

Habitat

Gouthwaite Reservoir is a long narrow water some 3 miles (4.8 km) long and a little under 0.5 miles (0.8 km) wide. It runs along the Nidd valley in a northwest to southeast direction and was constructed in 1899 as a compensation reservoir. It has never been subject to disturbance other than for a few anglers at the northern end or an occasional shoot during the winter months and has, in consequence, become a favourite feeding and

Gouthwaite Reservoir

resting place for many species of waterfowl and waders. It is bordered on the west side by the Pateley Bridge to Lofthouse road and rolling grazing land, and on the east side by higher land rising steeply to the adjacent heather moor of Dallowgill. The lower slopes of this scarp are used mainly for grazing sheep but there are some plantations of conifer and ample hardwoods along the field edges.

The northwestern end of the reservoir is best for birds and has an extensive area of *Juncus* marsh bordering the inflowing river channel and also some shallow lagoons. A large area of silted mud is exposed for much of the year but especially during the summer and autumn as the water level drops. This area is the favourite haunt of many waterfowl and waders at the appropriate season. The deeper open water immediately south of the mud is used by diving ducks and grebes mainly during the winter months.

Continuing northwards beyond the reservoir, the course of the infant River Nidd runs through a relatively narrow valley of grazing land which rises sharply on each side. Several large hanging conifer plantations attract Eurasian Sparrowhawks, an occasional Northern Goshawk and many Wood Pigeons. Green Woodpeckers are also resident in the valley.

Species

During the summer months, the borders of the reservoir are host to breeding Common Sandpipers, a few Yellow Wagtails, and Meadow Pipits. A few pairs of Great Crested Grebes attempt to nest annually but are often thwarted by falling water levels. Small numbers of Black-headed Gulls breed in the marsh, and Northern Lapwings, Common Redshanks, Great Ringed Plovers and occasional Little Ringed Plovers nest. Tufted Ducks and Common Teals are successful breeders and appear on the water with their broods of young during the summer.

The spring and autumn periods bring many passage birds, notably waterfowl and waders, their numbers augmenting the resident populations. Oystercatchers, Northern Lapwings, Common Snipe, Common Redshanks and Eurasian Curlews are present during the breeding season as well as being represented during passage along with Common Greenshanks and Ruffs. The less usual waders are always a possibility, depending on the weather conditions and the water levels. Diving duck numbers build up during the autumn and winter when flocks of Common Goldeneyes have peaked at around 40 birds in recent years. Common

Pochards and Tufted Ducks are also numerous and small numbers of Goosanders occur. Canada Geese breed on the marsh and on the adjacent moorland. During the autumn and winter, their numbers increase and the flock is often joined by occasional Pink-footed, Bean or Greylag Geese. A few feral Barnacle and Lesser Snow Geese frequent the area and are often at Gouthwaite. Small parties of both Whooper and Tundra Swans may drop in, often for only brief periods before moving on, as may parties of Common Scoters. Occasional divers and grebes also occur on the open water, Pied-billed Grebe having occurred in 1977. Assemblies of Grey Herons often reach double figures during the autumn and winter months.

Many birdwatchers scan the ridge on the far side of the reservoir for birds of prey and are often rewarded with up to six species in the course of a day's vigil during the autumn and winter, Common Buzzard, Rough-legged Buzzard, Hen Harrier, Marsh Harrier, Northern Goshawk, Eurasian Sparrowhawk, Peregrine Falcon, Common Kestrel and Merlin are regularly seen and the rare species seen in recent years include Honey-buzzard, Black Kite, Red Kite and Golden Eagle. Ospreys regularly pass through on spring passage and Short-eared Owls hunt over the moor edge on the far ridge.

Autumn gales have brought passing flocks of Kittiwakes and the occasional skua to the reservoir. Large numbers of gulls assemble in the shallows adjacent to the mud during late summer and winter, Lesser Black-backs (mainly autumn), Common and Black-headed being the most numerous with fewer Herring and Great Black-backs during the winter. Common and Arctic Terns pass through in varying numbers depending on the weather conditions but mainly in spring when easterly winds force passage birds inland. A few Black Terns may also be seen during these periods.

Timing

The light conditions for viewing over the reservoir are good, in that the sun is from behind, except for very early in the morning during the summer months. There is little or no disturbance to the birds and a visit at any time of day will be productive. Periods of westerly winds are best for looking for raptors when they hang on the updraughts from the west-facing ridge. Visits during late afternoon and evening can be good for autumn waders, especially after heavy rain and also for watching the gulls assembling in autumn and winter.

Access

To reach Gouthwaite Reservoir, leave Pateley Bridge on the road to Lofthouse and Middlesmoor and continue for 2.5 miles (4 km) to reach the start of the reservoir at Gouthwaite Lodge. After a further 1.5 miles (2.4 km) and just past Colt House Farm, there is a car park and picnic site on the left (voluntary contributions – £1 recommended) opposite which is a fenced viewing area inside the Reservoir boundary wall. There are two other similar areas which afford views over the northern end of the Reservoir before one reaches the village of Ramsgill. A telescope is recommended. The road can be very busy with both local and tourist traffic so one should take care when walking along the verges.

Calendar

Winter (October to March): Occasional divers and grebes, Great Cormorant, Grey Heron, Whooper and Tundra Swans, Canada Goose,

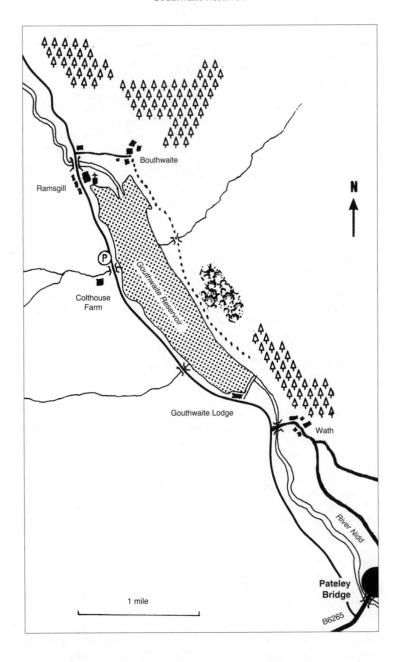

Pink-footed Goose (occasional), Lesser Snow Goose (occasional), Barnacle Goose, Eurasian Wigeon, Common Teal, Mallard, Northern Pintail, Common Pochard, Tufted Duck, Common Goldeneye, Goosander, Hen Harrier, Northern Goshawk, Eurasian Sparrowhawk, Common Buzzard, Rough-legged Buzzard, Merlin, Common Kestrel, Peregrine Falcon, Moorhen, Common Coot, Eurasian Curlew, European Golden

Plover, Northern Lapwing, Common Redshank, Dunlin, Common Snipe, Black-headed Gull, Common Gull, Herring Gull, Great Black-backed Gull, Stock Dove, Wood Pigeon, Pied Wagtail, Wren, Hedge Accentor, Robin, Blackbird, Fieldfare, Redwing, Mistle Thrush, Blue Tit, Great Tit, Magpie, Eurasian Jackdaw, Rook, Carrion Crow, Common Raven (scarce), Common Starling, Chaffinch, Greenfinch, Siskin, Common Redpoll, Yellowhammer.

Spring and autumn passage (March to early June and late July to October): Common Shelduck, Northern Shoveler, waders, Lesser Black-backed Gull, Common Tern, Arctic Tern, Black Tern (occasional), Common Swift, Sky Lark, Sand Martin, Barn Swallow, House Martin, Tree Pipit, Meadow Pipit, Yellow Wagtail, Northern Wheatear.

Spring and summer (April to August – breeding): Great Crested Grebe, Little Grebe, Canada Goose, Mallard, Common Teal, Northern Shoveler, Eurasian Sparrowhawk, Common Kestrel, Northern Lapwing, Common Snipe, Common Redshank, Eurasian Curlew, Common Sandpiper, Great Ringed Plover, Little Ringed Plover (occasional), Yellow Wagtail, Pied Wagtail, Tree Pipit, Meadow Pipit, Common Redstart, Willow Warbler, Spotted Flycatcher, Blue Tit, Great Tit, Chaffinch, Greenfinch and Reed Bunting, in addition to the other common resident breeding species.

54 SCAR HOUSE AND ANGRAM RESERVOIRS

OS Landranger Maps 98/99
Wensleydale/Northallerton
and Ripon

Habitat

These two upland reservoirs were built at the turn of the 19th Century to dam the River Nidd near to its source on Great Whernside which stands at a height of 2310 feet (704 m) above sea level. The approach road to the first (lower) reservoir, Scar House, is good tarmac and runs along the western side of a deep valley passing through upland grazing land with an ample scattering of mature deciduous trees and several plantations of conifer, mainly larch and some Scots pine. The grassland of the valley sides gives way to open heather moorland on the ridge tops. Beyond Scar House Reservoir, the surrounding area is open heather moorland reaching to Little Whernside which stands at a height of 1984 feet (605 m) above sea level and northwestwards to Angram Reservoir and Great Whernside.

Species

The lower reaches of the valley, after leaving the main Middlesmoor road, are fairly open with large deciduous trees and some conifers along the rivercourse. A waterfall on the right, some 200 yards (182 m) beyond the pay machine should be checked for Grey Wagtail and Dipper. Tree

Pipits, Common Redstarts, several species of warblers, Spotted Flycatchers and Pied Flycatchers are all present along this stretch. A large stand
of larch and Scots pine just beyond the waterfall is worth checking for
Common Crossbills. Continue until you come to a walled-up railway tunnel, 200 yards (180 m) beyond where there is a large stand of deciduous
trees at the entrance to Summerstone Farm; these trees are good for Common Redstarts and Pied Flycatchers. Green and Great Spotted Woodpeckers can be found in this section and Stock Doves and Mistle Thrushes
are familiar birds along the valley. Further along the road in the more desolate areas, Meadow Pipits, Whinchats, Northern Wheatears and an occasional Ring Ouzel can usually be found. Northern Lapwings, Common
Snipe, Eurasian Curlews and Common Redshanks all breed in the damp
hillside meadows and Red Grouse can be heard, if not always seen, calling from the heather moor.

During the autumn and winter months, several Common Buzzards
come into the valley to roost in one or other of three rectangular larch
plantations on the opposite side of the valley between the tunnel and the
car park; up to six birds have been counted in recent years. Flocks of Fieldfares frequent the trees and grassland from late autumn through to spring.

The two reservoirs are wild and bleak and are not very attractive to
waterfowl although occasional herds of Whooper and Tundra Swans
drop in for short periods and flocks of Kittiwakes have been recorded in
stormy autumn conditions. Common Sandpipers nest along the edges
and an occasional pair of Lesser Black-backed Gulls stays to breed.

Timing
Any time of the day is suitable for a visit but mid to late afternoon is the
best time to wait for the Common Buzzards arriving to roost during the
winter. April, May and June are perhaps the best time to visit, when the
birds are in song and displaying.

Access
To reach the reservoir access road, pass through the village of Lofthouse,
following the sign for Stean and Middlesmoor, and turn right after just 200
yards (180 m) onto a private Water Authority road signed Scar House
Reservoir. 50 pence is payable at a machine situated at a gate and buildings 200 yards (180 m) from the main road. Proceed along the road, stopping to view the river and wooded valley along the first section. After
passing the walled-up railway tunnel, park near the track to Summerstone
Farm, and walk down the hill to the river bridge. This track is good for
Common Redstarts, Spotted Flycatchers and Pied Flycatchers during the
spring and summer. Continuing along the road for a further 2 miles (3.2
km) brings you to a large car parking area within sight of the dam wall.
From here, public footpaths run along both sides of Scar House Reservoir
as far as Angram Reservoir, the path along the northeastern edge being
reached by crossing over the dam wall.

Calendar
Winter (October to March): Hen Harrier, Eurasian Sparrowhawk, Common Buzzard, Peregrine Falcon, Red Grouse, Stock Dove, Fieldfare, Redwing, Mistle Thrush.

Spring and summer (April to August): Common Kestrel, Northern Lapwing, Common Snipe, Woodcock, Eurasian Curlew, Common Redshank,

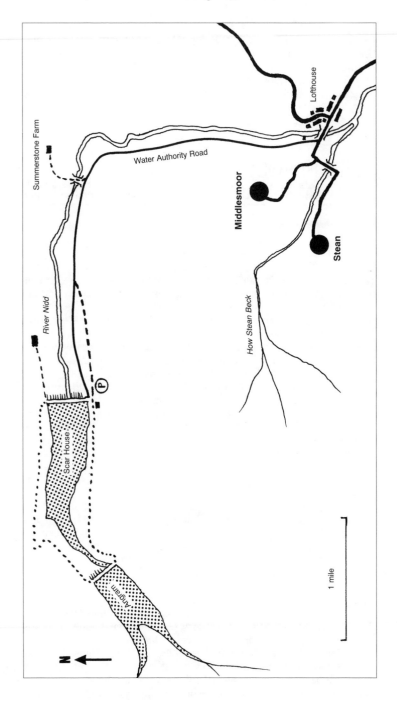

Common Sandpiper, Stock Dove, Wood Pigeon, Green Woodpecker, Great Spotted Woodpecker, Tree Pipit, Meadow Pipit, Yellow Wagtail, Grey Wagtail, Pied Wagtail, Dipper, Common Redstart, Whinchat, Northern Wheatear, Ring Ouzel, Blackbird, Mistle Thrush, Garden Warbler, Blackcap, Willow Warbler, Spotted Flycatcher, Pied Flycatcher, Eurasian Treecreeper.

55 LOFTHOUSE TO MASHAM

OS Landranger Map 99
Northallerton and Ripon

Habitat

The areas of heather moorland on each side of the road between Lofthouse and the reservoirs are the most extensive in the region and are managed for Red Grouse. The large open expanses of Pott Moor to the west and High Ash Head Moor to the east form part of the extensive Masham Moors which stretch in every direction relieved only by drystone walls and occasional gullies such as at Agill, the major valley along this moorland road. The heather moorland ends as one reaches the reservoirs and gives way to damp grassland with *Juncus* rush, used for sheep grazing, beyond which the valley opens out into grassland with farms and scattered deciduous trees before reaching the town of Masham.

Colsterdale is a very attractive valley running westwards for about 3 miles (4.8 km) from near Leighton. It is mainly sheep-grazing land with hedgerows and dry-stone walls, some plantations of conifer and much deciduous timber in the valley bottom and on the hillsides. The stream is lined with alders and there is a very fine avenue of large mature alders in one section. The valley is surrounded by the extensive Masham Moors.

Species

The moors in this area are famous for their Red Grouse, and the visitor is guaranteed several sightings at any season of the year. From the first cattle grid on the watershed some 2 miles (3.2 km) from Lofthouse, to the end of the heather at the second cattle grid some 2 miles (3.2 km) further on, is the best place to see this species. The first cattle grid is a good vantage point from which to scan the moors for harriers, buzzards and Short-eared Owls. Ring Ouzels frequent gullies and rocky outcrops, and Meadow Pipits are common breeding birds all over the upland areas. Common Cuckoos can be seen regularly over the open moorland in early summer as they search for pipits' nests in which to lay their eggs. European Golden Plovers, Northern Lapwings, Common Snipe, Eurasian Curlews and Common Redshanks all breed, either on the heather moor or in the adjacent rough grassland. Although heavily keepered, an occasional Merlin or Short-eared Owl can be seen during the breeding season. Birds of prey, which occur during the autumn and winter months include Hen Harrier, Northern Goshawk, Common Buzzard, Rough-legged Buzzard and Peregrine Falcon. A solitary Golden Eagle has frequented the

Red Grouse

area in recent winters. Small flocks of Snow Buntings are sometimes seen along the roadsides during periods of severe weather.

The wooded slopes between Leighton and Roundhill Reservoirs hold a few Pied Flycatchers and Common Redstarts during the summer. Goosanders breed in the vicinity and small numbers are often on Leighton Reservoir during the winter months. Common Sandpipers and Oystercatchers breed around the reservoir margins and a few passage waders may be seen at the appropriate season. The large pine trees near the reservoir keeper's house sometimes have a few crossbills. Large assemblies of Mallards and smaller numbers of other waterfowl and gulls occur on Leighton during the autumn and winter months. The alder-lined stream through Colsterdale is very good for passerines during the spring and summer when visitors include Common Redstart, Common Whitethroat, Blackcap, Willow Warbler and Spotted Flycatcher. The alders are frequented by feeding flocks of Siskins and Common Redpolls during the autumn and winter months.

Timing

The best time to undertake this moorland drive is during April, May and June when the Red Grouse are displaying and much in evidence. European Golden Plovers, Northern Lapwings, Common Snipe and Eurasian Curlews are also active at this time when the migrant passerines are also arriving back on their breeding grounds. Visits at any time of day are equally rewarding. Autumn and winter are the best times to see birds of prey, especially in Colsterdale where all the regularly recorded species have been seen in recent years.

Access

This route is the only exit from Upper Nidderdale and, after visiting Gouthwaite or Scar House Reservoirs (see sites 48 and 49), is recommended as an alternative to returning down the dale to Pateley Bridge. Starting at the village of Lofthouse, turn right onto the Masham road and pass the Crown Hotel on the right. Proceed through the narrow main street and up a steep and winding incline to reach the moortop at a cattle grid, 2 miles (3.2 km) from the village. Partway up the incline, stop at a small stone building on the right and look down the valley to Gouthwaite Reservoir and scan the ridges for birds of prey. Near the top of the incline, look for a wide gateway on the left at a right-hand bend, just after which is a track to the right signed 'Unsuitable for vehicles'. Park here and walk along to a gate and beyond. This walk is good for European Golden Plovers, Short-eared Owls, Northern Wheatears and Ring Ouzels. Do not trespass from the track onto the heather moor. Continue along the main road and reach the first cattle grid after which the road drops steadily downhill to a valley bottom at Agill. Park here, where Agill Beck passes under the road, and look for Ring Ouzels and Whinchats. Proceed to a second cattle grid, from where Leighton Reservoir is visible straight ahead as the road drops down. Park carefully along the roadside just past the track to Roundhill Reservoir. This overlooks the southern end of Leighton Reservoir and the moors beyond.

To reach Roundhill Reservoir, drive (or walk) back up the hill for 150 yards (135 m) along the minor access road which leads to the dam wall after 0.5 miles (0.8 km). The first large trees on the left are worth checking for Pied Flycatchers and Common Redstarts in the summer. Park near the reservoir keeper's house and walk the short distance to the dam wall to view the reservoir and the surrounding area.

Returning to the main road, continue along the edge of Leighton Reservoir where there are several parking places and 1 mile (1.6 km) after leaving the end of the water, look for a minor road to the left signed Colsterdale. Take this road, which runs along the north side of the valley for approximately 3 miles (4.8 km). About 1 mile (1.6 km) from the start of the dale, the road runs alongside an alder-lined stream and passes through an avenue of very large mature alder trees. There are two large grassy parking areas on the left by the stream in this section where one should stop to look for flocks of Siskins in winter and other passerines in spring and summer. After leaving the second parking place, there is a sharp double hairpin bend as the road climbs steeply uphill. Look for a parking area on the right, 500 yards (460 m) from the last parking area, from where a path leads through a gate and eventually onto heather moor. This walk is good for Red Grouse and also for birds of prey in the autumn and winter.

Continuing along the dale, there are several gates across the road in the final section before reaching the scattered farmsteads of Colsterdale village where the tarmac ends near a bridge. Park here by the stream from where a track leads onto the moorland which is another good area for Red Grouse. On leaving Colsterdale, keep left and continue along the main road, passing through the villages of Healey and Fearby to reach the town of Masham after 3.5 miles (5.6 km). Total distance of this drive, excluding the Colsterdale extension, is 11 miles (17.6 km). During the winter months, the upland stretch of the route between Lofthouse and Leighton Reservoir may be closed owing to heavy snowfalls.

Calendar

This includes the upland moors, the reservoirs and the valley towards Masham.

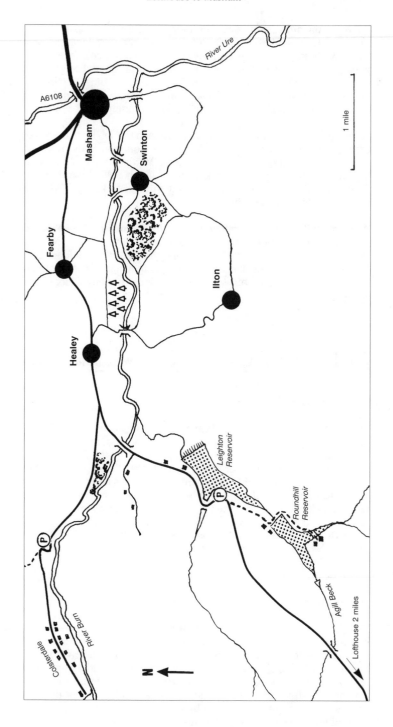

All year: Mallard, Goosander, Common Coot, Eurasian Sparrowhawk, Common Kestrel, Merlin (rare), Red Grouse, Common Pheasant, Stock Dove, Wood Pigeon, Tawny Owl, Short-eared Owl (scarce), Green Woodpecker, Great Spotted Woodpecker, Pied Wagtail, Wren, Hedge Accentor, Robin, Blackbird, Mistle Thrush, Long-tailed Tit, Blue Tit, Great Tit, Magpie, Eurasian Jackdaw, Rook, Carrion Crow, Common Starling, House Sparrow, Chaffinch, Greenfinch, Yellowhammer.

Spring and summer (March to August): European Golden Plover, Northern Lapwing, Eurasian Curlew, Common Snipe, Common Redshank, Common Cuckoo, Common Swift, Sky Lark, Sand Martin, Barn Swallow, House Martin, Meadow Pipit, Common Redstart, Whinchat, Northern Wheatear, Ring Ouzel, Song Thrush, Common Whitethroat, Blackcap, Willow Warbler, Spotted Flycatcher, Goldfinch, Linnet.

Autumn and winter (September to March): Common Teal, Common Pochard, Tufted Duck, Common Goldeneye, Hen Harrier, Northern Goshawk, Common Buzzard, Rough-legged Buzzard, Golden Eagle (occasional), Peregrine Falcon, Fieldfare, Redwing, Siskin, Common Redpoll, Common Crossbill (occasional), Snow Bunting (occasional).

56 HACKFALL WOODS

OS Landranger Map 99
Northallerton and Ripon

Habitat

This site comprises a large area of ancient woodland, at least 350 years old, along the 330 feet (100 m) deep gorge cut by the River Ure. The woods stretch along the river valley for 2 miles (3.2 km) upstream from the picturesque village of Mickley where the river is fairly wide, shallow and stony for much of the way. There are many old oaks, ash and cherry with ample understorey and dead timber, making this an excellent place for woodland birds. The Woodland Trust owns 112 acres (45 ha) on the northwest-facing slopes which is designated as a Site of Special Scientific Interest. New paths, bridges and board walks have been created to improve the access.

The nearby Nutwith and Roomer Common, is also worth a visit whilst in the area and a footpath leads onto this site from the parking area at the Hackfall Woods entrance (see 'Access' section below).

Species

The main attraction here is the proliferation of woodland birds which can be seen to advantage from the footpaths along the riverbank or along the wooded slopes. Eurasian Sparrowhawks breed along the valley and can often be seen displaying over the woods during the spring. Common Kestrels are resident and usually in evidence over the more open areas. Common Sandpipers breed along the river and a few pairs of Northern Lapwings nest in the adjacent fields. During the spring and early summer, Woodcocks should be looked for at dusk when they display along the slopes. Stock Doves and Wood Pigeons are typical birds here, the latter being very common. Common Cuckoos can be heard during the spring and summer. Tawny Owls are resident and several pairs nest along the valley.

The river holds Common Kingfisher, Dipper, Grey Wagtail, and Pied Wagtail. All three species of woodpeckers can be seen in the woods, Great Spotted being the most likely. Barn Swallows and House Martins nest in and around the villages and farmsteads. In addition to the resident titmice, thrushes and finches, the woods are host to many summer migrants including Tree Pipit, Common Redstart, Lesser Whitethroat, Common Whitethroat, Garden Warbler, Blackcap, Wood Warbler, Chiffchaff, Willow Warbler, Spotted Flycatcher and Pied Flycatcher. Hawfinch is rare but a possibility.

Timing
As for the other woodland sites, the best time to visit for the most species is during April, May and June when the summer migrants are settled in and the resident birds are singing and well in evidence. Winter visits can be rewarding for woodpeckers, Dippers, thrushes, titmice and finches.

Access
There are three main access points to the woods along the valley. The two entering that part owned by The Woodland Trust are reached from the village of Grewelthorpe, which lies 6 miles (9.6 km) northwest of Ripon. Enter Grewelthorpe, passing the village pond on the left, and come to The Hackfall public house immediately after which the road bends sharp right. Look for the first footpath into the woods on the right about 200 yards (180 m) from the bend. There are no official car parking facilities here and one should park back in the village and walk to the entrance. This entrance is marked with a Woodland Trust sign and also another sign recommending the second entrance, 0.5 miles (0.8 km) further along the road where there is a small car parking area at the entrance to Nutwith Common, opposite which is the signed entrance to Hackfall Woods. This footpath leads for 300 yards (275 m) to the top of the high south ridge overlooking the wooded valley from where a path signed 'Fisher Hall and Fountain Pond' leads down to the left and joins the riverside path after about 500 yards (460 m). Another path leads to the right along the ridge and is signed 'The Ruin and Alum Springs'. Before leaving the Hackfall Woods parking area, if time permits, it is worth walking, at least partway, along the footpath which leads from the car park for 1 mile (1.6 km) through the open mixed woodland on Nutwith and Roomer Common.

The third entrance, from where the path runs upstream alongside the river for 1 mile (1.6 km) to the Woodland Trust section, is reached from the village of Mickley. From Grewelthorpe, take the Ripon road and after 1.25 miles (2 km) turn left signed Mickley and West Tanfield. After 1 mile (1.6 km), where the road drops down a hill, look for a small but obvious roadside car parking area on the left, shortly before entering the village. There is a sign reading 'Public Footpath – Riverside Walk'. This is a very good walk for seeing most birds.

Calendar
All year: Mallard, Eurasian Sparrowhawk, Common Kestrel, Common Pheasant, Moorhen, Stock Dove, Wood Pigeon, Collared Dove, Tawny

Owl, Common Kingfisher, Green Woodpecker, Great Spotted Wood-pecker, Lesser Spotted Woodpecker, Grey Wagtail, Pied Wagtail, Dipper, Wren, Hedge Accentor, Robin, Blackbird, Mistle Thrush, Goldcrest, Long-tailed Tit, Marsh Tit, Coal Tit, Blue Tit, Great Tit, European Nuthatch, Eurasian Treecreeper, Eurasian Jay, Magpie, Eurasian Jackdaw, Rook, Carrion Crow, Common Starling, House Sparrow, Chaffinch, Greenfinch, Bullfinch, Hawfinch (scarce), Yellowhammer.

Spring and summer (April to August): Northern Lapwing, Common Sand-piper, Woodcock, Common Cuckoo, Common Swift (villages), Sky Lark, Barn Swallow, House Martin, Tree Pipit, Meadow Pipit, Common Red-start, Song Thrush, Lesser Whitethroat, Common Whitethroat, Garden Warbler, Blackcap, Wood Warbler, Chiffchaff, Willow Warbler, Spotted Flycatcher, Pied Flycatcher, Goldfinch, Linnet.

Winter (October to March): Fieldfare, Redwing, Siskin, Common Redpoll.

57 NOSTERFIELD GRAVEL PITS

OS Landranger Map 99
Northallerton and Ripon

Habitat

This site comprises two separate areas: a working gravel quarry with a large lake, and a disused quarry which is to be landscaped and devel-oped as a local nature reserve. Both can be conveniently viewed from the roadside.

Species

The open, deep water of the new lake attracts diving ducks and also grebes. Tufted Ducks, Common Pochards, Common Goldeneyes and a few Goosanders can be seen during the winter months, at which time an occasional party of Tundra or Whooper Swans may drop in. Any one of the rarer grebes or divers is a possibility in the late autumn and winter. Flocks of Greylag and Canada Geese frequent both areas, most regularly grazing around the old lagoons where flocks of Eurasian Wigeons can be seen during the winter. Both waters, but mainly the old lagoons, have occasional Northern Pintails and Northern Shovelers in autumn and win-ter as well as Mallards and Common Teals.

During the spring passage period from mid-March, large numbers of Oystercatchers assemble around the old lagoons, some pairs staying to nest, as do one or two pairs of Common Redshanks, Great and Little Ringed Plovers and Northern Lapwings. Common Shelducks pass through in spring and two or three pairs breed in the area. The shallow margins of the lagoons attract good numbers of passage waders in both spring and autumn. During May, if winds are from the east, Common, Arctic or Black Terns may drop in to feed before moving on. Gulls occur throughout the year; small numbers of Lesser Black-backed and Black-headed being present during the summer months, and the other large gulls, in addition, during the autumn and winter.

Both Red-legged and Grey Partridges occur in the area as do Wood Pigeons and Stock Doves, the latter often feeding around the lagoon edges where a flock of feral pigeons is usually to be seen. The short grassland is good for migrant Northern Wheatears, Meadow Pipits and Yellow Wagtails in spring and autumn. Corvids are common in the grassland with large flocks of Rooks and Eurasian Jackdaws usually in evidence. Tree Sparrows, Greenfinches, Goldfinches and Linnets are typical birds of the lagoon edges and the surrounding farmland, especially during the autumn from July to September. Small numbers of Yellowhammers and Reed Buntings frequent the area.

Access

To reach Nosterfield Gravel Pits, leave Ripon on the A6108 Masham road and after 6 miles (9.6 km) cross a narrow bridge over the River Ure into the village of West Tanfield. Turn right at a mini-roundabout and after 0.25 miles (0.4 km) turn left signed 'The North and Thirsk'. Continue for a further 0.5 miles (0.8 km) and come to the old lagoon on the left in a large depression. Park on the left in what was the old quarry entrance, now signed 'Ornithologists Car Park'.

On leaving this part of the complex, turn left onto the main road and drive 0.75 miles (1.2 km) to a 'T' junction. The large new lake is directly opposite this junction. Park on the grass verge to view the water and the surrounding fields.

A newly constructed earth bank has made viewing difficult but the water can be well seen from the roadside just west of the junction.

Calendar

Winter (October to March): Includes many resident species which are present throughout the year. Little Grebe, Great Crested Grebe, Grey Heron, Mute Swan, Tundra Swan (occasional), Whooper Swan, Pink-footed Goose (occasional), White-fronted Goose (occasional), Greylag Goose, Canada Goose, Eurasian Wigeon, Common Teal, Mallard, Northern Shoveler, Northern Pintail (scarce), Common Pochard, Tufted Duck, Common Goldeneye, Goosander (occasional), Eurasian Sparrowhawk,

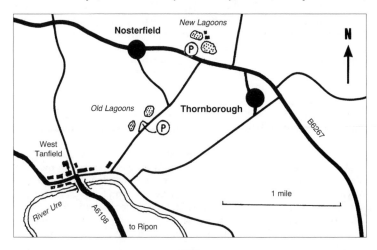

Common Kestrel, Red-legged Partridge (Chukar hybrids may occur), Grey Partridge, Common Pheasant, Moorhen, Common Coot, European Golden Plover, Northern Lapwing, Common Snipe, Black-headed Gull, Common Gull, Herring Gull, Great Black-backed Gull, Stock Dove, Wood Pigeon, Collared Dove, Sky Lark, Meadow Pipit, Pied Wagtail, Hedge Accentor, Robin, Blackbird, Fieldfare, Redwing, Mistle Thrush, Blue Tit, Great Tit, Magpie, Eurasian Jackdaw, Rook, Carrion Crow, Common Starling, House Sparrow, Tree Sparrow, Chaffinch, Greenfinch, Yellowhammer, Reed Bunting, Corn Bunting (scarce).

Spring and autumn passage (April to early June and August to October): Little Ringed Plover, Great Ringed Plover, Dunlin, Ruff, Eurasian Curlew, Common Redshank, Common Greenshank, Green Sandpiper, Common Sandpiper, gulls including Lesser Black-backed Gull, Common Tern, Arctic Tern, Black Tern, Common Swift, Yellow Wagtail, finches.

Spring and summer (April to August): Common Shelduck, Oystercatcher, Common Cuckoo, Sand Martin, Barn Swallow, House Martin, Song Thrush, Common Whitethroat, Willow Warbler, Goldfinch.

58 MARFIELD NATURE RESERVE (FORMERLY MASHAM GRAVEL PITS)

OS Landranger
Map 99
Northallerton
and Ripon

Habitat

Marfield Nature Reserve is a restored gravel-pit complex administered jointly by Redland Aggregates Ltd., English Nature, The National Rivers Authority, The Yorkshire Wildlife Trust and local naturalists. Two lakes and a series of smaller ponds and dykes with a large area of *Juncus* marsh make this an excellent place for birds. The surrounding countryside is mainly grazing and arable land with some small stands of timber and a small wood at the northern end of the Reserve. A wooded gully with oaks and ash near the southern car park is worth investigating, especially in spring for migrant warblers.

There are three hides: one overlooks the whole complex from a high bank at the northern end, another is similarly positioned on the western side and the third is at the southeastern corner of the main lake.

Species

This site is one of the best in the region for ease of access and diversity of species. A visit at any time of year can be worthwhile but the best periods are during the spring from April to early June and in late summer and autumn from mid-July to October when the species list can be excellent. The open water attracts many waterfowl throughout the year, but especially during the winter months. Greylag and Canada Geese, Mallards and Tufted Ducks are always present, their numbers being augmented from October onwards by Eurasian Wigeons, Common Teals, Northern Shovelers, Common Pochards, Common Goldeneyes, a few Goosanders and an occasional party of Whooper Swans. Moorhens and Common Coots can always be seen. A few Great Cormorants are present during the autumn and winter and a solitary Great Bittern has occurred in the *Juncus* marsh where Water Rail is a possibility in the autumn and winter months.

From late summer, gatherings of Lesser Black-backed Gulls frequent the Reserve as they migrate south and are joined by varying numbers of Common Gulls, Herring Gulls and Great Black-backed Gulls which outnumber them as the year advances. Black-headed Gulls are common throughout the year, large numbers breeding in the *Juncus* marsh opposite the north hide.

Both Great Crested and Little Grebes nest and Ruddy Duck is now usually present. During March, parties of Common Shelducks pass through the area, some staying to breed on the Reserve, their noisy display flights being a feature during April. Oystercatchers also pass through in good numbers at this time, several pairs staying to nest, along with Northern Lapwings, Common Redshanks, Great and Little Ringed Plovers and Common Sandpipers. Passage waders during spring and autumn may include all the regular migrant species, in numbers varying annually. The best time for seeing these is in the early mornings and also in the evenings, especially after heavy rain which forces them to drop down to rest and feed. Easterly winds during May sometimes bring migrating terns inland when a few Common, Arctic or Black may descend to feed over the water, often only briefly, before moving on.

The surrounding open country with stands of old timber has Common Kestrel and Stock Doves. Wood Pigeons are ever present. Both Red-legged and Grey Partridges can be found on the drier parts of the Reserve and also in the adjoining fields where corvids favour the short grass of the sheep pastures. Periods of cool, damp weather during late April and May regularly force hirundines to feed low over the water, often in large numbers, especially if this adverse weather coincides with their main arrival periods. Common Swifts are often similarly involved in May and June. Finch flocks frequent the rough ground in late summer when Greenfinches, Goldfinches and Linnets feed on the weed seeds. Warblers are often noticeable at this time as young birds start to wander.

Look for Eurasian Treecreepers in the wooded gully or on the old mature trees around the eastern edge of the Reserve. Great, Blue and Coal Tits and also finches are attracted to feeders by the side of the hide overlooking the main lake. Yellowhammers and Reed Buntings can usually be found throughout the year.

Timing

April to June and from late July to September are the best periods to visit for the highest number of species. Have regard for the wind direction as easterly winds during the spring period may bring terns down to feed over the water. The site is good for passage waders, particularly during the late summer and autumn when varying numbers of several species stop off to rest and feed, often only briefly before moving on. Early morning and also in the evening are the best times to see them. Late summer is also a good time for seeing finch flocks and migrating hirundines and warblers.

Waterfowl are present throughout the year, their numbers being swollen during the late autumn and winter months, unless frozen off.

Access

To reach Marfield, approach Masham either from Ripon on the A6108, or from the A1 (exit at Quernhow service station, 6 miles (9.5 km) south of Leeming Bar, on the B6267). Just before entering Masham, cross the humpbacked bridge over the River Ure and continue on the A6108, signed Middleham and Leyburn, for exactly 1 mile (1.6 km) and come to the first Reserve entrance on the right. Drive down the track for 300 yards (270 m) and bear left at two red-brick houses to park in a large open area. A sign indicates the entrance to the Reserve. Walk initially along the edge of the wooded gully on the right and join a gravelled path which leads to the hide at the southeastern corner of the lake. It is possible to continue along the eastern end of the lake, cross over a stile and walk round the grass field before another stile at the opposite corner leads back into the Reserve.

There is a second entrance to the Reserve some 0.5 miles (0.8 km) along the main A6108 which is the best way to reach the two elevated hides. Park on the right in a lay-by at the end of the narrow wood, or on a track just beyond the wood opposite Mile House Farm. Walk the short distance along the grass verge to the south side of the wood where there is a signed gate leading onto the Reserve. To reach the north hide, walk straight ahead alongside the wood for about 400 yards (360 m). For the west hide, walk to the right for 230 yards (200 m). Both these hides offer excellent views over the whole complex, the west hide being very good in the evenings when the sun is from behind. The north hide can be more easily reached by driving along the track opposite Mile House Farm for 300 yards (270 m) to a small car park from where a path leads the short distance to the hide. Marfield can be conveniently coupled with a visit to Thorp Perrow Arboretum (see site 59).

Calendar

All year: Little Grebe, Mute Swan, Canada Goose, Greylag Goose, Mallard, Tufted Duck, Eurasian Sparrowhawk, Common Kestrel, Red-legged Partridge, Grey Partridge, Moorhen, Common Coot, Northern Lapwing, Common Redshank, Black-headed Gull, Stock Dove, Wood Pigeon, Collared Dove, Sky Lark, Pied Wagtail, Blackbird, Mistle Thrush, Song Thrush, Blue Tit, Great Tit, Coal Tit, Eurasian Treecreeper, Magpie, Eurasian Jackdaw, Rook, Carrion Crow, Common Starling, House Sparrow, Chaffinch, Greenfinch, Linnet, Yellowhammer, Reed Bunting.

Spring and summer (April to September): Great Crested Grebe, Common Shelduck, Ruddy Duck, Oystercatcher, Great Ringed Plover, Little Ringed Plover, Common Sandpiper, Common Cuckoo, Common Swift, Sand Martin, Barn Swallow, House Martin, Sedge Warbler, Willow Warbler, Chiffchaff, Blackcap.

Spring and autumn passage (late March to early June and July to October): Osprey (occasional), Peregrine Falcon (occasional), Water Rail (possibly also in winter), good selection of waders, Lesser Black-backed Gull, occasional terns, Yellow Wagtail, warblers, hirundines.

Winter (October to March): Great Cormorant, Great Bittern (occasional),

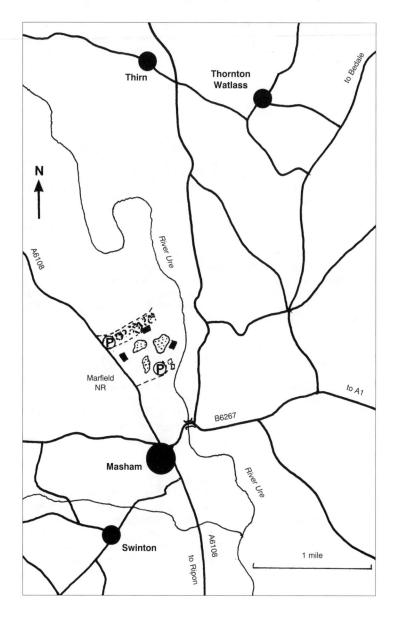

Whooper Swan (occasional), geese, Eurasian Wigeon, Common Teal, Northern Shoveler (also on passage), Common Pochard, Common Goldeneye, Goosander, Common Snipe, Eurasian Curlew, Common Gull, Herring Gull, Great Black-backed Gull, Fieldfare, Redwing.

59 THORP PERROW ARBORETUM

Habitat

This 85-acre (34 ha) arboretum is set in over 1000 acres (404 ha) of farmed parkland, owned and administered by Sir John Ropner. It is home to some of the largest and rarest trees in England and has also large areas of oak woodland and a pinetum which was planted between 1840 and 1870. The pathways through the woods are mown regularly during the summer months thus enabling easy access to all the areas. There is also a well-established lake.

Species

The various tree species attract a wide range of birds and the list is very good in consequence. The areas of open woodland have all the typical passerines associated with this habitat including Goldcrests, European Nuthatches, Eurasian Treecreepers, titmice, Wrens, Robins, Hedge Accentors, Blackbirds, Song Thrushes, Mistle Thrushes, Chaffinches, Greenfinches, Bullfinches and Common Starlings in addition to the summer visitors which include Common Redstart, Pied Flycatcher, Spotted Flycatcher, Willow Warbler, Chiffchaff, Garden Warbler and Blackcap. Common Cuckoo should be heard if not seen and Great Spotted Woodpecker is resident as are Coal Tits which frequent the Pinetum.

During the spring and summer, the lake has several pairs of Little Grebes, Common Coots, Moorhens, Tufted Ducks and an occasional Mute Swan. The larger resident birds which may be seen in the quieter parts of the woods are Eurasian Sparrowhawk, Common Kestrel, Tawny Owl, Woodcock, Wood Pigeon, Stock Dove, Eurasian Jay and Eurasian Jackdaw.

Timing

Spring (late April to early June) is the best time to visit when the songbirds are showing to advantage. A visit during the autumn and winter months, however, can be of interest. Although there are fewer woodland birds in evidence at this time, all the resident species are present in addition to the winter visitors. It is better to arrive as early in the day as possible during the spring period when the songbirds are at their best and before the visitors arrive, although pressure from this quarter is never too great.

Access

This site is situated just 4 miles (6.4 km) west of the A1 motorway between Bedale and Masham. Leave the A1 at Leeming Bar, 11 miles (17.6 km) south of Scotch Corner, to join the A684 to Bedale. Proceed through the town, following the Arboretum signs, and join the B6268. Look for a minor road on the left after 1 mile (1.6 km) signed for Well, Ripon and the Arboretum, the entrance to which is on the left after another 1 mile (1.6 km). It is open all the year round from dawn till dusk, entry being through a cafe situated next to the car parking area. Admission (at the time of writing) is £3 per adult, £2 for senior citizens and children, payable at the cafe

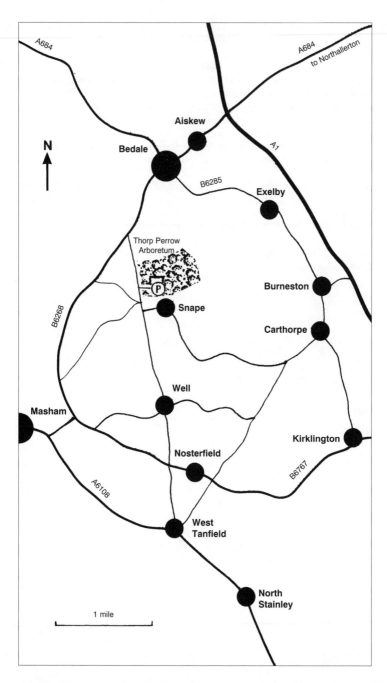

which is open from 10 am to 5 pm except in winter. There is an honesty box at a gate beside the cafe for those visiting outside these hours or during the winter months. There are several picnic tables once inside the grounds. Walk to the left and follow the track around the perimeter which passes through a cypress avenue, open deciduous woodland, the Pinetum and alongside the lake before returning to the cafe.

Calendar

All year: Little Grebe, Tufted Duck, Eurasian Sparrowhawk, Common Kestrel, Moorhen, Common Coot, Stock Dove, Wood Pigeon, Tawny Owl, Great Spotted Woodpecker, Wren, Hedge Accentor, Robin, Blackbird, Song Thrush, Mistle Thrush, Goldcrest, Long-tailed Tit, Marsh Tit, Coal Tit, Blue Tit, Great Tit, European Nuthatch, Eurasian Treecreeper, Eurasian Jay, Magpie, Eurasian Jackdaw, Rook, Carrion Crow, Common Starling, House Sparrow, Chaffinch, Greenfinch, Bullfinch.

Spring and summer (April to early August): Common Cuckoo, Common Swift (overhead), Barn Swallow, House Martin (overhead), Pied Wagtail, Common Redstart, Garden Warbler, Blackcap, Chiffchaff, Willow Warbler, Spotted Flycatcher, Goldfinch, Common Redpoll.

Winter (October to March): Mallard, Common Teal, Fieldfare, Redwing, Brambling, Siskin.

THE WASHBURN VALLEY, ILKLEY MOOR AND THE LEEDS/HARROGATE/ KNARESBOROUGH AREAS

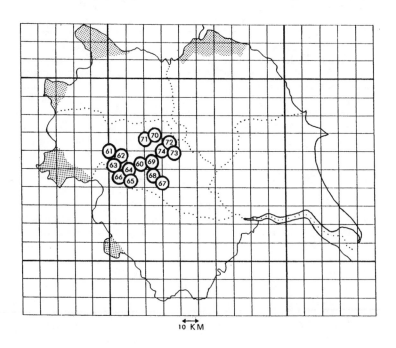

10 KM

60 THE WASHBURN VALLEY: FEWSTON, SWINSTY AND LINDLEY RESERVOIRS INCLUDING DOB PARK

OS Landranger
Map 104
Leeds and
Bradford

Habitat

This chain of three reservoirs lies along the valley of the River Washburn and stretches for 6.5 miles (10.2 km) from the village of Blubberhouses at the northern end, to near Farnley in the south. Access to a fourth reservoir known as Thruscross, two miles north of Blubberhouses, is difficult, and the water is used for boating; it is therefore not recommended. The two reservoirs at the northern end, Fewston and Swinsty, are separated by a causeway and are surrounded in the main with plantations of spruce, Scots pine and larch which cover the slopes down to the water's edge in many parts. There are also large areas of deciduous timber on the eastern side of Swinsty Reservoir. The Water Authority has provided car parking and picnic facilities at two sites by this reservoir. Recommended footpaths run through the woods on the northeastern side of Fewston Reservoir and along the western side of Swinsty Reservoir. A minor road runs along the northern edge of both waters providing access to the dividing causeway and also to the Stack Point picnic area on the north side of Swinsty.

Travelling further south down the valley to Lindley Reservoir, the main road runs through pastureland with some small patches of conifers. A large plantation of larch dominates the eastern side of the reservoir and the western edge is bordered by pastureland. A public footpath runs for 1 mile (1.6 km) along the entire length of the reservoir.

The area between Swinsty and Lindley Reservoirs, known as Dob Park, is a valley of pastureland 2 miles long (3.2 km) through which runs the River Washburn. There are some stands of deciduous woodland, the most interesting ones being Dob Park Wood on the western side of the river and Folly Hall Wood on the east, both good for woodland passerines.

Species

This is one of the most interesting sites in the region and it is certainly worth spending a whole day here. The large areas of water occasionally attract wandering divers and grebes during the autumn and winter months when such species are most likely to occur and Red-throated, Black-throated and Great Northern Divers have all been recorded in recent years. Occasional Great Cormorants call in during the winter. There is a small breeding colony of Grey Herons in Dob Park Wood and one or two birds can usually be seen along the valley. Resident flocks of Greylag and Canada Geese are sometimes joined by individuals or small parties of other geese. Lindley is the best reservoir for surface-feeding ducks, particularly Mallards, which regularly peak at 500 or more during the autumn and winter months, when smaller numbers of Eurasian Wigeons and Common Teals are usually present as well as a few Gadwalls, Northern Pintails and Northern Shovelers. Diving ducks favour the open water, Common Pochards and Tufted Ducks occurring in varying numbers throughout the year and Common Goldeneyes and Goosanders

Grey Herons

being present during the winter months. Any one of the more unusual sea ducks is always a possibility in autumn and winter.

The valley is a good place for birds of prey and in addition to the breeding Eurasian Sparrowhawks and Common Kestrels, there is the chance of seeing a lone Hen Harrier, Northern Goshawk or Common Buzzard during the non-breeding season and also an occasional Merlin from the adjacent moorland areas. Osprey is a possibility during the spring and autumn migration seasons. Red-legged Partridges, Grey Partridges and Common Pheasants are all resident and can be seen in the open ground surrounding the woods and along the valley. A few Common Coots occur and Moorhens are resident. Any of the usual passage waders may occur on spring and autumn migration but only in small numbers due to the lack of any significant areas of marginal mud. Breeding waders include Northern Lapwing, Common Snipe, Eurasian Curlew, Common Redshank and Common Sandpiper. Autumn and winter flocks of European Golden Plovers and Northern Lapwings can be found in pastureland around the area and both Common and Jack Snipes frequent marshy ground in Dob Park during the winter.

The large winter gull roost in Swinsty Reservoir regularly numbers many hundreds of birds, mainly Black-headed. Common and Herring with smaller numbers of Great Black-backed and an occasional Iceland or Glaucous. Some Lesser Black-backed Gulls are usually present, but mainly during the spring and autumn when birds are on migration. A few passage terns may feed over the water, often for only short periods before moving on, usually during May and early June and especially if the winds are from the east. Stock Doves and Wood Pigeons are resident in the valley, the latter being very common. Owls are represented by Little and Tawny which both breed, and by Short-eared which may hunt the open areas during the winter months. All three species of woodpeckers occur, Green being most frequent in the Dob Park area. Sky Larks return to the higher ground in the spring to breed and autumn flocks can also be seen in these areas. Large concentrations of feeding Sand Martins, Barn Swallows and House Martins sometimes occur over the water in spring and autumn, especially if the weather is cool and damp. Barn Swallows and House Martins breed in the villages or around the farms. Tree and Meadow Pipits both breed in the area, the latter also moving through in good numbers in both spring and autumn. Pied Wagtails, Grey Wagtails and Dippers nest along the course of the River Washburn and a few Yellow Wagtails are present in summer.

The woods hold several pairs of Eurasian Jays as well as Magpies, Eurasian Jackdaws, Rooks and Carrion Crows which are all common throughout the year. The woods are also good for Common Redstarts, warblers, Spotted and Pied Flycatchers, European Nuthatches, Eurasian Treecreepers and titmice. Flocks of Siskins and Common Redpolls can be seen in the alder trees in autumn and winter and Common Crossbills sometimes occur, mainly in the larch plantation alongside Lindley Reservoir.

Timing

The best time to visit this complex is during the period April to June when the maximum number of species is likely to be present. Visits during the autumn can be worthwhile for waterfowl, passage waders and some passerines. Most of the resident species are in evidence during the winter months as well as Fieldfares, Redwings and Bramblings. Viewing over the reservoirs is best during the mornings before the sun gets into the western sky, but the causeway between Fewston and Swinsty, and also the path along the western side of Swinsty, are good for viewing during the afternoons and evenings. The main winter gull roost on Swinsty Reservoir occasionally shifts to Fewston Reservoir if disturbed for any reason, but this is not usual.

Access

The Washburn Valley Reservoirs lie south of the A59 Harrogate to Skipton road, some 8 miles (12.8 km) west of Harrogate and 15 miles (24 km) east of Skipton. Approaching from Harrogate, proceed for 5 miles (13.6 km) to the Hopper Lane Hotel, after which continue down the hill for 350 yards (320 m) and park in a loop lay-by on the left. From here a public footpath leads through the conifer wood along the north shore of Fewston Reservoir. The path runs close to the water's edge for much of the way and affords good views over the reservoir. On returning to the lay-by, turn right onto the main road and drive back past the Hopper Lane Hotel 0.25 miles (0.4 km) beyond which is a minor road on the right. Follow this narrow and winding road which passes along the edge of the woodland and comes to the village of Fewston after 1 mile (1.6 km). Bear right in the village to a 'T' junction signed 'Timble and Otley'. This road crosses over the causeway where one should stop to view both reservoirs. On the other side of the causeway, turn left into Swinsty Moor car parking area after 150 yards (135 m); (toilets – not always open in the winter months). A path leads through a white gate to the left of the car park entrance and along the western shore of Swinsty Reservoir. This route passes through conifer woodland and an area of beech trees before reaching the dam wall after about 1 mile (1.6 km) and continues through Dob Park to Lindley Bridge.

To reach Lindley Reservoir by car from Swinsty Moor car park, return over the causeway and bear right, signed 'Norwood'. Pass the village church and come to Stack Point parking area on the right with picnic tables by the lakeshore. This is a good place from which to view Swinsty Reservoir and also to look for woodland passerines. On leaving the car

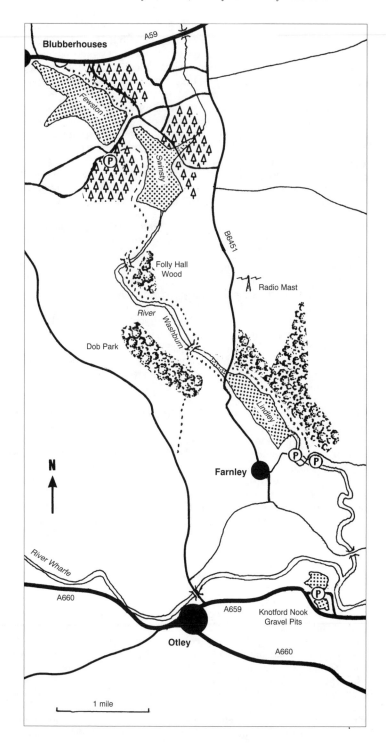

park, turn right and cross the bridge with a small arm of the reservoir to the left (sometimes dry in the summer) and continue for 0.75 miles (1.2 km) to a 'T' junction, having passed a fork to the right signed 'No through road'. Turn right at the main road signed 'Otley 5½' and continue for 5 miles (8 km) passing a radio mast on the left before descending a steep and winding hill to Lindley Reservoir. Park on the left in a wide entrance area just before the road bridge. From here, a public footpath leads south for 1 mile (1.6 km) along the whole length of the reservoir and alongside a larch plantation. This is a very good walk during the spring and early summer for passerines. Returning to the car park, proceed over Lindley Bridge and park carefully in a small gateway entrance on the right immediately over the bridge. The path through Dob Park leads northwards from here along an arm of the reservoir (often dry, except for the feeder river, during very dry summers). This shallow area has some emergent vegetation along its edges and is sometimes good for waterfowl and passage waders. The path now runs along the western side of the River Washburn for 0.5 miles (0.8 km) before crossing over the bridge to continue for a further 0.5 miles (0.8 km) to a small pack-horse bridge. Look for Dippers anywhere along the river. Continue for 0.5 miles (0.8 km) to Folly Hall Wood, good for Wood Warblers, Common Redstarts and Pied Flycatchers. At the northern end of the wood, cross over a third river bridge from where the path leads through an area of marshy ground, good for Common and Jack Snipes during the autumn and winter months. This path leads eventually to the dam wall of Swinsty Reservoir and through the woods on the western side to Swinsty Moor car park.

Total distance of the walk from Lindley Bridge to Swinsty Moor car park is just over 3 miles (5 km). *En route*, one can cross the pack-horse bridge and walk the 0.5 miles (0.8 km) to Dob Park Wood where there is a breeding colony of Grey Herons.

Another recommended walk during the spring and early summer starts at the southern end of Lindley Reservoir. To reach this area, follow the road from Lindley Bridge to Otley and after 5 miles (8 km), enter the village of Farnley. Where the main road swings to the right, turn left at Farnley School and proceed downhill for 0.75 miles (1.2 km) to a narrow bridge overlooking a trout farm. Park on the right, either just before or just after the bridge and take a footpath on the left, uphill from the bridge, signed 'Norwood Bottoms'. This path continues through woodland and open scrub for about 0.5 miles (0.8 km) before reaching the dam wall of the reservoir, from where it continues along the whole length of the water back to Lindley Bridge.

Calendar

This includes all three reservoirs and their environs.

Winter (October to March): occasional divers and the rarer grebes, Great Cormorant, Eurasian Wigeon, Gadwall (scarce), Common Teal, Northern Pintail (scarce) Northern Shoveler (mainly in spring), Greater Scaup (occasional), Long-tailed Duck (occasional), Common Scoter (occasional sometimes in summer), Common Goldeneye, Smew, Red-breasted Merganser (occasional) Goosander, Hen Harrier, Common Buzzard, Northern Goshawk, Merlin, European Golden Plover, Jack Snipe, Common Gull, Herring Gull, Iceland and Glaucous Gulls (roost on Swinsty) Great Black-backed Gull, Short-eared Owl, Fieldfare, Redwing, Brambling, Siskin (occasionally in summer also), Common Crossbill.

Spring and autumn passage (April to early June and August to October): Osprey, passage waders, Lesser Black-backed Gull, Common Tern, Arctic Tern, Meadow Pipit, Yellow Wagtail, Northern Wheatear.

Spring and Summer (April to August): includes several species which also occur on passage in both spring and autumn. Great Crested Grebe, Common Sandpiper, Eurasian Curlew, Common Redshank, Common Cuckoo, Common Swift, Sky Lark, Sand Martin, Barn Swallow, House Martin, Tree Pipit, Common Redstart, Song Thrush, Common Whitethroat, Garden Warbler, Blackcap, Wood Warbler, Chiffchaff, Willow Warbler, Spotted Flycatcher, Pied Flycatcher, Linnet, Goldfinch.

All year: Grey Heron, Greylag Goose, Canada Goose, Mallard, Common Pochard, Tufted Duck, Eurasian Sparrowhawk, Common Kestrel, Red-legged Partridge, Grey Partridge, Common Pheasant, Moorhen, Northern Lapwing, Common Snipe, Woodcock, Black-headed Gull, Stock Dove, Wood Pigeon, Little Owl, Tawny Owl, Common Kingfisher, Green Woodpecker, Great Spotted Woodpecker, Lesser Spotted Woodpecker (scarce), Grey Wagtail, Pied Wagtail, Dipper, Wren, Hedge Accentor, Blackbird, Mistle Thrush, Goldcrest, Long-tailed Tit, Marsh Tit, Willow Tit, Coal Tit, Blue Tit, Great Tit, European Nuthatch, Eurasian Treecreeper, Eurasian Jay, Magpie, Eurasian Jackdaw, Rook, Carrion Crow, Common Starling, House Sparrow, Chaffinch, Greenfinch, Common Redpoll, Bullfinch, Yellowhammer, Reed Bunting.

61 BARDEN AND EMBSAY MOORS AND RESERVOIRS

OS Landranger Map 104
Leeds and Bradford

Habitat

These two adjacent moors combine to make an extensive area of managed heather moorland with two large open reservoirs, the sloping stone banks of which are devoid of vegetation and not very suitable for birds except at the northwestern corner of the lower reservoir where the feeder stream enters. The area between the lower and upper reservoirs, however, has several gullies with bushes and rocky outcrops and is a most interesting area. There are two access points onto the moors from the main road, each with a map showing the footpaths.

Species

The number of species in this specialised habitat is inevitably small, but for those wishing to see the typical moorland birds, it is a good area with easy access and is a splendid scenic walk in fine weather. During the spring and summer months, typical birds of the moorland are Red Grouse, Common Pheasant, European Golden Plover, Northern Lapwing,

Eurasian Curlew, Meadow Pipit and Ring Ouzel, the best place to see the last species being the rough ground between the two reservoirs. Common Snipe, Common Redshanks and Common Sandpipers also nest in the area. Upwards of 1,000 pairs of Black-headed Gulls and 600 pairs of Lesser Black-backed Gulls breed around the upper reservoir.

During the winter months any of the other larger gulls may be seen on the reservoirs. Post-breeding assemblies of Northern Lapwings and Eurasian Curlews gather during July, from which time migrant pipits and wagtails may be seen around the reservoirs. At any time from September to March, there is always the chance of seeing Short-eared Owl or the occasional Hen Harrier, Common Buzzard, Rough-legged Buzzard, Merlin or Peregrine Falcon.

Timing
May and June are the best months to visit when the breeding birds are settled in and are displaying. July can be an interesting period for flocks of Northern Lapwings and Eurasian Curlews and also for migrants including a few waders and passerines around the reservoirs. Birds can be very scarce during the winter months but this is the best time to see the occasional bird of prey

Access
This site lies 15 miles (24 km) west of Harrogate, just off the B6160 opposite Bolton Abbey Woods. Travel north from Bolton Abbey and after

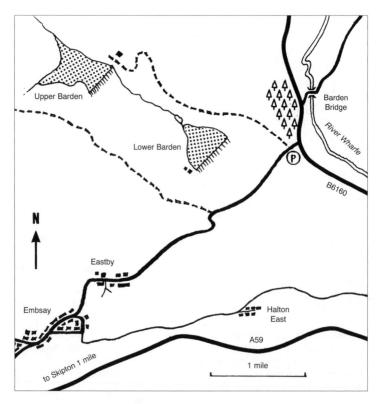

5 miles (8 km), just before reaching Barden Tower, look for a road to the left signed 'Embsay and Dales Railway'. This road runs along the southern edge of the moors and allows good views over the area including the lower reservoir, albeit from a distance. The first access track is on the right after only 50 yards (45 m) from the turn-off and is identified by a sign showing the footpaths, in a wide gateway. There is a small parking area on the opposite side of the road. Walk along this track and come to the start of the lower reservoir after 0.75 miles (1.2 km). The upper reservoir is another 2 miles (3.2 km) further on.

On returning to the car, proceed towards Embsay and Skipton for 1 mile (1.6 km) and come to the parking area on the right at the top of a hill from where there is a footpath across the moors (refer to the sign). The main road continues from here through the villages of Eastby and Embsay before reaching Skipton. If approaching from Skipton, enter the adjacent village of Embsay on Main Street and look for the left turning signed Barden.

Calendar

Spring and Summer (April to August): Includes several resident species which are present throughout the year. Canada Goose, Mallard, Common Kestrel, Red Grouse, Common Pheasant, Oystercatcher, European Golden Plover, Northern Lapwing, Eurasian Curlew, Common Snipe, Common Redshank, Common Sandpiper, Black-headed Gull, Lesser Black-backed Gull, Stock Dove, Common Cuckoo, Meadow Pipit, Pied Wagtail, Northern Wheatear, Ring Ouzel, Eurasian Jackdaw, Carrion Crow, Common Starling, Linnet.

Autumn and winter (September to March): Goosander, Hen Harrier, Common Buzzard, Rough-legged Buzzard, Merlin, Peregrine Falcon, Common Gull, Herring Gull, Great Black-backed Gull, Short-eared Owl.

62 BOLTON ABBEY ESTATE AND STRID WOODS

OS Landranger Map 104
Leeds and Bradford

Habitat

This well-wooded valley between Harrogate and Skipton runs along the course of the River Wharfe and consists of mature deciduous trees and some conifer and understorey. The area is ideal for woodland passerines and most of those associated with this habitat are represented. The river varies in width, being broad and shallow near the Abbey, and fast flowing through the woods, particularly along a stretch known as The Strid. The woods are bordered by sheep-grazing land and also open moorland to the north. Areas of open grassland run alongside the river on the south side and around the Abbey.

Species

Special birds found in the general area of the woodland include Green, Great Spotted and Lesser Spotted Woodpeckers, European Nuthatch, Eurasian Treecreeper, Pied Flycatcher, Common Redstart, Tree Pipit and Wood Warbler as well as the usual *Sylvia* and *Phylloscopus* warblers, titmice and finches. The river is good for Common Kingfisher, Grey Wagtail, Dipper and Common Sandpiper whilst the wider parts near the Abbey usually have Goosanders and Oystercatchers.

Timing

April to mid-June is the best time to visit for all the woodland species when they are in song and before the trees are in full leaf. Visits during the winter can be good for the resident woodland species. Goosanders with their broods of young are sometimes along the river near the Abbey in early summer. A visit during the evening could produce Woodcock, Little Owl and Tawny Owl.

Access

To reach Bolton Abbey, leave Harrogate on the A59, drive for 15 miles (24 km) and cross a bridge over the River Wharfe. Turn right at the roundabout into Bolton Abbey village and follow the B6160. Pass through a triple stone archway and after 0.5 miles (0.8 km) reach the Cavendish Pavilion Riverside car park on the right. The track leads down a slope to the open grassland in the valley where one can park by the river. Walk downstream along the river bank to the Abbey. A footbridge along the way crosses over the river into the wooded slopes opposite. Maps showing the nature trails for this and the next site are available at the respective car parks.

Returning to the road from the car park, turn right and continue for just over 1.5 miles (2.4 km) to the Strid Woods Car Park. From here, several nature trails lead along the river through some of the best woodland.

On returning again to the main road, turn right and continue for 0.75 miles (1.2 km) to Barden Tower, an imposing stone ruin on the right, immediately after which turn right onto a minor road signed for Appletreewick and Pateley Bridge. After 520 yards (475 m) come to the single-lane humpbacked Barden Bridge over the River Wharfe. Cross the bridge and temporarily park immediately on the left in a small area by the river to look for Common Sandpiper, Grey Wagtail and Dipper. Continue up the hill for 350 yards (320 m) and take a *very* sharp right-hand bend onto a single-lane road signed 'Hazelwood and Storiths'. On the left of this road, for the first mile (1.6 km), is open sheep-grazing land and moorland. At the end of this area, where there are some scattered trees just before a right-hand bend, look for Green Woodpeckers. The road now enters the hanging woodland with the river on the right. There are small parking places along the roadside from where one can look for the woodland specialities. This is a good alternative route, down the north side of the valley, back to the main A59 Harrogate/Skipton road.

Calendar

Spring and Summer (April to August): Goosander, Oystercatcher, Woodcock, Common Sandpiper, Common Cuckoo, Common Swift, Sand Martin, Barn Swallow, Tree Pipit, Common Redstart, Song Thrush, Lesser Whitethroat, Common Whitethroat, Garden Warbler, Blackcap, Wood Warbler, Chiffchaff, Willow Warbler, Spotted Flycatcher, Pied Flycatcher.

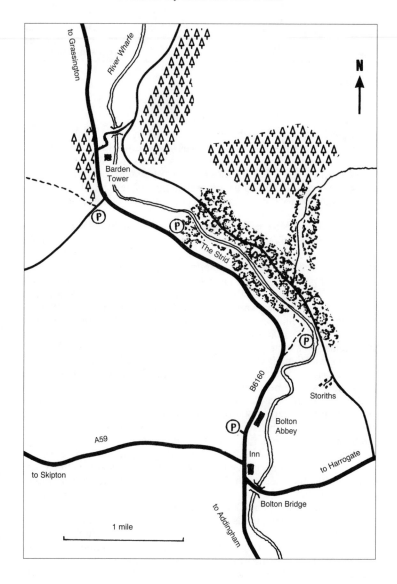

All year: Eurasian Sparrowhawk, Common Kestrel, Moorhen, Northern Lapwing, Black-headed Gull, Stock Dove, Wood Pigeon, Tawny Owl, Little Owl, Common Kingfisher, Green Woodpecker, Great Spotted Woodpecker, Lesser Spotted Woodpecker, Grey Wagtail, Pied Wagtail, Wren, Hedge Accentor, Robin, Blackbird, Mistle Thrush, Goldcrest, Long-tailed Tit, Marsh Tit, Coal Tit, Blue Tit, Great Tit, European Nuthatch, Eurasian Treecreeper, Eurasian Jay, Magpie, Eurasian Jackdaw, Carrion Crow, Rook, Common Starling, House Sparrow, Chaffinch, Greenfinch, Goldfinch, Siskin, Common Redpoll.

Winter (October to March): Fieldfare, Redwing, Brambling.

Habitat

Chelker Reservoir is an open sheet of water 0.75 miles (1.2 km) long and lying at 820 feet (228 m) above sea level. The surrounding area is mainly grazing land with a few scattered deciduous trees. There are small areas of reeds and a few willow bushes at the western end, but otherwise the banks are bare and offer little food or shelter for waterfowl. The main A65 Ilkley to Skipton road runs along the southern edge of the reservoir.

Species

The reservoir is sometimes very bleak and devoid of birds but at certain times of the year it can be quite productive. During the winter months, it is visited by several species of waterfowl and an occasional diver or one of the rarer grebes. Much of the reservoir is open deep water on which Common Pochards, Tufted Ducks, Common Goldeneyes and Goosanders are regularly present with an occasional Smew. It is sometimes visited by small flocks of Common Scoters and one or two Great Cormorants. It is not a good water for surface-feeding ducks but a few Eurasian Wigeons, Common Teals and Mallards are usually present in the winter. The local flocks of Greylag and Canada Geese sometimes feed around the edges and a solitary Grey Heron is often present. Both Little and Great Crested Grebes breed in small numbers.

During the autumn, Common Coots assemble in large flocks which regularly number up to 300 birds and more. During April and May, if brought down by adverse weather, especially from the east, Common, Arctic and Black Terns may pass through on migration. Some passage waders feed around the edges in both spring and autumn and the commoner gulls are usually in evidence during the autumn and winter. Common Sandpipers breed around the reservoir and Common Redshanks in the surrounding fields; both can also be seen feeding along the water's edge. Flocks of European Golden Plovers and Northern Lapwings congregate in the adjacent fields from late summer. Meadow Pipit is a common breeding and passage bird in the area and Reed Buntings breed around the reservoir. During the late spring and summer, Common Swifts often feed over the water during cool and wet weather, as do Sand Martins, Barn Swallows and House Martins, especially whilst on migration. Northern Wheatears can sometimes be seen in the surrounding fields during the spring and autumn.

Timing

A visit at any time of the year could produce interesting birds but spring, autumn and winter are the best times. The main road runs along the southern edge of the reservoir and the light is therefore good for viewing at any time of day.

Access

Leave Ilkley on the A65 road for Skipton and continue for 4 miles (6.4 km) to the reservoir on the right, identified by four white wind

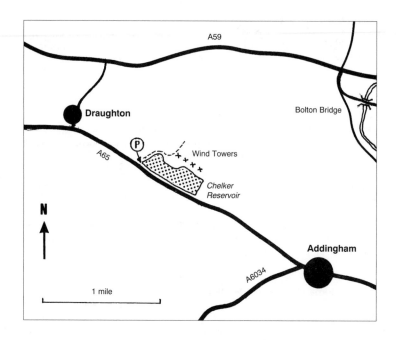

towers. Parking is difficult and one should proceed for 0.75 miles (1.2 km) along the side of the reservoir to park on the right next to the entrance gate. Do not park on the opposite side of the road in the entrance to Berwick Intake Farm. This western end of the reservoir has areas of reeds and willows and is better for lacustrine passerines. The main road is very busy and one should take care when walking along the narrow grass verges.

Calendar

Winter (October to April): Includes several species which are present throughout the year. Occasional divers and the rarer grebes, Great Cormorant, Grey Heron, Greylag Goose, Canada Goose, Eurasian Wigeon, Common Teal, Mallard, Common Pochard, Tufted Duck, Common Scoter (occasional; sometimes in summer also), Common Goldeneye, Smew (occasional), Goosander, Common Kestrel, Moorhen, Common Coot, European Golden Plover, Northern Lapwing (flocks from late summer), Black-headed Gull, Common Gull, Herring Gull, Great Black-backed Gull.

Spring and Summer (April to August): Oystercatcher, Common Sandpiper, Common Redshank, Sky Lark, Meadow Pipit (also on passage), Reed Bunting.

Spring and autumn passage (April to early June and August to October): Northern Shoveler, passage waders, Lesser Black-backed Gull, Common Tern, Arctic Tern, Black Tern, Common Swift, Sand Martin, Barn Swallow, House Martin, Yellow Wagtail, Pied Wagtail, Northern Wheatear.

Habitat

Middleton Woods comprises three areas of ancient woodland known as Coppy Wood, Stubham Wood and Hudson Wood. They cover an area of 110 acres (45 ha) and lie at an altitude of between 250 and 490 feet (75 m and 100 m) above sea level on the south-facing slope of the River Wharfe valley. They are mainly deciduous comprising oak, maple, silver birch, rowan and hawthorn with fewer beeches, willows and poplars. Elderberry and blackberry are abundant throughout and there are some stands of hazel, blackthorn and rhododendron. There are several areas of wet boggy ground, some small streams and a small pond. The woods are famous locally for the dense carpeting of bluebells during May.

Species

Woodland passerines are the main attraction of this site and most of the species associated with the habitat can be found here. European Nuthatches and Eurasian Treecreepers are resident and the titmice are well represented with Long-tailed, Marsh, Coal, Blue and Great being present throughout the year. Chaffinches, Greenfinches and Bullfinches are also resident. Hawfinches are seen occasionally and probably breed in the woods. Once the summer migrants have arrived and settled in during April and May, the woods become alive with the songs of Common Redstarts, Common Whitethroats, Garden Warblers, Blackcaps, Willow Warblers, Spotted Flycatchers and Tree Pipits. Smaller numbers of Lesser Whitethroats, Wood Warblers and Chiffchaffs occur. In addition, are the songs of the resident breeding species including Wrens, Hedge Accentors, Robins, Blackbirds, Song Thrushes, Mistle Thrushes, Chaffinches and Greenfinches. All three species of woodpeckers may occur, Great Spotted being the most likely.

Both Little and Tawny Owls reside along the valley the latter being vocal during the late autumn and early spring. Eurasian Sparrowhawks, Common Kestrels, Eurasian Jays and Eurasian Jackdaws all breed in the woods. An occasional Dipper is seen along the woodland streams or the adjacent River Wharfe and Common Cuckoos can be found in the marginal moorland areas above the wood.

Timing

The best time to visit Middleton Woods is during the spring and early summer from mid-April to June when the passerines are in full song. It is worthwhile paying an early morning visit at this time to hear the dawn chorus. Birds are sometimes sparse during the winter months but most of the resident species can usually be found in small numbers.

Access

To reach this site, enter the town of Ilkley on the A65 and turn north into New Brook Street at the main traffic lights. Pass over the river bridge and after 250 yards (230 m) turn right at Ilkley Cricket Ground. Continue past the swimming baths to reach a roadside parking place on the left opposite a narrow suspension footbridge over the River Wharfe after 0.5 miles (0.8 km). Entry onto the wooded slopes is over a stile, directly opposite the footbridge. Several paths lead through the woods (see map for site 65).

Calendar

Spring and summer (April to September): Woodcock, Common Cuckoo, Common Swift (overhead), Barn Swallow, House Martin (overhead), Tree Pipit, Common Redstart, Song Thrush, Common Whitethroat, Lesser Whitethroat (few), Garden Warbler, Blackcap, Wood Warbler (few), Chiffchaff (few), Willow Warbler, Spotted Flycatcher, Pied Flycatcher (scarce; usually in spring), Goldfinch, Linnet.

All year: Eurasian Sparrowhawk, Common Kestrel, Wood Pigeon, Little Owl, Tawny Owl, Green Woodpecker (scarce), Great Spotted Woodpecker, Lesser Spotted Woodpecker (scarce), Dipper (occasional), Wren, Hedge Accentor, Robin, Blackbird, Mistle Thrush, Goldcrest, Long-tailed Tit, Marsh Tit, Coal Tit, Blue Tit, Great Tit, European Nuthatch, Eurasian Treecreeper, Eurasian Jay, Magpie, Eurasian Jackdaw, Carrion Crow, Common Starling, House Sparrow, Tree Sparrow (scarce, but usually present in the sewage works across the river), Chaffinch, Greenfinch, Siskin, Common Redpoll, Bullfinch, Hawfinch (scarce).

65 ILKLEY MOOR AND TARNS

OS Landranger Map 104
Leeds and Bradford

Habitat

This area forms part of the extensive Rombalds Moor which stretches from Skipton southeastwards to Guiseley, a distance of some 10 miles (16 km). The open moor is composed of heather, bilberry, bracken and *Juncus* grassland. The lower slopes and the area around the main tarn have good patches of gorse, some elder and bramble, and there are several isolated clumps of trees scattered along the edges of the moors.

Species

Being close to the town of Ilkley, this is a convenient place for seeing most of the upland breeding species. Red Grouse are common and the breeding waders are European Golden Plover, Northern Lapwing, Eurasian Curlew, Common Redshank and Common Snipe with a few pairs of Dunlins. An occasional Short-eared Owl frequents the moors and Little Owls can be seen around the moor edges. Common Kestrels are usually in evidence and nest on the crags as do a few pairs of Stock Doves. Meadow Pipits and some Northern Wheatears pass through on spring and autumn migration, the former also breeding in good numbers.

During the summer, Ring Ouzels and Whinchats are relatively numerous and Willow Warblers are common in the trees and scrub along the edges of the moors. Grey Wagtails and Dippers are sometimes seen

Male Whinchat

along the upland streams or at the two tarns. A few pairs of Reed Buntings nest around the wetter patches on the moorland. Winter assemblies of Fieldfares, Redwings and Pied Wagtails regularly roost in the heather and dead bracken, and an occasional Hen Harrier may be seen at this time.

Timing
The moorland can be very bleak and desolate during the winter months, but during the spring and summer it is an extremely pleasant place for seeing the moorland species. The best times to visit are during the spring and autumn (late April to June and July to September). The area is very popular with walkers but is extensive enough to remain an important breeding habitat for many upland species. Early morning is perhaps the most productive time but visits at any time of day can be worthwhile.

Access
Leave the town of Ilkley on Wells Road which runs north off The Grove (main street) in the town centre next to The Midland Bank building, and proceed up the hill to reach a cattle grid after 500 yards (460 m). Just before the grid, turn left opposite a phone box into Crossbeck Road and immediately enter a car parking area on the right in front of a large building signed 'Bradford and Ilkley Community College – Hillside'. Proceed through a five-barred gate and follow the path to the left for 300 yards (275 m) to the Tarn, a man-made lake surrounded by a footpath. Several paths lead onto the moors from this area. On leaving the car park, turn left, cross the cattle grid and come to White Wells Museum on the left where one can park. From here, a footpath leads uphill towards the crags and to another small tarn. To reach the moors, continue along the main road and bear left onto a 'No through road' which climbs steadily uphill to reach the moor edge at the end of the tarmac after 0.5 miles (0.8 km). Park here and walk across the moors on the obvious tracks. The area is

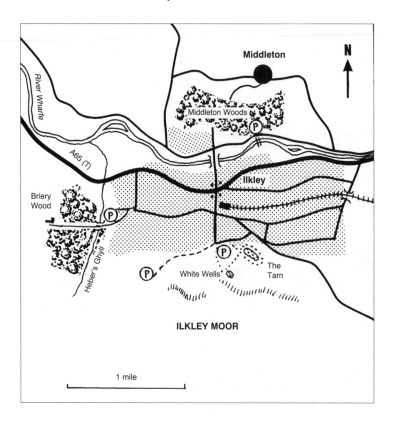

common land with unrestricted access. Halfway up the incline before coming to the end of the tarmac, look for a large gully on the left which is good for Ring Ouzels.

Calendar

This includes the open moorland, the moorland edges and the Tarns.

Spring and summer (late April to August): Includes several resident species which are present throughout the year. Mallard, Tufted Duck (occasional on the Tarn), Eurasian Sparrowhawk, Common Kestrel, Red Grouse, Grey Partridge (few), Common Pheasant, European Golden Plover, Northern Lapwing, Dunlin (few pairs), Common Snipe, Eurasian Curlew, Common Redshank, Stock Dove, Wood Pigeon, Collared Dove, Common Cuckoo, Little Owl, Short-eared Owl (scarce), Common Swift, Green Woodpecker (occasional), Great Spotted Woodpecker, Sky Lark, Barn Swallow, House Martin, Meadow Pipit, Pied Wagtail, Grey Wagtail, Wren, Hedge Accentor, Robin, Northern Wheatear, Whinchat, Ring Ouzel, Blackbird, Song Thrush, Mistle Thrush, Willow Warbler, Spotted Flycatcher, Magpie, Eurasian Jackdaw, Rook, Carrion Crow, Common Starling, House Sparrow, Chaffinch, Greenfinch, Linnet, Yellowhammer, Reed Bunting.

Winter (October to March): Hen Harrier (occasional), Fieldfare, Redwing, Pied Wagtail (roost on the moor).

66 HEBER'S GHYLL, ILKLEY

OS Landranger Map 104
Leeds and Bradford

Habitat
This is an area of excellent mature deciduous woodland with some scattered Scots pine and spruce, situated on the north-facing slopes at the edge of Ilkley Moor and at the western edge of the town of Ilkley. There are several footpaths leading up into the wooded slopes, the main one of which criss-crosses a stream over several rustic bridges as it climbs up the hillside.

Species
All the usual species associated with this mature woodland habitat can be found including most of the resident song birds and the summer visitors. It is a very good place for Common Redstarts, Garden Warblers, Blackcaps, Wood Warblers, Chiffchaffs, Willow Warblers, Spotted Flycatchers, Pied Flycatchers, European Nuthatches and Eurasian Treecreepers as well as the thrushes, titmice and finches. A few Common Crossbills are sometimes seen around the conifers during the winter months.

Timing
Late April to June is the best period to visit these woods for the highest number of species. Visits during the winter can also be interesting when the resident species and winter visitors are easy to see.

Access
From the centre of Ilkley, drive west along The Grove and at the end of the main shopping area, bear left into Grove Road. Continue for just over 0.5 miles (0.8 km) and turn left into Heber's Ghyll Drive. Proceed for 500 yards (460 m) and park on the left just before crossing a bridge with a stone parapet. Footpaths lead up into the wooded hillside from here, the main one, which runs straight up alongside the stream, being the best from which to see most of the birds. The woodland continues alongside the road for 500 yards (460 m) before coming to open sheep pasture where the road also ends (see map for site 65).

Calendar
All year: Eurasian Sparrowhawk, Wood Pigeon, Tawny Owl, Great Spotted Woodpecker, Lesser Spotted Woodpecker, Wren, Hedge Accentor, Robin, Blackbird, Mistle Thrush, Goldcrest, Long-tailed Tit, Marsh Tit, Coal Tit, Blue Tit, Great Tit, European Nuthatch, Eurasian Treecreeper, Eurasian Jay, Magpie, Eurasian Jackdaw, Rook, Carrion Crow, Common Starling, House Sparrow, Chaffinch, Greenfinch, Bullfinch, Hawfinch (scarce).

Spring and summer (late April to August): Common Cuckoo, Common Redstart, Song Thrush, Garden Warbler, Blackcap, Wood Warbler, Chiffchaff, Willow Warbler, Spotted Flycatcher, Pied Flycatcher.

67 ECCUP RESERVOIR

OS Landranger Map 104
Leeds and Bradford

Habitat

This large reservoir, built in 1897, has a surface area of 195 acres (79 ha) and is designated as a Site of Scientific Interest. The banks are fairly open with some willows and sallows along the edges and the whole reservoir is surrounded by a strip of mixed woodland set some little way back from the water's edge. Along the northern side it is mainly coniferous but there are some good stands of beech, oak, lime and silver birch along the southern shore, which can be viewed from the public footpath running between the woodland and the water. There are several good hedgerows in the adjacent farmland and also a golf course which abuts the south-eastern end.

Species

This water has attracted several lone divers and the rarer grebes over the years and any one of these is always a possibility during the autumn and winter months. The occasional Great Cormorant may drop in any time during the year and Grey Herons are often present. Small numbers of Greylag Geese occur and winter flocks of Canada Geese often number up to 750 birds. A few Common Shelducks are seen during the winter months and some also pass through on migration in the spring. Waterfowl are fairly well represented and the following species are usually present from September to April, mainly during the autumn period; some recent maxima are shown. Eurasian Wigeon (150), Gadwall (small numbers only), Common Teal (100 – usually fewer), Northern Pintail (few only), Northern Shoveler (20, mainly during the autumn), Common Pochard (50), Tufted Duck (100), Common Goldeneye (30) and Goosander (100). Occasional Ruddy Ducks appear from time to time.

Eurasian Sparrowhawks breed in the woods and can be seen throughout the year. The reservoir has no significant areas of muddy shoreline except perhaps during the late summer, and attracts only few passage waders in consequence. Some do drop in however, usually during May and from July to September.

A spectacular gull roost starts to build up during the early autumn and by September, Black-headed Gulls regularly number up to 6,000 birds and Common Gulls up to 1,000, gradually increasing to their peak numbers during the period January to March when there may be up to 15,000 and 5,000 respectively. Lesser Black-backed Gulls normally peak at around 300 birds during September and October, with Herring and Great Black-backed Gulls building up from October and reaching their maximum numbers during December and January with 4,000 and 1,000 birds respectively. An occasional Mediterranean, Iceland and Glaucous Gull may attend the roost during the winter months and a few Little Gulls sometimes appear on spring or autumn migration. Common, Arctic and Black Terns may pass through during May, usually with easterly winds.

The woodland and the adjacent hedgerows hold most of the common resident passerines in addition to the summer migrants which include Lesser Whitethroat, Common Whitethroat, Garden Warbler, Blackcap,

Chiffchaff, Willow Warbler and Spotted Flycatcher. During the autumn, a few Common Redstarts, Whinchats and Northern Wheatears pass through , the last two species being seen in the agricultural land to the west and north around Eccup Moor where small flocks of finches and Yellowhammers often occur during the autumn and winter. The titmice are well represented in the woodland with Long-tailed, Willow, Coal, Blue and Great Tits all breeding in the vicinity.

Timing

The reservoir is best visited during the autumn and winter months, from September to March, when the waterfowl are present and the gull roost is established. It is certainly worth investigating during May also when the warblers are in residence. The early autumn period can be similarly good for this group and also for passage chats and finch flocks. Early mornings or in the evenings are the best times to visit.

Access

Eccup Reservoir is conveniently situated on the northern edge of Leeds and some 8 miles (12.8 km) south of Harrogate. Travelling out of Leeds on the A61 Harrogate road, come to the traffic lights at Alwoodley Gates, just at the end of the Leeds suburbs (5 miles (4km) south of Harewood), and turn left into Alwoodley Lane, signed 'Adel'. Continue for exactly 1 mile (1.6 km), passing Sand Moor Golf Club, and come to Lakeland Drive on the right. Park carefully in this area and walk back for 35 yards (32 m) to a white gate signed Public Footpath with two vehicle No Entry signs. This track passes a plantation of pine trees on the left and the Golf Course on the right before coming to one of the reservoir lodges after 500 yards (460 m) from where the path leads to both left and right. The track to the right runs alongside the reservoir and the woodland for 1 mile (1.6 km) to a second lodge and eventually joins the A61 Leeds to Harrogate road. The track to the left runs alongside the main woodland area to join a footpath running north to Eccup village. Just before reaching the first lodge, look for a footpath on the right, through a gate between hedgerows which runs eastwards and eventually crosses the golf course to join Alwoodley Lane 700 yards (640 m) from the main traffic lights.

Calendar

This includes the reservoir, the surrounding woodland and the adjacent agricultural land.

All year: Great Crested Grebe, Grey Heron, Greylag Goose, Canada Goose, Mallard, Eurasian Sparrowhawk, Common Kestrel, Grey Partridge, Common Pheasant, Moorhen, Common Coot, Northern Lapwing, Black-headed Gull, Stock Dove, Wood Pigeon, Collared Dove, Tawny Owl, Green Woodpecker, Great Spotted Woodpecker, Grey Wagtail, Pied Wagtail, Wren, Hedge Accentor, Robin, Blackbird, Song Thrush, Mistle Thrush, Goldcrest, Long-tailed Tit, Willow Tit, Coal Tit, Blue Tit, Great Tit, Eurasian Treecreeper, Eurasian Jay, Magpie, Eurasian Jackdaw, Rook, Carrion Crow, Common Starling, House Sparrow, Tree Sparrow (sporadic), Chaffinch, Greenfinch, Goldfinch, Common Redpoll, Bullfinch, Yellowhammer.

Summer-breeding: Common Cuckoo, Common Swift, Sky Lark, Barn Swallow, House Martin, Lesser Whitethroat, Common Whitethroat, Garden

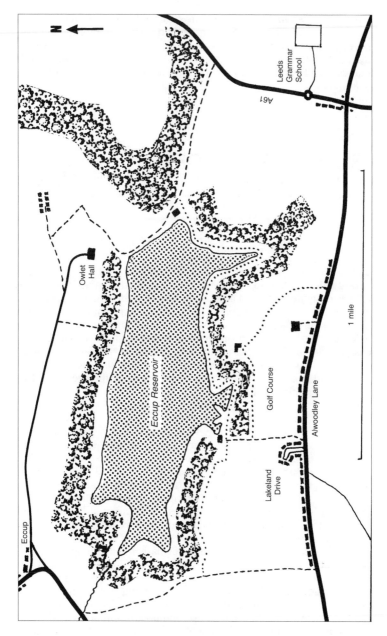

Warbler, Blackcap, Chiffchaff, Willow Warbler, Spotted Flycatcher.

Spring and autumn passage (April to early June and July to September):
Common Shelduck, Northern Shoveler, passage waders in small num-
bers, Little Gull, Lesser Black-backed Gull (also in the winter gull roost),
Common Tern, Arctic Tern, Black Tern, Meadow Pipit, Yellow Wagtail,
Common Redstart, Whinchat, Northern Wheatear, Linnet.

Winter (October to March): Eurasian Wigeon, Gadwall, Common Teal, Northern Pintail, Common Pochard, Tufted Duck, Common Goldeneye, occasional Smew and Red-breasted Merganser, Goosander, Ruddy Duck, Mediterranean Gull, Common Gull, Herring Gull, Iceland Gull, Glaucous Gull, Great Black-backed Gull, Fieldfare, Redwing, Brambling, Siskin.

68 KNOTFORD NOOK GRAVEL PITS

OS Landranger Map 104
Leeds and Bradford

Habitat

These two large restored gravel pit lagoons are situated 1.5 miles (2.4 km) east of Otley on the A659 Otley to Tadcaster road. The main lagoon is enclosed on the north and east by the River Wharfe which is lined with mature alders and some poplars. The outflow from a small sewage farm flows into the river near the northwestern end of the main lagoon. Open fields abut the western end and there is an area of rough grassland to the east. The second lagoon lies to the south and the two are separated by an old tarmac quarry road. This second lagoon is bordered by mature hedges and trees. Both sheets of water are fished by the Leeds and District Amalgamation of Anglers.

Species

This site is very well watched by local people and is a good area for birds throughout the year. Little and Great Crested Grebes nest and occasional divers and the rarer grebes occur during the winter months. Waterfowl are usually present in good numbers at this time including the usual surface-feeding and diving ducks. Smew is a regular visitor. A few grey Herons are usually present and a large gull roost builds up during the autumn and winter, consisting mainly of Black-headed and Common with fewer Herring and Great Black-backed and an occasional Iceland.

Migrant Common and Arctic Terns regularly move through in spring on easterly winds when Black Terns may pass also. The water is not noted for passage waders due to regular angling and a lack of marginal mud but a few inevitably drop in during the spring and autumn passage periods. Common Swifts assemble to feed over the water or along the roadside trees during cool and damp conditions in spring and early summer as do the hirundines. Common Kingfisher and Grey Wagtail can be seen along the river and Dipper is often near the sewage outflow. The riverside alders are good for Siskins and Common Redpolls during the autumn and winter.

Timing

A visit at any time of the year can be worthwhile, but spring and autumn are the most productive when passage migrants are moving through the area. Winter can be exceptionally good for waterfowl. The waters are very well used by fishermen and the margins are disturbed in consequence.

Access

To reach Knotford Nook, leave Otley to the east on the A659 and after 1.5 miles (2.4 km) look for a tarmac track on the left, signed 'Otley Waste Water Treatment Works', opposite a large red-brick farm building. The main lagoon is visible on the left after just a few yards. Park along the road and view the water from the several vantage points; do not climb the walls and approach the water's edge. Near the end of the main lagoon is the start of the second one on the opposite side of the road. The road continues in a loop back to the main road, passing close to the river at a bend some 0.75 miles (1.2 km) from the start. A public footpath runs along the river bank from here and continues along the northern end of the main lagoon and eventually to Otley. Park on the loop road near the river and walk along the riverbank at least as far as the sewage outflow. Total length of the tarmac loop road is just under 1 mile (1.5 km) (see map for site 60).

Calendar

Winter (October to March): Includes several resident species which are present throughout the year. Occasional divers and the rarer grebes, Little Grebe, Great Crested Grebe, Great Cormorant (occasional), Grey Heron, Mute Swan, Tundra and Whooper Swans (occasional), Greylag Goose, Canada Goose, Eurasian Wigeon, Gadwall (scarce), Common Teal, Mallard, Northern Pintail (scarce), Common Pochard, Tufted Duck, Common Goldeneye, Smew, Goosander, Ruddy Duck (scarce), Eurasian Sparrowhawk, Common Kestrel, Water Rail (occasional), Moorhen, Common Coot, European Golden Plover, Northern Lapwing, Common Snipe, Woodcock, Black-headed Gull, Common Gull, Herring Gull, Iceland Gull, Great Black-backed Gull, Stock Dove, Wood Pigeon, Collared Dove, Little Owl, Tawny Owl, Short-eared Owl (occasional), Common Kingfisher, Great Spotted Woodpecker, Lesser Spotted Woodpecker (scarce), Sky Lark, Grey Wagtail, Pied Wagtail, Dipper, Wren, Hedge Accentor, Robin, Blackbird, Fieldfare, Song Thrush, Redwing, Mistle Thrush, Goldcrest, Long-tailed Tit, Marsh Tit, Blue Tit, Great Tit, Eurasian Treecreeper, Magpie, Eurasian Jackdaw, Rook, Carrion Crow, Common Starling, House Sparrow, Tree Sparrow, Chaffinch, Brambling, Greenfinch, Goldfinch, Siskin, Common Redpoll, Bullfinch, Yellowhammer, Reed Bunting.

Spring and summer (April to August): Includes several species which also occur on passage in both spring and autumn. Common Cuckoo, Common Swift, Sand Martin, Barn Swallow, House Martin, Sedge Warbler, Lesser Whitethroat, Common Whitethroat, Garden Warbler, Blackcap, Chiffchaff, Willow Warbler, Spotted Flycatcher.

Spring and summer passage (April to early June and August to October): Common Shelduck, Northern Shoveler, Osprey, Oystercatcher, passage waders, Lesser Black-backed Gull, Common Tern, Arctic Tern, Black Tern, Meadow Pipit, Tree Pipit, Yellow Wagtail, Common Redstart, Whinchat, Northern Wheatear, Linnet.

Habitat

These two reservoirs, the western one of which is known locally as John of Gaunt's, are separated by a causeway and lie just 2 miles (3.2 km) east of Fewston Reservoir and the Washburn Valley. The surrounding land is mainly sheep pasture with dry-stone walls, plenty of gorse bushes and scattered mature oaks, ash and hawthorns, particularly along the northern edge of John of Gaunt's. There is a conifer plantation on the southern bank of the eastern reservoir and a larch plantation along its entire northern edge. John of Gaunt's is the best water for birds and has areas of emergent vegetation at the western end including water horsetail and amphibious bistort as well as marshy edges. During periods of dry weather in late summer and autumn, there may be small areas of exposed mud along the shorelines in this section.

Species

The area between the main road and the first reservoir is good for Eurasian Curlews which are common and breed here. The footpath along the northern edge of the two reservoirs is an excellent walk, particularly during the late spring and summer months. Stock Doves and Little Owls should be looked for in this part and also at the ruined farm building (see 'Access' below). The reservoirs have a pair of Great Crested Grebes, a few Mallards and several pairs of Tufted Ducks and Common Coots. A lone Grey Heron is often present. Common Sandpipers breed around the edges and a few non-breeding Black-headed Gulls are often present during the summer. Some passage waders call in, mainly during late July and September, especially if the water level is low and there are suitable muddy edges. Red-legged Partridge is a possibility in the adjacent pastures. Wood Pigeons are common in the conifers where Woodcocks can be seen 'roding' at dusk in the spring. Eurasian Sparrowhawks, Common Kestrels and both Green and Great Spotted Woodpeckers are resident.

The mature oaks, ash and hawthorns along the northern shore of John of Gaunt's, especially around the gullies and streams, are favoured by Common Redstarts and most of the common resident passerines (see 'Calendar' section). The site has attracted several rare birds including Pied-billed Grebe (1965), Slavonian Grebe (1992), Ferruginous Duck (1975/76), Long-billed Dowitcher (1976) and Golden Oriole (1992).

Timing

A visit at any time of the year can be worthwhile for the different groups of birds: April to early June for the residents and summer migrants; July to September for passage waders, waterfowl and passerines, and during the winter months (October to March) for waterfowl and winter thrushes.

Access

Beaver Dyke is situated south of the main A59 Harrogate to Skipton road, some 6 miles (9.5 km) west of Harrogate. The best approach, from either

Harrogate or Skipton, is along the A59 to where the B6451 Summerbridge to Otley road crosses, 7 miles (11.2 km) from Harrogate and 18 miles (28.8 km) from Skipton. Turn south here to Otley, proceed for just over 0.5 miles (0.9 km) and turn left onto a minor road. After 0.75 miles (1.2 km) look for a stile at a gateway on the right, marked with a waymarker arrow and a sign reading 'Dogs to be kept on lead', about 350 yards (320 m) before Willow House Farm. Park off the road on the grass verges near the stile.

The footpath passes between dry-stone walls through sheep pasture and meadows before coming to a fork after 700 yards (640 m). Take the left track, signed 'Pot Bridge and Beckwithshaw', which runs along the sloping sheep pasture above the first reservoir and passes a ruined farm building where one should look for Little Owl and Stock Dove. Just past here is a wooden seat overlooking the western part of the reservoir. Continue and come to a gate where a stream runs down a wooded gully, good for Common Redstarts. A little further along is the causeway between the two reservoirs, where one should stop to look over both areas of water and their banks before returning to the path to enter the larch plantation at the end of which the recommended walk ends, 1.25 miles (2 km) from the main road starting point.

Calendar

All year: Little Grebe, Grey Heron, Canada Goose, Mallard, Tufted Duck, Eurasian Sparrowhawk, Common Kestrel, Red-legged Partridge, Common Pheasant, Moorhen, Common Coot, Northern Lapwing, Stock Dove, Wood Pigeon, Little Owl, Tawny Owl, Green Woodpecker, Great Spotted Woodpecker, Wren, Robin, Hedge Accentor, Blackbird, Mistle Thrush, Long-tailed Tit, Coal Tit, Blue Tit, Great Tit, Eurasian Jay, Magpie, Eurasian Jackdaw, Rook, Carrion Crow, Common Starling, Chaffinch, Greenfinch, Linnet, Bullfinch.

Spring and summer (April to August): Great Crested Grebe, Eurasian Curlew, Common Sandpiper, Black-headed Gull (non-breeders), Sky Lark, Barn Swallow (also on passage), House Martin (also on passage), Meadow Pipit, Pied Wagtail, Common Redstart, Song Thrush, Willow Warbler, Goldcrest, Spotted Flycatcher.

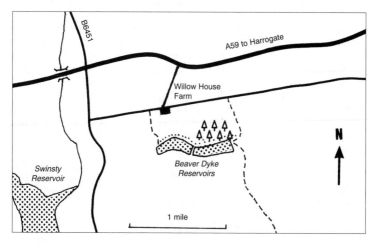

Spring and autumn passage (mainly autumn – April to early June and July to September): Any of the usual passage waders in small numbers only, depending on the presence of exposed mud and mainly during the autumn. Common, Arctic or Black Terns, hirundines.

Winter (October to March): Common Teal, Common Pochard, Common Goldeneye, Fieldfare, Redwing.

70 STUDLEY ROYAL PARK AND FOUNTAINS ABBEY

OS Landranger Map 99
Northallerton and Ripon

Habitat

Studley Park is owned by The National Trust and is an area of old and typical open parkland with large mature deciduous trees scattered over rolling grassland. It covers an area of 400 acres (162 ha) and is managed as a deer park where three species, Red, Sika and Fallow, can be seen. A lake near the northeastern entrance to the grounds of Fountains Abbey is bordered by open parkland with a large car parking area on the west side and by woodland on the east. A new visitor centre is situated close to the Abbey. The Abbey grounds, consisting of mature timber including many yew trees, running along both sides of the valley to Fountains Abbey, are excellent for birds. A large water garden with lawns covers much of the valley floor. The Abbey is situated in open grassland alongside the River Skell.

Species

The lake attracts Little and Great Crested Grebes and small numbers of waterfowl. The large trees in the adjacent parkland are home to Stock Doves, Eurasian Jackdaws and European Nuthatches. Titmice and finches are well represented and are attracted to feeders inside the entrance gate to Fountains Abbey grounds. Woodland passerines are the most interesting birds here and the mature timber and understorey is prime habitat for this group. The grounds are the best place in the region for Hawfinches, with gatherings of up to 50 birds being seen regularly during the winter months. Look for Grey Wagtails and Dippers on the River Skell by the Abbey which has many pairs of Eurasian Jackdaws and a population of feral pigeons. Nesting boxes in the woodland near the Abbey have breeding Pied Flycatchers. A pair of pinioned Whooper Swans breeds annually and often rears free-flying young.

Timing

A visit at any time of the year can be worthwhile, but spring (April to June) is perhaps the most rewarding time, when the birds are in song and easier to see. Hawfinches can be seen to advantage during the winter months, at which season the lake is better for waterfowl.

Male Pied Flycatcher

Access

Leave Ripon on the B6265 Pateley Bridge road and after 2 miles (3.2 km) turn left opposite a crucifix and pass through the village of Studley Roger to a cattle grid at the entrance to the deer park, 0.5 miles (0.8 km) from the main road. Drive through the park, passing through an archway by the deerherder's cottage, and continue to the parking area overlooking the lake (toilet facilities). The large trees above the car park are good for Hawfinches during the winter. It is possible to walk to Fountains Abbey from here; the entrance gate is just below the car park, from where a tarmac pathway leads through the grounds to the Abbey after about 1 mile (1.6 km). Look for Hawfinches in the large trees on both sides of the path anywhere from the entrance gate for the next 500 yards (460 m).

An alternative to walking to the Abbey through the grounds is to return to the main road through Studley Roger and turn left to reach a signed entrance on the left after 1 mile (1.6 km). Continue along this access road for a further 1 mile (1.6 km) to the visitor centre and car park. The Abbey is only a short walk from here. Entry into the deer park is free but a charge is made for cars (£1.50 in 1992 – refundable if a ticket to the Abbey grounds is subsequently bought and shown). The entrance charge to the Abbey Grounds for non National Trust members is between £2.50 and £3.50 depending on the season, payable at the Studley Park entrance gate or at the Visitor Centre.

Calendar

Spring and Summer (April to August): Little Grebe, Great Crested Grebe, Grey Heron, Greylag Goose, Canada Goose, Mallard, Tufted Duck, Eurasian Sparrowhawk, Common Kestrel, Common Pheasant, Moorhen, Common Coot, Common Sandpiper, Eurasian Curlew, Stock Dove, Wood Pigeon, Common Cuckoo, Tawny Owl, Common Swift, Common Kingfisher, Great Spotted Woodpecker, Lesser Spotted Woodpecker, Sand Martin, Barn Swallow, House Martin, Grey Wagtail, Pied Wagtail, Dipper,

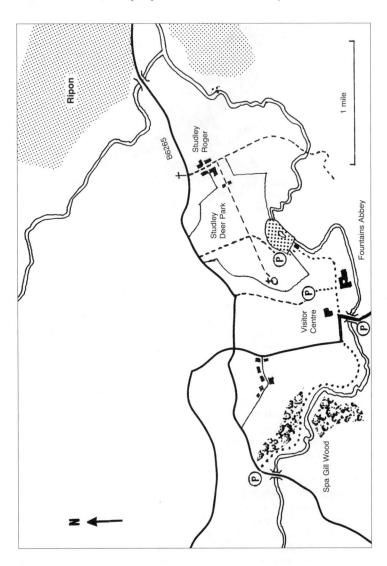

Common Redstart, Blackbird, Song Thrush, Mistle Thrush, Garden Warbler, Blackcap, Chiffchaff, Willow Warbler, Goldcrest, Spotted Flycatcher, Pied Flycatcher, Long-tailed Tit, Marsh Tit, Coal Tit, Blue Tit, Great Tit, European Nuthatch, Eurasian Treecreeper, Magpie, Eurasian Jackdaw, Rook Carrion Crow, Chaffinch, Greenfinch, Bullfinch, Hawfinch.

Autumn and winter (September to March): Common Teal, Common Pochard, Common Goldeneye, Black-headed Gull, Common Gull, Grey Wagtail, Fieldfare, Redwing, Brambling, Siskin and Common Redpoll, in addition to all the resident species including in the above section, which are present throughout the year.

71 SPA GILL WOOD, GRANTLEY

OS Landranger Map 99
Northallerton and Ripon

Habitat

This extensive strip of woodland runs along the sides of the River Skell upstream from Fountains Abbey. There are good stands of mature beech, alders, some plantations of conifers and several areas of wet boggy land beneath the riverside trees which attract many birds. The site is well worth a visit and is a most pleasant walk in spring and early summer.

Species

A very good place to see the woodland passerines, and many of those associated with this habitat are present. From mid-April, it is possible to see and hear Pied Flycatchers, Common Redstarts, most of the breeding *Sylvia* and *Phylloscopus* warblers including Wood Warblers which frequent the large beech trees just through the entrance gate. During the winter months, Green, Great and Lesser-Spotted Woodpeckers, European Nuthatches and Eurasian Treecreepers can all be found as well as Goldcrests, Long-tailed, Marsh, Coal, Blue and Great Tits.

Timing

Spring and early summer is the best time to visit the woods when the passerines are in full song and before the leaves are fully out. Visits during the winter months can also be interesting for the resident woodland species.

Access

To reach this site, leave Ripon on the B6265 road for Pateley Bridge and continue for 4 miles (6.4 km), passing the entrance to Studley Roger village after 1.5 miles (2.4 km), and come to a steep hill at a left bend. Before reaching the bottom of the hill, where a bridge crosses the River Skell, look for a narrow parking place on the roadside near a gateway on the right. The wide entrance gateway to the woods is on the opposite side of the road. The path leads through the woods alongside the river for 1.5 miles (2.4 km) to come out at Fountains Hall. The first 0.5 miles (0.8 km) is the best for woodland birds. The bridge on the main road is worth checking for Grey Wagtail and Dipper (see map for site 70).

Calendar

Spring and summer (April to August): Woodcock, Common Cuckoo, Common Redstart, Song Thrush, Lesser Whitethroat, Common Whitethroat, Garden Warbler, Blackcap, Wood Warbler, Chiffchaff, Willow Warbler, Spotted Flycatcher, Pied Flycatcher.

All year: Eurasian Sparrowhawk, Common Kestrel, Moorhen, Stock Dove, Wood Pigeon, Tawny Owl, Green, Great Spotted and Lesser Spotted Woodpeckers, Grey and Pied Wagtails, Wren, Hedge Accentor, Robin, Blackbird, Mistle Thrush, Goldcrest, Long-tailed, Marsh, Coal, Blue and Great Tits, European Nuthatch, Eurasian Treecreeper, Eurasian Jay, Magpie, Eurasian Jackdaw, Carrion Crow, Rook, Common Starling, Chaffinch, Greenfinch, Goldfinch, Siskin, Common Redpoll, Bullfinch.

72 COPGROVE LAKE

Habitat and Species

This small private lake is worth visiting if in the Knaresborough area. It has been recently dredged and a new earth bank along the western shore has temporarily eliminated the vegetation. A smaller area of open water under the bridge from the main lake has been much enlarged by the dredging and will be more attractive for dabbling ducks in due course. The eastern edge of the main lake is bordered by mature alder trees and there is a conifer plantation adjacent to the smaller area of water.

The lake usually holds some waterfowl during the autumn and winter including Common Teal, Mallard, Northern Shoveler, Eurasian Wigeon Common Pochard, Tufted Duck and Common Goldeneye. Little Grebe, Moorhen and Common Coot are resident. The surrounding trees are good for small passerines. There is a small collection of pinioned waterfowl.

Timing

A visit at any time between September and March can be worthwhile for ducks and also for passerines in the surrounding trees. Visits during the spring and summer months (April to August) can be very pleasant when both the waterbirds and the song birds are breeding. The light is good for viewing from the bridge at any time of day.

Access

Copgrove Lake is just 5 miles (8 km) north of Knaresborough and is reached by leaving the town on the A6055 Boroughbridge road. After leaving the built-up area (garage on the left) take a left fork after 0.5 miles (0.8 km) to Farnham. Turn right at a 'T' junction after 1 mile (1.6 km) then take the first left after 500 yards (460 m). After 1 mile (1.6 km) take a very sharp left turn at a junction and drop downhill to cross Occaney Beck. Continue to the next 'T' junction and turn left to reach the lake after 350 yards (320 m). Park just over the bridge on the right and view from this small lay-by or from the bridge.

Calendar

Autumn and winter (September to March): Includes several resident species which are present throughout the year. Little Grebe, Eurasian Wigeon, Common Teal, Mallard, Northern Shoveler, Common Pochard, Tufted Duck, Common Goldeneye, Common Pheasant, Moorhen, Common Coot, Stock Dove, Wood Pigeon, Great Spotted Woodpecker, Common Kingfisher, Wren, Hedge Accentor, Robin, Blackbird, Fieldfare, Redwing, Mistle Thrush, Long-tailed Tit, Marsh Tit, Coal Tit, Blue Tit, Great Tit, Eurasian Treecreeper, Magpie, Eurasian Jackdaw, Rook, Carrion Crow, Common Starling, Chaffinch, Siskin, Common Redpoll.

Spring and early summer (April to June): Common Cuckoo, Sand Martin, Barn Swallow, Song Thrush, Blackcap, Chiffchaff, Willow Warbler, Spotted Flycatcher, Goldfinch, Reed Bunting.

73 HAY-A-PARK GRAVEL PIT, KNARESBOROUGH

OS Landranger
Map 104
Leeds and Bradford

Habitat

Hay-a-Park is a disused gravel pit on the outskirts of Knaresborough and comprises a large area of open deep water at the northern end and a series of shallow reed-fringed lagoons at the southern end. The surrounding area to the north and east is mainly grazing land and rough grassland with hawthorn hedges and some mature trees, and that to the south and west is the built-up suburbs of the town. The banks of the main water are open with muddy or rocky shorelines.

Species

Hay-a-Park has become one of the most popular waters for Goosanders in Yorkshire and gatherings of up to 150 birds are regularly seen during the winter months. Common Pochards and Tufted Ducks are also common and a few Common Goldeneyes are usually present in winter when an occasional Red-breasted Merganser may appear.

A large flock of Canada and Greylag Geese is usually present and often attracts other species of geese such as Bean, Pink-footed, Lesser Snow and Barnacle, the last two species being of feral origin. Great Crested and Little Grebes breed and any one of the rarer grebes and divers may turn up during the non-breeding season.

The common waders pass through during spring and autumn and less usual ones in recent years have included Kentish Plover and Purple Sandpiper. The rough grassland and willow scrub is good for Reed Buntings and Sedge Warblers and there is a small colony of Reed Warblers in the *Phragmites* beds at the southern end. An evening visit could produce Water Rail. During the early spring passage period, flocks of Oystercatchers occur and Common Shelducks are regular visitors. A few Great

Male Goosander

215

Cormorants frequent the open water in autumn and winter and there is always the chance of seeing the rarer waterfowl. In recent years, less usual birds have included Black-throated Diver, Black-necked Grebe, Great Bittern, Greater Scaup, Bearded Tit and Penduline Tit. An occasional pair of Common Terns stays in the area during the summer months but rarely breeds here. Common, Arctic and Black Terns appear on passage when easterly winds bring them across country and an occasional Osprey passes through in the spring.

A resident population of mixed feral ducks and geese near a small island on the west side often attracts the wild waterfowl which then allow a close approach.

Timing

Early morning and evening are the best times to visit. The shoreline is subject to disturbance by anglers and dog walkers but they do not disturb the waterfowl on the open water. The Goosander numbers build up during the late afternoon in winter and the gulls assemble at this time. Visits at any time of the year can be of interest but obviously spring, autumn and winter are the most productive.

Access

To reach the gravel pit, leave Knaresborough on the A59 main York road and turn left at traffic lights at the bottom of the first hill as you leave the town, into Chain Lane. Continue for 0.5 miles (0.8 km) and turn right at the junction (parade of shops on the left) into Park Lane. Proceed for 300 yards (275 m) and park on the right just before a railway bridge or on the left of the road 150 yards (135 m) beyond the bridge. Enter the area at a fence beside a metal gate and walk along the obvious paths which circle the lagoons and the open water beyond.

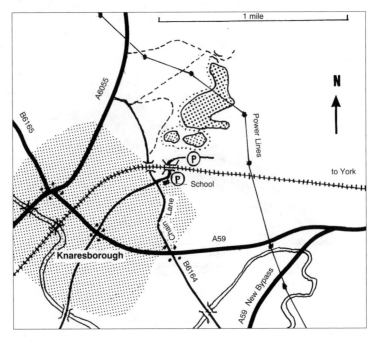

Calendar

Winter (October to March): Great Crested Grebe, Little Grebe, Great Cormorant, Greylag Goose, Canada Goose, Snow Goose (occasional), Eurasian Wigeon, Gadwall (scarce), Common Teal, Mallard, Common Pochard (some non-breeders in summer also), Tufted Duck, Common Goldeneye, Red-breasted Merganser (occasional), Goosander, Water Rail, Moorhen, Common Coot, Black-headed Gull, Common Gull, Herring Gull, Great Black-backed Gull, Fieldfare, Redwing, Tree Sparrow.

Spring and autumn passage (March to June and August to September): Osprey, waders, Common Tern, Arctic Tern, Black Tern, Common Swift, Sand Martin, Barn Swallow, House Martin, Meadow Pipit, Yellow Wagtail, Pied Wagtail, Northern Wheatear.

Spring and summer (April to August – breeding): Great Crested Grebe, Little Grebe, Canada Goose, Mallard, Tufted Duck, Moorhen, Common Coot, Northern Lapwing (adjacent fields), Common Sandpiper, Pied Wagtail, Wren, Hedge Accentor, Robin, Blackbird, Song Thrush, Mistle Thrush, Sedge Warbler, Reed Warbler, Garden Warbler, Blackcap, Willow Warbler, Magpie, Common Starling, Tree Sparrow, Chaffinch, Greenfinch, Yellowhammer, Reed Bunting.

74 THE NIDD GORGE: BILTON BECK WOODS; SCOTTON BANKS; CONYNGHAM HALL

OS Landranger
Map 104
Leeds and Bradford

Habitat

The Nidd Gorge is a steep-sided, well wooded valley administered by the Harrogate Borough Council as a conservation area. The Woodland Trust owns Bilton Beck Woods and Rudding Bottoms, an area of 47 acres (19 ha) at the western end of the complex. The enterprise is known as 'the Nidd Gorge Project' and the part covered by this chapter stretches from the Harrogate suburb of Bilton at its western end, eastwards to Knaresborough, a distance of just over 3 miles (5 km).

The Gorge was formed at the end of the last ice age as the result of a once great lake finally breaching the retaining ice sheets, when the escaping torrent carved the gorge which was to become the course of the River Nidd. The river is shallow and stony for much of its course through the gorge and the banks are clad with mature, and also regenerating, deciduous timber and ample stands of larch, spruce and Scots pine. The land to the north is mainly farmland and the suburb of Bilton abuts the western end. There are many fine ancient beech trees in the grounds of Conyngham Hall at Knaresborough.

Species

The wooded slopes along the River Nidd, especially those in the Scotton Banks section, are an extremely pleasant place to walk and look for woodland birds. The river has occasional Goosanders, which may breed along the valley, and resident Grey Wagtails and Dippers which can be seen almost anywhere along the Gorge, especially at the weir in Bilton Beck Woods. The other resident passerines are well represented and once the summer migrants have arrived, from April onwards, the woods are alive with their combined songs. An early morning visit to Scotton Banks is recommended at this time.

Displaying Eurasian Sparrowhawks can be seen over the wooded slopes during the spring and Common Kestrels are usually in evidence throughout the year. Green, Great Spotted and Lesser Spotted Woodpeckers are resident and European Nuthatches can be seen, particularly around the Conyngham Hall grounds. During the late evenings in spring and early summer, 'roding' Woodcocks can be seen flying up and down the valley and Tawny Owls can be heard calling.

The woodland warblers include Lesser Whitethroat, Garden Warbler, Blackcap and Chiffchaff, with Common Whitethroats and Willow Warblers occurring in the scrub areas around the perimeter where Tree Pipits are sometimes present. Spotted Flycatchers, Marsh Tits, Coal Tits, Eurasian Treecreepers and Bullfinches can be seen almost anywhere and Wrens, Robins and Chaffinches, are very common. During the autumn and winter months there is a chance of seeing one or two Hawfinches and small flocks of Bramblings around the large beech trees in Conyngham Hall grounds.

Timing

The best period to visit this area is during late April, May and June when the songbirds are at their best. Early mornings can be most profitable, especially to hear the dawn chorus. The grounds of Conyngham Hall are very popular with tourists during the summer months and one should try to visit on weekdays if possible and early in the day. Winter can be productive when most of the resident birds are easy to see, including the woodpeckers, Grey Wagtails, European Nuthatches and Dippers.

Access

It is possible to walk along the whole length of the Gorge on the riverside footpaths but for the purpose of this guide, I have recommended three different access points which can be reached by car.

The first is at the western end adjacent to the Harrogate suburb of Bilton and is reached by leaving the A59 Skipton Road through Harrogate at The Dragon public house, into Bilton Lane. Continue for 0.75 miles (1.2 km) to the end of the built-up estate and come to a small car park on the right (free). A 'Nidd Gorge Project' sign fixed to a wooden fence on the opposite side of the road marks the entrance. Walk northwestwards along the disused railway track, with open grass fields on each side, for just over 0.5 miles (1 km) before reaching the old railway viaduct over the River Nidd. One can walk onto the viaduct but not proceed beyond it. This is a good vantage point from which to view downstream and over the wooded banks. The footpath leads to the right just before the viaduct and continues along the side of a field before entering Bilton Beck Woods and dropping down to the riverbank. Walk along this riverside path for just over 0.5 miles (1 km) to where Milner's Lane turns off to the right shortly after passing a weir, and returns through the fields to The Gardener's Arms pub, just 220 yards (200 m) from the car park. It is, however, worth continuing along the riverbank path for a further 0.5 miles (0.8 km) to Rudding Bottoms before returning along Milner's Lane. Total distance from the car park to the viaduct and through Bilton Beck Woods to Rudding Bottoms and back along Milner's Lane is about 2 miles (3.5 km).

The second walk leads from the B6165 Knaresborough to Ripley road. Starting in Knaresborough at the junctions of the A59, the A6055 and the B6165, take the last of these and after 1.5 miles (2.4 km) look for the electricity pylon wires over the road, beneath which turn left into the car park (information board). Walk into the woodland from here for 250 yards (220 m) where the track bears left and after a further 100 yards (90 m) there is a footbridge over the river. Depending on the time available, one can continue along the left bank riverside path which passes through very good woodland for 1.5 miles (2.4 km) to rejoin the main B6165 via Lands Lane, just over 1.25 miles (2 km) nearer to Knaresborough. Alternatively, one can cross the footbridge, stopping on the bridge to view the river and the wooded valley, to join the riverside path which leads in both directions, the one to the right leading eventually to Rudding Bottoms and Bilton Beck Woods after 1.25 miles (2 km); the one to the left follows a loop in the river course and climbs uphill to the top of the gorge from where there are splendid views over the area after about 0.5 miles (800 m).

The third, and much more compact area, is Conyngham Hall grounds comprising open fields alongside the well-wooded riverbanks. This very popular tourist site lies at the western edge of Knaresborough just off the A59 Knaresborough to Harrogate road. On leaving the town and before crossing over the river bridge, turn right just after a pelican crossing into the signed grounds and car park (pay machines). Park on the grass at the far end of the car park near the picnic tables and walk a short distance upstream to cross a footbridge, after which the path bears left and returns along the opposite bank to the main road bridge at The World's End public house, a distance of about 1 mile (1.6 km).

Calendar

This includes the woods, the adjacent land and the river at all three sites.

All year: Mallard, Eurasian Sparrowhawk, Common Kestrel, Common Pheasant, Moorhen, Stock Dove, Wood Pigeon, Collared Dove, Tawny Owl, Common Kingfisher, Green Woodpecker, Great Spotted Woodpecker, Lesser Spotted Woodpecker, Grey Wagtail, Pied Wagtail, Dipper, Wren, Hedge Accentor, Robin, Blackbird, Song Thrush, Mistle Thrush, Goldcrest, Long-tailed Tit, Marsh Tit, Coal Tit, Blue Tit, Great Tit, European Nuthatch, Eurasian Treecreeper, Eurasian Jay, Magpie, Eurasian Jackdaw, Rook, Carrion Crow, Common Starling, House Sparrow, Chaffinch, Greenfinch, Bullfinch, Hawfinch (Conyngham Hall), Yellowhammer.

Spring and summer (April to August): Goosander, Woodcock, Common Sandpiper, Common Cuckoo, Common Swift (feeding overhead), Sky Lark, Sand Martin, Barn Swallow, House Martin, Tree Pipit, Common Redstart (scarce), Lesser Whitethroat, Common Whitethroat, Garden Warbler, Blackcap, Chiffchaff, Willow Warbler, Spotted Flycatcher, Goldfinch, Linnet.

Winter (October to March): Fieldfare, Redwing, Brambling, Siskin, Common Redpoll.

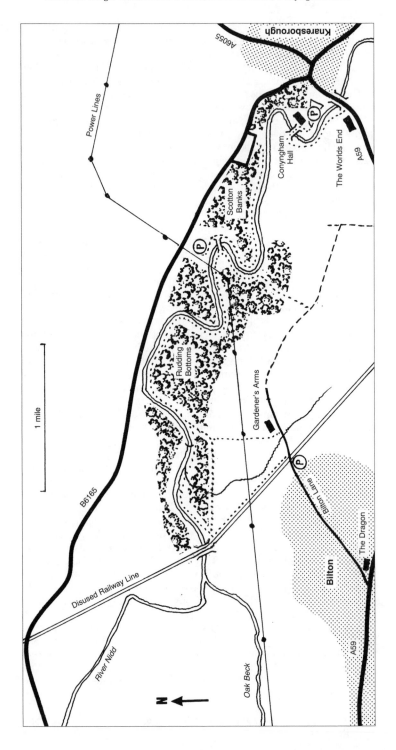

THE AIRE VALLEY

75 Fairburn Ings Nature Reserve
76 New Swillington Ings (Astley Lake)
77 Temple Newsam Park (Avenue Wood) and Skelton Lake
78 Allerton Bywater Lagoons and Lowther Lake
79 Mickletown Ings

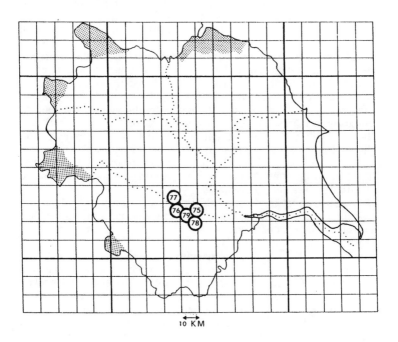

10 KM

75 FAIRBURN INGS NATURE RESERVE

Habitat

Conveniently situated alongside the A1 Motorway, Fairburn Ings is one of the best places for birdwatchers in the region. The area was first declared a Local Nature Reserve in 1968 and the RSPB became involved in 1976 with the appointment of a full-time warden. The reserve is now managed by the RSPB on behalf of the Leeds City Council.

The reserve consists of over 200 acres (81 ha) of open water, spoil heaps (tipped colliery waste), some areas of which are now clothed in deciduous trees, and low-lying wet pastureland. The wetlands are the result of mining subsidence which is ongoing and shallow lagoons at the northwestern end of the reserve are of fairly recent origin. An area of marshy ground for over a thousand years, subsequent drainage and the creation of a flood bank along the River Aire during the 18th Century, gradually reclaimed the land which was used for grazing stock. During the 19th Century, coal mining activities eventually led to subsidence and the land again became waterlogged. Permanent pools became established and gradually became deeper as others appeared along the valley. The land to the north of the reserve is mainly agricultural with some stands of mature deciduous timber.

Lying in a direct line between the Upper Humber Estuary and the Aire Gap through the Pennines, Fairburn Ings attracts many migrants as they cross the country in both directions.

Species

During the winter months, Fairburn is host to occasional divers and the rarer grebes. Great Crested and Little Grebes nest and Black-necked Grebe is an occasional summer visitor. Concentrations of waterfowl occur during the winter months and large numbers of Mallards, Common Teals, Tufted Ducks and Common Pochards can be seen annually with smaller numbers of Eurasian Wigeons, Gadwalls, Northern Pintails, Northern Shovelers and Common Goldeneyes. Small parties of Common Scoters often drop in during July and August, indicating a cross-country movement at that time. A few Garganeys are present during the summer months. The resident flock of Canada Geese and Mute Swans sometimes brings down other species of geese. Herds of Tundra and Whooper Swans appear annually during the winter and up to 100 Whoopers regularly occur. Several rare or unusual waterfowl have been recorded including American Wigeon, American Black Duck, Blue-winged Teal, Red-crested Pochard, Greater Scaup, Long-tailed Duck, Velvet Scoter and the three 'sawbills'. Ruddy Duck is now resident in small numbers and a pair of common Shelducks often stays to nest.

Strategically placed for cross-country migration, Fairburn has had its fair share of birds of prey including Common and Rough-legged Buzzards, Northern Goshawk, Honey-buzzard, Montagu's, Hen and Marsh Harriers, Red-footed Falcon, Lesser Kestrel and Peregrine Falcon whilst Osprey, Hobby and Merlin occur annually. Eurasian Sparrowhawk and Common Kestrel are resident.

Red-legged and Grey Partridges breed locally and the extensive lacustrine vegetation is good for winter Water Rails and resident Moorhens and Common Coots. Spotted Crakes have been recorded in several years, mainly during the autumn. During periods of spring and autumn migration, waders are well represented and the usual passage species can be seen, with rarer ones always a possibility.

A large gull roost during the winter months includes Black-headed, Common, Lesser Black-backed, Herring and Great Black-backed gulls with an occasional Iceland or Glaucous. Small parties of Kittiwakes sometimes pass through during the periods of adverse weather in both spring and autumn. Common, Arctic and Black Terns are regular visitors on migration and a small colony of Common Terns nests annually on the island in Main Bay. Roseate, Little and Sandwich Terns have also occurred.

Large concentrations of Common Swifts are a feature of the Ings between May and August with counts of up to several thousands in cool and damp conditions.

During the autumn, from late July to mid-September, Barn Swallows and Sand Martins gather in large numbers to roost in the reedbeds. Meadow Pipits and Yellow Wagtails pass through, mainly during the autumn, and roosts of the latter species usually develop in the reeds or other waterside vegetation. There is a good breeding population of Reed and Sedge Warblers and most of the common *Sylvia* warblers nest on the reserve. Both *Sylvia* and *Phylloscopus* warblers pass through from early April into May and at any time from July to mid-September. Reed Buntings are common breeding birds and counts of up to 100 in spring doubtless include some passage birds. A few pairs of Corn Buntings breed in the area and small numbers sometimes roost in the reedbeds during the early months of the year.

Over 260 species have been recorded on the reserve with an annual total of around 170 including 65 regular breeding species.

Timing

A visit at any time of year can be worthwhile for birds of the particular season. Winter can be exceptionally good for waterfowl, and both spring and autumn are good for passage waders, terns and migrant passerines. May and June are interesting for the breeding species and there is always the chance of seeing a southern vagrant at this time. Viewing from the road along the northern edge of the reserve can be difficult due to the light conditions, unless there is cloud cover. The three hides along the spoil heaps on the south side are better for light at any season.

Access

Fairburn Ings is adjacent to the A1 Motorway and lies some 4 miles (6.4 km) north of the A1/M62 junction. Approaching from the south, bear left into Fairburn village and come to the Cut Road parking area on the left in Caudle Hill. Approaching from the north, leave the motorway, signed 'Fairburn ¼', and cross over the motorway bridge into the village. Turn right immediately past the Waggon and Horses public house into Gauk Street (signed 'Castleford') and turn right at a 'T' junction down Caudle Hill to reach the Cut Road parking area after 100 yards (91 m). From this car park, walk down Cut Road and along 'The Cut', a lane bordered by large and mature hawthorns, good for warblers in spring and autumn. One can view the open water of Village Bay from here; a good area for

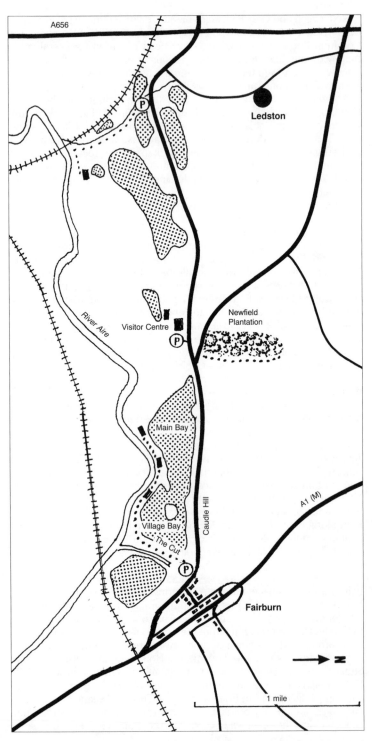

A656

Ledston

River Aire

Visitor Centre

Newfield
Plantation

Main Bay

Caudle Hill

A1 (M)

Village Bay

The Cut

Fairburn

N

1 mile

waterfowl and passage terns. The track continues to the right along the spoil heaps on the south side, to three hides overlooking an island and the Main Bay. The light is best from this side.

Returning to the car park, proceed along the road and stop at the swan-feeding lay-by after 1 mile (1.6 km). View the open Main Bay from here. The visitor centre is 0.5 miles (0.8 km) further along the road on the left (keep left at a fork in the road). From the visitor centre, one can walk to The Pickup Hide, overlooking a shallow scrape, good for waterfowl and waders. A boardwalk to this hide and also circling the adjacent marshy area is designed to accommodate wheelchair users. One mile (1.6 km) further along the road are some shallow reed-fringed lagoons on the right, also good for waterfowl and waders, especially during the autumn. A foot-path from a third parking area on the left at the western end of the reserve, 0.5 miles (0.8 km) from the start of these shallow pools, leads to a hide overlooking a small lagoon. A footpath along the eastern edge of New-field Plantation is reached by bearing right at the fork just before the vis-itor centre (signed Ledston and Kippax). The plantation is worth checking for woodland species.

Leaflets with a map of the Reserve are available at the visitor centre.

Calendar

Spring and summer (April to August – breeding): Includes several resident species which are present throughout the year. Mute Swan, Canada Goose, Common Shelduck, Mallard, Gadwall, Garganey (scarce), Com-mon Pochard, Tufted Duck, Eurasian Sparrowhawk, Common Kestrel, Red-legged Partridge, Grey Partridge, Water Rail (elusive), Moorhen, Common Coot, Little Ringed Plover, Northern Lapwing, Common Snipe, Common Redshank, Black-headed Gull, Common Tern, Collared Dove, Turtle Dove, Little Owl, Tawny Owl, Common Swift, Common Kingfisher, Sky Lark, Sand Martin, Barn Swallow, House Martin, Meadow Pipit, Yel-low Wagtail, Pied Wagtail, Wren, Hedge Accentor, Robin, Whinchat, Blackbird, Song Thrush, Mistle Thrush, Grasshopper Warbler (sporadic), Reed Warbler, Sedge Warbler, Blackcap, Garden Warbler, Common Whitethroat, Lesser Whitethroat, Willow Warbler, Long-tailed Tit, Willow Tit, Blue Tit, Great Tit, Magpie, Carrion Crow, Common Starling, House Sparrow, Tree Sparrow, Chaffinch, Greenfinch, Goldfinch, Linnet, Bullfinch, Yellowhammer, Reed Bunting, Corn Bunting.

Winter (October to March): Occasional divers and the rarer grebes, Grey Heron, Tundra Swan, Eurasian Wigeon, Common Teal, Northern Pintail, Common Goldeneye, Smew, Goosander, Merlin, European Golden Plover, Mediterranean Gull (occasional), Common Gull, Lesser Black-backed Gull, Herring Gull, Iceland and Glaucous Gulls (occasional), Great Black-backed Gull, Kittiwake (occasional during gales), Fieldfare, Redwing, Eurasian Jackdaw, Rook.

Spring and autumn passage (April to early June and July to October): In addi-tion to those migrants which breed on the Reserve: Common Shelduck, Northern Shoveler, Marsh Harrier, Hen Harrier, Northern Goshawk (occa-sional), Osprey, most of the passage waders with sub-rarities annually, occasional gale-blown skuas in autumn, Little Gull, Common Tern, Arctic Tern, Black Tern, occasional Roseate, Little and Sandwich Terns, Common Cuckoo, Common Swift, hirundines, Tree Pipit, Meadow Pipit, Yellow Wag-tail, Pied Wagtail, Common Redstart, Whinchat, Northern Wheatear.

Habitat

The sheet of open shallow floodwater known as Astley Lake is part of the old Swillington Ings, an area of slag heaps and subsidence flashes, lying to the south of the now deserted village of Astley, and favoured by bird-watchers since the 1940s. It has changed markedly over the years and most of the old and established lagoons have gone, but part of the western area, wherein lies the new lake, was regraded and developed as a reserve by British Coal in 1987.

The gently sloping banks are relatively bare save for some areas of *Juncus* rushes and there are 14 small islets of varying character, designed to attract different groups of birds; some are suitable for breeding Common Terns, Moorhens and Common Coots, others are ideal for loafing water-fowl and waders and all offer food and some shelter for many species. Immediately to the west are two areas of water known as Park Lake and Oxbow Lake. The banks of the River Aire, which runs eastwards in front of the hide, are mainly open grass with some willow bushes. There is a copse of alder and birch, known as Fleet Plantation, just upstream from the hide. To the northwest of Astley Lake is a large area of mature decid-uous timber, part of Swillington Park.

Species

Being part of the large complex of subsidence flashes and lakes along the Aire Valley, New Swillington Ings is an excellent place for birds. Both Little and Great Crested Grebes breed, the latter species often reaching double figures during the spring. During the 1940s, several pairs of Black-necked Grebes nested at the old Swillington Ings along Astley Lane and occasional birds pass through today; there were three in full summer plumage in June 1992. Great Cormorants are becoming relatively numer-ous along the valley and are present almost daily throughout the year, numbers peaking at between 20 and 30 birds during the winter months. A few Grey Herons are usually present. A pair or two of Mute Swans breed annually and both Tundra and Whooper Swans call in during the autumn and winter months. Small flocks of Greylag Geese are sometimes present and Canada Geese are resident and breed at Astley Lake. A few Common Shelducks nest and some are usually present throughout the year.

Eurasian Wigeons frequent the area during the winter months and their numbers often reach between 200 and 400 birds. Most of the usual water-fowl can be seen during the winter including the following, with some approximate recent maxima in brackets; Gadwall (140), Common Teal (300), Mallard (200), Northern Pintail (10), Northern Shoveler (150), Common Pochard (400), Tufted Duck (500), Common Goldeneye (100), Goosander (30) and Ruddy Duck (155 at the now drained St Aidan's in February 1991, the county's largest gathering). Rarer ones have been Ring-necked Duck (1991), Ferruginous Duck (1991), Common Scoter (small numbers occasionally), Smew and Red-breasted Merganser. Occa-sional Garganeys are seen in spring and autumn. Eurasian Sparrowhawk and Common Kestrel are resident breeding species and Merlin is seen

Great Ringed Plover

fairly regularly during the autumn and winter months. There are a few records of more unusual birds of prey each year, including Common Buzzard, Osprey, Hobby and Peregrine Falcon.

Both Red-legged and Grey Partridges can be seen around the lakes. An occasional Water Rail is heard during the winter months and Moorhens and Common Coots are common residents, flocks of the latter species often numbering between 100 and 150 birds during the late autumn. During the peak spring and autumn migration seasons, small numbers of waders pass along the Aire Valley and are well represented at New Swillington. Most of the regular species occur including Little and Great Ringed Plovers, Grey Plover, Red Knot, Sanderling, Little Stint, Dunlin, Ruff, Black-tailed and Bar-tailed Godwits, Whimbrel, Eurasian Curlew, Spotted Redshank, Common Redshank, Common Greenshank, Green Sandpiper, Wood Sandpiper, Common Sandpiper and Turnstone. Rarer ones in recent years have been Temminck's Stint, Pectoral Sandpiper and Spotted Sandpiper.

Occasional Little Gulls occur with passage Common, Arctic and Black Terns during late April to May. Up to four pairs of Common Terns have stayed to breed on the small islets at Astley Lake in recent years and a few Sandwich Terns have been seen, usually during April and May.

Large numbers of Common Swifts hawk for insects over the water during late May and June, and again in early August before their main departure. Common Kingfisher is seen regularly and Green Woodpecker is a possibility around Fleet Plantation. Sand Martins are common over Astley Lake during late April and again in late July and August, their numbers varying with the weather and the particular season. Migrant Meadow Pipits, Yellow Wagtails and Pied Wagtails, including some 'White' Wagtails, are usually present during the spring and autumn seasons and Water Pipits have become regular visitors during March each year. Northern Wheatears find the open ground to their liking and some pass through each year during April and May, the later ones being on their way to breeding grounds beyond the British Isles.

A few Sedge and Reed Warblers can be seen in the area, usually around Fleet Lane Pond, and Willow Warblers breed in Fleet Plantation. Up to 120 Carrion Crows gather around Astley Lake in the winter evenings, prior to going to roost. Finches are fairly numerous with Chaffinches, Greenfinches and Goldfinches being the most common. Siskins and Common Redpolls are also present in small numbers during the autumn and winter months. Yellowhammers and Reed Buntings breed in the area.

Timing

The periods March to early June and late July to October are best for the largest number of species when the passage migrants augment the numbers of resident birds. The hide faces north and the light is therefore good throughout the day. Winter visits will always provide good numbers of waterfowl and some resident waders and it is certainly worth calling in during the winter afternoons to witness the gulls assembling to roost.

Access

Travelling south on the A1, take the A642 to Wakefield, 8 miles (12.8 km) south of Wetherby. Continue through Garforth and Swillington, cross over the River Aire and pass under a railway bridge on entering Oulton. Before the road bears to the right in the centre of the town, look for Fleet Lane on the left just past Kwik-Save Supermarket and opposite the Old Masons Arms public house. This road passes under a narrow railway bridge and then over the Aire and Calder Canal before reaching the hide and car park adjacent to the Bayford Oil Terminal after 1.25 miles (2 km). The stilted hide is set on the south bank of the River Aire and overlooks the river and the lake beyond. A telescope is recommended. A footpath runs along the banks of the river and one can walk westwards to Fleet Plantation, or eastwards to Fleet Lane Pond and Lemonroyd Lock.

The hide is managed on behalf of British Coal by the New Swillington Ings Bird Group and is open to the public at weekends and on bank holidays. It is kept locked at other times but the lock combination is available to bona fide visiting birdwatchers and will be given on request by any members on site, or on application to the Secretary, Peter Griffin, 4 Fleet Lane, Oulton, LS26 8HX. At the time of writing, there is no official access to the north side of the river but British Coal intend to reopen a public footpath around the lakes which, unfortunately, may cause disturbance to the waterbirds. Visitors are therefore asked to keep to the south side of the river and view from the hide and the riverbanks. Please do not enter the lake area from the north.

Calendar

All year: Little Grebe, Great Crested Grebe, Great Cormorant, Grey Heron, Mute Swan, Canada Goose, Common Shelduck, Gadwall, Common Teal, Mallard, Northern Shoveler, Common Pochard, Tufted Duck, Ruddy Duck, Eurasian Sparrowhawk, Common Kestrel, Red-legged Partridge, Grey Partridge, Common Pheasant, Moorhen, Common Coot, Northern Lapwing, Black-headed Gull, Stock Dove, Wood Pigeon, Collared Dove, Common Kingfisher, Green Woodpecker, Sky Lark, Meadow Pipit, Grey Wagtail, Pied Wagtail, Wren, Hedge Accentor, Robin, Blackbird, Song Thrush, Mistle Thrush, Long-tailed Tit, Willow Tit, Blue Tit, Great Tit, Eurasian Jay, Magpie, Eurasian Jackdaw, Carrion Crow, Common Starling, Tree Sparrow, Chaffinch, Greenfinch, Goldfinch, Bullfinch, Yellowhammer, Reed Bunting.

Summer (late March to August): Common Swift, Yellow Wagtail, Sedge Warbler, Reed Warbler, Willow Warbler, Linnet.

Spring and autumn passage (late March to early June and late July to October): Black-necked Grebe (occasional), Garganey, Osprey, Merlin

228

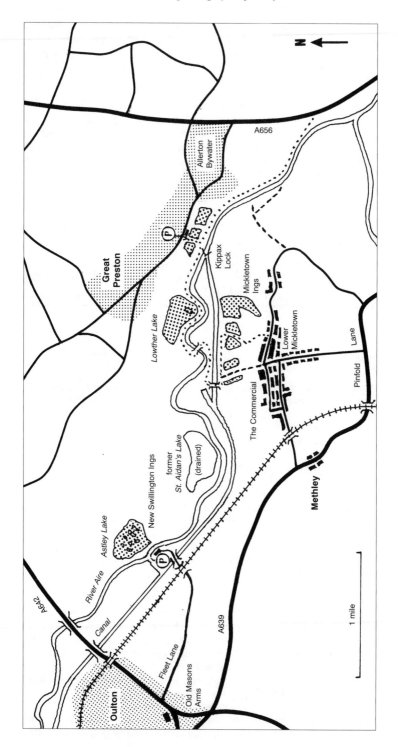

(in winter also), Hobby, most of the usual passage waders (see 'Species' section), Little Gull, Lesser Black-backed Gull, Common Tern, Arctic Tern, Black Tern, Sandwich Tern (occasional), Turtle Dove, Common Cuckoo, Sand Martin (also breeds), Barn Swallow, House Martin, Yellow Wagtail, Pied Wagtail (some 'Whites', annually), Spotted Flycatcher.

Winter (October to March): Tundra Swan, Whooper Swan, Eurasian Wigeon, Northern Pintail, Common Goldeneye, Goosander, Peregrine Falcon, Water Rail, European Golden Plover, Common Snipe, Common Gull, Herring Gull, Iceland Gull, Glaucous Gull, Great Black-backed Gull, Water Pipit (almost annual in March), Fieldfare, Redwing, Goldcrest, Siskin, Common Redpoll.

77 TEMPLE NEWSAM PARK (AVENUE WOOD) AND SKELTON LAKE

OS Landranger
Map 104
Leeds and Bradford

Habitat

Avenue Wood stretches for 1 mile (1.6 km) westwards from the access road and is an excellent place for woodland birds. The main tree species are oak and beech with some silver birch and a mixture of other traditional species with a good understorey. The wood is surrounded in the main by agricultural land.

Skelton Lake is a large shallow lake lying some 2 miles (3.2 km) southwest of Avenue Wood. It is set in a shallow basin amongst open grassland and is bordered by the River Aire on its southern edge and by various industrial complexes to the north. Many saplings have been planted around the north and west edges, but, at the moment, the shallow lake edges are completely open and there are six islands. A hardcore road circles the lake from which very good views can be had of the whole area, especially from an elevated section near a small plantation at the northeast corner.

Species

Avenue wood is very good for woodland birds and most of those associated with this habitat can be seen. Both Stock Doves and Wood Pigeons breed, the latter species being numerous during the winter months. Tawny Owls are resident and can be heard calling, mainly during the late autumn and early spring. All three species of woodpecker occur, Great Spotted being the most numerous and Lesser Spotted being seen most regularly during the early months of the year. During the late spring and summer months, once the migrants are settled in, one should walk the narrow pathways through the wood which are good for songbirds including Garden Warblers, Blackcaps, Chiffchaffs, Willow Warblers, Spotted

Flycatchers and all the common resident species. The titmice can be numerous, especially during the autumn and winter months when flocks of Long-tailed, Blue and Great Tits are regularly present. Coal Tits are seen occasionally. European Nuthatches and Eurasian Treecreepers are typical birds, albeit in small numbers, and can be seen to advantage during the winter months.

Skelton Lake is an excellent place for waterbirds with breeding Great Crested Grebes and most of the usual ducks being present at the appropriate season. Common Pochards and Tufted Ducks occur in good numbers during the winter months and also to a lesser degree during the summer. Ruddy Ducks are now regularly present. Other species which can be seen in the autumn and winter months include Little Grebe, Common Goldeneye, Goosander, Mallard, Common Teal and Eurasian Wigeon with Northern Pintails, Northern Shovelers and Gadwalls occurring in smaller numbers. Smew has been recorded. Large assemblies of Common Coots are a feature of the autumn and winter months and some stay to nest. Several pairs of Mute Swans are resident and small parties of Whooper Swans sometimes drop in during the late autumn and winter. Small flocks of Greylag and Canada Geese are regularly present and sometimes attract other species of geese. Large numbers of gulls frequent the site in winter and may include one of the 'white-winged' species. Several pairs of Common Terns nest on the islands and can be seen to advantage from the road along the southern edge as they pass low overhead to fish in the River Aire. At times of passage, particularly in May, migrating Common Terns and a few Arctic Terns sometimes appear over the water to feed before continuing their journey, and Black Terns may appear similarly, particularly with easterly winds, their stay often being of brief duration before moving on.

The shallow edges are very good for passing waders and all the usual species can be expected and regularly occur, mainly during July to September. Great and Little Ringed Plovers, Northern Lapwings, Common Redshanks and Common Sandpipers nest around the lake. A solitary Grey Heron may be seen and the potential for any vagrant species is great: a Pied-billed Grebe occurred in June 1997. Common Kestrel is resident and Eurasian Sparrowhawk is sometimes seen flying over. During the spring and autumn passage periods, especially if the weather is cold and damp, large numbers of Common Swifts and hirundines may gather to feed low over the water. Common Whitethroats are relatively numerous in the areas of scrub, Blackcaps breed in the small plantation and Sedge Warblers nest in the thick vegetation, mainly along the banks of the River Aire. Several pairs of Sky Larks and a few pairs of Meadow Pipits nest in the grassland. Linnets are common, and during the late summer and autumn, flocks of Greenfinches and Goldfinches join them to feed on the weed seeds.

Timing

As for all the woodland habitat, the best time to visit Avenue Wood is during the period of late April to June for the maximum number of species. Visits during the late autumn and winter, however, can be rewarding for woodpeckers, winter thrushes, titmice and finches.

Skelton Lake is worth a visit at any time of year, each season having its particular attractions. Early morning, or during the evenings, are often the best times for seeing migrating birds during the spring and autumn passage periods.

Access

To reach Avenue Wood, leave the A1 onto the A642 Wakefield road (as for new Swillington Ings) and after passing through Garforth and Swillington, look for the Bridge Farm Hotel on the right just before crossing the River Aire bridge. Turn sharp right here and continue for 1.25 miles (2 km) to reach the start of the woodland which runs alongside the road for 0.5 miles (0.8 km). There is good roadside parking along most of this length. Halfway along is the main entrance into the park at The Avenue, a wide park road with woodland on either side. There are also four access points through the roadside fence, two before and two after the main gate, from where paths run through the actual wood.

If approaching from the south via Oulton, pass under a railway bridge and over the canal and river bridges just before coming to the Bridge

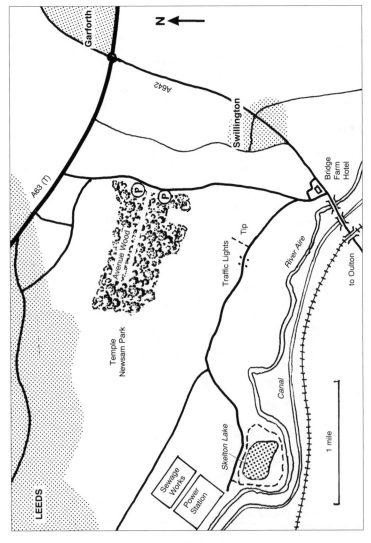

Farm Hotel turn-off as above. If approaching from Leeds, leave the ring road onto the A63 to Selby and take the right-hand exit from the first roundabout at Sainsbury's supermarket. The woods are on the right after 0.75 miles (1.2 km). Do not follow the sign for Temple Newsam House at the last roundabout on the ring road before reaching Austhorpe.

Skelton Lake is reached by approaching from the A1 via Garforth or from the south via Oulton on the A642 and taking the road alongside the Bridge Farm Hotel, as for Avenue Wood. After 0.5 miles (0.8 km) bear left (signed Newsam Green and Waste Disposal Site Only). Continue for just over 2 miles (3.2 km), passing through a set of traffic lights where the road narrows at a farm, and come to the lake entrance gate (unsigned) on the left. The lake is visible shortly before one reaches the gate. Drive into the site and along the hardcore road which circles the lake. The site is being developed as a permanent reserve and will eventually be signed. At the time of writing, major road works are in progress and the access details may change.

Calendar

This includes Avenue Wood and Skelton Lake.

All year: Great Crested Grebe, Great Cormorant, Grey Heron, Mute Swan, Greylag Goose, Canada Goose, Mallard, Common Pochard, Tufted Duck, Ruddy Duck, Eurasian Sparrowhawk, Common Kestrel, Moorhen, Common Coot, Northern Lapwing, Black-headed Gull, Stock Dove, Wood Pigeon, Collared Dove, Common Kingfisher, Sky Lark, Meadow Pipit, Pied Wagtail, Wren, Hedge Accentor, Robin, Blackbird, Song Thrush, Mistle Thrush, Blue Tit, Great Tit, European Nuthatch, Magpie, Eurasian Jackdaw, Carrion Crow, Common Starling, House Sparrow, Chaffinch, Greenfinch, Linnet, Reed Bunting.

Summer: Great Ringed Plover, Little Ringed Plover, Common Redshank, Common Sandpiper, Common Swift, Yellow Wagtail, Sedge Warbler, Common Whitethroat, Blackcap, Willow Warbler.

Spring and autumn passage (late March to early June and July to October): waders, Lesser Black-backed Gull, Common Tern, Arctic Tern, Black Tern, Turtle Dove, Common Cuckoo, Sand Martin, House Martin, Barn Swallow, Yellow Wagtail.

Winter: Occasional diver or rarer grebe, Whooper Swan, Eurasian Wigeon, Northern Pintail, Common Goldeneye, Goosander, Smew (occasional), Common Snipe, Common Gull, Herring Gull, Iceland or Glaucous Gull (occasional), Great Black-backed Gull, Fieldfare, Redwing.

78 ALLERTON BYWATER LAGOONS AND LOWTHER LAKE

OS Landranger
Maps 104 and 105
Leeds and Bradford/York

Habitat

The three shallow lagoons at Allerton Bywater are adjacent to the village and are set in open grassland between the road and the River Aire. The largest, eastern lagoon, has no trees around its margins and offers excellent uninterrupted views over the whole water area. The centre lagoon has some willows, and *Phalaris, Glyceria* and *Typha* at its western end, and the third, western lagoon, is surrounded by sallows and also has large areas of reeds and grasses. The two eastern lagoons are surrounded by raised grassy banks. The banks of the River Aire have some willows and the land across the river is mainly arable. The site is very compact and easy to work.

Lowther Lake is a fairly new, landscaped opencast coal site, just 0.5 miles (0.8 km) upstream from Allerton Bywater. There are increasing areas of reeds and sallows around the southern shoreline and the lake will become more attractive to birds as the vegetation increases.

Species

These lagoons are a very good place for seeing waterfowl at close range during the autumn and winter months. Most of the common species occur including Common Teal, Mallard, Tufted Duck, Common Pochard, Common Goldeneye and Ruddy Duck. Rare ones in recent years have been Ferruginous Duck and Ring-necked Duck. A few pairs of Little and Great Crested Grebes breed annually as do one or two pairs of Mute Swans, an occasional pair of Common Pochards and two or three pairs of Ruddy Ducks. Small numbers of passage waders call in during the spring and autumn migration seasons, but are regularly disturbed and quickly move on. It is best to visit early in the morning for these species. Sedge Warblers and Reed Buntings nest around the western end of the complex.

The surrounding grassy banks are ideal for migrant Meadow Pipits, Pied Wagtails and Yellow Wagtails during April and May and again in the autumn. Large numbers of Sand Martins, Barn Swallows and House Martins as well as Common Swifts feed over the water during the period of their first arrival in late April and early May, especially if the weather is cool or damp.

Lowther Lake has little emergent vegetation save for some reeds and sallow bushes along its southern shore and is disturbed by fishermen. Nevertheless, it is worth a visit, particularly during the spring. Great Crested Grebe numbers build up to around ten or 15 birds during February and March with one or two pairs staying to breed. A pair of Mute Swans nests annually and Sedge Warblers breed around the margins. Small numbers of the commoner waterfowl are usually present and there is always the chance of seeing an unusual species, the Lake having attracted Ferruginous Duck, Velvet Scoter and a passing Marsh Harrier.

Timing

A visit to this complex at any time of the year can be worthwhile, especially during the spring and autumn when migration is in progress. Waterfowl are always in evidence during the winter months, unless frozen off, and the resident species at Allerton Bywater Lagoons are relatively confiding, being used to the many local people who regularly walk along the banks. The light is good for viewing from the raised riverside path at any time of day. Early morning is the best time to visit for passage waders before they are disturbed.

Access

To reach this site, leave Castleford to the north on the A656 and after 0.75 miles (1.2 km) from the main roundabout at the northern edge of the town, take a turning to the left signed 'Allerton Bywater Colliery'. This road continues through the village, at the western end of which look for a Murco Garage opposite Allerton Grange Residential Home and turn left at the side of the garage onto a track signed 'Public Footpath', to a small car parking area behind the garage. The footpath leads from here through a gate and across a causeway between two of the three lakes to join a path which runs along the banks of the river.

If approaching from Fairburn Ings Reserve, drive along the northern side of the Ings to where the road joins the A656 and proceed straight across to Allerton Bywater. Continue for 0.5 miles (0.8 km) to a 'T' junction and turn right. The lagoons are now visible on the left before reaching the garage and car park after 550 yards (500 m). Walk upstream along the river bank for about 0.5 miles (0.8 km) to Lowther Lake. The high retaining bank can be seen from the lagoons, upstream from Kippax Lock. A footpath circles the lake. One can continue westwards along the river bank path from here, cross over a footbridge and pass the mining machinery to a second footbridge over the canal at the start of Mickletown Ings (see site 79). Total distance of the walk from Allerton Bywater to Mickletown Ings and back is approximately 3 miles (4.8 km) (see map for site 76).

Calendar

This includes both sites.

All year: Mute Swan, Canada Goose, Common Pochard, Tufted Duck, Ruddy Duck, Moorhen, Common Coot, Reed Bunting.

Spring and summer (April to August): Little Grebe, Great Crested Grebe, Northern Lapwing, Common Swift, Sedge Warbler.

Spring and autumn passage (April to early June and late July to October): Northern Shoveler, the usual passage waders in small numbers, Sand Martin, Barn Swallow, House Martin, Meadow Pipit, Pied Wagtail, Yellow Wagtail.

Winter (October to March): Great Cormorant, Grey Heron, Common Teal, Mallard, Common Goldeneye, Common Snipe.

79 MICKLETOWN INGS

OS Landranger Maps 104 and 105
Leeds and Bradford/York

Habitat

This area of ancient marshland, lying near to the confluence of the Rivers Aire and Calder, has changed much over the years due in part to drainage and the subsequent change of land character. The whole area is dealt with in great detail by Richard Brook in his admirable *Birds of the Aire Valley Wetlands* published in 1976. The complex comprises several shallow lagoons with extensive areas of *Juncus, Glyceria, Phalaris* and *Phragmites* reeds around the margins and also stands of thornscrub, willow and sallow. The site is botanically very rich and has been well surveyed and documented. It is bordered to the north by the Aire and Calder Canal and to the south by the village of Mickletown and the Lower Mickletown Road.

Species

Both Little and Great Crested Grebes nest on the Ings and up to three pairs of Mute Swans nest annually. Breeding ducks include a few pairs of Gadwalls, Northern Shovelers, Common Pochards, Tufted Ducks and several pairs of Ruddy Ducks. An occasional pair of Water Rails has nested and birds are often heard calling during the winter months but rarely seen. There is a small breeding colony of Black-headed Gulls. One or two pairs of Little Owls are resident in the vicinity and can sometimes be seen during the daytime. A few pairs of Yellow Wagtails and an occasional pair of Grasshopper Warblers breed in the area. Between ten and 20 pairs of Sedge Warblers and up to 20 pairs of Reed Warblers breed annually, the best place to see the latter species being the reed-filled lagoon along Pit Lane on the left-hand side of the track before reaching the canal bank.

During the autumn migration season, hirundines pass along the Aire Valley in good numbers and daily assemblies at Mickletown have included up to 1,500 Sand Martins and 5,000 Barn Swallows in recent years. Meadow Pipits, Pied Wagtails and Yellow Wagtails also pass through in both spring and autumn when their numbers may be large depending on their being grounded by adverse weather. The rough ground bordering the Ings is very suitable for autumn finch flocks which are a regular feature here. The waterfowl numbers build up in the autumn when assemblies of Common Teals often number 100 birds, Tufted Ducks up to 200 birds and Common Pochards up to 300. Scarce waterfowl in recent years have been Ferruginous Duck, Greater Scaup, Long-tailed Duck and Smew.

Moorhens and Common Coots are resident with numbers of the latter species increasing to 500 birds and more during the winter months. Great Cormorants are becoming regular visitors to the waters along the valley and some appear at Mickletown. There is very little marginal mud suitable for passage waders but a few always call in during the spring and autumn periods, including most of the regular passage species. Ruffs have reached double figures. An occasional Green Sandpiper can be seen during the winter when a few Common Snipe and Common Redshanks also occur. A solitary Jack Snipe may be flushed during March or April.

There has been a small roost of Long-eared Owls during recent winters and a lone Short-eared Owl may be seen hunting over the adjacent rough ground. Common, Arctic and Black Terns may appear on passage during April and May, usually on winds from the east, and especially with rain. The bushes and rough ground surrounding the Ings are good for breeding warblers including Common Whitethroat, Lesser Whitethroat, Blackcap and Willow Warbler. One or two pairs of Willow Tits are normally present in the summer.

Timing

This wetland area is best visited during April, May and June when the summer visitors are back in territory and the passage migrants are in evidence. Visits during the autumn and winter can also be worthwhile particularly for waterfowl and finch flocks.

Access

Mickletown Ings is reached by taking the A639 eastwards from Oulton, near Rothwell, or northwestwards from Castleford. Approaching from Rothwell, continue for 2 miles (3.2 km) and pass through the village of Methley. After a further 1 mile (1.6 km) turn left into Pinfold Lane and enter Lower Mickletown. Approaching from Castleford, cross the River Calder just after leaving the built-up area and come to Pinfold Lane after 0.75 miles (1.2 km). At the end of Pinfold Lane, turn left at the 'T' junction (phone box) and park near The Commercial pub. Walk down Pit Lane which is adjacent to the pub and come to the first lagoons on both sides of the track after 300 yards (275 m). Continue towards the new footbridge and, on reaching the canal bank, turn right to follow the canal for 500 yards (460 m) to a signed vehicle passing point from where a footpath leads to the right through the rough ground and passes over a causeway between two areas of water (there is no public access round the large eastern lagoon). This track eventually bears left and passes alongside ploughed land back to the village along the unsigned Cutler Lane, joining the main road opposite Ings Drive. Walk to the right for 300 yards (275 m) to reach The Commercial pub. This round trip takes in all the best habitats and is a very good walk during the spring and early summer.

Instead of returning to Mickletown village from the Ings, it is possible to walk back along the canal footpath to the new footbridge and cross over to the north side where the path continues over a second footbridge passing Lowther Lake and finally coming to Allerton Bywater lagoons, a distance of some 1.5 miles (2.4 km); see site 78.

On leaving Mickletown by car, continue eastwards through the village along Lower Mickletown Road to rejoin the main A639 Castleford road after a long loop of 1.5 miles (2.4 km); (see map for site 76).

Calendar

All year: Mute Swan, Red-legged Partridge, Grey Partridge, Water Rail, Moorhen, Common Coot, Black-headed Gull, Wood Pigeon, Collared Dove, Little Owl, Wren, Hedge Accentor, Robin, Blackbird, Willow Tit, Blue Tit, Great Tit, Magpie, Eurasian Jackdaw, Rook, Carrion Crow, Common Starling, House Sparrow, Tree Sparrow, Chaffinch, Greenfinch, Bullfinch, Yellowhammer, Reed Bunting.

Spring and summer (April to August): Little Grebe, Great Crested Grebe, Canada Goose, Gadwall, Garganey (occasional), Northern Shoveler,

Common Pochard, Tufted Duck, Ruddy Duck, Common Kestrel, Northern Lapwing, Common Cuckoo, Common Swift, Sky Lark, Yellow Wagtail, Grasshopper Warbler (sporadic), Sedge Warbler, Reed Warbler, Common Whitethroat, Lesser Whitethroat, Blackcap, Willow Warbler, Goldfinch. Most of these species also occur on passage in both spring and autumn.

Spring and autumn passage (April to early June and late July to October): Most of the regular passage waders in small numbers, Lesser Black-backed Gull, Common Tern, Arctic Tern, Black Tern, Sand Martin, Barn Swallow, House Martin, Meadow Pipit, Pied Wagtail, Whinchat, Northern Wheatear, Linnet.

Winter (October to March): Great Cormorant, Grey Heron, Common Teal, Mallard, Eurasian Sparrowhawk, Water Rail (sometimes breeds), Jack Snipe, Common Snipe, Green Sandpiper, Common Redshank, Common Gull, Herring Gull, Great Black-backed Gull, Long-eared Owl, Short-eared Owl, Fieldfare, Redwing.

THE LOWER DERWENT VALLEY

80 Moorlands Wood Reserve
81 Wheldrake Ings Lower Derwent Valley NNR
82 Wheldrake Wood (Black Plantation)
83 North Duffield Carrs, Aughton Ings and Bubwith Ings
84 Skipwith Common
85 Strensall Common
86 Bishop Wood, near Selby
87 Southfields Reservoirs
88 Carlton Towers Lake

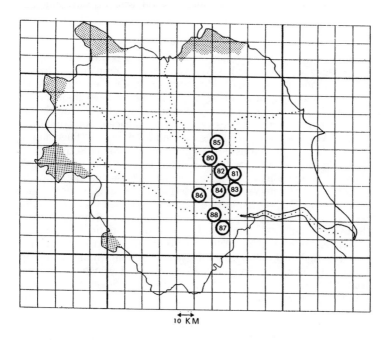

10 KM

Habitat

This 17-acre (6.8 ha) reserve, once a large ornamental garden, has been owned and administered by volunteers of the Yorkshire Wildlife Trust since 1955. It consists of well-maintained mature mixed woodland including many oaks, beech, birch, lime, chestnut, maples, rowan, cherry and several *acers* in addition to the conifers which include spruce, fir, pine, larch and hemlock. The understorey is mainly rhododendron and azaleas which attract many visitors to the Reserve during May and June. There are three small ponds within the wood, which is surrounded by open agricultural land.

Species

Visits throughout the year can be good when most of the resident woodland species are to be found. An occasional Grey Heron drops in to feed by the ponds and Common Moorhens are usually in their vicinity, although breed only occasionally. Eurasian Sparrowhawk frequents the area and regularly breeds in the wood as does Tawny Owl. Wood Pigeons are common and Stock Doves visit from the adjacent farmland. Great Spotted Woodpeckers can be heard, and seen, around their nesting holes. Wrens are numerous, along with Hedge Accentors, Robins, Blackbirds, Chaffinches and the titmice which include Long-tailed, Marsh, Coal, Blue and Great. European Nuthatch is scarce but Eurasian Treecreeper is usually recorded. Eurasian Jays are fairly common being very noisy and obvious during the summer when their young are on the wing, at which time family parties of titmice may be seen moving through the wood. Listen for Goldcrests around the coniferous trees.

From late April, summer visitors are Common Cuckoo, Common Swift (overhead), Barn Swallow (adjoining fields), Garden Warbler, Blackcap, Chiffchaff, Willow Warbler (very few) and Spotted Flycatcher. During the winter, Fieldfares and Redwings appear along with Siskins which can be sporadic in their occurrence.

Timing

The most productive period to visit this site is during April, May and June for the most species and the birdsong. Autumn and winter visits are worthwhile, however, for the resident woodland species.

Try to be in the wood as early as possible in the morning during the spring and early summer when the song is at its best. Viewing is easy from the wide footpaths.

Access

From the York ring-road, take the A19 Thirsk/Northallerton road and after 1 mile (1.6 km) turn right at The Blacksmith's Arms pub for Skelton. Pass through the village and after 2 miles (3.2 km), look for an open parking area at a wide verge on the left alongside the wood and just before the entrance gate. The Reserve is open daily and entry is free except during May and June when a small charge is made (including YWT members).

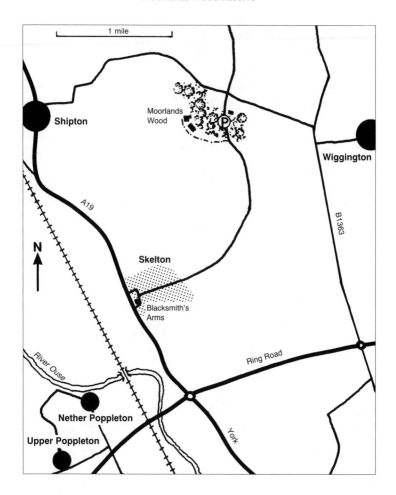

The woodland paths, being wide and well maintained, are suitable for wheelchairs.

Calendar

All year: Grey Heron (occasional), Eurasian Sparrowhawk, Common Kestrel, Stock Dove, Wood Pigeon, Tawny Owl, Great Spotted Woodpecker, Wren, Hedge Accentor, Robin, Blackbird, Song Thrush (scarcer in winter), Mistle Thrush, Goldcrest, Long-tailed Tit, Marsh Tit, Coal Tit, Blue Tit, Great Tit, European Nuthatch (scarce), Eurasian Treecreeper, Eurasian Jay, Magpie, Carrion Crow, Common Starling, Chaffinch, Greenfinch, Common Redpoll.

Spring and summer (April to August): Eurasian Curlew (adjoining fields), Common Cuckoo, Common Swift (overhead), Barn Swallow, Garden Warbler, Blackcap, Chiffchaff, Willow Warbler (very few), Spotted Flycatcher.

Winter (October to March): Fieldfare, Redwing, Siskin.

81 WHELDRAKE INGS LOWER DERWENT VALLEY NNR

OS Landranger Map 105
York

Habitat

This area is owned by the Yorkshire Wildlife Trust and forms a major part of the Lower Derwent Valley National Nature Reserve. It is one of the best areas for winter waterfowl in the region. The extensive water meadows lie in the widest part of the flood plain of the valley and are a scarce habitat owing to a traditional type of management based on hay-cropping and grazing with no use of chemicals. The botanically rich meadows receive a rich deposit of river silt from the annual inundations which vary in depth according to the autumn and winter rains; in very dry winters there may be no open floodwater along the valley.

The River Derwent is lined with mature crack willows and sallows and the banks are well vegetated with willowherbs, thistles and some *Typha*. Mature hawthorn hedges and thickets adjacent to the car parking area and a large area of rough ground upstream from the bridge, consisting in the main of hairy willowherb, creeping thistle and nettles, are good for passerines, especially warblers during the summer and finches in the autumn. A large sheet of open water in the centre of the reserve area is surrounded by trees and some reeds.

Species

Wheldrake Ings has much to offer the birdwatcher throughout the year. The large expanse of water meadows, overlooked by a hide, is home to several interesting species during the summer months. Controlled water levels ensure the correct conditions for breeding waterfowl and waders which include Mute Swan, Greylag Goose, Canada Goose, Common Shelduck, Eurasian Wigeon (few), Gadwall, Common Teal (few), Mallard, an occasional pair of Northern Pintails, Garganey (few), Northern Shoveler, Tufted Duck, Common Pochard, Ruddy Duck (rare), Northern Lapwing, Common Snipe, Eurasian Curlew and Common Redshank. Many species of passage waders occur in both spring and autumn with some lingering late into the spring, including a few Black-tailed Godwits and Ruffs. Moorhens and Common Coots are numerous and Water Rail is a possibility. Several pairs of Little Grebes breed and an occasional pair of Great Crested Grebes. Any one of the divers or one of the rarer grebes may turn up if the water level is high during the winter months and Black-necked Grebe occurs on passage almost every spring, a pair having stayed to nest in recent years. A few Great Cormorants occur each year and Grey Herons are regular visitors from a nearby breeding colony.

During the late autumn and winter months large numbers of waterfowl arrive to spend the winter on the Ings, their numbers depending on the severity of the weather and the water levels. Small numbers of both Tundra and Whooper Swans are present during most winters. Flocks of Eurasian Wigeons regularly number up to 5,000 birds with more on occasions, and the other regular species at this time, with some recent maxima in brackets, are as follows: Gadwall (50), Common Teal (4,500),

Black-tailed Godwits

Mallard (5,000), Northern Pintail (200), Northern Shoveler (250), Common Pochard (2,000), Tufted Duck (150), Common Goldeneye (30) and Goosander (30). Small parties of grey geese may call in for short periods during the autumn and winter; Bean, Pink-footed and White-fronted occurring almost annually.

A solitary Marsh Harrier may be seen passing through during spring or autumn and an occasional Hen Harrier occurs during the winter months. There is a fair chance of seeing Northern Goshawk in the area, mainly during the autumn and winter, and Eurasian Sparrowhawk is resident and common. Occasional Ospreys pass through during spring and autumn. Common Kestrel is resident and Merlin and Peregrine Falcon are sometimes seen during the winter. One or two Hobbies are recorded annually in late summer.

Red-legged and Grey Partridges are resident in the area. The large areas of lush grassland are perfect for Common Quails and one or two have been heard calling in recent years with breeding proved in 1989. In addition to the passage waders which find the area much to their liking, there are several wintering species, and these, with some approximate recent maxima in brackets, are as follows: European Golden Plover (6,000), Northern Lapwing (5,000), Dunlin (200), Ruff (50), Common Snipe, Eurasian Curlew (100) and Common Redshank (40).

Black-headed Gulls nest out on the marshes and large numbers assemble to roost during the winter months when up to 5,000 and more can be seen. Common, Herring and Great Black-backed Gulls also occur and their numbers are often large. Lesser Black-backed Gulls occur on passage in both spring and autumn, mainly the latter. During easterly winds, particularly with rain in April and May, passage terns may appear, mainly Common, with fewer Arctic and some Black. A few Little Gulls may also appear in these conditions. Large numbers of Wood Pigeons occur in the winter and Stock Doves are usually to be seen. Turtle Doves breed in the area. Barn Owls are scarce but the sighting of a hunting bird at dusk is always a possibility. Little Owls are resident and Short-eared Owl may be seen hunting over the Ings during the winter months.

During the spring and early summer, many Common Swifts feed over the meadows, or pass through in adverse weather, when their numbers can be impressive. Common Kingfisher breeds in the river banks and may be seen flying along the river course or across the Ings. The area is an excellent feeding place for hirundines during the spring and autumn migration periods when Sand Martins, Barn Swallows and House Martins all occur in large numbers. On 23rd August 1990, 300 Barn Swallows were present and their number increased next day to 20,000 during a thunder-storm; the majority quickly moved on. A few pairs occasionally breed in the hides. Meadow Pipits and Yellow Wagtails are typical passerines of the open grassland during the summer and many also pass on migration when Northern Wheatears also move through.

Warblers are well represented and the following species are present during the summer; some approximate numbers of pairs present in the area are given in brackets: Grasshopper Warbler (few), Sedge Warbler (up to 70 pairs), Reed Warbler (30 pairs), Lesser Whitethroat (few), Com-mon Whitethroat (20 pairs), Blackcap (fairly common) and Willow War-bler (60 pairs). The *Sylvia* and *Phylloscopus* warblers occur mainly in the trees and scrub along the rivercourse. The titmice can be seen well here, Long-tailed, Marsh, Willow, Blue and Great Tits all occurring throughout the year, mainly along the river. Autumn flocks of Chaffinches, Green-finches, Goldfinches and Linnets occur throughout the area and Yel-lowhammers, Reed Buntings and Corn Buntings are resident.

Some rare species recorded along the whole of the Lower Derwent Valley in more recent years have been Purple Heron (January), Eurasian Spoonbill (May), American Wigeon (May/June), American Golden Plover (April and July), Corn Crake (June and July), Common Crane (April and May; three birds in 1986), Stone Curlew (August), Pectoral Sandpiper (September), Red-necked Phalarope (August), Great Skua (April), Mediterranean Gull (February and April), Caspian Tern (May), European Bee-eater (May), Richard's Pipit (June) and Bearded Tit (November).

Timing

A visit at any time of the year can be worthwhile. Spring is good for breed-ing waterfowl and waders, as well as passage waders, passerines and the chance of a southern rarity. The summer is a relatively quiet period but there are always some interesting birds to be seen as well as a wealth of flowers. The best time is perhaps during the autumn when the hordes of waterfowl start to arrive, and when the migrants are moving through. Dur-ing the winter, depending on the severity of the weather, the numbers of swans and ducks can be spectacular.

Access

To reach Wheldrake Ings, leave the York ring road to the south onto the A19 Selby road. After exactly 1 mile (1.6 km) turn left to Wheldrake signed 'Wheldrake 4 and Thorganby 6½'. After 3.5 miles (5.6 km), enter the village of Wheldrake and continue straight on towards Thorganby. Having passed through Wheldrake, and following a sharp right bend, turn left after 0.5 miles (0.8 km) onto a tarmac track (unsigned). Look for two

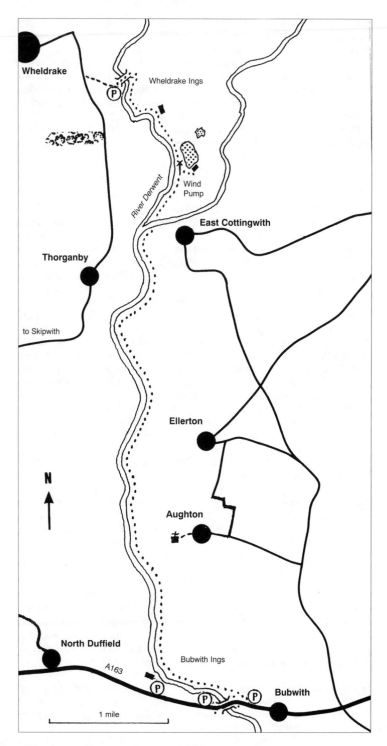

old stone gateposts with pointed tops. The car parking area is reached after 0.25 miles (0.4 km). Park here and walk across the bridge over the river and turn right over a stile. Please keep to the well marked riverside path which runs adjacent to the water meadows. There are four public hides, the first one, a little over 0.25 miles (0.5 km) from the car park has two levels and overlooks the main ings. The third hide is recommended and overlooks a large area of open water about 0.5 miles (0.8 km) further along the river bank to the left of a wind pump.

During the breeding season from 1st April to 30th June, access is restricted to Yorkshire Wildlife Trust members only who may be asked to show their membership cards.

Calendar

Winter (October to March): Includes many resident species which are present throughout the year. Occasional divers and the rarer grebes, Little Grebe, Great Crested Grebe, Great Cormorant, Grey Heron, Mute Swan, Tundra Swan, Whooper Swan, occasional grey geese, Greylag Goose, Canada Goose, Common Shelduck, Eurasian Wigeon, Gadwall, Common Teal, Mallard, Northern Pintail, Northern Shoveler, Common Pochard, Tufted Duck, an occasional sea duck, Common Goldeneye, Goosander, Ruddy Duck (scarce), Hen Harrier, Northern Goshawk, Eurasian Sparrowhawk, Common Kestrel, Merlin, Peregrine Falcon, Red-legged Partridge, Grey Partridge, Common Pheasant, Water Rail, Moorhen, Common Coot, European Golden Plover, Northern Lapwing, Dunlin, Ruff, Common Snipe, Eurasian Curlew, Common Redshank, Black-headed Gull, Common Gull, Lesser Black-backed Gull (scarce), Herring Gull, Great Black-backed Gull, Stock Dove, Wood Pigeon, Collared Dove, Barn Owl (scarce), Little Owl, Short-eared Owl, Common Kingfisher, Great Spotted Woodpecker, Sky Lark, Meadow Pipit, Pied Wagtail, Wren, Hedge Accentor, Robin, Blackbird, Fieldfare, Song Thrush (scarce), Redwing, Mistle Thrush, Long-tailed Tit, Marsh Tit, Willow Tit, Blue Tit, Great Tit, Magpie, Eurasian Jackdaw, Rook, Carrion Crow, Common Starling, House Sparrow, Tree Sparrow, Chaffinch, Brambling, Greenfinch, Goldfinch, Siskin, Linnet, Common Redpoll, Bullfinch, Yellowhammer, Reed Bunting, Corn Bunting.

Spring and summer (April to August): Includes several species which also occur on passage in both spring and autumn. Little Grebe, Great Crested Grebe (scarce), Grey Heron, Mute Swan, Greylag Goose, Canada Goose, Eurasian Wigeon (few pairs), Gadwall, Common Teal (very few pairs), Mallard, Garganey (few pairs), Northern Shoveler, Common Pochard (few pairs), Tufted Duck, Ruddy Duck (scarce), Eurasian Sparrowhawk, Common Kestrel, Red-legged Partridge, Grey Partridge, Common Quail (scarce), Common Pheasant, Water Rail (scarce), Moorhen, Common Coot, Northern Lapwing, Common Snipe, Eurasian Curlew, Common Redshank, Turtle Dove, Common Cuckoo, Common Swift, Sand Martin, Barn Swallow, House Martin, Yellow Wagtail, Grasshopper Warbler, Sedge Warbler, Reed Warbler, Lesser Whitethroat, Common Whitethroat, Garden Warbler, Blackcap, Willow Warbler, Spotted Flycatcher.

Spring and autumn passage (April to early June and late July to October): Marsh Harrier, Osprey, passage waders, Little Gull, Lesser Black-backed Gull, Common Tern, Arctic Tern, Black Tern, Whinchat, Northern Wheatear, Chiffchaff.

82 WHELDRAKE WOOD (BLACK PLANTATION)

OS Landranger
Map 105; York

Habitat
This plantation of Scots pine and spruce with scattered oaks and silver birch is surrounded by agricultural land and lies just 1.5 miles (2.4 km) northwest of the village of Wheldrake. It is worth combining with a visit to the Lower Derwent Valley, particularly during the spring and early summer. There is a Forest Enterprise car park from where a main ride and several tracks lead through the young forest.

Species
Although the number of species is not great in this specialised habitat, it is nevertheless a pleasant site during the spring and early summer and also in the autumn. Most of the commoner migrants which include Turtle Dove, Tree Pipit, Blackcap, Garden Warbler, Chiffchaff, Willow Warbler and Spotted Flycatcher.

Tawny Owl occurs in the area and may be heard at dusk. Long-eared Owl, although scarce, is a possibility, its mournful hoots in the early spring often being the only indication of its presence. Both Green and Great Spotted Woodpeckers are resident as is Eurasian Jay. During the autumn, Siskins and Common Redpolls should be present and Common Crossbills, although very sporadic in their occurrence, are a possibility.

Timing
As stated above, spring and early summer are the most productive periods to visit, and early morning and evening recommended.

Access
On entering the village of Wheldrake from the west, take the second road to the left, North Lane, continue through a housing estate for about 700 yards (550 m) and turn left into Broad Highway, a minor 'no through road' running through agriculture and signed for the village hall (just before the primary school). Continue for 1.5 miles (2.4 km), passing Hardmoor Farm and the Keeper's Cottage on the left before arriving at the Wheldrake Forest car park.

Calendar
This includes the surrounding agricultural land.

All year: Eurasian Sparrowhawk, Common Kestrel, Red-legged Partridge, Grey Partridge, Common Pheasant, Northern Lapwing, Stock Dove, Wood Pigeon, Tawny Owl, Long-eared Owl (scarce), Green Woodpecker, Great Spotted Woodpecker, Wren, Hedge Accentor, Robin, Blackbird, Mistle Thrush, Goldcrest, Coal Tit, Blue Tit, Great Tit, Eurasian Treecreeper, Eurasian Jay, Magpie, Eurasian Jackdaw, Rook, Carrion Crow, Common Starling, Chaffinch, Greenfinch, Siskin, Common Redpoll, Bullfinch, Yellowhammer.

Spring and summer (April to September): Turtle Dove, Common Cuckoo,

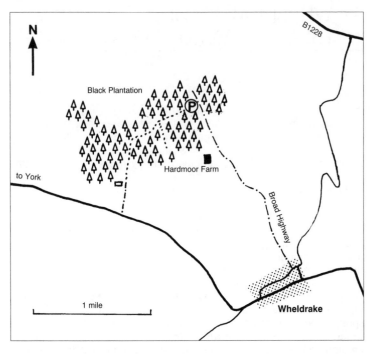

Tree Pipit, Song Thrush, Blackcap, Garden Warbler, Chiffchaff, Willow Warbler, Spotted Flycatcher, Linnet, Goldfinch.

Winter (October to March): Fieldfare, Redwing, Brambling.

83 NORTH DUFFIELD CARRS, AUGHTON INGS AND BUBWITH INGS: LOWER DERWENT VALLEY NNR

OS Landranger
Map 105
York

Habitat

This area comprises a series of flood-meadows on the east bank of the River Derwent between the villages of Aughton and Bubwith, to the south of Wheldrake Ings. It differs mainly from that area in the fact that there are no controls over the water levels and only at times of severe flooding in autumn and winter does the water inundate the meadows which are grazed and cut for hay during the summer. A hide overlooks a large pool with some *Typha* on the western bank of the river adjacent to the A19 York to Selby road.

Species

During the winter months, if the floodwater covers the area, the wild swans and other waterfowl can be seen to advantage on Aughton Ings. The flood-water is open and thus attractive to swans and diving ducks and there is more chance to see a rarity such as the occasional diver or one of the rarer grebes and diving ducks. With the exception of some of the breeding waterfowl and passerines the Bubwith area has basically the same species list as Wheldrake. Northern Lapwings, Common Snipe, Eurasian Curlews and Common Redshanks breed in the meadows during the summer months. A Common Crane appeared in May 1984 and three in May 1986.

Timing

Autumn and winter are the best times to visit the area but the numbers of waterfowl depend entirely on the presence of floodwater. Spring and summer can be very pleasant, especially for seeing the displaying waders. The hide faces northeast and the light is good for viewing at any time of the day.

Access

This area is reached by turning left on leaving Wheldrake Ings car park and proceeding to the village of Skipwith. Look for the Hare and Hounds pub, just beyond which, fork left signed 'Bubwith 4 and North Duffield 1½'. Continue through North Duffield and come to a 'T' junction signed Bubwith. Turn left onto the A163 and look for a car park on the left after 0.75 miles (1.2 km). Park here and walk the 150 yards (15 m) to a hide overlooking a large pool on the west bank of the river and also the flooded meadows beyond (winter only when the water is out). The hide has a ramp and is suitable for wheelchair users. On leaving the car park, turn left and continue for 0.5 miles (0.8 km) to a bridge over the River Der-went (permanent traffic lights). There are small car parking areas on the left, just before and just after the bridge. Walk northwards on the east bank of the river along the raised floodbank at least as far as Aughton Church, 2 miles (3.2 km) from the bridge, and view the flood meadows on the right (see map for site 81).

Calendar

With the exception of some of the breeding waterfowl and the passerines associated with the tree-lined river banks at Wheldrake, the species list for the Bubwith/North Duffield area is the same as for that site.

84 SKIPWITH COMMON
OS Landranger Map 105
York

Habitat

This remnant of ancient oak and birch woodland is situated some 7 miles (11.2 km) southeast of York. The Yorkshire Wildlife Trust leases some 600 acres (242 ha) which is designated as a reserve. The area is very flat, lying between 25 and 33 feet (approx 27 m) above sea level with sandy soils, some areas of impervious clay, large areas of peat and several permanent ponds. There are stands of mature Scots pines and some plantations of other conifers. The open heath areas were at one time being invaded by birch and Scots pine due to the cessation of grazing but this was re-established in 1984; Hebridean sheep are now used to control the vegetation and maintain the open heathland.

Species
The area is one of the few places in the region where European Nightjars can be seen or heard. Woodcocks are also fairly common during the breeding season and can be seen roding at dusk. A few pairs of Long-eared Owls are resident on the Common and their young are often heard calling in the spring. Black-headed Gulls breed in small colonies around the pools where Mallards and Common Snipe also nest. The oak and birch woodland is host to Eurasian Sparrowhawks, Turtle Doves, several species of warblers with Grasshopper Warbler (scarce), Lesser Whitethroat, Common Whitethroat, Garden Warbler, Blackcap, Chiff-chaff and Willow Warbler as well as Tree Pipits, Common Redstarts, Spotted Flycatchers, Goldcrests, Eurasian Treecreepers and most of the titmice. Eurasian Jays are usually in evidence. All three woodpeckers occur with Green and Great Spotted as breeding species. During the winter months, small numbers of waterfowl, including Mallards, Common Teals and a few Eurasian Wigeons frequent the pools.

Timing
The best time to visit is during April, May and June when the passerines are in song. Dusk is obviously the time to listen and watch for European Nightjars and Woodcocks.

Access
Skipwith Common can be reached from either the village of Skipwith or from the main A19 York to Selby road near the village of Riccall. After leaving Wheldrake, proceed through the village of Thorganby and enter Skipwith. Pass The Hare and Hounds pub on the left and bear right across the main road to take a track at the end of the triangular village green. This leads into the woodland and passes the first reserve boundary sign after 0.25 miles (0.4 km). Proceed along the track and come to an open area after another 0.25 miles (0.4 km). It is worth stopping here to look for passerines and also to listen for European Nightjars and Woodcocks at dusk. Continue along for a further 0.5 miles (0.8 km) passing a large stand of mature Scots pines on the right, and come to the junction of four tracks, identified by a large reserve sign on a section of fence. This is the best place to start for European Nightjars but do not park here. Bear right along the unsigned King Rudding Lane and pass a large old disused wartime runway on the left before reaching the official car park on the right, 100 yards (90 m) beyond the edge of the woodland. This is another section of runway opposite two new battery-hen units. Walk back into the wood from here to the track junction and take the track to the right of the reserve sign to the open heath after about 200 yards (180 m). An evening watch from here during May or June should produce both European Nightjar and Woodcock. Any other area of open heathland in the vicinity should also be checked for these species.

Approaching along the A19 from York, look for King Rudding Lane on the left opposite the bypassed village of Riccall. The official car park is

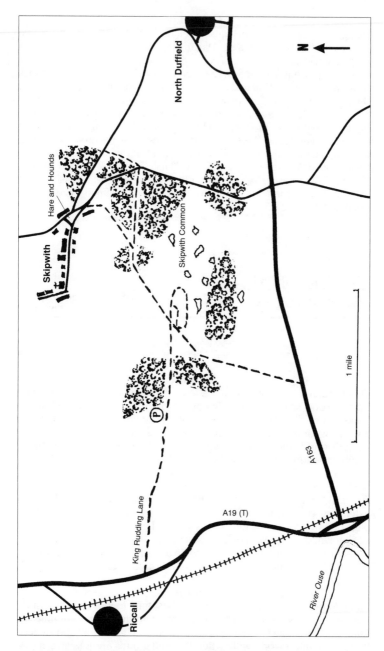

1.25 miles (2 km) along this lane. Walk from here to the track junction as described above. Total distance from the A19 turn off to the track junction is 1.75 miles (2.8 km) and from the village of Skipwith through the woods is 1 mile (1.6 km). Visitors are asked to keep to the paths and not walk over the heaths. Midges can be very bad at dusk and one should be adequately prepared.

Calendar

Spring and summer (April to August): Includes all the resident species which can be seen throughout the year. Mallard, Eurasian Sparrowhawk, Common Kestrel, Red-legged Partridge, Grey Partridge, Common Pheasant, Moorhen, Northern Lapwing, Woodcock, Eurasian Curlew, Black-headed Gull, Stock Dove, Wood Pigeon, Collared Dove, Turtle Dove, Common Cuckoo, Tawny Owl, Long-eared Owl, European Nightjar, Green Woodpecker, Great Spotted Woodpecker, Lesser Spotted Woodpecker (scarce), Tree Pipit, Wren, Hedge Accentor, Robin, Common Redstart, Blackbird, Song Thrush, Mistle Thrush, Grasshopper Warbler (scarce), Lesser Whitethroat, Common Whitethroat, Garden Warbler, Blackcap, Chiffchaff, Willow Warbler, Goldcrest, Spotted Flycatcher, Long-tailed Tit, Marsh Tit, Willow Tit, Coal Tit, Blue Tit, Great Tit, Eurasian Treecreeper, Eurasian Jay, Magpie, Eurasian Jackdaw, Rook, Carrion Crow, House Sparrow, Chaffinch, Greenfinch, Goldfinch, Bullfinch, Yellowhammer, Reed Bunting.

85 STRENSALL COMMON

OS Landranger Map 100
Malton and Pickering

Habitat

This 105-acre reserve is one of the few remaining lowland heaths in the Vale of York (see also site 84, Skipwith Common), and is owned by the Yorkshire Wildlife Trust. It consists of both wet and dry heath with birch and oak woodland, and there are often large areas of standing water, particularly during the winter months, parts of the Reserve, however, being damp underfoot for much of the year.

Species

Strensall Common is similar in habitat to Skipwith (site 84) but is not so extensive. The list of species is also similar to that site including a few pairs of Woodcocks and Eurasian Nightjars. Long-eared Owl, however, is not known to occur. Most of the resident species can be seen also during the autumn and winter months. Juvenile birds, including titmice and warblers, are in evidence during late June, July and August.

Timing

As for Skipwith Common (site 84), the best time to visit is during April, May and June when the birds are in song, and during the evenings for Eurasian Woodcocks and possibly European Nightjars. July and August, however, can be worthwhile when the young birds are foraging in parties, especially the titmice and also groups of warblers.

Access

Leave the York ring-road on the western side of the city, near a bridge over the River Foss onto a minor road signed Earswick and Strensall. This road bypasses the village of Strensall after 1 mile (1.6 km) with Strensall

Army Camp on the right, and after a further 1 mile (1.6 km) comes to a cattle grid. The Reserve starts here and runs for 1 mile (1.6 km) on the left of the road. The land on the right of the road is a military training area and shooting range, and should not be entered. Park in an open space near the cattle grid or along a track with a Reserve sign about 100 yards (90 m) further along on the left. Walk from here along the track, cross a railway line and continue along the edge of the woodland, coming eventually to a gate which leads onto the common.

On returning to the car, one can drive along the main road to the end of the Reserve and just before a second cattle grid and a small bridge, park near the Reserve sign and walk into the woods from here.

Calendar

With the exception of Long-eared Owl, the list is the same as for site 84.

86 BISHOP WOOD, NEAR SELBY

OS Landranger Map 105
York

Habitat

This site is part of a once great stretch of ancient woodland where Common Buzzards and Common Ravens nested during the 19th Century. It is still an interesting area with plenty of large trees including oak, beech, lime, silver birch, ash and sycamore in addition to several large stands of conifers and some open boggy patches. The wood is surrounded by flat agricultural land.

Species

During the spring and summer months when most of the common resident birds and summer migrants are in song and actively nesting, this is a very interesting place to visit. Eurasian Sparrowhawks breed in the wood and may be seen along the rides. Common Kestrels hunt over the adjacent open ground where Red-legged and Grey Partridges should be looked for. A few Northern Lapwings nest in the fields where feeding Stock Doves can also be seen. Wood Pigeons are very numerous at all seasons. The deciduous parts of the wood are excellent for small birds where Wrens, Robins, Blackbirds, Song Thrushes, Coal, Blue and Great Tits and Chaffinches are common, in addition to the summer visitors which include Lesser Whitethroat, Garden Warbler, Blackcap, Chiffchaff, Willow Warbler and Spotted Flycatcher.

Birds can be relatively scarce during the winter months but during autumn and early winter one can see small flocks of titmice, Goldcrests, Eurasian Treecreepers and finches as well as the winter thrushes.

Timing

As for all woodland sites, the best time to visit is during late April, May and June for the most species, and particularly early in the morning or during the evening.

Access

Bishop Wood lies 4 miles (6.4 km) west of Selby and is best reached from either Cawood or Sherburn in Elmet. Travel north from Selby on the B1223 and reach Cawood after 4 miles (6.4 km). Take the B1222 to Sherburn and look for the entrance to the wood on the left after 2.5 miles (4 km), just before crossing the railway bridge. The entrance is signed 'Bishop Wood – Park Nook'. Drive along the wide unmade forestry track for 500 yards (460 m) to the car parking area just inside the wood from where a track leads through a gate and eventually joins other tracks which intersect the 2 square miles (5 square km) of woodland.

Calendar

This includes the woodland and the surrounding agriculture.

All year: Eurasian Sparrowhawk, Common Kestrel, Red-legged Partridge, Grey Partridge, Common Pheasant, Stock Dove, Wood Pigeon, Tawny Owl, Great Spotted Woodpecker, Wren, Hedge Accentor, Robin, Blackbird, Mistle Thrush, Goldcrest, Coat Tit, Blue tit, Great Tit, Eurasian

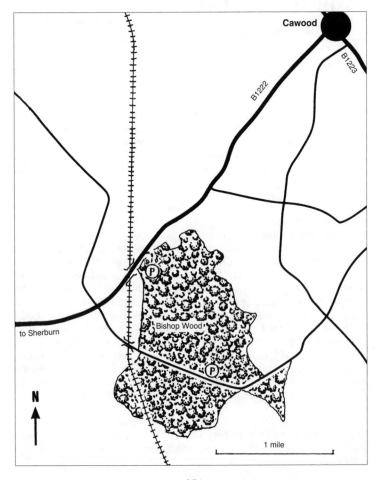

Treecreeper, Eurasian Jay, Magpie, Eurasian Jackdaw, Rook, Carrion Crow, Common Starling, Chaffinch, Greenfinch, Bullfinch, Yellow-hammer.

Spring and summer (April to August): Northern Lapwing, Common Cuckoo, Sky Lark, Song Thrush, Lesser Whitethroat, Garden Warbler, Blackcap, Chiffchaff, Willow Warbler, Spotted Flycatcher, Linnet.

Winter (October to March): Fieldfare, Redwing, Brambling.

87 SOUTHFIELDS RESERVOIRS

OS Landranger Map 111
Sheffield and Doncaster

Habitat

These two large man-made compensation reservoirs feed the Aire and Calder Navigation Canal which runs along their southern boundary. They were completed in 1911 and cover an area of 120 acres (48 ha) being divided by a narrow bund and surrounded by banks along which there are paths used mainly by fishermen. The bund and surrounding grass banks are clothed in willowherbs and other tall plants with a few small bushes, and there is also some emergent vegetation around the water's edge.

Species

The winter months produce good numbers of waterfowl including Goosanders which have increased in recent years with a peak count of 202 birds in February 1996. Common Goldeneyes are usually present during the winter months in varying numbers. Other waterfowl, occurring less regularly or in smaller numbers, include Common Teal, Northern Pintail, Northern Shoveler, Gadwall and an occasional Red-breasted Merganser. Small flocks of both Whooper and Tundra Swans sometimes drop in during the late autumn and winter months when skeins of Pink-footed or Greylag Geese may also pass over.

Three species of divers have been seen, Great Northern being added to the list in 1996 and the three rarer grebes have occurred. Great Cormorants are usually present and the reservoirs have attracted Shag, Eurasian Spoonbill, Purple Heron and Little Egret. Regular watching over the years has produced records of several birds of prey including Honey-buzzard, Black Kite, Red Kite, Marsh, Hen and Montagu's Harriers, Northern Goshawk and Common Buzzard in addition to Osprey which occurs regularly on passage and also the resident Eurasian Sparrowhawk and Common Kestrel. Peregrine Falcon and Merlin are often recorded and Hobby is seen fairly regularly each year.

A winter gull roost consisting of Great Black-backed, Lesser Black-backed, Herring, Common and Black-headed Gulls often attracts Glaucous, Iceland and Mediterranean Gulls which are being recorded with increasing frequency. Flocks of up to 1,000 each of Northern Lapwings and European Golden Plovers are a feature of the surrounding area at this time.

The summer months can be relatively quiet with only a few breeding Mallards, Moorhens and an occasional pair of Great Crested Grebes, Little Grebes and Common Coots. The surrounding hedgerows and the rank vegetation, however, have breeding Common and Lesser Whitethroats, Willow Warblers and Sedge Warblers, with a few pairs of Grasshopper Warblers in most years, in addition to the commoner resident passerines. Eurasian Curlews and Northern Lapwings breed in the surrounding fields with a pair of Oystercatchers nesting in 1996. A pair of Common Shelducks hatched ten ducklings on the adjacent Went Ings in 1995.

April to early June and late July to October are good periods for passage migrants, some interesting species having been recorded over the years. Although there are no significant areas of mud suitable for feeding waders, several species are recorded annually at times of passage, usually flying over but often circling the water before continuing, although some do stop to rest and feed along the edges. Common Sandpipers are regular and other species which may be encountered include Eurasian Curlew, Common Greenshank, Ruff, Oystercatcher and Dunlin with occasional Turnstone, Bar-tailed and Black-tailed Godwits, Whimbrel, Great and Little Ringed Plovers. During periods of easterly winds, particularly in the spring, terns may appear over the water including Common, Arctic and Black with an occasional Sandwich or Little. A few Little Gulls may also pass through during the same conditions. Common Swifts and the three hirundine species assemble over the open water as they pause to feed whilst on passage, especially during periods of cold winds or rain in late April and May and again during late summer.

The autumn period, as well as being good for passage waders, is also a good time for assemblies of waterfowl which increase at this time. During July and August, warblers of several species frequent the hedgerows and tall vegetation along with a few Whinchats, Spotted Flycatchers and the resident Reed Buntings and Yellowhammers. Flocks of Linnets, Greenfinches and Goldfinches gather to feed on weed seeds around the reservoirs in the late summer. During September and early October, Meadow Pipits and Sky Larks pass overhead, the latter often being in evidence also during the winter months, along with Northern Lapwings, when they are forced to shift their feeding locations due to frost or snow. The winter thrushes may be seen flying over in flocks during October and November as they continue westwards following their arrival along the coast in easterly winds. Corn Buntings are most in evidence during the winter months.

Timing

The open deep water makes this a good autumn and winter site when the numbers of waterfowl are high and an occasional diver or rare grebe may be seen. Visits during the spring and autumn migration seasons can be very productive for waders and terns, the latter especially with easterly winds in spring. Southfield is a popular water for sailing, windsurfing and angling with some disturbance to birds on the open water and along the banks as a consequence. Viewing from the south side adjacent to the canal is best as the sun is from behind for most of the day. A telescope is essential.

Access

Leaving Snaith, west of Goole, travel eastwards on the A645 towards Rawcliffe and after passing through the small villages of West and East

256

Cowick, turn right at a mini-roundabout onto the A614, signed Sykehouse and Askern. After 1 mile (1.6 km), turn right onto a minor road, again signed Sykehouse and Askern. Pass the track signed to Beever Sailing Club on the right and after about 0.5 miles (0.8 km), turn right immediately before a metal bridge (Beevers Bridge) over the Aire and Calder Navigation Canal, onto a track which runs alongside the canal for 0.5 miles (0.8 km) to the fishermen's car park, where it is permitted to leave one's car. If approaching along the M18, leave the motorway at junction 6, signed Thorne, and travel northwards on the A614 for about 4 miles (6.4 km). After crossing two bridges, turn left onto the minor road as above and come to the metal Beevers Bridge.

From the car park, walk up onto the reservoir banking and proceed to the left along the canal bank from where there are excellent views over both reservoirs. It is not possible to walk along the full southern edge of the western reservoir due to an outlet into the canal but there are adequate views from the southeastern corner. To walk around the western reservoir, one must proceed to the northern side and along a field-edge at the back of the sailing clubhouse, the compound of which is private.

Calendar

All year: Little Grebe, Great Crested Grebe, Great Cormorant, Grey Heron, Mute Swan, Mallard, Eurasian Sparrowhawk, Common Kestrel, Red-legged Partridge, Grey Partridge, Common Pheasant, Moorhen, Common Coot, Stock Dove, Wood Pigeon, Collared Dove, Little Owl, Tawny Owl, Common Kingfisher, Green Woodpecker, Great Spotted Woodpecker, Sky Lark (also on passage), Wren, Hedge Accentor, Robin, Blackbird, Song Thrush, Mistle Thrush, Long-tailed Tit, Blue Tit, Great Tit, Eurasian Jay, Magpie, Eurasian Jackdaw, Rook, Carrion Crow, Common Starling, House Sparrow, Tree Sparrow, Chaffinch, Greenfinch, Goldfinch, Linnet, Bullfinch, Yellowhammer, Reed Bunting, Corn Bunting (mainly winter).

Spring and autumn passage (April to early June and late July to October): Common Shelduck, Northern Shoveler, raptors, waders, gulls, Common Tern, Arctic Tern, Black Tern, Common Swift, Sand Martin, Barn Swallow, House Martin, Tree Pipit, Meadow Pipit, Yellow Wagtail, Whinchat, Northern Wheatear, Reed Warbler, Common Whitethroat, Lesser Whitethroat, Garden Warbler, Blackcap, Chiffchaff, Spotted Flycatcher.

Summer – breeding: Great Crested Grebe, Common Shelduck (occasional), Mallard, Moorhen, Oystercatcher, Eurasian Curlew and Northern Lapwing (surrounding fields), Turtle Dove, Common Cuckoo, Pied Wagtail, Yellow Wagtail, Grasshopper Warbler, Sedge Warbler, Common Whitethroat, Lesser Whitethroat, Willow Warbler (also on passage), plus the commoner resident passerines.

Winter: divers, rarer grebes, Tundra Swan, Whooper Swan, Pink-footed Goose (occasional skeins over), Greylag Goose, Eurasian Wigeon, Gadwall, Common Teal, Northern Pintail, Common Pochard, Tufted Duck, Greater Scaup (occasional), Long-tailed Duck (occasional), Common Scoter (occasional – also on passage), Common Goldeneye, Smew (occasional), Goosander, Red-breasted Merganser (occasional), Water Rail, gulls at roost, Fieldfare, Redwing, Goldcrest, Siskin.

88 CARLTON TOWERS LAKE

Habitat
This lake, which lies on both sides of the road, is surrounded by mature deciduous trees and is adjacent to farmland and close to the River Aire.

Species
The lake is worth a visit if in the area, especially during the autumn and winter months when the waterfowl are most in evidence. Assemblies of gulls from the surrounding agricultural land gather at this time to drink and bathe. The trees hold several passerine species associated with this lakeside habitat including titmice, thrushes and finches during the autumn and winter, and some warblers in the summer.

Timing
A visit in the spring would be worthwhile, mainly for the migrant and resident passerines in the wooded areas and the breeding birds on and around the lake. Winter is a good time for a short visit to view the lake for waterfowl and gulls, in addition to the woodland passerines.

Access
Carlton Towers is alongside the A1041 Snaith to Selby road. Travelling north from Snaith the lake is on the right just before the village of Carlton. Shortly after leaving Snaith, a bailey bridge crosses the River Aire, 0.5 miles (0.8 km) beyond which is the lake. After crossing over the bailey bridge, look for an open area on the right at a left-hand bend after 200 yards (180 m). Park here and walk along the roadside footpath for about 400 yards (360 m) to view the lakes and the surrounding land.

Calendar
Winter (October to March): Little Grebe, Grey Heron, Mute Swan, Greylag and Canada Geese, waterfowl, Common Kestrel, Moorhen, Common Coot, Northern Lapwing, European Golden Plover, gulls, Stock Dove, Wood Pigeon, Collared Dove, Great Spotted Woodpecker, Sky Lark, Wren, Hedge Accentor, Robin, Blackbird, Fieldfare, Redwing, Mistle Thrush, Goldcrest, Long-tailed Tit, Blue Tit, Great Tit, Eurasian Treecreeper, Magpie, Eurasian Jackdaw, Rook, Carrion Crow, Common Starling, House Sparrow, Tree Sparrow, Chaffinch, Greenfinch, Yellowhammer.

Summer (April to August): Common Swift, Sand Martin, Barn Swallow, House Martin, Yellow Wagtail, Song Thrush, Sedge Warbler, Blackcap, Willow Warbler, Spotted Flycatcher and Linnet in addition to the winter list above, except for European Golden Plover, Fieldfare and Redwing.

THE DONCASTER AREA

89 Thorpe Marsh
90 Potteric Carr Nature Reserve
91 Thorne Moors NNR
92 Sprotborough Flash and The Don Gorge
93 Wombwell Ings and Broomhill Ings
    93A Old Moor Wetlands
94 Denaby Ings
95 Thrybergh Country Park

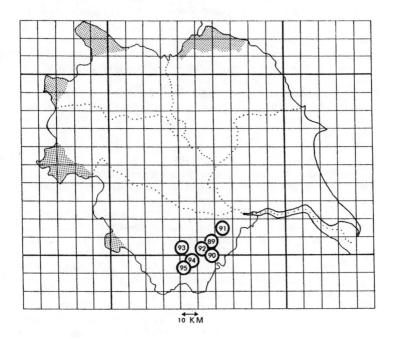

10 KM

Habitat

This extensive reserve has been created adjacent to Thorpe Marsh Power Station on land owned by National Power and is administered by them and The Yorkshire Wildlife Trust. There are many interesting habitats, some of which, such as the ridge and furrow pasture at Reedholme, being of ancient origin contrasting with the newly created Thorpe Mere, a large lake with two islands and marginal vegetation ideal for waterfowl and passerines. There are several smaller ponds on the reserve and on the adjacent land, the largest being Applehurst Pond, created during the early part of the century as the result of excavations to provide material for the railway embankments. An old disused embankment, clothed in trees and scrub, mainly silver birch, bisects the Reserve and is an ideal habitat for small passerines. The artificial embankments surrounding the lake are covered in grasses and shrubs with areas of silver birch, alder and oak.

The whole area has been carefully planned and developed and is well managed by the Yorkshire Wildlife Trust and National Power to maintain suitable habitats for a wide variety of birds as well as plants, insects and mammals.

Species

The diverse habitats make Thorpe Marsh an ideal place to spend a full day. The lake has breeding Little and Great Crested Grebes, Mute Swans, Greylag and Canada Geese, Mallards and an occasional pair of Tufted Ducks. During the autumn and winter months a few Great Cormorants drop in to rest and feed and Grey Herons are present in small numbers throughout the year. Both Tundra and Whooper Swans may visit the lake in winter along with several species of waterfowl including the following with some recent maxima shown: Eurasian Wigeon (160), Gadwall (single figures), Common Teal (300), Mallard (500), Northern Pintail (scarce), Northern Shoveler (few), Common Pochard (20), Tufted Duck (70) and a few Common Goldeneyes, Goosanders and Ruddy Ducks.

Eurasian Sparrowhawks and Common Kestrels are resident and breed on the reserve and an occasional Common Buzzard, Osprey or Merlin may occur at times of migration.

Red-legged Partridges, Grey Partridges and Common Pheasants nest in the area and Water Rail is often seen during the winter. Moorhens and Common Coots are present throughout the year.

Several species of waders occur on passage as well as Little Ringed Plover, Northern Lapwing, Common Snipe and Common Redshank, which breed on the reserve. Black-headed, Common, Lesser Black-backed, Herring and Great Black-backed Gulls occur mainly during the winter months when assemblies on the lake may be large. A few Common and Arctic Terns may pass through during the spring and autumn migration periods depending on the weather conditions. Turtle Doves nest and Wood Pigeons are numerous. Owls are well represented and five species are usually recorded each year: Barn, Little, Tawny, Long-eared and Short-eared all occurred in 1990. A few Long-eared Owls roost on the reserve in the winter months when an occasional Short-eared may be seen hunting over the area. Common Kingfisher is regularly seen on the lake, the ponds or along the Eau Beck. Green Woodpecker is resident and breeds locally, Great Spotted is a regular visitor and Lesser Spotted is a possibility.

Migrant hirundines, Yellow and Pied Wagtails, Meadow Pipits, Common Redstarts, Whinchats, Northern Wheatears and several species of warblers can be seen during the spring and autumn migration periods of April to early June and August to October. Breeding warblers are Sedge, Reed, Lesser Whitethroat, Common Whitethroat, Blackcap, Chiffchaff and Willow Warbler. Titmice are attracted to feeders near the Field Centre where baited areas are visited by Chaffinches, Bramblings and Green-finches as well as many Tree Sparrows in the winter. The silver birches and alders along the old railway embankment are good for Siskins and Common Redpolls in the autumn. Bullfinches, Yellowhammers and Reed Buntings are resident.

Timing

A visit at any time of the year can be worthwhile as the varied habitats attract a wide variety of birds at all seasons. For the largest number of species, April, May and early June is the best period, when the migrants are passing through or settling in and are singing. Autumn and winter are good for waders and waterfowl as well as for flocks of finches and the immigrant winter thrushes.

Access

Travel north from Doncaster on the A19 and after 2 miles (3.2 km) turn right into Bentley onto the road for Barnby Dun. The Power Station is reached on the left after a little under 3.5 miles (5.5 km) from Bentley having passed through the village of Arksey. Before reaching the power

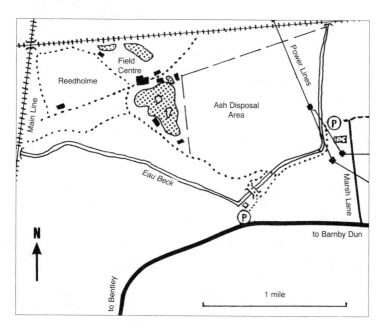

station and just before a rise in the road, look for a small gravel area on the left and park here (or on a wide bare verge opposite). Proceed through a wooden gate and along a hardcore track which leads to the right passing an old blockhouse to reach a new metal bridge after about 150 yards (135 m) where signs direct one to the Reserve pathway. If this parking area is full, or if preferring to park away from the main road, continue along the road to the power station entrance, signed Thorpe Marsh and Nature Reserve, and proceed along the straight tarmac access road, passing the works buildings on the right and some rectangular ponds on both sides of the road. Where the road bears right, park in an open area on the left. A wooden gate leads onto a wide cinder track at the end of which is an electricity pylon and a sign marking one access point to the Reserve. Walk past the sign along a short slightly raised cinder path to some bushes and two marker posts. Continue down the banking and over a small footbridge. The path continues to the left along the top of Eau Beck Bank and comes to the metal bridge as above from where one joins the main cinder path which continues alongside a wide ditch on the left and a raised embankment on the right. Walk for about 0.5 miles (0.8 km) and come to the first hide on the right, overlooking the main lake. On leaving the hide, turn right, and the Field Centre is reached after about 200 yards (180 m).

There are several footpaths around the area and several other hides overlooking the lake, the ponds and the pastures at Reedholme. Access to the Reserve is by permit only (valid for one year) which can be obtained on request by sending a stamped and addressed envelope to The Permit Secretary, The Yorkshire Wildlife Trust, 10 Toft Green, York YO1 1JT. Information leaflets giving details of the Reserve and showing the footpaths and positions of the hides are available at the Field Centre; volunteer wardens are usually on site.

Calendar

Winter (October to March): Includes some species which are present in small numbers throughout the year. Little Grebe, Great Crested Grebe, Great Cormorant, Tundra Swan (occasional), Whooper Swan, Eurasian Wigeon, Gadwall, Common Teal, Common Pochard, Tufted Duck, Common Goldeneye, Goosander, Water Rail, European Golden Plover, Jack Snipe, Woodcock, Green Sandpiper, Common Gull, Herring Gull, Great Black-backed Gull, Little Owl, Long-eared Owl, Short-eared Owl, Grey Wagtail, Common Stonechat (occasional), Fieldfare, Redwing, Goldcrest, Coal Tit, Brambling, Siskin, Common Redpoll.

All year: Grey Heron, Mute Swan, Greylag Goose, Canada Goose, Mallard, Eurasian Sparrowhawk, Common Kestrel, Red-legged Partridge, Grey Partridge, Common Pheasant, Moorhen, Common Coot, Northern Lapwing, Common Snipe, Common Redshank, Black-headed Gull, Lesser Black-backed Gull, Stock Dove, Wood Pigeon, Barn Owl (scarce), Tawny Owl, Common Kingfisher, Green Woodpecker, Great Spotted Woodpecker, Sky Lark, Meadow Pipit, Pied Wagtail, Wren, Hedge Accentor, Robin, Blackbird, Song Thrush, Mistle Thrush, Long-tailed Tit, Willow Tit, Blue Tit, Great Tit, Eurasian Treecreeper, Eurasian Jay, Magpie, Eurasian Jackdaw, Rook, Carrion Crow, Common Starling, House Sparrow, Tree Sparrow, Chaffinch, Greenfinch, Goldfinch, Linnet, Bullfinch, Yellowhammer, Reed Bunting.

Spring and summer (April to August): Includes several species which also occur on passage in both spring and summer. Ruddy Duck (scarce), Little

Ringed Plover, Turtle Dove, Common Cuckoo, Common Swift, Sand Martin, Barn Swallow, House Martin, Grasshopper Warbler, Sedge Warbler, Reed Warbler, Lesser Whitethroat, Common Whitethroat, Garden Warbler, Blackcap, Chiffchaff, Willow Warbler.

Spring and autumn passage (April to June and August to October): Common Shelduck, Osprey, Merlin (occasional), Oystercatcher, Dunlin, Whimbrel, Eurasian Curlew, Common Greenshank, Common Sandpiper, several other passage waders, gulls, Common Tern, Arctic Tern, Black Tern (occasional), Yellow Wagtail, Common Redstart, Whinchat, Spotted Flycatcher.

90 POTTERIC CARR NATURE RESERVE

OS Landranger Map 111
Sheffield and Doncaster

Habitat

This area of remnant carrland lies only 2.25 miles (3.6 km) southeast of the centre of Doncaster. It is a shallow basin averaging only 34 feet (10 m) above sea level comprising peat, marl and clay to a depth of between 6 and 12 feet (2 m and 4 m). Up to 300 years ago, the area formed part of the extensive fenland, some of which was successfully drained for agricultural use before subsequently mining subsidence during the early part of the present century caused many areas to revert to wet carrland. The Reserve area is intersected by disused and operative railway embankments.

The 300-acre (120 ha) Reserve, first set up in 1968 by The Yorkshire Wildlife Trust with the co-operation of British Rail and the local authorities, is now actively managed by the YWT and its team of volunteer wardens. The creation and maintenance of varied habitats including the planting of indigenous trees and the control of vegetation necessitated by the vigorous colonisation by trees and shrubs, particularly willow, has helped to make this one of the most valuable reserves in the region. Large areas of silver birch are now established on waste ground and on disused railway embankments with oak and alder colonising new areas and becoming established. The open water provides important habitats for many species of birds as well as for aquatic plants and insects. *Phragmites* reeds and bulrushes have become established in several areas, providing an important habitat for many life forms. There are some stands of mature woodland, open expanses of grassland and scrub, as well as the traditional carrland which once covered the entire area of flat land between the Rivers Don and Trent.

Species

The diverse habits attract a wide variety of birds and a total of 180 species has been recorded including several rarities such as Little Egret, Eurasian Spoonbill, Red-crested Pochard, Ferruginous Duck, Red-footed Falcon,

Common Crane, Pectoral Sandpiper and Marsh Warbler. The unprece-
dented breeding by a pair of Little Bitterns in 1984 brought the total number of breeding species to 85. Little and Great Crested Grebes nest on the
Reserve and an occasional Black-necked Grebe occurs in spring or
autumn. Great Cormorant and Great Bittern may both occur sporadically
during the winter when Grey Heron is a regular visitor. Mute Swans are
resident and both Tundra and Whooper Swans drop in during the winter
as do a few Pink-footed and Greylag Geese. Common Shelducks regularly
pass through during the spring migration season. The winter months are
good for waterfowl, when many birds assemble to add to the Reserve's
breeding populations; Eurasian Wigeons, Gadwalls, Common Teals, Mallards, Northern Pintails, Northern Shovelers, Common Pochards, Tufted
Ducks and Common Goldeneyes usually being present in good numbers.
Ruddy Ducks now spend the summer here.

During the spring and autumn migration periods, it is possible to see a
lone Marsh or Hen Harrier hunting over the carrs and there is always the
chance of seeing a wandering Northern Goshawk, Common Buzzard,
Osprey, Merlin or Hobby at these times. Eurasian Sparrowhawk and Common Kestrel are both resident and nest in the area. Red-legged and Grey
Partridges are resident as are Common Pheasant, Water Rail, Moorhen
and Common Coot.

Passage waders include all the usual species in addition to Northern
Lapwing, Common Snipe, Woodcock and Common Redshank which
breed on the Reserve. During periods of easterly winds, mainly in the
spring, Common, Arctic and Black Terns may arrive and feed over the
water; an occasional Little Gull is seen in the autumn.

Black-headed Gull is a common breeding species. Common, Lesser
Black-backed, Herring and Great Black-backed Gulls are regular visitors
in the winter when an occasional Iceland or Glaucous Gull may turn up.
Stock Doves, Wood Pigeons and Collared Doves are resident and Turtle
Doves and Common Cuckoos are present during the summer months.
Five species of owls are regularly recorded, Barn Owl being the least
likely, but Little, Tawny and Long-eared all nest in the reserve area, Short-
eared Owl may be seen hunting over the carrs during the autumn and
winter. Common Kingfisher is regularly seen around the lakes and ponds
and both Green and Great Spotted Woodpeckers are resident. The site is
very good for warblers and nine species breed annually. During the
autumn, thousands of Sand Martins and Barn Swallows congregate to
roost in the reedbeds on their journey south and large numbers of Common Swifts can be seen moving south over the area during late August.
The resident titmice include Long-tailed, Willow, Coal, Blue and Great
with Bearded Tits being seen on occasions. Eurasian Jay is a fairly common breeding species and the resident seed-eating passerines are Tree
Sparrow, Chaffinch, Greenfinch, Goldfinch, Linnet, Common Redpoll,
Bullfinch, Yellowhammer, Reed Bunting and Corn Bunting.

Timing

From the foregoing, it will be seen that a visit at any time of the year can
be worthwhile but the best period for numbers of species is during the
spring (April to early June) when passage migrants are on the move and
when the summer visitors have arrived and are in song. The summer
months can be interesting for breeding waterbirds and warblers. The
autumn brings passage waders and an influx of waterfowl and winter
thrushes, Bramblings and Siskins.

Access

To reach Potteric Carr Reserve, leave the M18 Motorway at Junction 3 onto the A6182 and after 1 mile (1.6 km) come to a roundabout and take the third exit, signed 'No through road'. Turn right after 50 yards (45 m) into the Reserve car park. Approach from Doncaster town centre, take the A6182 and come to the same roundabout.

A permit is needed for access to the Reserve; a requirement of Railtrack as a condition for allowing the crossing of railway tracks at the three crossing points. Permits, for which a small charge is made, are available from the Yorkshire Wildlife Trust Ltd, 10, Toft Green, York YO1

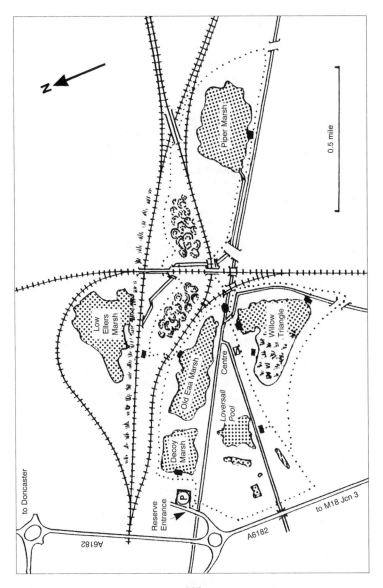

1JT. The Reserve facilities include 5 miles (8 km) of footpaths, eight viewing hides (three of which are suitable for wheelchair users) and a Field Centre with cafe, picnic area and toilets. This is open on Sundays throughout the year including Bank Holidays (except Christmas and New Year). Light lunches can be arranged for groups if adequate notice is given. A guide to the nature walks on the Reserve is available from the YWT office in York.

Calendar

Winter (October to March): Includes some species which are present in small numbers throughout the year. Great Cormorant, Grey Heron, Tundra Swan, Whooper Swan, Pink-footed Goose (occasional), Eurasian Wigeon, Northern Pintail, Common Goldeneye, Smew (occasional), Redbreasted Merganser (occasional), Goosander, Merlin, Jack Snipe, Common Gull, Lesser Black-backed Gull, Herring Gull, Iceland and Glaucous Gulls (occasional), Great Black-backed Gull, Kittiwake (occasional, usually following gales), Short-eared Owl, Grey Wagtail, Common Stonechat, Fieldfare, Redwing, Goldcrest, Brambling, Siskin.

All year: Little Grebe, Great Crested Grebe, Mute Swan, Greylag Goose, Canada Goose, Gadwall, Common Teal, Mallard, Common Pochard, Tufted Duck, Eurasian Sparrowhawk, Common Kestrel, Red-legged Partridge, Grey Partridge, Common Pheasant, Water Rail, Moorhen, Common Coot, Northern Lapwing, Common Snipe, Woodcock, Blackheaded Gull, Stock Dove, Wood Pigeon, Collared Dove, Little Owl, Tawny Owl, Long-eared Owl, Common Kingfisher, Green Woodpecker, Great Spotted Woodpecker, Sky Lark, Meadow Pipit, Pied Wagtail, Wren, Hedge Accentor, Robin, Blackbird, Song Thrush, Mistle Thrush, Longtailed Tit, Willow Tit, Coal Tit, Blue Tit, Great Tit, Eurasian Treecreeper, Eurasian Jay, Magpie, Eurasian Jackdaw, Rook, Carrion Crow, Common Starling, House Sparrow, Tree Sparrow, Chaffinch, Greenfinch, Goldfinch, Linnet, Common Redpoll, Bullfinch, Yellowhammer, Reed Bunting, Corn Bunting.

Spring and summer (April to August): Includes several species which also occur on passage in both spring and autumn. Garganey, Ruddy Duck, Little Ringed Plover, Great Ringed Plover, Common Redshank, Turtle Dove, Common Cuckoo, Common Swift, Sand Martin, Barn Swallow, House Martin, Tree Pipit, Yellow Wagtail, Whinchat, Grasshopper Warbler, Sedge Warbler, Reed Warbler, Lesser Whitethroat, Common Whitethroat, Garden Warbler, Blackcap, Chiffchaff, Willow Warbler, Spotted Flycatcher.

Spring and autumn passage (April to June and August to October): Blacknecked Grebe (occasional, mainly in spring), Common Shelduck, Marsh Harrier (occasional), Osprey, Hobby (occasional), waders, Common Tern, Arctic Tern, Black Tern (on easterly winds), hirundines, Common Redstart, Northern Wheatear, Pied Flycatcher (rare.).

91 THORNE MOORS NNR

Habitat

Thorne Moors is part of a formerly more extensive area of wetland which occupied the floodplain of the Humberside Levels several thousand years ago. The whole complex is the largest expanse of lowland raised bog in Britain, covering an area of 8201 acres (3318 ha). A large area of abandoned peat workings is managed as National Nature Reserve by English Nature, of which Thorne Moors forms an important part. The drier parts are clothed in birch with bracken and heather, and the wetter parts have Sphagnum mosses, cranberry, cross-leaved heath are hare's tail cottongrass. There are areas of fen with *Phragmites*, reed-mace, willows and sallows, and also strips of woodland comprising pedunculate oak, ash, hawthorn and sycamore.

Species

The specialised topography of the Reserve with the adjoining arable land and the waste ground around the edges and in the Thorne Colliery area, combine to provide a wide range of habitats for many species including some specialities.

This is the most northerly place in Britain where the Rufous Nightingale breeds regularly with up to three or four pairs being present annually. A pair of Hobbys spends the summer here and European Nightjars have numbered up to 20–25 singing males in recent years. Listen for Rufous Nightingales in the thick scrub on the right about 300 yards (270 m) beyond the entrance to the Reserve in the area of Bell's Pond. The best place to see the Hobbys is in the Mill Drain area (see map). European Nightjars may be heard and seen in most of the open areas towards evening when Woodcocks may also be seen as they indulge in their display flights. Common Snipe is a familiar breeding bird and can be observed 'drumming' over the area. A lone Jack Snipe may be flushed from the drain sides during the winter months.

Both Sedge and Reed Warblers breed in and around the areas of reed and willow scrub and several pairs of Grasshopper Warblers are recorded each year. Willow Warblers are generally common and the areas of thick scrub attract Garden Warblers, Blackcaps, Lesser and Common Whitethroats and also Chiffchaffs. Other summer visitors associated with the heathland habitat are Whinchat and Tree Pipit which should be looked for around the old tramways towards the Southern Boundary Drain. An occasional Common Stonechat may be seen during the late autumn and winter. A few pairs of Yellow Wagtails frequent the area during the late summer and Pied Wagtail is resident. Common Cuckoo is usually in evidence during the spring and early summer.

Wood Pigeons are sometimes common in the winter when large numbers roost in the stands of trees. Stock Doves regularly fly over the moor and a few pairs of Turtle Doves breed. Collared Doves occur in small numbers around the adjacent agricultural land. The owls are well represented, Tawny and Little being the most likely to be encountered although a lone Barn Owl is sometimes recorded during the summer.

Long-eared Owl is a scarce resident and seldom seen. During the winter months, one or two Short-eared Owls are present and hunt over the open moor. Green Woodpeckers are recorded regularly and an occasional Great Spotted Woodpecker frequents the larger timber.

Coveys of both Red-legged and Grey Partridges occur along the old tramways or in the adjacent arable fields. A few pairs of Little Grebes, Common Teals, Mallards, Moorhens and Common Coots breed along the drains and around the larger ponds, where a lone Grey Heron is often present. Flocks of Common Teals and Mallards may number up to 150 and sometimes more during the winter. Water Rail is a resident, more often heard than seen, being regular during the winter when its squeals emanate from the wet cover. During the spring, and more particularly the autumn, small numbers of passage waders drop in to rest and feed by the larger areas of water on the moor. Green Sandpipers favour the edges of the drains during the late summer and autumn, mainly in August.

Birds of prey are regularly seen and apart from the Hobbys mentioned above and also Eurasian Sparrowhawk and Common Kestrel, both of which are resident, there have been isolated records of several larger species. Marsh Harriers occur annually, most frequently between April and September, but may be encountered at any time of year. Hen Harrier is also a regular visitor, mainly from November to April, when a lone bird may hunt over the moor. Merlins are often seen in the winter from October to February and an occasional Peregrine Falcon may appear over the Reserve at any time from August to March.

There is a breeding colony of Black-headed Gulls at Mill Drain Marsh with 2–300 birds during the spring and early summer. Willow Tit is a characteristic bird of the lowland birch moors and several pairs breed at Thorne. Long-tailed, Blue and Great Tits also occur and a few pairs of Eurasian Jays are resident.

Carrion Crows patrol the moor and large numbers often assemble to roost during the winter months. Young Common Starlings gather to form roosts in the summer, with immigrant winter visitors swelling the ranks during the late autumn, when large flights can be seen in the evenings on their way to roosts in the area. Common Redpoll is resident and several pairs breed. Finches gather on the waste ground around the edge of the Reserve to feed on weed seeds in late summer when Greenfinches, Goldfinches and Linnets are often in good numbers. Barn Swallows nest in old buildings on and adjacent to the moor and large numbers often roost in the reedbeds, with fewer Sand Martins, in late summer and autumn.

Timing

A visit at any time of year can be worthwhile but the spring period, April to June, is the best when the resident and migrant songbirds are showing to advantage. During the late summer and autumn months one can expect to see small numbers of waterfowl and the usual passage waders, in addition to an occasional bird of prey. Meadow Pipits, Sky Larks and other migrant passerines can be seen on passage through the Reserve area during the period August to October.

The site is excellent for flowers, dragonflies and especially butterflies during the summer (July and August).

Access

From the M62, leave the motorway at junction 35 onto the M18 and after 5 miles (8 km), exit at junction 6 signed Thorne (A614). Come to a round-

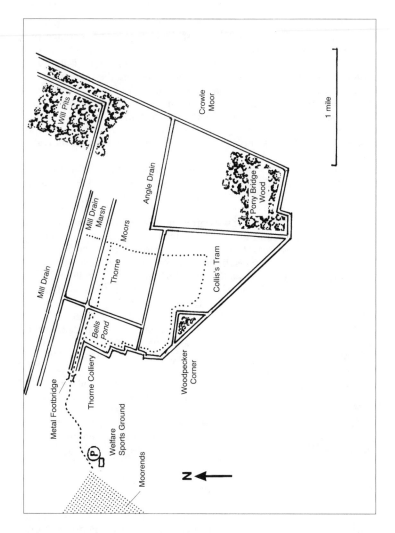

about at the end of the slip road and take the first sharp left onto a minor road (sign: Vehicle Distribution Centre) which runs north, parallel to the M18, and after 1.5 miles (2.4 km), turn right at a 'T' junction and right again at a second 'T' junction. Pass over a level crossing and enter the village of Moorends. Look for Grange road which is the second on the left and proceed to the end where there is a large locked metal gate across the road to Thorne Colliery. Bear right here into a cinder car parking area which belongs to the Welfare Sports Ground. Parking is allowed by agreement. There is a barrier at the entrance which is open from 0830 to 1630 Monday to Friday, 0800 to 1200 on Saturday and 0800 to 1400 on Sundays. It would be necessary to park at the east end of Grange Road if intending to stay on the moors after 1630, or if arriving very early in the morning.

From the car park, walk along the road leading to Thorne Pit and take the first left (at an electricity pylon) along a short tarmac road which joins the main access road to the pit. Cross this road and continue along a gravel track marked Public Footpath which runs alongside a ditch and the fenced spoil-heaps. On reaching a small derelict red-brick bridge, proceed straight on (do not bear right) onto a narrow path which skirts arable land and comes to a metal footbridge and an English Nature sign which marks the start of the Reserve. Distance from the car park to the bridge is 1.25 miles (2 km). From here, a network of paths, most which are along the dyke sides or on the old tramways, criss-cross the moors. One must, however, return eventually to the footbridge which is the only point of access. Keep to the pathways and do not cross the moorland, some areas of which can be difficult and sometimes dangerous with deep water channels.

Details of the recommended route (5 miles: 8 km), shown on the accompanying map, are as follows. From the start of the Reserve at the metal bridge, walk east for 1.25 miles (2 km), crossing seven short stretches of board walk along the path, part of which is lined with rhododendron bushes. After the last boardwalk, there is a 'T' junction. Turn right here and then almost immediately left to continue for a further 0.75 miles (1.2 km) to a cross-track. Walk initially to the left towards the area of Mill Drain Marsh which is the best place to see Hobby. Return to the cross-track and continue south along the tramway, identified by old wooden sleepers, and come to a red sign 'Danger Deep Water' after 0.75 miles (1.2 km) which marks the Southern Boundary Drain. Proceed straight on for about 300 yards (270 m) and turn right along Collis's Tramway which leads to the southwest boundary at Woodpecker Corner after 1 mile (1.6 km), before turning north for a further 1 mile (1.6 km), passing Bell's Pond area, just before rejoining the original track 300 yards (270 m) east of the metal bridge.

During the summer months, mosquitoes, midges and biting flies can be a problem and one should be suitably prepared especially in the evenings. During the winter months, the wet peatland may be difficult for walking and strong footwear should be worn. For further information contact the Site Manager, English Nature, Humber to Pennines Team, Northgate, Wakefield, West Yorkshire WF1 3BJ (Tel: (01924) 387010).

Calendar
This includes the adjoining fields and wasteland.

All year: Little Grebe, Grey Heron, Common Teal, Mallard, Eurasian Sparrowhawk, Common Kestrel, Red-legged Partridge, Grey Partridge, Common Pheasant, Water Rail, Moorhen, Common Snipe, Woodcock, Black-headed Gull, Stock Dove, Wood Pigeon, Collared Dove, Barn Owl (scarce), Little Owl, Tawny Owl, Common Kingfisher (scarce), Green Woodpecker, Great Spotted Woodpecker, Sky Lark, Meadow Pipit (scarcer in winter), Pied Wagtail, Wren, Hedge Accentor, Robin, Blackbird, Song Thrush, Mistle Thrush, Long-tailed Tit, Willow Tit, Blue Tit, Great Tit, Eurasian Jay, Magpie, Eurasian Jackdaw, Rook (adjoining fields), Carrion Crow, Common Starling, House Sparrow, Tree Sparrow (scarce), Chaffinch, Greenfinch, Goldfinch, Linnet, Common Redpoll, Bullfinch, Yellowhammer, Reed Bunting.

Spring and summer (April to early August): Hobby, Common Coot, Turtle Dove, Common Cuckoo, European Nightjar, Common Swift, Sand Martin, Barn Swallow, House Martin, Tree Pipit, Yellow Wagtail, Whinchat, Rufous Nightingale, Common Redstart (scarce), Grasshopper Warbler,

Sedge Warbler, Reed Warbler, Lesser Whitethroat, Common Whitethroat, Garden Warbler, Blackcap, Chiffchaff, Willow Warbler, Spotted Fly-catcher.

Spring and autumn passage (April to early June and late July to October): Northern Shoveler, Marsh Harrier, Merlin, Peregrine Falcon, waders, Lesser Black-backed Gull, Northern Wheatear, Common Redstart, Ring Ouzel (scarce in spring).

Winter (October to March): Hen Harrier, Merlin, Peregrine Falcon, Common Gull, Jack Snipe, Short-eared Owl, Common Stonechat (scarce), Fieldfare, Redwing, Goldcrest (scarce), Brambling, Siskin.

92 SPROTBOROUGH FLASH AND THE DON GORGE

**OS Landranger Map 111
Sheffield and Doncaster**

Habitat

The small Sprotborough Flash Reserve, administered by The Yorkshire Wildlife Trust, lies alongside the River Don and was formed as the result of mining subsidence which flooded during the winter of 1924. The river level was subsequently raised to improve navigation and as more land flooded, the original flash became deeper. The water now covers an area of 22 acres (9 ha) and is surrounded by reedmace and *Phragmites* reeds as well as brambles, willows, sallows, hawthorns and larger trees. Lying to the north of the Flash is a large stand of woodland consisting of two adjoining areas known as Pott Ridings Wood and Sprotborough Planta-tion. On the south side of the river is the steep-sided and heavily-wooded Don Gorge, a very good area for woodland birds.

Species

The number of species recorded annually in these combined areas varies between 120 and 130. Both Little and Great Crested Grebes breed on the Flash and Grey Herons are always present (one pair nested in 1992). Two pairs of Ruddy Ducks and several pairs of Gadwalls have nested in recent years. Both Eurasian Sparrowhawks and Common Kestrels are resident and regularly seen. An occasional Water Rail is recorded during the win-ter months and Moorhens and Common Coots are resident breeding species. Although not a very suitable place for migrating waders, having little or no exposed mud, some open areas are created by ongoing habi-tat management and these attract small numbers of several species annu-ally, mainly during the autumn.

Gulls are evident during the winter months; Black-headed and Com-mon being the most numerous with smaller numbers of Herring and a few Great Black-backs. Some Lesser Black-backed gulls pass through, mainly during the spring migration period. Small numbers of Common Terns are recorded in most years. Stock Doves, Wood Pigeons and Collared Doves are resident and a few Turtle Doves are present in the summer. Little and Tawny Owls both breed in the area. Common Kingfisher is often seen from the hides and all three species of woodpeckers nest in the vicinity.

During the spring and autumn migration seasons, flocks of hirundines feed over the Flash along with Common Swifts. The area is very good for warblers and the visitor may see up to eight species in a day during the spring and summer; Sedge and Reed Warblers around the Flash, Lesser and Common Whitethroats, Garden Warblers, Blackcaps, Chiffchaffs and Willow Warblers in the scrub and the woodlands. Eurasian Jays are resident and fairly common and Tree Sparrows are regularly present, mainly during the winter months. Most of the resident finches can be seen including Hawfinch, a few pairs of which breed in the deciduous woodland.

Timing

This compact Reserve and the nearby woodland in the Don Gorge holds a wide variety of birds and is certainly a good place to visit, especially during April, May and June for the highest number of species. A visit during the winter months can be worthwhile for waterfowl and most of the resident passerines in addition to the winter thrushes and finches. The woods in the Don Gorge are very popular during the summer months and also on fine days at other times, attracting lots of people but most of the woodland birds are little disturbed. The hides alongside the Flash are open to the public and are well used. There is little or no disturbance to the actual water area and its environs.

Access

Sprotborough Flash and the Don Gorge can be easily reached from the A1 Motorway. Leave the motorway onto the A630 for Rotherham at a junction just 3 miles (4.8 km) to the west of Doncaster and after 0.5 miles (0.8 km) come to traffic lights and turn right for Sprotborough. After just over 1 mile (1.6 km), the road drops down the steep slopes of the Gorge from where several public footpaths lead through the deciduous woodlands. Continuing downhill by car, cross a bridge over the River Don, followed by a second bridge over a canal, after which turn immediately left and park after 50 yards (45 m) in an obvious small roadside parking area on the left beside the canal. From here, walk along the canal bank, passing The Boat Inn, and after about 100 yards (90 m) come to a YWT Reserve sign at the start of the Flash. The pathway continues along the riverbank with the Flash on the right screened by a raised banking. There are three hides, the first one being simply an open-backed shelter, the second and third ones, named 'Kingfisher' and 'Heron' respectively, are large and of standard construction affording good views over the water and the woodland beyond.

Access to the woodland on the north side of the Flash is along a track in front of a row of cottages beside The Boat Inn and through a farm gate where a Reserve sign shows the various footpaths through the woods. These woods are private but are wardened by the YWT under an agreement with the owners and there are several permissive footpaths along which one can walk.

Calendar

This includes The Flash and the woodlands in Don Gorge.

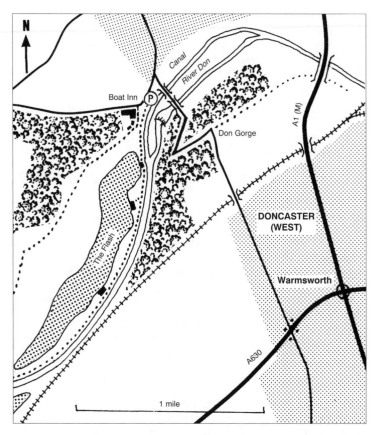

Winter (October to March): Includes several resident species which are present throughout the year. Little Grebe, Grey Heron, Mute Swan, Canada Goose, Eurasian Wigeon, Gadwall, Common Teal, Mallard, Northern Shoveler, Common Pochard, Tufted Duck, Ruddy Duck, Eurasian Sparrowhawk, Common Kestrel, Grey Partridge, Common Pheasant, Water Rail (scarce), Moorhen, Common Coot, European Golden Plover, Northern Lapwing, Common Snipe, Woodcock, Black-headed Gull, Common Gull, Herring Gull, Great Black-backed Gull (few), Stock Dove, Wood Pigeon, Collared Dove, Little Owl, Tawny Owl, Green Woodpecker, Great Spotted Woodpecker, Lesser Spotted Woodpecker, Sky Lark, Meadow Pipit, Pied Wagtail, Wren, Hedge Accentor, Robin, Blackbird, Fieldfare, Song Thrush, Redwing, Mistle Thrush, Goldcrest, Long-tailed Tit, Willow Tit, Coal Tit, Blue Tit, Great Tit, Eurasian Treecreeper, Eurasian Jay, Magpie, Rook, Carrion Crow, Common Starling, House Sparrow, Tree Sparrow, Chaffinch, Greenfinch, Goldfinch, Siskin, Common Redpoll, Bullfinch, Yellowhammer, Reed Bunting, Corn Bunting (scarce).

Summer (April to August): Great Crested Grebe, Turtle Dove, Common Cuckoo, Common Swift, Common Kingfisher, Sand Martin, Barn Swallow, House Martin, Sedge Warbler, Reed Warbler, Lesser Whitethroat, Common Whitethroat, Garden Warbler, Blackcap, Chiffchaff, Willow Warbler, Spotted Flycatcher, Linnet.

Spring and autumn passage (April to early June and August to October):
Little Ringed Plover, Dunlin, Common Greenshank, Green Sandpiper,
Common Sandpiper (any of the other regular passage waders may
occur), Lesser Black-backed Gull and Yellow Wagtail, in addition to
some of the summer visitors which also occur on passage.

93 WOMBWELL INGS AND BROOMHILL INGS

OS Landranger
Map 111 Sheffield
and Doncaster

Habitat

Wombwell Ings is a local authority reserve and consists of a large open
lagoon set in pastureland, with little vegetation, which allows easy viewing.
The water level at both Wombwell and Broomhill varies according to the
season and during the summer months there are good areas of marginal
mud, ideal for waders. There is a smaller pond at Wombwell which has
large stands of reedmace. Broomhill Ings is a Yorkshire Wildlife Trust
Reserve and is administered jointly by them and the Barnsley Metropolitan
Borough Council. The main sheet of water is 10 acres (4 ha) in extent and
reaches a maximum depth of about 8 feet (2.8 m). A visitor centre and hide
were recently burned down by vandals. There is a hide at Wombwell Ings.

Species

These two almost adjacent reserves are well watched by local people and
have an impressive bird list of 218 species with up to 160 being recorded
annually in recent years.

Little and Great Crested Grebes both breed, numbers of the former
species often reaching double figures during the autumn. Great Cormorants visit the area and one or two can usually be seen during the winter months. Grey Herons are always present, their numbers peaking in
August. A pair of Mute Swans breeds annually and small numbers of Tundra Swans may drop in during the winter at which time Whooper Swans
occur regularly on Broomhill Ings. Small numbers of Greylag Geese and
up to 80 Canada Geese are resident. Common Shelducks are usually present in small numbers throughout the year.

The area is good for waterfowl and up to 200 Eurasian Wigeons regularly spend the winter in the Wombwell Ings area. A few Gadwalls are
present throughout the year and a pair occasionally nests. Common Teals
pass through during the autumn when their numbers reach up to 300
birds, that number usually staying throughout the winter. Mallards are
present all year with peak numbers in autumn when around 300 birds are
usual. Small numbers of Northern Pintails pass through, mainly during
spring and autumn, when a few Garganeys may appear also. Gatherings
of Common Pochards, Tufted Ducks, Common Goldeneyes and
Goosanders are never large but some are always present in the winter; a
few pairs of Tufted Ducks breed in the area and some pairs of Ruddy
Ducks nest annually, usually on Wombwell Ings.

Eurasian Wigeon

Eurasian Sparrowhawk and Common Kestrel are both resident in the area and other passing raptors in recent years have included Osprey, Merlin, Hobby and Peregrine Falcon. Moorhens and Common Coots are numerous with regular counts of up to 200 Common Coots during the spring and autumn. Most of the passage waders are recorded during both migration seasons and flocks of European Golden Plovers and Northern Lapwings regularly number between 500 and 1,000 birds during the winter.

Gulls frequent the area with all the usual species being represented in addition to an occasional Iceland Gull. Easterly winds, particularly with rain, during May sometimes bring down migrating Common, Arctic and Black Terns which feed over the water, often for only short periods before moving on. A pair of Common Terns has nested on an artificial raft at Broomhill in recent years. Large numbers of Stock Doves are recorded each year with several hundreds feeding on stubble fields during the autumn; an exceptional 1,000 birds were counted flying over to roost in December 1990. Turtle Doves can be seen during the summer months. Five species of owls have been recorded in the area but most are very scarce and difficult to see, except for an occasional Short-eared hunting over the area during the non-breeding season.

The area is a good feeding place for Common Swifts which often gather over the open water in adverse weather conditions, and many of which doubtless breed in the nearby suburbia. A roost of Barn Swallows at Wombwell Ings has peaked at 15,000 in autumn. Passage of pipits, wagtails and a few Northern Wheatears is evident every spring and autumn; a roost of 242 Yellow Wagtails at Wombwell Ings in August 1990 was exceptional. Autumn gatherings of Goldfinches and Linnets on Wombwell Ings regularly number up to 200 or more of each species and numbers of Corn Buntings also regularly reach that figure in winter.

Timing

Visits during the winter months can be worthwhile for seeing waterfowl, especially the herd of Whooper Swans, but the spring and autumn migration periods (April to early June and late July to October) are the best for numbers of species. There is very little disturbance to Broomhill Ings and a visit at any time of day can be good. Periods of easterly winds with rain during May and early June are likely to bring down migrating terns and hirundines.

Access

These two reserves lie some 5 miles (8 km) east of Barnsley. Leave the A1 (M) at junction 37, 4 miles (6.4 km) north of the M18 junction 2, onto the A635 to the west for Dearne and Barnsley. After 6 miles (9.6 km), having passed through Hickleton and Goldthorpe, come to a roundabout and turn left onto the A6195 signed 'Wath, Wombwell and Hoyland'. Continue for 1.25 miles (2 km) to a second roundabout and take the third exit for Broomhill. Come to the Old Moor Tavern on the left after just under 0.5 miles (0.7 km) where the main road bends to the left. To reach Womb-well Ings, turn right here onto a short stretch of tarmac road and cross a small bridge over Bulling Dyke, after which turn immediately left into a car park, identified by children's swings. Walk along the left side of the adjoining field, and then along the side of Bulling Dyke and below a raised embankment, to the hide.

On leaving the car park, turn right onto the main road and pass through Broomhill village, just after which the water of Broomhill Ings is visible on the right. The signed car park is on the right, 175 yards (160 m) from the last houses.

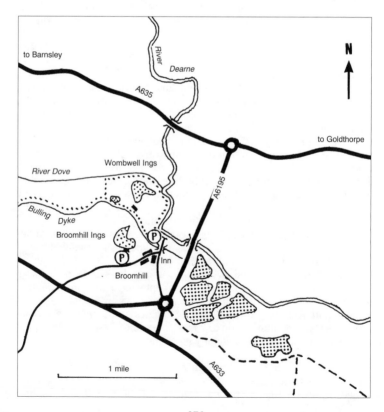

Calendar
This includes both sites.

Winter (October to March): Includes several resident species which occur throughout the year. Little Grebe, Great Crested Grebe, Great Cormorant, Grey Heron, Mute Swan, Tundra Swan, Whooper Swan, Greylag Goose, Canada Goose, Common Shelduck, Eurasian Wigeon, Gadwall, Common Teal, Mallard, Northern Pintail, Northern Shoveler, Common Pochard, Tufted Duck, Common Goldeneye, Goosander, Ruddy Duck, Eurasian Sparrowhawk, Common Kestrel, Merlin (occasional), Red-legged Partridge, Grey Partridge, Water Rail (mainly late autumn, occasionally during the summer), Moorhen, Common Coot, European Golden Plover, Northern Lapwing, Jack Snipe, Common Snipe, Green Sandpiper, Black-headed Gull, Common Gull, Herring Gull, Iceland Gull (occasional), Great Black-backed Gull, Stock Dove, Wood Pigeon, Collared Dove, Little Owl, Tawny Owl, Long-eared Owl (scarce), Short-eared Owl, Common Kingfisher, Green Woodpecker, Great Spotted Woodpecker, Sky Lark, Wren, Hedge Accentor, Robin, Blackbird, Fieldfare, Song Thrush, Redwing, Mistle Thrush, Goldcrest, Long-tailed Tit, Willow Tit, Blue Tit, Great Tit, Magpie, Eurasian Jackdaw, Rook, Carrion Crow, Common Starling, House Sparrow, Tree Sparrow, Chaffinch, Greenfinch, Goldfinch, Linnet, Yellowhammer, Reed Bunting, Corn Bunting.

Spring and summer (April to August): Includes several species which also occur on passage in both spring and autumn. Little Ringed Plover, Common Tern, Turtle Dove, Common Cuckoo, Common Swift, Sand Martin, Barn Swallow, House Martin, Yellow Wagtail, Pied Wagtail, Whinchat, Grasshopper Warbler (sporadic), Sedge Warbler, Reed Warbler, Lesser Whitethroat, Common Whitethroat, Blackcap, Chiffchaff, Willow Warbler.

Spring and autumn passage (April to early June and August to October): Hen Harrier (occasional), Osprey, Oystercatcher, passage waders, Little Gull, Lesser Black-backed Gull, Common Tern, Arctic Tern, Black Tern, Meadow Pipit, Northern Wheatear, Spotted Flycatcher.

93A OLD MOOR WETLANDS

OS Landranger Map 111
Sheffield and Doncaster

This new complex, incorporating the former Wath Ings' is due to open in February 1998. When completed, it will form an important link in the chain of wetland habitats in this region and will be one of the major sites for waterfowl and waders in the county. (See map for site 93.)

Habitat
This small reserve of approximately 100 acres (40.5 ha) is managed by the Yorkshire Wildlife Trust. It is situated on the north side of the River Dearne and includes a large sheet of shallow water known as the Main Ing, and a smaller sheet on the eastern end known as Cadeby Flash. There is much deciduous timber including many dead elm trees on the reserve. The embankment along the southern edge of the Main Ing is clothed in mature trees including hawthorns, rowans, alders and sycamores. Much of the reserve is covered by *Glyceria* marsh which is grazed by cattle. The Main Ing has extensive areas of *Typha* and *Glyceria* as well as other lacustrine vegetation, providing ample food for waterfowl during the winter months. Several mature crack willows line the river bank.

Species
A bird list of 169 species makes this compact reserve well worth a visit. The Main Ing is very suitable for breeding waterbirds and it is possible to see Little and Great Crested Grebes, Mallards, Gadwalls, Northern Shovelers, Tufted Ducks, Moorhens and Common Coots during the summer months. Common Kingfisher is also resident. The trees along the embankment and around the main water areas are good for woodpeckers and passerines. Both Green and Great Spotted Woodpeckers occur and Long-eared Owl is often reported. Eurasian Treecreepers and Willow Tits can be seen and most of the usual warblers, including Sedge and Reed, and also finches, are present during the breeding season. During the winter months, the Main Ing is good for waterfowl and the wooded areas contain most of the titmice and finches, in addition to immigrant thrushes.

Timing
Spring and early summer is perhaps the best period to visit the reserve when the resident birds are displaying and the newly arrived migrants are in song. A visit at any time from late July to October can be worthwhile for passage waterfowl and waders. The winter months are good for waterfowl, immigrant thrushes and finches as well as the resident woodland species.

Access
Denaby Ings is reached from Mexborough on the A6023. On leaving the town centre, look for a left fork signed 'Denaby Ings Nature Reserve' and proceed along Pastures Road for 0.5 miles (0.8 km) and look for a second sign pointing to the right which marks the entrance to the car park which is alongside the road. Walk from the car park back to the road to a set of concrete steps on the right which lead up to a small visitor centre and to a nearby hide overlooking the Main Ing.

A Nature Trail leads from the car park along the main road, passing over a bridge, and after 440 yards (400 m), turns right through a gate and along a footpath parallel to Pastures Lane. A path leads from the visitor centre along the top of the sluice embankment for 540 yards (500 m) to another hide and continues over a sluice gate, bearing left to Cadeby Flash after 330 yards (300 m).

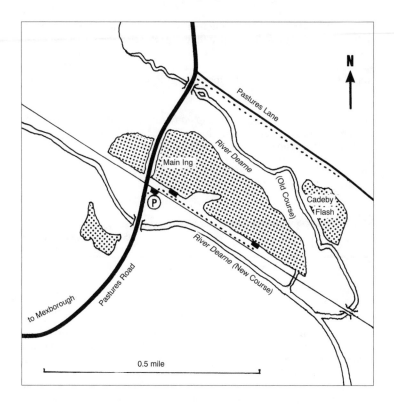

0.5 mile

Calendar

Winter (October to March): Grey Heron, Tundra Swan, Whooper Swan, grey geese (occasional), Eurasian Wigeon, Common Teal, Northern Pintail, Common Goldeneye, Merlin, European Golden Plover, Jack Snipe, Common Snipe, Woodcock, Common Redshank, Green Sandpiper, Common Gull, Herring Gull, Great Black-backed Gull, Long-eared Owl, Short-eared Owl, Grey Wagtail, Common Stonechat, Fieldfare, Redwing, Brambling, Siskin. A few of the above are resident species and occur throughout the year.

Spring and summer (April to August; breeding): Includes several species which also occur on passage during both spring and autumn. Little Grebe, Great Crested Grebe, Mute Swan, Canada Goose, Mallard, Garganey (rare), Northern Shoveler, Common Pochard, Tufted Duck, Eurasian Sparrowhawk, Common Kestrel, Red-legged Partridge, Grey Partridge, Common Pheasant, Moorhen, Common Coot, Little Ringed Plover, Northern Lapwing, Black-headed Gull, Stock Dove, Wood Pigeon, Collared Dove, Turtle Dove, Common Cuckoo, Little Owl, Tawny Owl, Common Swift, Common Kingfisher, Green Woodpecker, Great Spotted Woodpecker, Lesser Spotted Woodpecker (rare), Sand Martin, Barn Swallow, House Martin, Sky Lark, Tree Pipit, Meadow Pipit, Yellow Wagtail, Pied Wagtail, Wren, Hedge Accentor, Robin, Whinchat, Blackbird, Song Thrush, Mistle Thrush, Grasshopper Warbler (sporadic), Sedge Warbler, Reed Warbler, Lesser Whitethroat, Common Whitethroat,

Garden Warbler, Blackcap, Chiffchaff, Willow Warbler, Goldcrest, Spotted Flycatcher, Long-tailed Tit, Willow Tit, Blue Tit, Great Tit, Eurasian Treecreeper, Common Starling, Eurasian Jay, Magpie, Eurasian Jackdaw, Rook, Carrion Crow, House Sparrow, Tree Sparrow, Chaffinch, Greenfinch, Goldfinch, Linnet, Common Redpoll, Bullfinch, Yellowhammer, Reed Bunting, Corn Bunting.

Spring and autumn passage (April to early June and late July to October): Passage waders, Common Tern, Arctic Tern, Black Tern, Common Redstart, Northern Wheatear.

95 THRYBERGH COUNTRY PARK

OS Landranger Map 111
Sheffield and Doncaster

Habitat

Thrybergh Country Park is adjacent to the A630 Doncaster to Rotherham road and is bordered to the south by undulating arable land. The water is fairly deep with a bare open shoreline, except for the eastern corner and along the southern arm where there is some waterside vegetation. The main water is fished and also used for water sports during the summer months (April to September) but the two arms of the reservoir are protected by lines of buoys and are undisturbed except for people walking along the perimeter footpath.

Species

Waterfowl during the winter months are perhaps the main attraction here and at any time from October to March, good numbers of ducks frequent the water. Great Crested Grebes are usually present throughout the winter and an occasional Great Cormorant is seen. Grey Herons are regular visitors. The numbers of waterfowl can be quite impressive and the main ones, with some recent maxima in brackets, are: Mallard (120), Common Pochard (175) and Tufted Duck (155), in addition to which small numbers of Eurasian Wigeons, Common Teals, Gadwalls, Northern Shovelers, Common Goldeneyes and Goosanders are often present. A pair of Mute Swans, a small flock of Canada Geese, Moorhens and Common Coots are resident.

The arable fields to the south attract flocks of European Golden Plovers (1,000 in January 1993) and also Northern Lapwings. Gulls assemble during the late afternoons in winter, Black-headed being the most numerous (4,000 in January 1993) with smaller numbers of Common, Herring and Great Black-backed and sometimes a few Lesser Black-backed. Flocks of Stock Doves sometimes reach double figures and Wood Pigeons are numerous. Finches are well represented with all the usual commoner species being recorded each autumn and winter, in addition to Yellowhammers and Reed Buntings. Pied Wagtails frequent the shoreline and Sky Larks favour the arable fields at this time. Common Stonechat was seen during the winter of 1992/93.

During the spring and autumn migration seasons, a few passage waders may be seen in the more secluded areas, and passerines in the bushes and trees around the southern shores. Common Swifts and hirundines hawk for insects over the water, particularly during cool weather whilst they are on migration, and passage terns may occur on easterly winds. During April and May, parties of migrating Meadow Pipits, Yellow Wagtails and Pied Wagtails, including an occasional 'White' Wagtail, frequent the grassy banks of the reservoir.

Timing

Being a popular recreational water during the summer months, Thrybergh is really a winter birdwatching site and from October to March can be an excellent place for seeing waterfowl at fairly close range. The light is not really a problem at any time of day as the path from the car park continues around the western end and circles both arms of the reservoir. The waterfowl usually congregate at the eastern end. Visits during April/May and August/September will produce passage migrants and these periods are not without interest in spite of the disturbance to the main water area.

Access

This area is certainly worth a visit during the winter months and with such easy access, is recommended, especially for viewing waterfowl.

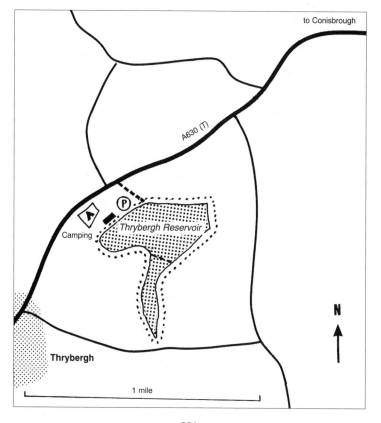

Leave the A1(M) west of Doncaster onto the A630 for Rotherham and continue for 5.5 miles (8.8 km), passing through Conisbrough, before coming to the Country Park entrance on the left just before entering Thrybergh. The car park is just 200 yards (180 m) from the main road and overlooks the reservoir. There is a visitor centre (not always open) where a list of current bird sightings is sometimes displayed in the window. There are toilet facilities and several picnic tables near the water's edge as well as a field for mobile caravans and camping. A footpath circles the lake but access to the eastern end is prohibited during the winter months (October to March) in order to prevent disturbance to the waterfowl in their preferred area. This does not restrict viewing, however, as the entire main water can be viewed from the car park or from the western shore.

Calendar

Winter (October to March): Little Grebe, Great Crested Grebe, Grey Heron, Great Cormorant (occasional), Mute Swan, Canada Goose, Common Shelduck, Eurasian Wigeon, Gadwall, Common Teal, Mallard (including several feral types), Northern Pintail (scarce), Northern Shoveler, Common Pochard, Tufted Duck, Common Goldeneye, Goosander, Eurasian Sparrowhawk, Common Kestrel, Grey Partridge, Moorhen, Common Coot, European Golden Plover, Northern Lapwing, Common Snipe, Black-headed Gull, Common Gull, Herring Gull, Lesser Black-backed Gull (few), Great Black-backed Gull, Stock Dove, Wood Pigeon, Collared Dove, Little Owl, Tawny Owl, Sky Lark, Meadow Pipit (also on passage), Wren, Hedge Accentor, Robin, Common Stonechat (irregular), Blackbird, Fieldfare, Song Thrush, Redwing, Mistle Thrush, Blue Tit, Great Tit, Magpie, Eurasian Jackdaw, Rook, Carrion Crow, Common Starling, House Sparrow, Chaffinch, Greenfinch, Goldfinch, Linnet, Yellowhammer, Reed Bunting.

Spring and autumn passage (April to early June and August to October): Common Tern, Arctic Tern, Black Tern, Common Cuckoo, Common Swift, Sand Martin, Barn Swallow, House Martin, Yellow Wagtail, Whinchat, Northern Wheatear, Sedge Warbler, Common Whitethroat, Blackcap, Willow Warbler.

THE SOUTHERN PENNINES

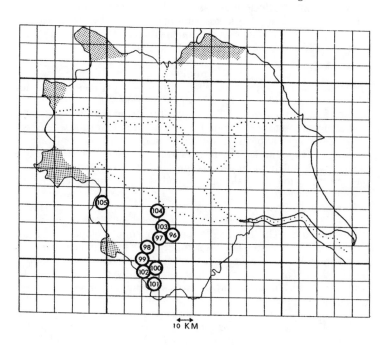

10 KM

96 WINTERSETT RESERVOIR; COLD HIENDLEY RESERVOIR; ANGLERS' PARK LAKE; HAW PARK

OS Landranger
Maps 110/111
Sheffield and
Huddersfield/
Doncaster

Habitat

This complex has several varied habitats and is one of the best places for birdwatching in the area. The shoreline of Wintersett Reservoir varies from open grazing and arable land to deciduous woodland, hedgerows, some marsh and willow scrub and open rocky shore. Cold Hiendley Reservoir, a long thin water stretching westwards from Wintersett, is surrounded by mature deciduous trees and thick waterside vegetation. The relatively new Anglers' Park Lake is surrounded mainly by open grassland and some areas of young trees and rough ground. The nearby Haw Park is an extensive area, consisting mainly of large conifers.

Species

The large areas of open water at Wintersett and Anglers' Park Lake attract occasional divers and the rarer grebes during the autumn and winter months and also many waterfowl at this time. Great Crested and Little Grebes are resident and their numbers during the autumn and winter regularly reach 30 to 40 birds, usually on Wintersett where several pairs of each species breed annually. One or two Black-necked Grebes occur during the spring and autumn periods. Small numbers of Great Cormorants pass through in the spring and autumn and a few Grey Herons are present throughout the year.

Tundra and Whooper Swans are regularly seen during the period October to March and grey geese including several Pink-footed and a few White-fronted and Greylags often drop in. Common Shelducks are regular visitors, mainly during the late spring. Surface-feeding ducks are well represented; Eurasian Wigeons at Anglers' Park Lake regularly number up to 100 birds and more. Small numbers of Gadwalls, Common Teals, Northern Pintails and Northern Shovelers frequent all three lake areas during the non-breeding season with an occasional Garganey during the late spring or autumn. Common Pochards favour the open water of Anglers' Park Lake and winter gatherings regularly number around 200 birds with up to 400 on occasions. Tufted Ducks are common and winter flocks of up to 300 and 400 are regular; small numbers breed on Wintersett. Good numbers of Common Goldeneyes spend the winter on the lakes and Goosanders assembling to roost on Anglers' Park Lake often number up to 20 birds. Ruddy Ducks can be seen in small numbers throughout the year.

An occasional Marsh Harrier may pass through during the spring, and Osprey is a regular visitor on passage at this time. Eurasian Sparrowhawks and Common Kestrels are resident in the area and there is always the chance of seeing Merlin during the winter or Hobby during the late summer and autumn.

Red-legged and Grey Partridges breed locally and a few Water Rails are seen during the winter months, usually in the marshy areas near the bridge on the western edge of Wintersett Reservoir. Most of the usual passage waders occur mainly during April/May/June and August/September, and have included Little Stint, Purple Sandpiper, Black-tailed Godwit, Bar-tailed Godwit and Turnstone in recent years. Single Arctic Skuas have passed through during some autumns. A Pomarine Skua was seen in October 1989 and a Long-tailed Skua in September 1991.

Gulls are well represented and rarer species in recent years have been Mediterranean, Sabine's and Kittiwake; a few Little Gulls pass through during the spring and autumn. A large roost of gulls on either Wintersett or Anglers' Park Lake regularly holds up to several thousands, mainly Black-headed, Lesser Black-backed and Herring with fewer Common, Great Black-backed and an occasional Iceland or Glaucous. Easterly winds during May and June bring passage terns to the area and Common, Arctic and Black are regular visitors with an occasional Sandwich or Little Tern.

Owls are well represented with Little, Tawny and Long-eared resident in small numbers and Short-eared occurring during the autumn and winter; Barn Owl is scarce. Common Kingfisher is a possibility and all three species of woodpeckers are resident in the general area.

Spring and autumn passage during April/May and August/September brings pipits, wagtails and warblers which move through on migration. Both Sedge and Reed Warblers breed at Wintersett as do Lesser Whitethroat, Common Whitethroat, Garden Warbler, Blackcap, Chiffchaff and Willow Warbler. Arrivals of immigrant thrushes during October and November bring many Blackbirds, Fieldfares and Redwings into the area.

A total of 222 species recorded since 1945 reflects the excellence of this area.

Timing

Winter is a good time to visit for waterfowl, but spring (April to early June) and autumn (August to October) are the best times for seeing most species when passage waders and migrant passerines are moving through. There is some disturbance at Wintersett from boating and windsurfing, mainly at the weekends, but the water is extensive and some birds are always to be seen. The waterfowl tend to leave Wintersett when disturbed and fly to the nearby Anglers' Park Lake. It is worth spending a full day at this complex, especially during the spring or autumn passage periods.

Access

To reach this area, starting with Wintersett Reservoir, leave Wakefield to the south on the A61 and after 1.75 miles (2.8 km) turn left for Ryhill at The Three Houses pub into Chevet Lane. Continue under a railway arch, passing the conifers of Haw Park on the left and take the next left after another 1 mile (1.6 km) signed 'Cold Hiendley and Ryhill'. Continue for another 1 mile (1.6 km) and turn left at a sign for Anglers' Country Park. Wintersett Reservoir is visible on the left before reaching a small bridge over the eastern arm of the water, 0.5 miles (0.8 km) from the turning. Stop at this bridge and view the open water to the left and the small Botany Bay to the right.

To reach Anglers' Country Park, continue along the road for a little under 0.5 miles (0.8 km) and turn left (signed) to reach the car park after another 0.5 miles (0.8 km). A well marked path leads from the car park through a gate (information board) and circles the lake. Proceed in a clockwise direction having passed a shallow scrape and an area of rough ground on the left, which is worth checking for waders and passerines at

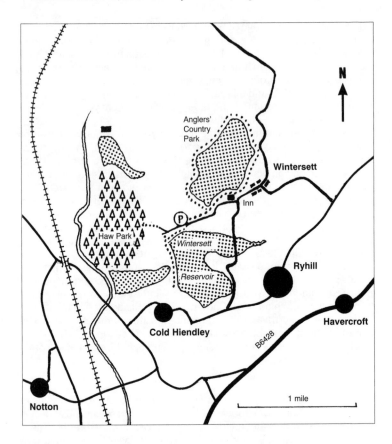

the appropriate season. The path passes a hide and returns eventually to the car park. From here, one can walk across the road and down a short track to the West Riding Sailing Club compound and bear right for 50 yards (45 m) to view Wintersett Reservoir from the northern edge. A path continues along the northwestern edge of the water, through a strip of deciduous trees and eventually to a bridge. This is a good vantage point from which to view the open water and also the smaller Cold Hiendley Reservoir to the west. The bridge also overlooks an area of marshy ground and bushes, good for passerines.

It is also possible to reach the bridge by turning right outside Anglers' car park and walking along the road (for fishermen's cars only) which runs parallel to the strip of woodland and finally to the bridge after 0.5 miles (0.8 km). A track forking right through a metal gate, partway along this road, leads to Haw Park where several paths lead through the coniferous woodland. On leaving Anglers' car park by car, turn left to reach The Anglers Retreat pub and the village of Wintersett after 0.5 miles (0.8 km).

Calendar

This includes all four sites.

Winter (October to March): Includes many resident species which are present throughout the year. Occasional divers and the rarer grebes, Little

286

Grebe, Great Crested Grebe, Great Cormorant, Grey Heron, Mute Swan, Tundra Swan, Whooper Swan, Pink-footed Goose (occasional), Greylag Goose, Canada Goose, Eurasian Wigeon, Gadwall, Common Teal, Mallard, Northern Pintail, Northern Shoveler, Common Pochard, Tufted Duck, Common Goldeneye, Smew (occasional), Goosander, Ruddy Duck, Hen Harrier (rare), Eurasian Sparrowhawk, Common Kestrel, Merlin, Red-legged Partridge, Grey Partridge, Common Pheasant, Water Rail, Moorhen, Common Coot, European Golden Plover, Northern Lapwing, Jack Snipe, Common Snipe, Woodcock, Mediterranean Gull, Black-headed Gull, Common Gull, Lesser Black-backed Gull, Herring Gull, Great Black-backed Gull, Iceland Gull, Glaucous Gull, Stock Dove, Wood Pigeon, Barn Owl (rare), Little Owl, Tawny Owl, Long-eared Owl, Short-eared Owl (occasional), Common Kingfisher, Green Woodpecker, Great Spotted Woodpecker, Lesser Spotted Woodpecker (rare), Sky Lark, Grey Wagtail, Pied Wagtail, Wren, Hedge Accentor, Robin, Common Stonechat, Blackbird, Fieldfare, Song Thrush, Redwing, Mistle Thrush, Goldcrest, Long-tailed Tit, Willow Tit, Coal Tit, Blue Tit, Great Tit, Eurasian Treecreeper, Eurasian Jay, Magpie, Eurasian Jackdaw, Rook, Carrion Crow, Common Starling, House Sparrow, Tree Sparrow, Chaffinch, Brambling, Greenfinch, Goldfinch, Siskin, Linnet, Common Redpoll, Bullfinch, Yellowhammer, Reed Bunting, Corn Bunting.

Spring and summer (April to August): Includes several species which also occur on passage in both spring and autumn. Little Ringed Plover, Turtle Dove, Common Cuckoo, Common Swift, Sand Martin, Barn Swallow, House Martin, Tree Pipit, Meadow Pipit, Yellow Wagtail, Common Redstart, Whinchat, Sedge Warbler, Reed Warbler, Lesser Whitethroat, Common Whitethroat, Garden Warbler, Blackcap, Chiffchaff, Willow Warbler, Spotted Flycatcher.

Spring and autumn passage (April to early June and August to October): Marsh Harrier (rare), Osprey, Hobby, waders, Common Tern, Arctic Tern, Black Tern, Northern Wheatear.

97 BRETTON COUNTRY PARK AND SCULPTURE PARK

**OS Landranger Map 110
Sheffield and
Huddersfield**

Habitat

The Bretton complex is an 18th-Century landscaped park with large areas of mature woodland and two lakes alongside the River Dearne. There are many fine oaks and beech trees set amongst the open pasture, part of which is grazed by sheep and cattle. The mixed woodland around the lakes is a nature reserve administered by The Yorkshire Wildlife Trust. The park falls into three main sections: the Country Park, the Sculpture

Park and the YWT Reserve. The Country Park covers 96 acres (38 ha) and is mainly open parkland running along the north bank of the River Dearne. The Sculpture Park is set in well-wooded parkland adjacent to Bretton Hall which was built in 1720 and is now administered as a College of Higher Education. The Nature Reserve covers an area of 150 acres (60 ha) and comprises all the coniferous and deciduous woodland surrounding the lakes.

Species

The well-established deciduous woodland and the mature oaks and beeches standing in the open parkland are very good for all the species associated with that habitat. All three species of woodpeckers occur along with European Nuthatches, Eurasian Treecreepers, titmice, Hawfinches and most of the other finches including Siskins and Common Redpolls at the appropriate season. During the summer months, most of the regular woodland warblers can be seen including Common and Lesser Whitethroats (usually scarce), Garden Warbler, Blackcap, Willow Warbler and Chiffchaff. The open parkland around the College and in the Sculpture Park also holds most of these species.

The lakes are relatively undisturbed and have breeding Little and Great Crested Grebes, Moorhens and Common Coots. During the winter months small numbers of waterfowl frequent both lakes and Canada Geese are present throughout the year. There is a breeding colony of Grey Herons in the Park and birds are usually to be seen, particularly in spring.

Timing

The spring period (April to early June) is certainly the best time to visit Bretton Park when the resident passerines are in song and the summer visitors are settled in. A walk through the parkland and the woodland at this time can be very productive. Both the Country Park and particularly the Sculpture Park can be very busy during the summer months and especially at weekends.

Access

This area is conveniently situated alongside the M1 motorway, some 15 miles (24 km) south of Leeds and a similar distance north of Sheffield. Leave the motorway at junction 38 and take the A637 Huddersfield road to the north. After just 0.5 miles (0.8 km) look for the entrance to Bretton Country Park on the left where there is free car parking, a visitor centre and toilet facilities. Paths lead from here into the Park. Information leaflets are available at the visitor centre.

Starting at the small gate leading from the car park, walk to the right and down the grass slopes to the dam wall where the footpath crosses a hump-backed bridge and the Dam Head, to continue as a permissive footpath through the well-wooded slopes of Oxley Bank Wood, part of the YWT Reserve. The remainder of the woodland in this area is not open to the general public but a permit can be obtained from the College for which a charge is made. Please keep to the woodland footpath. One can walk along the north bank of the River Dearne and into the Sculpture Park, a distance of about 0.5 miles (0.8 km) from the bridge.

To reach the Sculpture Park and the grounds of Bretton College by car, drive from the Country Park entrance for 1 mile (1.6 km) to the village of West Bretton and turn left at a war memorial. The College

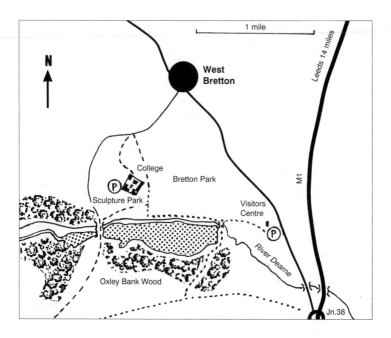

entrance is reached after just over 0.25 miles (0.4 km). Parking near the College is free. The Sculpture Park is open to the public, free of charge, from 10 am to 6 pm during the summer months and until dusk during the winter.

Calendar

Spring and summer (April to August): Includes several resident species which are present throughout the year. Little Grebe, Great Crested Grebe, Grey Heron, Canada Goose, Mallard, Common Kestrel, Common Pheasant, Moorhen, Common Coot, Stock Dove, Wood Pigeon, Collared Dove, Common Cuckoo, Tawny Owl, Little Owl, Common Swift, Common Kingfisher (scarce), Green Woodpecker, Great Spotted Woodpecker, Lesser Spotted Woodpecker, Sky Lark, Sand Martin, Barn Swallow, House Martin, Tree Pipit, Wren, Hedge Accentor, Robin, Blackbird, Song Thrush, Mistle Thrush, Lesser Whitethroat (occasional), Common Whitethroat (occasional), Garden Warbler, Blackcap, Chiffchaff, Willow Warbler, Spotted Flycatcher, Long-tailed Tit, Willow Tit, Coat Tit, Blue Tit, Great Tit, European Nuthatch, Eurasian Treecreeper, Eurasian Jay, Magpie, Eurasian Jackdaw, Rook, Carrion Crow, Common Starling, House Sparrow, Tree Sparrow, Chaffinch, Greenfinch, Goldfinch, Linnet, Bullfinch, Yellowhammer, Reed Bunting.

Autumn and winter (September to March): Waterfowl, gulls, Fieldfare, Redwing, Brambling, Siskin, Common Redpoll, Hawfinch.

98 INGBIRCHWORTH RESERVOIR

OS Landranger Map 110
Sheffield and Huddersfield

Habitat

This reservoir is set amongst grassland with dry-stone walls, at an altitude of 820 feet (250 m) above sea level and lies just 0.5 miles (0.8 km) from the main A629 Huddersfield to Sheffield road. A minor road passes close to the water's edge along the eastern and southern boundaries and there is a car park and several picnic tables overlooking the reservoir at the northern end. There is a thin strip of deciduous woodland between the road and the water's edge along the southwestern shore.

Being one of over 100 reservoirs in this part of the southern Pennines, many of which have no easy access for the birdwatcher, and lying just 10 miles (16 km) south of the centre of Huddersfield, Ingbirchworth is recommended.

Species

During the winter months, occasional divers and any one of the rarer grebes may turn up, and Great Northern Diver, Red-necked, Slavonian and Black-necked Grebes have occurred during recent years. Waterfowl include most of the usual diving and surface-feeding ducks as well as small numbers of Greater Scaup and Common Scoters which are seen occasionally. Some waders occur during both migration seasons and in addition to the more usual passage species, rare ones in recent years have been Spotted Sandpiper and Grey Phalarope. Both Iceland and Glaucous Gulls have occurred. As at any of the reservoirs along the Pennine Chain, Common, Arctic and Black Terns may call in to feed whilst on passage, mainly during April and May. Little Grebe, Great Crested Grebe and Tufted Duck are breeding species and Moorhens and Common Coots are resident.

The fields west of the reservoir, in the area of Whitley Common, regularly attract small trips of Dotterels during the spring. The meadows around the reservoir have breeding Eurasian Curlews, Northern Lapwings and Common Redshanks. In years when Common Quails are more numerous than usual, the adjacent meadows have attracted them and the species may have bred within 0.5 miles (0.8 km) of the reservoir boundary. During the spring migration season (April to early June) Common Swifts, hirundines, Meadow Pipits, Yellow Wagtails and Northern Wheatears pass through.

Timing

A visit at any time during the winter months will produce several species of waterfowl and the chance of a diver or one of the rarer grebes. April, May and early June can be good for passerines and other passage migrants including some waders which occur more regularly during the autumn (late July to September). Viewing from the car park area on the north side of the reservoir can be difficult on bright sunny days during the winter months as one is looking into the light. It is then better to view from the road along the southern edge.

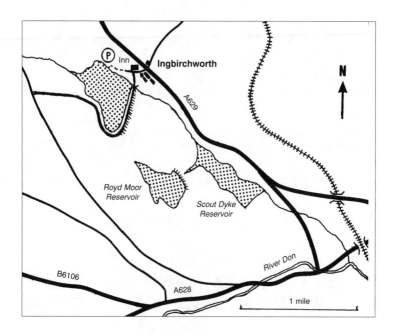

Access

Leave the M1 at junction 37 and take the A628 for Manchester and Peni-
stone. Continue for 5 miles (8 km) to a roundabout and turn right onto
the A629 Huddersfield road. Come to the village of Ingbirchworth after
2.5 miles (4 km) and look for a sign on the left to The Fountain Inn. Turn
left here, pass the pub, and where the road bears left to cross the dam
wall, proceed straight forward onto the track which leads to the car park
after about 100 yards (90 m). From the car park, a footpath leads to the
right alongside the water's edge and follows the northern edge of the
reservoir to join the main road at the northwestern corner. The reservoir
can also be viewed from this road by walking southeastwards from here.
The road circles the reservoir and returns over the dam wall to the car
park entrance track.

Calendar

Winter (October to March): Grey Heron, Eurasian Wigeon, Common Teal,
Northern Shoveler, Common Pochard, Tufted Duck, Greater Scaup
(small numbers fairly regularly), Common Scoter (occasional), Common
Goldeneye, Eurasian Sparrowhawk, Merlin, European Golden Plover,
Common Snipe, Common Redshank, Black-headed Gull, Common Gull,
Herring Gull, Lesser Black-backed Gull, Iceland Gull (occasional),
Glaucous Gull (occasional), Great Black-backed Gull, Kittiwake
(sporadic, usually during storms), Grey Wagtail, Fieldfare, Redwing,
Goldcrest, Coal Tit, Brambling, Common Redpoll and Bullfinch, in addi-
tion to the common resident species which are present throughout the
year.

Summer – breeding (April to July): Little Grebe, Great Crested Grebe, Mallard, Tufted Duck, Common Kestrel, Red-legged Partridge, Grey Partridge,
Moorhen, Common Coot, Northern Lapwing, Eurasian Curlew, Stock

Dove, Wood Pigeon, Collared Dove, Little Owl, Sky Lark, Barn Swallow, House Martin, Meadow Pipit (occurs on passage also), Pied Wagtail, Wren, Hedge Accentor, Robin, Whinchat, Blackbird, Song Thrush, Mistle Thrush, Sedge Warbler (few), Blackcap, Willow Warbler, Willow Tit, Blue Tit, Great Tit, Magpie, Eurasian Jackdaw, Rook, Carrion Crow, Common Starling, House Sparrow, Chaffinch, Greenfinch, Goldfinch, Linnet, Yellowhammer, Reed Bunting.

Spring and autumn passage (April to early June and late July to October): Little Ringed Plover, Great Ringed Plover, Dotterel, any of the other regular passage waders may occur, Common Tern, Arctic Tern, Black Tern, Common Cuckoo, Common Swift, Sand Martin, Barn Swallow, House Martin, Yellow Wagtail, Northern Wheatear.

99 LANGSETT RESERVOIR, MIDHOPE MOOR AND LOW MOOR VIEWPOINT

OS Landranger
Map 110
Sheffield and
Huddersfield

Habitat
This reservoir, like so many others in the southern Pennines, is surrounded by large conifer plantations which reach down to the water's edge in many places. The edges have little or no areas of mud suitable for passage waders. Lying to the southwest is Midhope Moor, an extensive area of open heather moor which can be overlooked from the road at the Low Moor viewpoint.

Species
The three major habitats which make up this site; the reservoir, the conifer plantations and the open moorland, provide the birdwatcher with a wide variety of species in a relatively small area.

The reservoir has breeding Little Grebes, and a few Great Crested Grebes occur occasionally. Small parties of Whooper Swans may call in during the late autumn and winter months when skeins of Pink-footed Geese are sometimes seen over the area. Common Teals, Mallards and Tufted Ducks breed around the reservoir and several other species occur on passage including Common Shelduck, Eurasian Wigeon, Northern Pintail, Northern Shoveler, Red-breasted Merganser and Goosander. Tufted Ducks, Common Goldeneyes and a few Common Pochards are usually present during the winter.

A lone Hen Harrier, Rough-legged Buzzard, Merlin or Peregrine Falcon may be seen over the moors from the Low Moor viewpoint during the winter and an occasional Osprey investigates the reservoir during migration. Northern Goshawk is a possibility in winter around the woodland areas in addition to Eurasian Sparrowhawk and Common Kestrel which are resident breeding species. Red Grouse breed on the open

Fieldfares

moorland and Grey Partridges and Common Pheasants occur around the moorland edges. Other breeding species in this habitat are European Golden Plover, Northern Lapwing, Common Snipe, Eurasian Curlew and Common Redshank with Common Sandpipers breeding around the reservoir.

Tawny Owls and Little Owls reside in the area and a pair of Short-eared Owls sometimes nests on the moors. Both Green and Great Spotted Woodpeckers are resident. The moors and the fringing fields have breeding Meadow Pipits, Ring Ouzels and a few pairs of Twites, and the woodland areas have most of the common breeding passerines including Tree Pipits, Wood Warblers, Pied Flycatchers and Common Crossbills, the last named species varying in numbers according to the particular year. Following the crossbill invasion in 1982, several Parrot Crossbills were recorded and some pairs stayed to breed in the general area.

Timing

The best times to visit are during the spring and early summer and also during the autumn. The spring and summer periods will provide most of the breeding species which can be readily seen around the moors or along the woodland walks. Autumn and early winter is the best period to watch from the Low Moor viewpoint for birds of prey and Red Grouse.

Access

To reach this site, leave the M1 motorway at junction 35A onto the A616 for Huddersfield and continue for 10 miles (16 km) to the village of Langsett. On entering the village look for a minor road on the left, signed 'Strines and Derwent Valley', which passes over the dam wall of Langsett Reservoir after only about 200 yards (180 m). Park on the dam road to view the reservoir and the conifer woods to the right. There is a small car park in the village alongside the main road about 100 yards (90 m) west

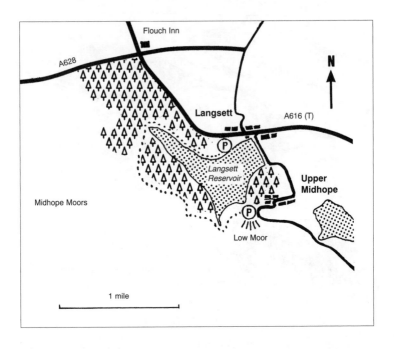

of the reservoir turning, from where a footpath leads through the woods to circle the reservoir. Continue along the dam road by car, enter the village of Upper Midhope and turn sharp right, signed 'Strines', and come to a sharp left bend after only about 400 yards (360 m). Park here in a wide area on the right, identified by a sign reading 'Privilege Footpath'. This is a good place from which to view the open expanse of Low Moor, and beyond, for raptors and Red Grouse. The privilege footpath leads from here through the woods surrounding Langsett Reservoir, crossing over Blackwell Beck, then turning westwards onto the moors before returning to cross the Little Don River and finally to the car park in the village. Distance from the Low Moor viewpoint to the village car park is about 3 miles (4.8 km).

Calendar

This includes the reservoir, the conifer plantations and the open moorland.

All year: Little Grebe, Grey Heron, Common Teal, Mallard, Tufted Duck, Eurasian Sparrowhawk, Common Kestrel, Red Grouse, Grey Partridge, Common Pheasant, Moorhen, Common Coot, Northern Lapwing, Common Snipe, Woodcock, Black-headed Gull, Stock Dove, Wood Pigeon, Collared Dove, Little Owl, Tawny Owl, Green Woodpecker, Great Spotted Woodpecker, Grey Wagtail, Pied Wagtail, Dipper, Wren, Hedge Accentor, Robin, Blackbird, Song Thrush, Mistle Thrush, Goldcrest, Long-tailed Tit, Willow Tit, Coal Tit, Blue Tit, Great Tit, Eurasian Treecreeper, Eurasian Jay, Magpie, Eurasian Jackdaw, Carrion Crow, Common Starling, House Sparrow, Tree Sparrow, Chaffinch, Greenfinch, Siskin, Linnet, Twite, Common Redpoll, Common Crossbill (can be very common in good years), Bullfinch, Yellowhammer, Reed Bunting.

Spring and summer (April to August): European Golden Plover, Eurasian Curlew, Common Redshank, Common Sandpiper, Common Cuckoo, Short-eared Owl, Sky Lark, Barn Swallow, House Martin, Tree Pipit, Meadow Pipit (also on passage), Common Redstart, Whinchat, Northern Wheatear, Ring Ouzel, Common Whitethroat, Garden Warbler, Blackcap, Wood Warbler, Chiffchaff, Willow Warbler, Spotted Flycatcher, Pied Flycatcher.

Winter (October to March): Whooper Swan, Pink-footed Goose, Common Pochard (few), Common Goldeneye, Hen Harrier, Northern Goshawk, Rough-legged Buzzard, Merlin, Peregrine Falcon, Common Gull, Lesser Black-backed Gull, Herring Gull, Iceland Gull (occasional), Glaucous Gull (occasional), Great Black-backed Gull, Fieldfare, Redwing, Rook, Brambling.

Spring and autumn passage (April to early June and August to October): Great Crested Grebe, Great Cormorant (occasional), Common Shelduck, Eurasian Wigeon, Northern Pintail, Great Scaup (occasional), Common Scoter (occasional), Red-breasted Merganser, Goosander, Osprey, Oystercatcher, Great Ringed Plover, Common Swift.

100 BROOMHEAD MOOR AND RESERVOIR

OS Landranger Map 110
Sheffield and Huddersfield

Habitat

Broomhead Moor is a large area of open heather moor and forms part of the extensive moors which stretch along the southern Pennines from Holmfirth, south to the Derbyshire border. It is bordered to the north by the Ewden Beck which runs through a narrow valley clothed in deciduous trees and continues eastwards to enter Broomhead Reservoir. The reservoir is set in a wide valley and is surrounded by conifer plantations and some stands of deciduous timber.

Species

The habitats in this area are almost exactly the same as at Langsett and Midhope, comprising the reservoir, the conifer plantations and the extensive Broomhead Moor. With very few exceptions, the species list is the same as for site 99. The reservoir attracts some Northern Shovelers on passage, a few pairs of Dunlins breed on Broomhead Moor and European Nuthatches frequent the stands of deciduous woodland.

Timing

Spring and early summer are the best times for most species when the resident and migrant breeding species are settled in. The autumn and winter can be good for birds of prey on Broomhead Moor and around the conifer plantations.

Access

After leaving Langsett and the Low Moor viewpoint, continue southeast-wards for 2 miles (3.2 km) before dropping steeply downhill to cross the Ewden Beck. The deciduous trees along this narrow valley are worth investigating for passerines in the spring and summer. Continue uphill and look for a small stand of large mature Scots pines and larches on the right and park beside a stone wall at the entrance gate to Broomhead Moor (opposite Broomhead Hall on the map). A footpath proceeds west-wards from here along the edge of the open heather moor and along the southern edge of the Ewden Valley.

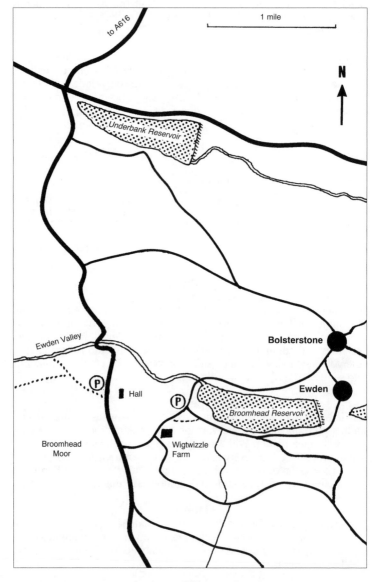

To reach Broomhead Reservoir, continue along the road and after just under 0.5 miles (0.8 km) turn left, signed 'Bolsterstone and Stocksbridge'. Keep left at a junction after 1.25 miles (0.4 km) in the area of Wigtwizzle Farm and reach the reservoir after a further 0.5 miles (0.8 km). Park on the left opposite a road junction, signed 'Bradfield', and walk to the bridge to view the water and the trees to the left where the Ewden Beck enters the reservoir. The Bradfield road along the southern edge of the reservoir is worth investigating and offers good views over the water and of the conifer plantations. There are two parking areas along this road, the first one on the right just 350 yards (32 m) from the junction and the other on the left after a little over 0.5 miles (0.9 km). A bridleway leads from this car park through the woods along the edge of the reservoir as far as the dam wall.

Calendar
See under Langsett and Midhope Moor (site 99).

101 REDMIRES RESERVOIRS, WYMING BROOK AND THE RIVELIN VALLEY

OS Landranger
Map 110
Sheffield and
Huddersfield

Habitat
This complex is situated at the northern edge of the Peak District National Park, some 6 miles (9.6 km) west of Sheffield. Conifer plantations abut the northern and western edges of the reservoirs and there are large tracts of open heather and bracken moorland to the north and south. The well-wooded Rivelin Valley and the Wyming Brook area lie just to the north of the reservoirs.

Species
Any time from July to October can be very good for watching birds passing through the area, particularly waders which may include most of the regular passage species including Common Redshanks, Little Stints, Curlew Sandpipers, Ruffs and Dunlins, with occasional godwits and any one of the rarer species being a possibility. The breeding waders are European Golden Plover, Northern Lapwing, Eurasian Curlew, Common Sandpiper, Common Redshank and Common Snipe.

During September and early October, many hundreds of Meadow Pipits pass over as they leave the high ground on their journey southwards. Visible migration is often quite impressive as finches, thrushes and other passerines pass overhead. From mid-October onwards, thousands of Fieldfares and Redwings may pass, depending on the right conditions for their arrival along the coast. Chaffinches, Bramblings, Linnets, occasional Twites and possibly a few Snow Buntings and Lapland Longspurs are also involved in these movements. A solitary Water Pipit has been recorded around the reservoir edges during recent winters.

Waterfowl numbers build up during the autumn when Tufted Ducks, Common Pochards and Common Goldeneyes are usually present in good numbers along with Eurasian Wigeons, Mallards, Common Teals and perhaps a few Northern Shovelers and Northern Pintails. Any one of the divers, rarer grebes or sea ducks is a possibility during the winter months. A pair of Red-breasted Mergansers has stayed to breed in recent years and a lone bird may be seen on the western reservoir during the summer. Eurasian Sparrowhawks and Common Kestrels are resident breeding species. A passing Osprey is possible during May or June and Merlin or Hen Harrier can sometimes be seen over the moorland during the autumn and winter months. Red Grouse can be watched from the footpaths across the moors throughout the year and a pair of Short-eared Owls regularly breeds in this area.

A roost of gulls builds up from July including many Lesser Black-backed and Black-headed Gulls which are joined in winter by Common, Herring and Great Black-backed Gulls. Keep an eye out for Yellow-legged Gull, which has been seen here in recent years.

The woods along the Rivelin Valley and Wyming Brook are good for passerines and a few pairs of Wood Warblers breed there. Siskins and Common Crossbills can also be seen during the breeding season.

Timing

This complex has something to offer the birdwatcher throughout the year but the best time to visit, for the most species, is during the period July to October. Passage waders regularly occur in good numbers, particularly if the water level is low. The best time to witness visual passerine migration is during September and October, mainly during the early mornings. Visits during the winter months can be productive for waterfowl and possible birds of prey.

Access

Travel west from Sheffield on the A57 and about 2 miles (3.2 km) from the city centre, look for The Crosspool Tavern on the right, opposite which is Redmires Road, signed 'Lodge Moor and Redmires'. Proceed along this road, passing the Hallamshire Golf Club on the right after just over 1 mile (1.7 km) and then Lodge Moor Hospital on the left after a further 1 mile (1.6 km), after which continue for 1.5 miles (2.4 km) and come to the Wyming Brook car park on the right at the bottom of the hill. One can walk north from here through the woods to Rivelin Dams, a distance of about 1 mile (1.6 km). This footpath continues westwards along the Rivelin Valley before turning south to cross the open moorland to the main Redmires Reservoir car park, a round trip of about 3 miles (4.8 km).

On leaving the Wyming Brook car park, turn right and drive for 0.75 miles (1.2 km) to the main Redmires car park. The footpath leading north from here crosses open moorland for 1 mile (1.6 km) before turning eastwards along the Rivelin Valley and finally back to the Wyming Brook car park (see above). There is a detailed map at each car park showing the various footpaths. One can walk, or drive, to the right from the main car park along a tarmac road around the end of the reservoir from which there are uninterrupted views over the water. This road ends at the southwestern corner of the reservoir, but a public byway continues westwards, passing conifer woodland and onto the open moor leading to Stanedge Pole, an ancient wooden marker, and eventually to the top of the impressive escarpment of Stanage Edge, a distance of just over 1 mile (1.7 km).

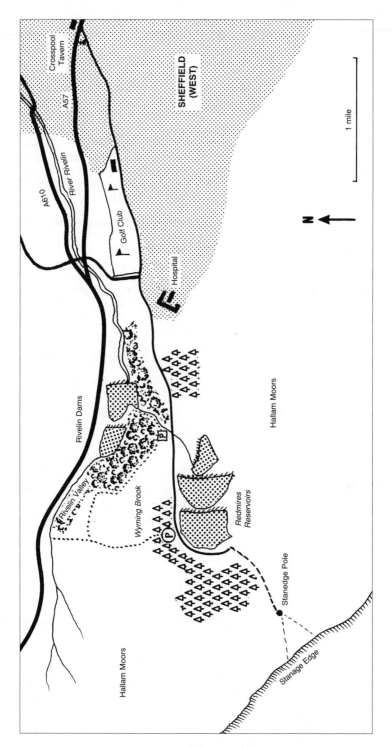

Calendar

This includes the reservoirs and the woodland along Wyming Brook and the Rivelin Valley.

All year: Grey Heron, Common Teal, Mallard, Tufted Duck, Eurasian Sparrowhawk, Common Kestrel, Red Grouse, Grey Partridge, Common Pheasant, Moorhen, Black-headed Gull, Stock Dove, Wood Pigeon, Collared Dove, Tawny Owl, Little Owl, Green Woodpecker, Great Spotted Woodpecker, Grey Wagtail, Pied Wagtail, Wren, Hedge Accentor, Robin, Blackbird, Mistle Thrush, Goldcrest, Long-tailed Tit, Willow Tit, Coal Tit, Blue Tit, Great Tit, Eurasian Treecreeper, Eurasian Jay, Magpie, Eurasian Jackdaw, Rook, Carrion Crow, Common Starling, House Sparrow, Tree Sparrow, Chaffinch, Greenfinch, Goldfinch, Siskin, Common Redpoll, Common Crossbill, Bullfinch, Yellowhammer, Reed Bunting.

Summer – breeding: Includes some species which also occur on passage in spring and autumn. Red-breasted Merganser (sporadic), European Golden Plover, Northern Lapwing, Common Snipe, Woodcock, Eurasian Curlew, Common Redshank, Common Sandpiper, Turtle Dove (scarce), Common Cuckoo, Short-eared Owl, Sky Lark, Barn Swallow, Tree Pipit, Meadow Pipit, Yellow Wagtail, Common Redstart, Whinchat, Northern Wheatear, Ring Ouzel, Song Thrush, Common Whitethroat, Garden Warbler, Blackcap, Wood Warbler (Wyming Brook), Chiffchaff, Willow Warbler, Spotted Flycatcher, Linnet, Twite.

Spring and autumn passage (April to early June and July to October): Northern Shoveler, Osprey, Merlin, Oystercatcher, Great Ringed Plover, Grey Plover, Red Knot, Sanderling, Little Stint, Curlew Sandpiper, Dunlin, Ruff, Black-tailed Godwit, Bar-tailed Godwit, Whimbrel, Spotted Redshank, Common Greenshank, Green Sandpiper, Lesser Black-backed Gull, Common Swift, Sand Martin, Barn Swallow, House Martin, Tree Pipit, Yellow Wagtail, Lapland Longspur (occasional), Snow Bunting (occasional).

Winter (October to March): Occasional divers and the rarer grebes, Eurasian Wigeon, Northern Pintail, Common Pochard, Greater Scaup, Common Scoter, Common Goldeneye, Goosander, Hen Harrier, Common Gull, Herring Gull, Great Black-backed Gull, Fieldfare, Redwing, Brambling.

102 THE STRINES AREA: HOLLING DALE PLANTATION AND FOULSTONE MOOR

OS Landranger
Map 110
Sheffield and
Huddersfield

Habitat

This area is included primarily for the easy access to open heather moor and the large conifer plantations. Holling Dale and the adjacent Bole Edge plantations are large areas of conifers bordering onto the open heather of Foulstone Moor to the west and Bradfield Moor to the north. These areas of heather moor form part of the extensive Broomhead, Midhope, Langsett and Thurlstone Moors which stretch northwards from here for 10 miles (16 km) to Holmfirth. The peak of Black Tor, at the western edge of Foulstone Moor, reaches a height of 1765 feet (538 m) above sea level.

The southern Pennines

Species

This area of extensive plantations of conifers is one of the best places in the region to see Common Crossbills which are relatively numerous in good 'crossbill' years. The woods and the adjoining moors are good for birds of prey, and several species are recorded annually. There is a fair chance of seeing a Northern Goshawk over the plantations during the autumn and winter months and an occasional Common Buzzard, Merlin or Peregrine Falcon may occur over the moorland at this time. Eurasian Sparrowhawk and Common Kestrel both breed locally.

The moors have breeding Red Grouse, European Golden Plovers, Northern Lapwings and Eurasian Curlews. Woodcocks nest in the area and should be looked for at dusk when they display over the open areas of woodland. Both Little and Tawny Owl are resident as are Great Spotted Woodpecker and Eurasian Treecreeper.

The mixed woodland on the hillsides has breeding Tree Pipits, Common Redstarts, Wood Warblers and Willow Warblers. Meadow Pipits are

301

numerous on the moorland. Goldcrests, Eurasian Jays, Siskins, and Common Redpolls are other characteristic breeding birds of the wooded slopes and clearings.

Timing

As with all the sites which are primarily woodland, the best time to visit for the highest number of species is during the spring and early summer. The moorland is also good at this time when the breeding waders are back in territory and are displaying. The autumn and winter months can be interesting for birds of prey and flocks of thrushes and finches.

Access

This area lies just 5 miles (8 km) south of Broomhead Reservoir and is well worth combining with a visit to that site. From Broomhead Reservoir, return past Wigtwizzle Farm to the main road and turn left. After 0.5 miles (0.8 km) keep right at a fork beyond which the road drops down a steep hill to cross over Agden Bridge and continues for a further 3 miles (4.8 km) passing Thornseat Lodge on the right just before skirting the western edge of Bole Edge plantation. The road now drops down to a hairpin bend at Strines Dike. Just before reaching the bend, park on the right in an open area with silver birch trees beside a conifer plantation. One can view the ridges and surrounding plantations from here. A footpath leads for 0.5 miles (0.8 km) through Holling Dale plantation before coming to the open Foulstone Moor and continues across the heathermoor to Black Tor after a further 1 mile (1.6 km).

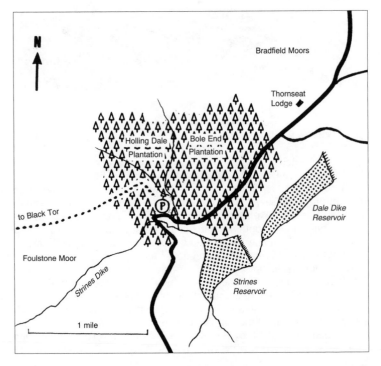

Calendar

All year: Eurasian Sparrowhawk, Common Kestrel, Red Grouse, Common Pheasant, Northern Lapwing, Woodcock, Stock Dove, Wood Pigeon, Little Owl, Tawny Owl, Great Spotted Woodpecker, Meadow Pipit, Pied Wagtail, Wren, Hedge Accentor, Robin, Common Stonechat (scarce), Blackbird, Song Thrush, Mistle Thrush, Goldcrest, Coal Tit, Blue Tit, Great Tit, Eurasian Treecreeper, Eurasian Jay, Magpie, Rook, Carrion Crow, Common Starling, House Sparrow, Chaffinch, Goldfinch, Siskin, Common Redpoll, Common Crossbill, Bullfinch, Yellowhammer.

Spring and Summer (late March to August): European Golden Plover, Eurasian Curlew, Common Cuckoo, Common Swift, Sky Lark, Barn Swallow, House Martin, Tree Pipit, Whinchat, Northern Wheatear, Wood Warbler, Willow Warbler, Spotted Flycatcher, Linnet.

Autumn and winter (September to March): Northern Goshawk, Common Buzzard, Peregrine Falcon, Fieldfare, Redwing, Brambling, Greenfinch.

103 PUGNEYS COUNTRY PARK

OS Landranger Maps 110/111
Sheffield and
Huddersfield/Doncaster

Habitat

Pugneys is a restored sand and gravel working formerly known as Durker Sand Quarries and consists of one large and two smaller lakes surrounded in the main by open fields with a small wood to the southwest.

The largest of the three lakes is used primarily for leisure activities but is good for waterbirds during the winter months. To the south of the main lake is a smaller area of water designated as a reserve. This has a reedbed and other waterside vegetation, which is lacking around the large lake, and is a better area for migrants and breeding birds, especially passerines. There is also a small lake to the northwest of the main lake known as Cawoods. The complex is owned by the Wakefield Metropolitan Borough Council.

Species

The large sheet of open water, with its two satellites, has a bird list of 204 species. Like others in the region, it attracts many waterbirds, especially during the winter months. An occasional diver or rarer grebe is recorded annually, and both Little and Great Crested Grebes occur throughout the year. Great Cormorants are often present in small numbers, mainly during spring and autumn, and a few Grey Herons regularly feed along the shoreline.

Mute Swans are common and a few Tundra and Whooper Swans are recorded during most winters. Large numbers of Canada Geese frequent the area during the non-breeding season and some Common Shelducks pass through on spring migration. The ducks, which often favour the smaller Reserve lake, occur in good numbers. Flocks of Eurasian Wigeons often reach up to 100 birds in the winter, and Gadwalls, Common Teals, Mallards and Northern Shovelers are usually to be seen, the largest numbers occurring during the autumn. Gatherings of diving ducks are a feature of the lakes and there are often up to 100 Common Pochards. The site is good for Tufted Ducks and between 200 and 500 can be seen during the winter period when Common Goldeneyes usually number around 20 birds. The numbers of Ruddy Ducks build up during the autumn with up to 20 birds regularly present and a pair has nested in recent years.

Eurasian Sparrowhawks and Common Kestrels are resident in the area. One or two Water Rails spend the winter around the Reserve lake and flocks of Common Coots regularly number 250 birds. Flocks of European Golden Plovers on the open grass fields often number 1,000 birds during the winter when flocks of Northern Lapwings gather also. Passage waders are usually well represented with most of the usual species being recorded annually. Little Ringed Plovers breed on the site.

A winter roost of gulls regularly holds up to 5,000 or more Black-headed Gulls with smaller numbers of Common, Herring and Great Black-backed and an occasional Iceland or Glaucous Gull. Lesser Black-backed Gulls pass through on spring and autumn migration. Common, Arctic and Black Terns stop off to feed whilst on spring migration, usually on easterly winds and especially after rain. A pair of Common Terns has stayed to breed in recent years.

Large gatherings of Common Swifts assemble to feed over the water, usually during periods of cool, damp weather in May and June. Meadow Pipits, Yellow Wagtails, Pied Wagtails and Northern Wheatears pass through the area on spring migration when they frequent the short grass around the lakes. Sedge and Reed warblers breed at the smaller Reserve lake.

Timing

Visits during the winter months (October to March) can be very good for waterbirds. During the summer, and particularly at weekends, the main lake and surrounding area is subject to much disturbance from boating and visitors and it is advisable to go there early in the mornings. The periods of spring and autumn migration (late March to May and late July to September) are the best times to visit for the most number of species.

Access

Pugneys is reached from exit 39 of the M1 motorway. Take the A636 for Wakefield and after 0.75 miles (1.2 km) come to a roundabout (signed 'Pugneys Country Park') and reach the park entrance gate after 100 yards (90 m). This leads straight into a car park adjacent to the main lake (free parking and toilet facilities). Footpaths circle the main lake, which covers an area of 75 acres (30 ha), and lead to the smaller Reserve lake on the opposite side near a small wood. To reach this area, walk to the right from the car park round the western end of the lake to the wood where a path leads to the lakeshore and a hide after about 100 yards (90 m).

Calendar

Winter (October to March): Includes many resident species which occur throughout the year. Occasional divers and rarer grebes, Little Grebe, Great Crested Grebe, Great Cormorant, Grey Heron, Mute Swan, Tundra

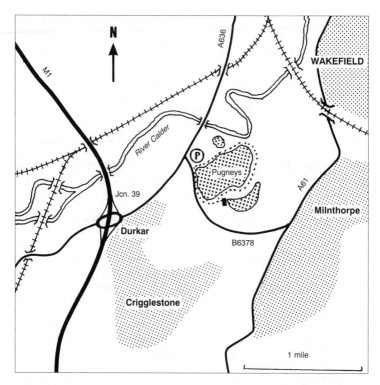

Swan, Whooper Swan, occasional grey geese, Canada Goose, Eurasian Wigeon, Gadwall, Common Teal, Mallard, Northern Pintail (scarce), Northern Shoveler, Common Pochard, Tufted Duck, Greater Scaup (scarce), Common Goldeneye, Smew (scarce), Red-breasted Merganser (scarce), Goosander, Ruddy Duck, Eurasian Sparrowhawk, Common Kestrel, Water Rail, Moorhen, Common Coot, Oystercatcher (occasional), European Golden Plover, Northern Lapwing, Dunlin, Common Snipe, Common Redshank, Mediterranean Gull, Black-headed Gull, Common Gull, Herring Gull, Iceland Gull, Glaucous Gull, Great Black-backed Gull, Stock Dove, Wood Pigeon, Little Owl, Common Kingfisher, Great Spotted Woodpecker, Sky Lark, Pied Wagtail, Fieldfare, Redwing, Willow Tit, Blue Tit, Great Tit, Long-tailed Tit, Magpie, Eurasian Jackdaw, Rook, Carrion Crow, Common Starling, Tree Sparrow, House Sparrow, Greenfinch, Siskin, Yellowhammer, Reed Bunting.

Spring and summer (April to August): Includes several species which also occur on passage during both spring and autumn. Little Ringed Plover, Common Redshank, Common Tern, Common Cuckoo, Common Swift, Sand Martin, Barn Swallow, House Martin, Meadow Pipit, Yellow Wagtail, Blackbird, Song Thrush, Mistle Thrush, Sedge Warbler, Reed Warbler, Common Whitethroat, Lesser Whitethroat, Garden Warbler, Blackcap, Chiffchaff, Willow Warbler, Goldfinch.

Spring and autumn passage (April to early June and August to October): Passage waders, Common Tern, Arctic Tern, Black Tern, Common Redstart, Whinchat, Northern Wheatear, Spotted Flycatcher.

104 ARDSLEY RESERVOIR

Habitat

This relatively bare and open reservoir, adjacent to the town of East Ard-sley, is set in grazing land with stone walls and some scattered deciduous timber. There is a small wood below the dam wall at the southern end and another to the north. The shoreline is fairly open with few small trees save for a line of willows along the eastern edge. A large slag heap cur-rently dominates the northeastern end of the reservoir but the open-cast mining at this site is due to cease shortly when the area will be restored to farmland with additional planting of hedgerows and trees.

Species

Ardsley Reservoir has a list of 175 species which has included several inter-esting birds over the years. The open and exposed water is attractive to wandering divers and three species have occurred. Sea ducks frequently call in and have included Common Eider, Velvet Scoter, Common Scoter and Greater Scaup in addition to both races of Brent Goose. Common Goldeneye is the most frequent winter duck, their numbers peaking dur-ing March when small numbers of Goosanders also occur. Common Pochards and Tufted Ducks occur in small numbers but the surface-feed-ing ducks are relatively scarce due to the lack of shallow margins.

A large gull roost builds up during the winter months and attracts all the larger species including Iceland and Glaucous Gulls which are seen fairly regularly from late December to February. Mediterranean Gull and Kitti-wake have also been recorded. A fine adult Yellow-legged Gull was found dying on the ice in January 1987 and remains the only Yorkshire specimen of this recently separated species. Lesser Black-backed Gulls are scarce until the spring when passage birds arrive in large numbers, mainly of the British race. Great Crested Grebes pass through at this time and there have been three records of Slavonian Grebe. A few Great Cormorants, Grey Herons and occasional wild swans drop in during most winters.

There are no really suitable areas of mud along the shorelines to attract passing waders until the late summer but a few are seen each year dur-ing the spring and autumn, Eurasian Curlew, Common Redshank and Common Sandpiper being the most frequent. The passage of Common, Arctic and Black Terns occurs here, as elsewhere, during May, usually with easterly winds. A Caspian Tern appeared in May 1989.

Many Meadow Pipits pass through *en route* to their moorland breeding areas from mid-March into April at which time departing Fieldfares and Redwings are usually evident. Migrant Pied Wagtails have included some 'Whites' during April and May. Small parties of Twites are sometimes seen in spring as they pass through on their way to higher ground. Wildfowl are more frequent during the autumn with most of the common species being represented including Eurasian Wigeons, Common Teals and Mal-lards with fewer Northern Pintails and Northern Shovelers, in addition to the diving ducks.

The water has attracted some birds in recent years which are rare inland including two Leach's Storm Petrels, an Avocet, Purple Sandpiper and Arctic Skua. Cool damp weather during the spring and autumn migrating seasons often brings down large numbers of Common Swifts and hirundines to feed low over the water. Meadow Pipits can be particularly numerous during September when they are moving south from their breeding areas on the higher ground.

The reservoir is subject to disturbance during the summer months, and this, coupled with the barren nature of the water's edge, reduces the number of breeding species. A few Great Crested Grebes are usually present however and attempt to breed, as do Mallards, Moorhens and occasionally Common Coots. Below the dam wall is Haigh Hall Spring Wood, a small area of deciduous timber which has breeding Tawny Owls, Great Spotted Woodpeckers, Eurasian Jays, Blackcaps, Willow Warblers, Great Tits, Blue Tits and Chaffinches. A solitary Little Owl can sometimes be seen on the stone walls in this area. To the north of the reservoir is Red Wood which has breeding Spotted Flycatchers, Blackcaps, Willow Warblers and Tree Sparrows. The banks of the reservoir and the surrounding farmland hold a few breeding pairs of Northern Lapwings, Sky Larks, Common and Lesser Whitethroats, Yellowhammers and Reed Buntings.

Timing
There is a certain amount of disturbance around the reservoir, except during the winter months, and early morning visits are recommended. The best times of the year to visit are during the spring and autumn migration seasons for the most species. It is worthwhile calling in during winter afternoons to witness the gulls assembling to roost, at which time there is always the chance of seeing a diver, rarer grebe or one of the sea ducks.

Access
Leave the M1 at junction 41 and take the A650 for Bradford, also signed 'Morley'. After 1.25 miles (2 km), turn left into Westerton Road opposite a large building (Thomas Ambler & Son) and then left again just over 0.5 miles (0.9 km) at Westerton Road Post Office into Haigh Moor Road. Continue for 500 yards (460 m) to the reservoir entrance on the left, just beyond a row of houses. At the time of writing there is no parking at the reservoir, so one should park carefully off Haigh Moor Road in one of the side streets and walk down the Water Authority track to reach the reservoir after 200 yards (180 m). An all-weather footpath circles the reservoir from which there are uninterrupted views of the water.

Calendar
This includes the reservoir, the surrounding farmland and the two small woods.

All year: Mallard, Moorhen, Common Coot, Little Owl, Tawny Owl, Great Spotted Woodpecker, Wren, Hedge Accentor, Robin, Blackbird, Mistle Thrush, Blue Tit, Great Tit, Magpie, Eurasian Jackdaw, Carrion Crow, Common Starling, House Sparrow, Tree Sparrow, Chaffinch, Greenfinch, Yellowhammer, Reed Bunting.

Spring and summer (April to August): Great Crested Grebe, Northern Lapwing, Common Swift, Barn Swallow, House Martin, Sky Lark, Lesser Whitethroat, Common Whitethroat, Blackcap, Willow Warbler, Spotted Flycatcher.

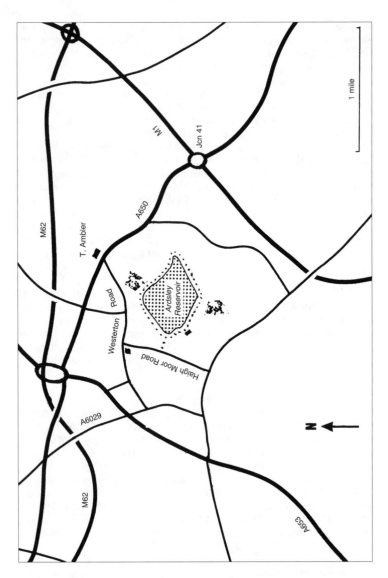

Spring and autumn passage (April to early June and late July to October): Eurasian Wigeon, Common Teal, Northern Pintail, Northern Shoveler, Common Scoter, Common Sandpiper, any of the other passage waders are a possibility depending on the water level, Lesser Black-backed Gull, Common Tern, Arctic Tern, Black Tern, Sand Martin, Barn Swallow, House Martin, Meadow Pipit, Pied Wagtail, Northern Wheatear.

Winter (October to March): Divers and the rarer grebes, Great Cormorant, wild swans (occasional), sea ducks (occasional), Common Pochard, Tufted Duck, Common Goldeneye, Black-headed Gull, Common Gull, Herring Gull, Iceland and Glaucous Gulls (fairly regular), Great Black-backed Gull, Grey Wagtail, Fieldfare, Redwing.

105 HARDCASTLE CRAGS

Habitat

This site is owned by The National Trust and covers an area of 300 acres (121 ha). It comprises the two steep-sided wooded valleys of Hebden Dale and Crimsworth Dene, each with a stream running through it, and lying just 1.5 miles (2.4 km) northwest of the town of Hebden Bridge. The woodland was planted during the 19th Century and consists mainly of Scots pine, beech, oak, silver birch and sycamore with ample understorey. The crags are rocky outcrops above the woodland and there are disused mill ponds.

Species

The birds found here are typically those associated with mature deciduous woodland and the site is certainly worth a visit for this group of species, particularly during the spring (April to early June) when the summer visitors have arrived and, together with the resident passerines, are in song and showing to advantage.

Eurasian Sparrowhawks breed in the woods and Common Kestrels can be seen along the upper crags and over the adjacent ground. Stock Doves and Wood Pigeons are resident, and during the summer months Common Cuckoos are present. Several pairs of Tawny Owls breed along the valleys and can be heard calling mainly during the spring and autumn. Both Green and Great Spotted Woodpeckers frequent the area and Dippers may be seen along the streams. Common Redstarts breed, along with Lesser Whitethroats, Garden Warblers, Blackcaps, Wood Warblers, Chiffchaffs and Willow Warblers. There are also Spotted Flycatchers and a few pairs of Pied Flycatchers. Eurasian Treecreepers are resident. The thrushes, titmice and finches are also well represented (see the 'Calendar' section below).

Timing

The best time to visit is during the period mid-April to early June when the resident songbirds and the summer visitors are at their best. It is worth going early in the day to hear the dawn chorus. The site is very popular with tourists and the car parks can be crowded, especially at weekends and during fine weather. The evenings can be very pleasant and worthwhile for woodland birds.

Access

To reach Hardcastle Crags, travel west from Halifax for 5 miles (8 km) on the A646 to the town of Hebden Bridge where there are National Trust signs in the town centre. These direct you to the A6033 Keighley Road, along which continue for just 0.75 miles (1.2 km) and bear left (National Trust sign) to reach the car parks after a further 0.5 miles (0.8 km). There are two car parking areas, both surrounded by woodland and each having a map showing the area and the footpaths. The upper, overflow car park is recommended. There are 3 miles (4.8 km) of tracks and paths through the woods and a 2-mile (3.2-km) walk around the crags.

Information leaflets are available (65 pence) from the Regional Office, 27 Tadcaster Road, Dringhouses, York YO2 2QG. Guided walks are also possible, details of which can be obtained from The Warden on Halifax (01422) 844518.

Calendar

Spring and summer (April to August – breeding): Includes the resident species which are also present throughout the year. Eurasian Sparrowhawk, Common Kestrel, Stock Dove, Wood Pigeon, Common Cuckoo, Tawny Owl, Green Woodpecker, Great Spotted Woodpecker, Dipper, Wren, Hedge Accentor, Robin, Common Redstart, Blackbird, Song Thrush, Mistle Thrush, Lesser Whitethroat, Garden Warbler, Blackcap, Wood Warbler, Chiffchaff, Willow Warbler, Spotted Flycatcher, Pied Flycatcher, Long-tailed Tit, Marsh Tit, Blue Tit, Great Tit, Eurasian Treecreeper, Eurasian Jay, Magpie, Eurasian Jackdaw, Carrion Crow, Common Starling, House Sparrow, Chaffinch, Greenfinch, Bullfinch.

GLOSSARY OF TERMS

Auk A collective name given to the Common Guillemot, Razorbill, Puffin and Little Auk.

Carrland Area of waterlogged, reedy ground with emergent trees, mainly of alder or willow.

Commoner Gulls Collective name for the Black-headed, Common, Lesser Black-backed, Herring and Great Black-backed Gulls.

Crepuscular Mainly active at dawn or dusk.

Clough A rocky and often wooded moorland gully in the southern part of the Yorkshire Pennines (see Gill).

Diurnal Mainly active during the hours of daylight.

Diving Duck A duck such as Tufted Duck, Common Pochard or any of the sea ducks, which dive below the surface to feed on weeds, invertebrates and shellfish.

Drain A narrow man-made watercourse, created to drain the surrounding land (see Dyke).

Drift Migrant Term applied mainly to migrant passerines which have been 'drifted' off their intended course by adverse winds.

Dyke A man-made drainage ditch (see Drain).

Eruption A mass exodus of birds, usually from their natal areas and mainly associated with high population levels and/or food shortage, e.g. Bohemian Waxwing, Bearded Tit (see Irruption).

Fall (of migrants) A sudden arrival, usually overnight but regularly continuing into the morning, of migrant passerines which have been, or are being, grounded by adverse weather as soon as they reach the coast. Mainly an autumn phenomenon.

Feral Term applied to a species either having been released or escaped from captivity and successfully living in a wild state.

Flash An area of open floodwater, usually occurring in pastureland and often only temporary.

Gill (or Ghyll) A rocky moorland gully in the northern part of the Yorkshire Pennines.

Grey Geese A collective name for Bean, Pink-footed, White-fronted, Lesser White-fronted and Greylag Geese.

Hirundine A member of the swallow or martin families.

Ings Areas of low-lying wet meadow usually adjacent to rivers and often resulting from mining subsidence.

Irruption A mass arrival of birds from another area, usually associated with high population levels and/or food shortage in their natal regions (see Eruption).

Larger Gulls Collective name for Lesser Black-backed, Herring, Iceland, Glaucous and Great Black-backed Gulls.

Leaf Warbler A member of the *Phylloscopus* group, e.g. Willow Warbler, Chiffchaff, Pallas's Leaf Warbler or Yellow-browed Warbler etc.

Loafing A term applied to gulls or waterfowl resting on land after feeding or bathing.

Nocturnal Mainly active during the hours of darkness.

Overshooting A term usually applied to spring migrants which are blown further north than their intended destination by strong winds from the southern quarter.

Passage Migrant Birds which pass through an area at times of both spring and autumn migration on their way to and from their summer quarters, e.g. Black Tern and Meadow Pipit.

Passerine A perching bird. Includes the larks, swallows, pipits, wagtails, chats, thrushes, warblers, flycatchers, titmice, shrikes, crows, starlings, sparrows, finches and buntings.

Raptor Name given to diurnal birds of prey, i.e. eagles, hawks and falcons.

Rarer Grebes Includes Red-necked, Slavonian and Black-necked Grebes.

Roding The crepuscular display flight of the Woodcock during which it flies with a peculiar deliberate wing action and uttering a short grunting note.

Redhead Name given to females and immature male sawbills (see below) and Common Goldeneyes in which the plumage of the first-year male resembles that of the female and is almost indistinguishable in the field.

Sawbill The collective name given to the Red-breasted Merganser, Goosander and Smew.

Scar A long ridge of exposed rock along the top of a hillside, or lines of tilted stratified rocks exposed near the shore at low tide.

Scrape A shallow man-made and water-filled excavation aimed primarily at providing habitat for waterfowl and waders. Also a small depression made by ground-nesting birds in which to lay their eggs – 'nest scrape'.

Sea Ducks Includes those ducks which are normally associated with coastal waters, e.g. Greater Scaup, Long-tailed Duck, Common Eider and Common Scoter.

Seawatching A very popular pursuit in which one scans the sea for passing seabirds, mainly divers, shearwaters, petrels, waterfowl, gulls, terns and skuas.

Surface-feeding Duck A duck, such as Common Teal or Mallard, which feeds by sifting food particles from, or just below, the water surface. Also dabbling duck.

Tarn An upland sheet of water, either natural or man-made but not a reservoir.

Vagrant A bird many miles from its normal range and a term usually applied to species from North America and Asia.

Visual Migration The diurnal movements of birds migrating overhead which can be witnessed, mainly during the autumn, at migrational focal points along the coast and inland.

Wader A collective name for the sandpipers, plovers and curlews etc. Also shorebird.

White-winged Gulls Name given to Iceland and Glaucous Gulls.

Wild Swans Tundra and Whooper Swans as opposed to the introduced Mute Swan.

Winter Thrushes Refers mainly to Fieldfares and Redwings but can also be applied to incoming autumn flocks of Blackbirds and Song Thrushes.

Wreck A term used for the sudden appearance onshore or inland, of storm-blown seabirds which normally spend their time out at sea, e.g. petrels and auks.

FURTHER READING LIST

The following books give detailed information for several of the areas included in this publication:

Brook R.L. (1976) *The Aire Valley Wetlands*. Wakefied Naturalists' Society.

Chislett R. (1953) *Yorkshire Birds*. A. Brown and Sons.

Clunas A.J. and Shorrock B. (1991) *Birds around Malham*. The Naturalist Vol.116 pp.73–91.

Dickens R.F. and Pickup J.D. (1973) *Fairburn and its Nature Reserve*. Dalesman.

Dickens R.F. and Mitchell W.R. (1978) *Birdwatching in Yorkshire*. Dalesman.

Elliott S.C. (1989) *Bird Watching in East Yorkshire, The Humber and Teesmouth*. C. Ward and Co. Ltd.

Hornbuckle J. and Herringshaw D. (1985) *Birds of the Sheffield Area*. Sheffield Bird Study Group and Sheffield City Libraries.

Lewis D.B. (Editor) (1991) *The Yorkshire Coast*. Normandy Press.

Limbert M., Mitchell R.D. and Rhodes R.J. (1986) *Thorne Moors – Birds and Man*. Doncaster and District Ornithological Society.

Mather John R. (1986) *The Birds of Yorkshire*. Croom Helm.

Morgan N. (1996) *The Birds of the Northallerton and Richmond Area*. Privately published.

Nelson T.H. (1907) *The Birds of Yorkshire*. A. Brown and Sons.

Pashby B.S. (1985) *John Cordeaux – Ornithologist*. Spurn Bird Observatory Committee.

Pashby B.S. (1988) *A List of the Birds of Spurn 1946–1985*. Spurn Bird Observatory Committee.

Rhodes R.J. (1967) *Birds of the Doncaster District*. Doncaster and District Ornithological Society.

Spencer K.G. (1973) *Birds in Lancashire*. Turner and Earnshaw Ltd.

Vaughan R. (1974) *Birds of the Yorkshire Coast*. Hendon Publishing.

The Yorkshire Naturalists' Union Annual Reports.

LIST OF SPECIES RECORDED IN YORKSHIRE AND NORTH HUMBERSIDE

This list includes all the 426 species which have been officially accepted onto the County List. Some have occurred on one occasion only and, in some cases, many years ago. There are, in addition, some exciting records of rare seabirds by very reliable and experienced observers, which have not yet been accepted by the National Rarities Committees and these have not been included.

Order and nomenclature follows that of Voous K.H., *List of Recent Holarctic Bird Species* (1973 and 1977) as amended.

The English names are those published by *British Birds* magazine in 1993 with the old name, if different, shown in brackets.

English name	Scientific name	English name	Scientific name
Red-throated Diver	*Gavia stellata*	Glossy Ibis	*Plegadis falcinellus*
Black-throated Diver	*Gavia arctica*	Eurasian Spoonbill	*Platalea leucorodia*
Great Northern Diver	*Gavia immer*	(Spoonbill)	
White-billed Diver	*Gavia adamsii*	Mute Swan	*Cygnus olor*
Pied-billed Grebe	*Podilymbus podiceps*	Tundra Swan	*Cygnus columbianus*
Little Grebe	*Tachybaptus ruficollis*	(Bewick's Swan)	
Great Crested Grebe	*Podiceps cristatus*	Whooper Swan	*Cygnus cygnus*
Red-necked Grebe	*Podiceps grisegena*	Bean Goose	*Anser fabalis*
Slavonian Grebe	*Podiceps auritus*	Pink-footed Goose	*Anser brachyrhynchus*
Black-necked Grebe	*Podiceps nigricollis*	White-fronted Goose	*Anser albifrons*
Black-browed	*Diomedia*	Lesser White-fronted	*Anser erythropus*
Albatross	*melanophris*	Goose	
Fulmar	*Fulmarus glacialis*	Greylag Goose	*Anser anser*
Soft-plumaged Petrel	*Pterodroma mollis*	(Grey Lag Goose)	
Capped Petrel	*Pterodroma hasitata*	Snow Goose	*Anser caerulescens*
Bulwer's Petrel	*Bulweria bulwerii*	Canada Goose	*Branta canadensis*
Cory's Shearwater	*Calonectris diomedea*	Barnacle Goose	*Branta leucopsis*
Great Shearwater	*Puffinus gravis*	Brent Goose	*Branta bernicla*
Sooty Shearwater	*Puffinus griseus*	Red-breasted Goose	*Branta ruficollis*
Manx Shearwater	*Puffinus puffinus*	Egyptian Goose	*Alopochen*
Mediterranean	*Puffinus yelkouan*		*aegyptiacus*
Shearwater		Ruddy Shelduck	*Tadorna ferruginea*
Little Shearwater	*Puffinus assimilis*	Common Shelduck	*Tadorna tadorna*
Wilson's Storm Petrel	*Oceanites oceanicus*	(Shelduck)	
(Wilson's Petrel)		Mandarin Duck	*Aix galericulata*
European Storm Petrel	*Hydrobates pelagicus*	Eurasian Wigeon	*Anas penelope*
(Storm Petrel)		(Wigeon)	
Leach's Storm Petrel	*Oceanodroma*	American Wigeon	*Anas americana*
(Leach's Petrel)	*leucorhoa*	Gadwall	*Anas strepera*
Northern Gannet	*Morus bassanus*	Common Teal (Teal)	*Anas crecca*
(Gannet)		Mallard	*Anas platyrhynchos*
Great Cormorant	*Phalacrocorax carbo*	American Black Duck	*Anas rubripes*
(Cormorant)		Northern Pintail	*Anas acuta*
Shag	*Phalacrocorax*	(Pintail)	
	aristotelis	Garganey	*Anas querquedula*
Great Bittern (Bittern)	*Botaurus stellaris*	Blue-winged Teal	*Anas discors*
American Bittern	*Botaurus lentiginosus*	Northern Shoveler	*Anas clypeata*
Little Bittern	*Ixobrychus minutus*	(Shoveler)	
Night Heron	*Nycticorax nycticorax*	Red-crested Pochard	*Netta rufina*
Striated Heron	*Butorides striatus*	Common Pochard	*Aythya ferina*
(Green-backed Heron)		(Pochard)	
Squacco Heron	*Ardeola ralloides*	Ring-necked Duck	*Aythya collaris*
Cattle Egret	*Bubulcus ibis*	Ferruginous Duck	*Aythya nyroca*
Little Egret	*Egretta garzetta*	Tufted Duck	*Aythya fuligula*
Great White Egret	*Egretta alba*	Greater Scaup (Scaup)	*Aythya marila*
Grey Heron	*Ardea cinerea*	Lesser Scaup	*Aythya affinis*
Purple Heron	*Ardea purpurea*	Common Eider (Eider)	*Somateria mollissima*
Black Stork	*Ciconia nigra*	King Eider	*Somateria spectabilis*
White Stork	*Ciconia ciconia*	Steller's Eider	*Polysticta stelleri*

List of Species Recorded in Yorkshire and North Humberside

English name	Scientific name	English name	Scientific name
Harlequin Duck	*Histrionicus histrionicus*	Oystercatcher	*Haematopus ostralegus*
Long-tailed Duck	*Clangula hyemalis*	Black-winged Stilt	*Himantopus himantopus*
Common Scoter	*Melanitta nigra*		
Surf Scoter	*Melanitta perspicillata*	Avocet	*Recurvirostra avosetta*
Velvet Scoter	*Melanitta fusca*	Stone-curlew	*Burhinus oedicnemus*
Bufflehead	*Bucephala albeola*	Cream-coloured Courser	*Cursorius cursor*
Common Goldeneye (Goldeneye)	*Bucephala clangula*	Collared Pratincole	*Glareola pratincola*
Hooded Merganser	*Mergus cucculatus*	Black-winged Pratincole	*Glareola nordmanni*
Smew	*Mergus albellus*	Little Ringed Plover	*Charadrius dubius*
Red-breasted Merganser	*Mergus serrator*	Great Ringed Plover (Ringed Plover)	*Charadrius hiaticula*
Goosander	*Mergus merganser*	Killdeer Plover (Killdeer)	*Charadrius vociferus*
Ruddy Duck	*Oxyura jamaicensis*		
Honey-buzzard (Honey Buzzard)	*Pernis apivorus*	Kentish Plover	*Charadrius alexandrinus*
Black Kite	*Milvus migrans*	Greater Sand Plover	*Charadrius leschenaultii*
Red Kite	*Milvus milvus*		
White-tailed Eagle	*Haliaeetus albicilla*	Dotterel	*Charadrius morinellus*
Marsh Harrier	*Circus aeruginosus*	Pacific Golden Plover	*Pluvialis fulva*
Hen Harrier	*Circus cyaneus*	American Golden Plover	*Pluvialis dominica*
Pallid Harrier	*Circus macrourus*		
Montagu's Harrier	*Circus pygargus*	European Golden Plover (Golden Plover)	*Pluvialis apricaria*
Northern Goshawk (Goshawk)	*Accipiter gentilis*		
Eurasian Sparrowhawk (Sparrowhawk)	*Accipiter nisus*	Grey Plover	*Pluvialis squatarola*
Common Buzzard (Buzzard)	*Buteo buteo*	Northern Lapwing (Lapwing)	*Vanellus vanellus*
Rough-legged Buzzard	*Buteo lagopus*	Red Knot (Knot)	*Calidris canutus*
Golden Eagle	*Aquila chrysaetos*	Sanderling	*Calidris alba*
Osprey	*Pandion haliaetus*	Semi-palmated Sandpiper	*Calidris pusilla*
Lesser Kestrel	*Falco naumanni*		
Common Kestrel (Kestrel)	*Falco tinnunculus*	Red-necked Stint	*Calidris ruficollis*
		Little Stint	*Calidris minuta*
Red-footed Falcon	*Falco vespertinus*	Temmick's Stint	*Calidris temminckii*
Merlin	*Falco columbarius*	Least Sandpiper	*Calidris minutilla*
Hobby	*Falco subbuteo*	White-rumped Sandpiper	*Calidris fuscicollis*
Eleanora's Falcon	*Falco eleonorae*		
Gyr Falcon	*Falco rusticolus*	Baird's Sandpiper	*Calidris bairdii*
Peregrine Falcon (Peregrine)	*Falco peregrinus*	Pectoral Sandpiper	*Calidris melanotus*
		Sharp-tailed Sandpiper	*Calidris acuminata*
Red Grouse	*Lagopus lagopus*	Curlew Sandpiper	*Calidris ferruginea*
Black Grouse	*Tetrao tetrix*	Purple Sandpiper	*Calidriu maritima*
Red-legged Partridge	*Alectoris rufa*	Dunlin	*Calidris alpina*
Grey Partridge	*Perdix perdix*	Broad-billed Sandpiper	*Limicola falcinellus*
Common Quail (Quail)	*Coturnix coturnix*	Stilt Sandpiper	*Micropalama himantopus*
Common Pheasant (Pheasant)	*Phasianus colchicus*	Buff-breasted Sandpiper	*Tryngites subruficollis*
Water Rail	*Rallus aquaticus*	Ruff	*Philomachus pugnax*
Spotted Crake	*Porzana porzana*	Jack Snipe	*Lymnocryptes minimus*
Little Crake	*Porzana parva*		
Baillon's Crake	*Porzana pusilla*	Common Snipe (Snipe)	*Gallinago gallinago*
Corn Crake (Corncrake)	*Crex crex*		
		Great Snipe	*Gallinago media*
Moorhen	*Galinula chloropus*	Long-billed Dowitcher	*Limnodromus scolopaceus*
Common Coot (Coot)	*Fulica atra*		
Common Crane (Crane)	*Grus grus*	Woodcock	*Scalopax rusticola*
Little Bustard	*Tetrax tetrax*	Black-tailed Godwit	*Limosa limosa*
Houbara Bustard	*Chlamydotis undulata*	Hudsonian Godwit	*Limosa haemastica*
Great Bustard	*Otis tarda*	Bar-tailed Godwit	*Limosa lapponica*
		Whimbrel	*Numenius phoepus*

List of Species Recorded in Yorkshire and North Humberside

English name	Scientific name	English name	Scientific name
Eurasian Curlew (Curlew)	*Numenius arquata*	Pallas's Sandgrouse	*Syrrhaptes paradoxus*
Spotted Redshank	*Tringa erythropus*	Rock Dove	*Columba livia*
Common Redshank (Redshank)	*Tringa totanus*	Stock Dove	*Columba oenas*
Marsh Sandpiper	*Tringa stagnatilis*	Wood Pigeon (Woodpigeon)	*Columba palumbus*
Common Greenshank (Greenshank)	*Tringa nebularia*	Collared Dove	*Streptopelia decaocto*
Lesser Yellowlegs	*Tringa flavipes*	Turtle Dove	*Streptopelia tutur*
Green Sandpiper	*Tringa ochropus*	Oriental Turtle Dove (Rufous Turtle Dove)	*Streptopelia orientalis*
Wood Sandpiper	*Tringa glareola*	Great Spotted Cuckoo	*Clamator glandarius*
Terek Sandpiper	*Xenus cinereus*	Common Cuckoo (Cuckoo)	*Cuculus canorus*
Common Sandpiper	*Actitis hypoleucos*		
Spotted Sandpiper	*Actitis macularia*	Black-billed Cuckoo	*Coccyzus erythrophthalmus*
Turnstone	*Arenaria interpres*		
Wilson's Phalarope	*Phalaropus tricolor*	Yellow-billed Cuckoo	*Coccyzus americanus*
Red-necked Phalarope	*Phalaropus lobatus*	Barn Owl	*Tyto alba*
Grey Phalarope	*Phalaropus fulicarius*	Eurasian Scops Owl (Scops Owl)	*Otus scops*
Pomarine Skua	*Stercorarius pomarinus*	Eagle Owl	*Bubo bubo*
		Snowy Owl	*Nyctea scandiaca*
Arctic Skua	*Stercorarius parasiticus*	Little Owl	*Athene noctua*
		Tawny Owl	*Strix aluco*
Long-tailed Skua	*Stercorarius longicaudus*	Long-eared Owl	*Asio otus*
		Short-eared Owl	*Asio flammeus*
Great Skua	*Stercorarius skua*	Tengmalms's Owl	*Aegiolus funereus*
Mediterranean Gull	*Larus melanocephalus*	European Nightjar (Nightjar)	*Caprimulgus europaeus*
Laughing Gull	*Larus atricilla*	Chimney Swift	*Chaetura pelagica*
Franklin's Gull	*Larus pipixcan*	White-throated Needletail	
Little Gull	*Larus minutus*		*Hirundapus caudacutus*
Sabine's Gull	*Larus sabini*		
Bonaparte's Gull	*Larus philadelphia*	Common Swift (Swift)	*Apus apus*
Black-headed Gull	*Larus ridibundus*	Alpine Swift	*Apus melba*
Ringed-billed Gull	*Larus delawarensis*	Little Swift	*Apus affinis*
Common Gull	*Larus canus*	Common Kingfisher (Kingfisher)	*Alcedo atthis*
Lesser Black-backed Gull	*Larus fuscus*	Blue-cheeked Bee-eater	*Merops superciliosus*
Herring Gull	*Larus argentatus*	European Bee-eater (Bee-eater)	*Merops apiaster*
Yellow-legged Gull	*Larus cachinnans*		
Iceland Gull	*Larus glaucoides*	European Roller (Roller)	*Coracias garrulus*
Glaucous Gull	*Larus hyperboreus*		
Great Black-backed Gull	*Larus marinus*	Hoopoe	*Upupa epops*
Ross's Gull	*Rhodostethia rosea*	Wryneck	*Jynx torquilla*
Kittiwake	*Rissa tridactyla*	Green Woodpecker	*Picus viridis*
Ivory Gull	*Pagophila eburnia*	Great Spotted Woodpecker	*Dendrocopus major*
Gull-billed Tern	*Gelochelidon nilotica*	Lesser Spotted Woodpecker	*Dendrocopus minor*
Caspian Tern	*Sterna caspia*		
Lesser Crested Tern	*Sterna bengalensis*	Short-toed Lark	*Calendrella brachdactyla*
Sandwich Tern	*Sterna sandvicensis*		
Roseate Tern	*Sterna dougallii*	Crested Lark	*Galerida cristata*
Common Tern	*Sterna hirundo*	Wood Lark (Woodlark)	*Lullula arborea*
Arctic Tern	*Sterna paradisaea*		
Bridled Tern	*Sterna anaethetus*	Sky Lark (Skylark)	*Alauda arvensis*
Little Tern	*Sterna albifrons*	Horned Lark (Shore Lark)	*Eremophila alpestris*
Whiskered Tern	*Chlidonias hybridus*		
Black Tern	*Chlidonias niger*	Sand Martin	*Riparia riparia*
White-winged Black Tern	*Chlidonias leucoptera*	Barn Swallow (Swallow)	*Hirundo rustica*
Common Guillemot (Guillemot)	*Uria aalge*	Red-rumped Swallow	*Hirundo daurica*
Razorbill	*Alca torda*	House Martin	*Delichon urbica*
Black Guillemot	*Cepphus grylle*	Richard's Pipit	*Anthus novaeseelandiae*
Little Auk	*Alle alle*		
Puffin	*Fratercula arctica*	Tawny Pipit	*Anthus campestris*

English name	Scientific name	English name	Scientific name
Olive-backed Pipit	*Anthus hodgsoni*	Blyth's Reed Warbler	*Acrocephalus dumetorum*
Tree Pipit	*Anthus trivialis*		
Petchora Pipit	*Anthus gustavi*	Marsh Warbler	*Acreocephalus palustris*
Meadow Pipit	*Anthus pratensis*		
Red-throated Pipit	*Anthus cervinus*	Reed Warbler	*Acrocephalus scirpaceus*
Rock Pipit	*Anthus petrosus*		
Water Pipit	*Anthus spinoletta*	Great Reed Warbler	*Acrocephalus arundinaceus*
Yellow Wagtail	*Motacilla flava*		
Citrine Wagtail	*Motacilla citreola*	Olivaceous Warbler	*Hippolais pallida*
Grey Wagtail	*Motacilla cinerea*	Booted Warbler	*Hippolais calligata*
Pied Wagtail	*Motacilla alba*	Icterine Warbler	*Hippolais icterina*
Bohemian Waxwing (Waxwing)	*Bombycilla garrulus*	Melodious Warbler	*Hippolais polyglotta*
		Marmora's Warbler	*Sylvia sarda*
Dipper	*Cinclus cinclus*	Dartford Warbler	*Sylvia undata*
Wren	*Troglodytes troglodytes*	Spectacled Warbler	*Sylvia conspicillata*
		Subalpine Warbler	*Sylvia cantillans*
Hedge Accentor (Dunnock)	*Prunella modularis*	Sardinian Warbler	*Sylvia melanocephala*
		Desert Warbler	*Sylvia nana*
Alpine Accentor	*Prunella collaris*	Orphean Warbler	*Sylvia hortensis*
Rufous-tailed Scrub Robin (Rufous Bush Robin)	*Cercotrichas galactotes*	Barred Warbler	*Sylvia nisoria*
		Lesser Whitethroat	*Sylvia curruca*
		Common Whitethroat (Whitethroat)	*Sylvia communis*
Robin	*Erithacus rubecula*		
Thrush Nightingale	*Luscinia luscinia*	Garden Warbler	*Sylvia borin*
Rufous Nightingale (Nightingale)	*Luscinia megarhynchos*	Blackcap	*Sylvia atricapilla*
		Greenish Warbler	*Phylloscopus trochiloides*
Bluethroat	*Luscinia svecica*		
Black Redstart	*Phoenicurus ochrurus*	Arctic Warbler	*Phylloscopus borealis*
		Pallas's Leaf Warbler (Pallas's Warbler)	*Phylloscopus proregulus*
Common Redstart (Redstart)	*Phoenicurus phoenicurus*	Yellow-browed Warbler	*Phylloscopus inornatus*
Whinchat	*Saxicola rubetra*		
Common Stonechat (Stonechat)	*Saxicola torquata*	Radde's Warbler	*Phylloscopus schwarzi*
Isabelline Wheatear	*Oenanthe isabellina*	Dusky Warbler	*Phylloscopus fuscatus*
Northern Wheatear (Wheatear)	*Oenanthe oenanthe*	Bonelli's Warbler	*Phylloscopus bonelli*
		Wood Warbler	*Phylloscopus sibilatrix*
Pied Wheatear	*Oenanthe pleschanka*	Chiffchaff	*Phylloscopus collybita*
Black-eared Wheatear	*Oenanthe hispanica*	Willow Warbler	*Phylloscopus trochilus*
Desert Wheatear	*Oenanthe deserti*	Goldcrest	*Regulus regulus*
Rock Thrush	*Monticola saxatilis*	Firecrest	*Regulus ignicapillus*
White's Thrush	*Zoothera dauma*	Spotted Flycatcher	*Muscicapa striata*
Ring Ouzel	*Turdus torquatus*	Red-breasted Flycatcher	*Ficedula parva*
Blackbird	*Turdus merula*		
Eyebrowed Thrush (Eye-browed Thrush)	*Turdus obscurus*	Mugimaki Flycatcher	*Ficedula mugimaki*
		Collared Flycatcher	*Ficedula albicollis*
		Pied Flycatcher	*Ficedula hypoleuca*
Dark-throated Thrush (Black-throated Thrush)	*Turdus ruficollis*	Bearded Tit	*Panurus biarmicus*
		Long-tailed Tit	*Aegithalos caudatus*
		Marsh Tit	*Parus palustris*
Fieldfare	*Turdus pilaris*	Willow Tit	*Parus montanus*
Song Thrush	*Turdus philomelos*	Crested Tit	*Parus cristatus*
Redwing	*Turdus iliacus*	Coal Tit	*Parus ater*
Mistle Thrush	*Turdus viscivorus*	Blue Tit	*Parus caeruleus*
Cetti's Warbler	*Cettia cetti*	Great Tit	*Parus major*
Lanceolated Warbler	*Locustella lanceolata*	European Nuthatch (Nuthatch)	*Sitta europaea*
Grasshopper Warber	*Locustella naevia*		
River Warbler	*Locustella fluviatilis*	Eurasian Treecreeper (Treecreeper)	*Certhia familiaris*
Savi's Warbler	*Locustella luscinioides*		
		Short-toed Treecreeper	*Certhia brachydactyla*
Aquatic Warbler	*Acreocephalus paludicola*	Penduline Tit	*Remiz pendulinus*
		Golden Oriole	*Oriolus oriolus*
Sedge Warbler	*Acrocephalus schoenobanus*	Isabelline Shrike	*Lanius isabellinus*
		Red-backed Shrike	*Lanius collurio*
		Lesser Grey Shrike	*Lanius minor*

List of Species Recorded in Yorkshire and North Humberside

English name	Scientific name
Great Grey Shrike	*Lanius excubitor*
Woodchat Shrike	*Lanius senator*
Eurasian Jay (Jay)	*Garrulus glandarius*
Magpie	*Pica pica*
Nutcracker	*Nucifraga caryocatactes*
Red-billed Chough (Chough)	*Pyrrhocorax pyrrhocorax*
Eurasian Jackdaw (Jackdaw)	*Corvus monedula*
Rook	*Corvus frugilegus*
Carrion Crow	*Corvus corone*
Common Raven (Raven)	*Corvus corax*
Common Starling (Starling)	*Sturnus vulgaris*
Rosy Starling (Rose-coloured Starling)	*Sturnus roseus*
House Sparrow	*Passer domesticus*
Tree Sparrow	*Passer montanus*
Red-eyed Vireo	*Vireo olivaceus*
Chaffinch	*Fringilla coelebs*
Brambling	*Fringilla montifringilla*
European Serin (Serin)	*Serinus serinus*
Greenfinch	*Carduelis chloris*
Goldfinch	*Carduelis carduelis*
Siskin	*Carduelis spinus*
Linnet	*Carduelis cannabina*
Twite	*Carduelis flavirostris*
Common Redpoll (Redpoll)	*Carduelis flammea*
Arctic Redpoll	*Carduelis hornemanni*
Two-barred Crossbill	*Loxia leucoptera*

English name	Scientific name
Common Crossbill (Crossbill)	*Loxia curvirostra*
Parrot Crossbill	*Loxia pityopsittacus*
Common Rosefinch (Scarlet Rosefinch)	*Carpodacus erythrinus*
Pine Grosbeak	*Pinicola enucleator*
Bullfinch	*Pyrrhula pyrrhula*
Hawfinch	*Coccothraustes coccothraustes*
Blackpoll Warbler	*Dendroica striata*
Song Sparrow	*Zonotrichia melodia*
White-crowned Sparrow	*Zonotrichia leucophrys*
White-throated Sparrow	*Zonotrichia albicollis*
Dark-eyed Junco	*Junco hyemalis*
Lapland Longspur (Lapland Bunting)	*Calcarius lapponicus*
Snow Bunting	*Plectrophenax nivalis*
Pine Bunting	*Emberiza leucocephalus*
Yellowhammer	*Emberiza citrinella*
Cirl Bunting	*Emberiza cirlus*
Rock Bunting	*Emberiza cia*
Ortolan Bunting	*Emberiza hortulana*
Rustic Bunting	*Emberiza rustica*
Little Bunting	*Emeriza pusilla*
Yellow-breasted Bunting	*Emberiza aureola*
Reed Bunting	*Emberiza schoeniclus*
Black-headed Bunting	*Emberiza bruniceps*
Corn Bunting	*Miliaria calandra*
Rose-breasted Grosbeak	*Pheucticus ludovicianus*

LIST OF ORGANISATIONS, SOCIETIES AND BIRD CLUBS

National

Royal Society for the Protection of Birds
The Lodge, Sandy, Bedfordshire SG19 2DL
(Tel: 01767-680551).

North of England Regional Office, E Floor,
Milburn House, Dean Street,
Newcastle-upon-Tyne NE1 1LE
(Tel: 0191-232-4148).

British Trust for Ornithology
The Nunnery, Nunnery Place,
Thetford, Norfolk IP24 4PU
(Tel: 01842 750050).

British Ornithologists' Union
c/o The Natural History Museum,
Sub-department of Ornithology, Tring,
Hertfordshire HP23 6AP (Tel: 0442-890080).

British Birds Rarities Committee
The Secretary, M.J. Rogers, Bag End,
Churchtown, Towednack, Cornwall
TR26 3AZ (Tel: 01736-796223).

Wildfowl and Wetlands Trust
Slimbridge, Gloucester GL2 7BT
(Tel: 01453-890333).

World Wild Fund for Nature
Panda House, Weyside Park, Godalming,
Surrey GU7 1XR (Tel: 01483-426444).

Royal Society for Nature Conservation
The Green, Witham Park, Waterside South,
Lincoln LN5 7JR (Tel: 01522-544400).

Friends of the Earth
26 Underwood Street, London N1 7JQ (Tel:
0171-490-1555).

Greenpeace UK
Canonbury Villas, 5 Caledonian Road,
London N1 9DX (Tel: 0171-837-7557).

English Nature (formerly Nature
Conservancy Council)
Northminster House, Peterborough
PE1 1VA (Tel: 01733-340345).

National Trust
36 Queen Anne's Gate, London SW1H 9AS
(Tel: 0171-222-9251).

Yorkshire Regional Office, 'Goddards',
27 Tadcaster Road, Dringhouses, York YO2
2QG (Tel: 01904-702021).

Woodland Trust
Autumn Park, Dysart Road, Grantham,
Lincolnshire NG31 6LL (Tel: 01476-74297).

Forestry Commission
231 Corstophine Road, Edinburgh
EH12 7AT (Tel: 01131-334-0303).

North of England Region, 1a Grosvenor
Terrace, York YO3 7BD (Tel: 01904-620221).

North York Moors Forest District Office,
42 Eastgate, Pickering, North Yorkshire
YO18 7DU (Tel: 01751 72771).

County

Yorkshire Wildlife Trust
10 Toft Green, York YO1 1JT
(Tel: 01904-659570).

Yorkshire Naturalists' Union

YNU Ornithological Recorders
Vice-county 61 (East Yorkshire)
W.F. Curtis, 'Farm Cottage', Church Lane,
Atwick, Great Driffield (Tel: 01964-532477)
(Temporarily until new appointment).

Vice-county 62 (North Yorkshire – East)
D. Bywater, 2 High Moor Way, Eastfield,
Scarborough (Tel: 01723 582619).

Vice-county 63 (South Yorkshire)
J.E. Dale, 158 Lindley Moor Road,
Huddersfield HD3 3UE (Tel: 01484 652453).

Vice-county 64 (West Yorkshire)
P. Singleton, 61 Parkland Drive,
Leeds LS6 4PP (Tel: 0113-682473).

Vice-county 65 (North Yorkshire – West)
N. J. Morgan, 'Linden', Church View,
Ainderby Steeple, Northallerton DL7 9PU
(Tel: 01609-770168).

Birdline North-east (Up-to-date rare bird
information service)
(Tel: 01891 700246).

Spurn Bird Observatory
The Warden, SBO, Kilnsea, via Partrington,
Hull, North Humberside HU12 OUG.

RSPB Reserves

Fairburn Ings
The Warden, 2 Springholm, Caudle Hill,
Fairburn, Knottingley, West Yorkshire

Blacktoft Sands
The Warden, 'Hillcrest', Whitgift,
Near Goole, North Humberside.

Hornsea Mere
The Warden, 11 Carlton Avenue, Hornsea,
North Humberside HU18 1JQ.

Bempton Cliffs
Same as for Hornsea Mere

Local Natural History Societies and Bird Clubs

Visitors staying in a particular area for any length of time may wish to contact the local organisation and the following is a list of societies and clubs with the addresses of the current secretaries, which may of course change at any time. Some publish a detailed Annual Report.

Barnsley Bird Study Group,
114 Everill Gate Lane, Broomhill,
Wombwell, Barnsley S73 OYJ.

Barnsley Naturalist and Scientific Society,
48 South Yorkshire Buildings,
Silkstone Common, Barnsley S75 4RJ.

Beverley Naturalists' Society,
44 Thurstan Road, Beverley HU17 8LS.

Bradford Naturalists' Society,
23 St Matthews Road, Bankfoot,
Bradford BD5 9AB.

Bradford Ornithological Group,
8 Longwood. Avenue, Bingley,
West Yorkshire.

Castleford and District Naturalists' Society,
31 Mount Avenue, Hemsworth, Pontefract
WF9 4QE.

Craven Conservation, 'Drumochter',
Stackhouse Lane, Giggleswick, Settle,
BD24 ODL.

Craven Naturalist and Scientific
Association, 2 Birchlands Avenue, Wilsden,
Bradford BD15 OHA.

Crosshills Naturalists' Society,
6 Main Street, Bradley, Keighley.

C.M. Rob Natural History Society,
Tanfield House, South Kilvington, Thirsk
YO7 2NL.

Darlington and Teesdale Naturalists' Field
Club, 10 Pentland Grove, Darlington,
Co. Durham DL3 8BA.

Doncaster Ringing Group, 41 Jossey Lane,
Scawthorpe, Doncaster DN5 9DB.

Doncaster and District Ornithological
Society, 1 Lindrick Road, Hatfield
Woodhouse, Doncaster DN7 6PF.

Doncaster Naturalists' Society,
42 Greenleaf Avenue, Wheatley Hill,
Doncaster DN2 5RF.

Filey Brigg Ornithological Group,
31 Wharfedale, Filey YO14 ODG.

Goole and District Natural History Society,
11 Thorntree Lane, Goole,
North Humberside DN14 6CJ.

Halifax Birdwatchers Club, 14 Moorend
Gardens, Pellon, Halifax HX2 OSD.

Halifax Scientific Society, 11 Upper Bell
Hall, Halifax HX1 3ED.

Harrogate and District Naturalists' Society,
6 Rossett Park Road, Harrogate HG2 9NP.

High Batts Nature Reserve, 37 Firs Crescent,
Harrogate HG2 9HF.

Hornsea Countryside Society, 6 Greenacre
Park, Hornsea, East Yorkshire.

Hornsea Bird Club, 44 Rolston Road,
Hornsea, East Yorkshire.

Huddersfield Birdwatchers' Club,
15 Dene Road, Skelmanthorpe,
Huddersfield HD8 9BU.

Hull Natural History Society,
3 Kingsmead, Woodmansey HU17 OTF.

Keighley Naturalists' Society, 'Wyndways',
Hob Hill, Stanbury BD22 OHE.

Leeds Birdwatchers' Club, 2 Woodhall Park
Gardens, Leeds LS28 7XQ.

Leeds Naturalists' Club and Scientific
Association, Woodland Villa,
86 Bachelor Lane, Horsforth,
Leeds LS18 5NF.

Leeds Urban Wildlife Group,
1 Ashleigh Road, West Park,
Leeds LS16 5AX.

Milnsbridge Naturalists' Society,
20 Varley Road, Slaithwaite, Huddersfield,
South Yorkshire.

Mirfield Naturalists' Society,
145 Old Bank Road, Dewsbury WF12 7AQ.

New Swillington Ings Bird Group,
4 Fleet Lane, Oulton, Leeds LS26 8HY.

Rotherham Naturalists' Society,
57 New Road, Firbeck, Worksop,
Nottinghamshire S81 9JY.

Rotherham and District Ornithological
Society, 18 Maple Place, Chapeltown,
Sheffield S30 4QW.

Ryedale Natural History Society,
5 Granary Court, Pickering YO18 7HA.

Scarborough Field Naturalists' Society,
4 Whin Bank, Scarborough YO12 5LE.

Sheffield Bird Study Group,
6 Den Bank Crescent, Crosspool,
Sheffield S10 5PD.

Sorby Natural History Society,
12 Endcliffe Vale Avenue,
Sheffield S11 8RX.

South Holderness Countryside Society,
16 Dawney Road, Bilton, Hull HU11 4HB.

Teesmouth Bird Club, 67 Marine Drive,
Hartlepool, Cleveland.

Upper Wharfedale Field Society,
'Summers Barn', Carrs End Lane,
Grassington, Skipton BD23 5BB.

320

Wakefield Naturalists' Society,
5 Ashdale, Walton Lane, Sandal,
Wakefield WF2 6EW.

Wharfedale Naturalists' Society,
2 Victoria Grove, Ilkley LS29 9BN.

Whitby Naturalists' Club, 13 Carr Hill Lane,
Briggsworth, Whitby.

Yoredale Natural History Society,
'Chimneys', Castle Hill, Middleham,
Leyburn DL8 4RD.

York Ornithological Club, 9 Fairway,
Clifton, York YO3 6QA.

CODE OF CONDUCT FOR BIRDWATCHERS

Today's birdwatchers are a powerful force for nature conservation. The number of those of us interested in birds rises continually and it is vital that we take seriously our responsibility to avoid any harm to the birds.

We must also present a responsible image to non-birdwatchers who may be affected by our activities and particularly those on whose sympathy and support the future of birds may rest.

There are 10 points to bear in mind:
1. The welfare of birds must come first
2. Habitat must be protected.
3. Keep disturbance to birds and their habitat to a mimimum.
4. When you find a rare bird think carefully about whom you should tell.
5. Do not harass rare migrants.
6. Abide by the bird protection laws at all times.
7. Respect the rights of landowners.
8. Respect the rights of other people in the countryside.
9. Make your records available to the local bird recorder.
10. Behave abroad as you would when birdwatching at home.

Welfare of birds must come first

Whether your particular interest is photography, ringing, sound recording, scientific study or just birdwatching, remember that the welfare of the bird must always come first.

Habitat protection

Its habitat is vital to a bird and therefore we must ensure that our activities do not cause damage.

Keep disturbance to a minimum

Birds' tolerance of disturbance varies between species and season. Therefore, it is safer to keep all disturbance to a minimum. No birds should be disturbed from the nest in case opportunities for predators to take eggs or young are increased. In very cold weather disturbance to birds may cause them to use vital energy at a time when food is difficult to find. Wildfowlers already impose bans during cold weather: birdwatchers should exercise similar discretion.

Rare breeding birds

If you discover a rare bird breeding and feel that protection is necessary, inform the appropriate RSPB Regional Office, or the Species Protection Department at the Lodge. Otherwise it is best in almost all circumstances to keep the record strictly secret in order to avoid disturbance by other birdwatchers and attacks by egg-collectors. Never visit known sites of rare breeding birds unless they are adequately protected. Even your presence may give away the site to others and cause so many other visitors that the birds may fail to breed successfully.

Disturbance at or near the nest of species listed on the First Schedule of the Wildlife and Countryside Act 1981 is a criminal offence.

Copies of *Wild Birds and the Law* are obtainable from the RSPB, The Lodge, Sandy, Beds. SG19 2DL (send two 2nd class stamps).

Rare migrants

Rare migrants or vagrants must not be harassed. If you discover one, consider the circumstances carefully before telling anyone. Will an influx of birdwatchers disturb the bird or others in the area? Will the habitat be damaged? Will problems be caused with the landowner?

The Law

The bird protection laws (now embodied in the Wildlife and Countryside Act 1981) are the result of hard campaigning by previous generations of birdwatchers. As birdwatchers we must abide by them at all times and not allow them to fall into disrepute.

Respect the rights of landowners

The wishes of landowners and occupiers of land must be respected. Do not enter land without permission. Comply with permit schemes. If you are leading a group, do give advance notice of the visit, even if a formal permit scheme is not in operation. Always obey the Country Code.

Respect the rights of other people

Have proper consideration for other birdwatchers. Try not to disrupt their activities or scare the birds they are watching. There are many other people who also use the countryside. Do not interfere with their activities and, if it seems that what they are doing is causing unnecessary disturbance to birds, do try to take a balanced view. Flushing gulls when walking a dog on a beach may do little harm, while the same dog might be a serious disturbance to a tern colony. When pointing this out to a non-birdwatcher be courteous, but firm. The non-birdwatchers' goodwill towards birds must not be destroyed by the attitudes of birdwatchers.

Keeping records

Much of today's knowledge about birds is the result of meticulous record keeping by our predecessors. Make sure you help to add to tomorrow's knowledge by sending records to your county bird recorder.

Birdwatching abroad

Behave abroad as you would at home. This code should be firmly adhered to when abroad (whatever the local laws). Well behaved birdwatchers can be important ambassadors for bird protection.

This code has been drafted after consultation between the British Ornithologists' Union, British Trust for Ornithology, the Royal Society for the Protection for Birds, the Scottish Ornithologists' Club, the Wildfowl and Wetlands Trust and the Editors of British Birds.

Further copies may be obtained from The Royal Society for the Protection of Birds, The Lodge, Sandy, Beds SG19 2DL.

INDEX OF PLACE NAMES
BY SITE NUMBER

INDEX OF SPECIES BY SITE NUMBER

86–94, 96, 97, 99,
101–105
Green 2, 26–29, 33–37,
40, 45, 46, 48, 53–56, 60,
62, 64, 65, 67, 69, 71, 74,
76, 77, 82, 84, 87, 89–94,
96, 97, 99, 101, 105
Lesser Spotted 26, 34, 40,
56, 60, 62, 64, 66, 68, 70,

71, 74, 77, 84, 89, 92, 94,
96, 97
Wren 2, 3, 5–9, 15–18, 20,
21, 23, 24, 26–29, 31–40,
45–51, 53, 55, 56, 58–60,
62, 64–69, 71–77, 79–82,
84, 86–99, 101, 102, 104,
105
Wryneck 6, 9, 17

Yellowhammer 2–9, 11, 12,
15–21, 23, 24, 27–29,
31–34, 38–40, 42, 51, 53,
55–58, 60, 65, 67, 68,
73–76, 79, 81, 82, 84,
86–99, 101, 1049